WORDSWORTH, COMMODIFICATION AND SOCIAL CONCERN

This new reading of Wordsworth's poetry, by leading critic David Simpson, centers on its almost obsessive representation of spectral forms and images of death in life. Wordsworth is reacting, Simpson argues, to the massive changes in the condition of England and the modern world at the turn of the century: mass warfare; the increased scope of machine-driven labor and urbanization; and the expanding power of commodity form in rendering economic and social exchange more and more abstract, more and more distant from human agency and control. Reading Wordsworth alongside Marx and Derrida, Simpson examines the genesis of an attitude of concern which exemplifies the predicament of modern subjectivity as it faces suffering and distress.

DAVID SIMPSON is G. B. Needham Distinguished Professor of English, University of California, Davis.

CAMBRIDGE STUDIES IN ROMANTICISM

Founding editor
PROFESSOR MARILYN BUTLER, *University of Oxford*

General editor
PROFESSOR JAMES CHANDLER, *University of Chicago*

Editorial Board
JOHN BARRELL, *University of York*
PAUL HAMILTON, *University of London*
MARY JACOBUS, *University of Cambridge*
CLAUDIA JOHNSON, *Princeton University*
ALAN LIU, *University of California, Santa Barbara*
JEROME MCGANN, *University of Virginia*
SUSAN MANNING, *University of Edinburgh*
DAVID SIMPSON, *University of California, Davis*

This series aims to foster the best new work in one of the most challenging fields within English literary studies. From the early 1780s to the early 1830s a formidable array of talented men and women took to literary composition, not just in poetry, which some of them famously transformed, but in many modes of writing. The expansion of publishing created new opportunities for writers, and the political stakes of what they wrote were raised again by what Wordsworth called those "great national events" that were "almost daily taking place": the French Revolution, the Napoleonic and American wars, urbanization, industrialization, religious revival, an expanded empire abroad and the reform movement at home. This was an enormous ambition, even when it pretended otherwise. The relations between science, philosophy, religion, and literature were reworked in texts such as *Frankenstein* and *Biographia Literaria*; gender relations in *A Vindication of the Rights of Woman* and *Don Juan*; journalism by Cobbett and Hazlitt; poetic form, content and style by the Lake School and the Cockney School. Outside Shakespeare studies, probably no body of writing has produced such a wealth of comment or done so much to shape the responses of modern criticism. This indeed is the period that saw the emergence of those notions of "literature" and of literary history, especially national literary history, on which modern scholarship in English has been founded.

The categories produced by Romanticism have also been challenged by recent historicist arguments. The task of the series is to engage both with a challenging corpus of Romantic writings and with the changing field of criticism they have helped to shape. As with other literary series published by Cambridge, this one will represent the work of both younger and more established scholars, on either side of the Atlantic and elsewhere.

For a complete list of titles published see end of book.

WORDSWORTH, COMMODIFICATION AND SOCIAL CONCERN

The Poetics of Modernity

DAVID SIMPSON

CAMBRIDGE UNIVERSITY PRESS

CAMBRIDGE UNIVERSITY PRESS
Cambridge, New York, Melbourne, Madrid, Cape Town, Singapore, São Paulo, Delhi

Cambridge University Press
The Edinburgh Building, Cambridge CB2 8RU, UK

Published in the United States of America by Cambridge University Press, New York

www.cambridge.org
Information on this title: www.cambridge.org/9780521898775

© David Simpson 2009

This publication is in copyright. Subject to statutory exception
and to the provisions of relevant collective licensing agreements,
no reproduction of any part may take place without
the written permission of Cambridge University Press.

First published 2009

Printed in the United Kingdom at the University Press, Cambridge

A catalogue record for this publication is available from the British Library

Library of Congress Cataloguing in Publication data
Simpson, David, 1951–
Wordsworth, commodification and social concern : the poetics of modernity / David Simpson.
p. cm. – (Cambridge studies in romanticism ; no. 79)
Includes bibliographical references and index.
ISBN 978-0-521-89877-5 (hardback)
1. Wordsworth, William, 1770–1850–Criticism and interpretation. 2. Wordsworth, William, 1770–1850–Knowledge–Social history. 3. Wordsworth, William, 1770–1850–Political and social views. 4. Social history in literature. 5. Social change in literature. 6. Great Britain–Social conditions–19th century. 7. Literature and society–England–History–19th century. I. Title. II. Series.
PR5892.S58S56 2009
821'.7–dc22   2008046625

ISBN 978-0-521-89877-5 hardback

Cambridge University Press has no responsibility for the persistence or
accuracy of URLs for external or third-party internet websites referred to
in this publication, and does not guarantee that any content on such
websites is, or will remain, accurate or appropriate.

For Margie

Contents

Acknowledgments	*page* viii
Introduction: the ghost and the machine: spectral modernity	1
1 At the limits of sympathy	17
2 At home with homelessness	54
3 Figures in the mist	83
4 Timing modernity: around 1800	116
5 The ghostliness of things	143
6 Living images, still lives	174
7 The scene of reading	206
Notes	235
Bibliography	260
Index	274

Acknowledgments

I have been thinking and writing about Wordsworth more or less constantly for thirty years, and consequently there are many debts and inspirations I cannot hope to recover from the depths of time. For those I can remember, and which have been most recently helpful in writing this book, I thank John Barrell, Steven Blevins, David Clark, Paul Fry, Geoffrey Hartman, Alysia Garrison, Timothy Morton, Gerhard Richter and Scott Shershow. Various audiences have entertained and helpfully responded to presentations that have now come to printed form in this book: at Cambridge, Yale, Berkeley, Santa Cruz, Davis, Liverpool, Zürich and Tübingen. Among my hosts on these occasions, I am grateful to Peter de Bolla, Geoffrey Hartman, Annie McClanahan, Chris Connery, Gerhard Richter and Scott Shershow, Jonathan Bate, Angela Esterhammer and Patrick Vincent, and Christoph Reinfandt. I thank also the two readers who reported on the manuscript for the Press, and Linda Bree and James Chandler for welcoming it to their series. Earlier versions of parts of chapters 2 and 5 will appear in a volume published by *Studien zur Englischen Romantik* and in *Studies in Romanticism*. Anna Pruitt helped me prepare the final copy of the manuscript. The office staff of the English Department at UC Davis has been a constant source of support. I am particularly indebted to Terry Antonelli, to Melissa Lovejoy (who took the photograph on the cover), and to Ron Ottman, who keeps my computers working. What I owe to Margaret Ferguson is by now beyond description: to begin to make my silence visible I have dedicated this book to her.

INTRODUCTION

The ghost and the machine: spectral modernity

William Wordsworth had good cause to be preoccupied by death. His mother died a month before his eighth birthday and his father when he was thirteen. Later in life he suffered the devastating loss of two children, Thomas and Catherine, as well as of his beloved brother John. Such personal tragedies were less exceptional then than they are now among those similarly circumstanced, but they affected him deeply, and they go some way toward explaining why his poetry is haunted by ghostly apparitions, figures of death-in-life, of life shadowed and sometimes claimed by death. In addition the early support for his promising but still uncertain career came from a legacy established by the death of his friend Raisley Calvert.

There was more, much more, that was not personal but which Wordsworth registered in deeply idiosyncratic terms. He became a poet during a period of global warfare involving massive mobilizations of armies and navies and appalling fatalities, many from military combat but many more from the sickness and disease contracted abroad and carried home by the discharged and disabled veterans of foreign wars. Death-dealing economic changes also darkened his imaginative horizon: rural depopulation and the increasing spread of mechanized labor and factory discipline that damaged human bodies just as visibly as did weapons of war. At first glance Wordsworth's poetry looks nothing like Blake's impassioned vision of dark satanic mills, but on closer inspection it registers similar and perhaps even more pervasive marks of weakness and of woe. Alongside the dancing daffodils and blooming celandines a brooding darkness makes abode, albeit one made harder to see because the poet's view of the world is so often complicated by anxieties of self-projection and self-doubt that can seem distracting or self-deceiving, but are better understood as reflecting a general condition of radically disoriented subjectivity. The chosen vales of Wordsworth's rural dwellers are haunted by spectral personifications of Britain's expanding military–industrial

I

complex, tragically alienated figures like Michael, Margaret, or Leonard Ewbank, and by ghostly conjurations that, like "Lucy," seem hardly to have subsisted at all as ordinary flesh and blood. A similarly spectral identity informs the poet's representations of himself.

David Ferry long ago noticed the uncanniness of this poetry, pronouncing its author "not the poet of the human heart, nor of the relations between human beings" but one aspiring to an ideal communion made up of "the dead speaking to the dead."[1] Ferry made a crucial turn away from the restorative Wordsworth celebrated by Matthew Arnold, a turn followed up in Geoffrey Hartman's argument for a connection between the secular, creative imagination that was the poet's best gift to posterity and the dark and liminal places where transitions between life and death seemed imminent or actually to occur.[2] Hartman's Wordsworth headed off the violence of apocalypse with a turn to nature, but only at the cost of internalizing a sublime experience of the self that could be as terrifying as anything in the natural or political world. In the 1980s Wordsworth criticism took a political-historical turn, often convicting him of moral failure or escapism of the sort summed up in Jerome McGann's memorable and influential claim that "between 1793 and 1798 Wordsworth lost the world merely to gain his own immortal soul."[3] The major energy of this criticism was devoted to pointing out the significance of Wordsworth's displacements and silences, often interpreted as resulting from conscious decisions and ethical failures. The analytical power of his language and of the positioning of his narrators and protagonists as indicators of a crisis of ethical subjectivity itself, one not open to mere good faith solutions but articulating a profound alienation that could be stated and explored but not surpassed, was often missed. Lost too was the deep bite of Wordsworth's self-critique, one that goes much beyond the self-deceptions of mere false consciousness, one that poses questions we have yet to come to terms with. Paul de Man gave us a Wordsworth significantly emptied of ontological consolations not by history but by the logic of language itself, while McGann reintroduced both history and the ontological consolation as the evidence for Wordsworth's moral derelictions.[4] What has been less commonly explored is the historical construction of Wordsworth's ontological emptiness. By about 1800 Wordsworth's best poetry, sensing the pressure of "a multitude of causes unknown to former times," discovers that it may have lost not only the world but also any sure sense of the poet's place in it, along with anything we might conventionally identify as an immortal soul.[5] The sequence of ghostly encounters and death-in-life images that results renders this poetry prospectively contemporary with our own present and indeed with our foreseeable future because the conditions that generated it have not gone away.

Our own specters come en masse. We are seemingly obsessed with theorizing refugees, nomads and displaced (and sometimes resurgent) multitudes as the governing figures of a global postmodern condition.[6] Wordsworth's wanderers tend to come singly, so that one might see in his fear (and avoidance) of crowds a resistance to modern massification, a displacement or mystification of what was before his eyes. The oppressive and frightening crowds of London and Paris indeed typify a historical condition whose emergent realities Wordsworth was consistently anxious to avoid. His preferred communities depend upon a political economy founded in small groups. Nonetheless, the very singularity of his nomads and refugees stands for many others, and the common forms of their alienation bespeak a general condition that is implicitly multitudinous. In this respect they might be seen as conforming to another of the major types of our contemporary social imagination, the *Muselmann* or figure of bare life, of death-in-life, historically generated by reports on conditions in the concentration camps by Primo Levi and others and subsequently theorized by Giorgio Agamben as the prescient denomination of a coming common fate.[7] Like the *Muselmann*, Wordsworth's solitaries often seem to be on the point of leaving life behind, staring blankly at a future not describable or imaginable by the rest of us, verging upon a condition of sheer animality. Some of them, like the old Cumberland beggar, maintain complete silence and do nothing to alleviate the uncertainties in those who behold them about the nature and extent of their obligations to respond. Others – the majority – talk back, but thereby proliferate rather than resolve these uncertainties; at the most one might say that they open a question and generate a discomfort which we have yet to find a way of appeasing. Eric Santner has discovered the same openness to an as yet undescribable ethics in modern literature between Rilke and Sebald; and one could indeed propose the long narrative of Jacques Austerlitz in Sebald's last novel as a protracted response to the question Wordsworth poses to the leech-gatherer: why are you here and what is it that you do?[8] Wordsworth's minimalist examples are perhaps even more recalcitrant than those of his successors in offering solutions, for there is next to nothing of a conventionally restorative humanism about his determination to represent persons in a state of exigent singularity.

This book argues that the ghost-ridden dark and twilight zones of Wordsworth's poetry not only embody a metaphysical intuition about the death-directedness of all life, making him the precursor of a (late) Freud, a Heidegger or a Sartre, but that they also and most profoundly explore the processes and consequences of modernization experienced at one of its most critical transitions. These processes impose figures of death on Wordsworth's life; they are critical to the formation of his sense of hauntedness. Wordsworth, I claim, had a profound poetic understanding of the condition of England around 1800, specifically of its evolution into a culture governed by industrial time, machine-driven labor and commodity form: the culture whose profile would eventually be theorized much later by Guy Debord in *The Society of the Spectacle*. A full understanding of the power and persistence of these conjunctions may be still to come: this is the argument of Jacques Derrida's *Specters of Marx*, a book that woke me up to a remarkable confluence of interests between Wordsworth and Marx on the matter of ghosts, and that made me see how Debord's theory of the spectacle also requires a recognition of spectrality. Derrida turned to Marx as a corrective response to the turn away from Marx*ism* after 1989; he confronted the triumphalism of the neoliberal "West" with a demand for reading Marx again (or for the first time) and issued a warning that what was deemed historically redundant could be conjured up instead as yet to happen. Reading Marx again after Derrida, and Wordsworth again after both, opens up a new way of understanding the historical affiliations between and determinations among spectral figures, commodities, factory time, machine labor, global war and poetic imagery. It sets us thinking again about the death-in-life aura that resides at the heart of so many Wordsworthian encounters. This seems especially to be the case where the poems address matters of social concern and has made me ask whether we might find in their historically prescient imaging of the ghostliness of the commodity form some clues about those still unresolved meanings and directions that make many of Wordsworth's poems still urgently undecidable. If so, then Wordsworth in turn can tell us something about how Marx handled the task of writing and how Marx himself experienced and represented the figurative imagination – his own and that of others – working within a culture of mature commodity capitalism.

I claim this as a poetics of modernity, although I do not mean to say that everything about the modern world or its poetry is packed into Wordsworth's work. But I do think that certain core components of modernity, those now associated with what is often called postmodernity (better conceived in the context of this argument as late modernity) are staged in Wordsworth's poems with a remarkable and specific intensity.

Wordsworth appealed to Mill and Arnold because of his premodern inclinations; they saw him as the poet of nature and elementary feeling who was capable of offering an antidote to the modern world. But these doctrinal and experiential positions are underpinned and shadowed by darker intuitions which do not lend themselves to ready consolation. In using the word *concern* in my subtitle, I intend to capture the unresolved nature of the questions Wordsworth raises about suffering and sympathy. To be concerned usually means not having an answer, not having finished with an issue, being in a state of suspended attention that may produce a resolution but has not done so yet. The word also usefully signals the reflexive component of Wordsworth's poetry, which is so often about itself and its own making. When one is concerned about something or someone, then one is speaking not only about a condition or situation in the world but also and always about one's attitude to it. Heidegger's *Besorgen* (concern) and its attendant terms "circumspection" [*Umsicht*] and "solicitude" [*Fürsorge*] capture some of this indecisiveness, which in Wordsworth often veers into bad faith.[9] Concern means being involved and attentive and aware of oneself being so; aware also that concern is not of itself enough, that it does not solve anything. Concern is not the stuff of science, nor a support system for a utopian scheme to come. It is outside the law, even when the law appears to cover some elements of its challenge. And it is never enough. It is generated by the coexistence of radical subjectivity (acute awareness of how and what one feels) with radical injustice or suffering, and it cannot bridge the gap. I call its role in Wordsworth's writing a *poetics* because I think that what is at issue is not just a contingent overlap between a few interesting poems but a paradigm that recurs across many of the best-known works. The poems I discuss in detail are few, but they stand for and point to others and represent, I think, an important structuring energy for much of Wordsworth's poetry. Much of that energy comes from insights into the operations of commodity form, itself the ghostly heart of all sorts of communications and exchanges in the modern world.

Commodification, by which I here mean to reference the extended development of commodity form (Marx's *Warenform*) by around 1800, is the hardest of my terms to explain up front; it is the one that requires lengthy exposition and an accumulation of instances to be made apparent, for the commodity cannot itself be either seen or felt: its form is ghostly. Marx's declaration is famous and is to be taken very seriously: "a commodity appears at first sight an extremely obvious, trivial thing. But its analysis brings out that it is a very strange thing, abounding in metaphysical subtleties and theological niceties." As such it carries with it a "secret" that we must try to decipher.[10] It seems easy enough to think about consumption and consumerism: we can track them through items, things in the world, and connect them readily enough with familiar moral discourses about luxury and expense, as many eighteenth-century writers did. The debate about consumption invokes human bodies and human desires, wants and needs, visible causes and urgent effects. We know, more or less, what Wordsworth and others thought and felt about these matters, and we have a number of histories of such responses.[11] The commodity form is harder to understand. We have indeed come a long way since W. J. T. Mitchell remarked, in 1986, that with some notable exceptions analysis of the commodity had "played a relatively minor role in the study of culture."[12] But despite a now widespread invocation of the importance of commodification in all walks of life, what it is and how it works are hardly common knowledge. It is particularly hard to understand the unseen operation of commodity *form*, which does not depend upon the desires or intentions of human subjects.[13] Alienation and reification can be all too comfortably discussed in relation to individual subjects and individual things, but only by ignoring the intricacies of a commodity form that puts them into complex, abstract relations and can even seem to make them dance.

Commodities can and do appear as things, but *as* commodities they are abstractions and lead a virtual life conducted according to the constantly shifting protocols of commodity form which significantly determine modern social relations. The commodity is created by an abstraction from both production and use value, and it has a historical existence: Lefebvre calls this "concrete abstraction."[14] Insofar as the individual commodity is a thing, it can be seen, but what is not visible is its embeddedness in the value form and in the system of equivalences that makes all things transposable into other things, most obviously into money. A thing leaves the visible world when it becomes a commodity (in which human labor has only a "phantom-like objectivity") and only briefly returns to earth at the moment when its use value is accessed and consumed by a purchaser.[15] Lukács thought that all problems in the modern world (which he too thought had come into being at the turn of the nineteenth century) could be traced back to these "invisible forces" of commodity form [*Warenstruktur*] – invisible but all-powerful and rendering the human subject a helpless onlooker.[16] Helplessness in the face of powers that are sensed as phantom forces but never fully embodied (while never settling into the consoling forms of approved religiosity) generates radical concern; we see by glimpses and sometimes not at all, and we are never sure that what we can see is what matters most.

No one takes kindly to being deemed a helpless onlooker; such a condition seems to diminish or deny the power of human agency, denying us options for intervention or even rational theorization because the forces that move the world are not visible and cannot thus be formulated as a politics. Political protest did occur, of course, as it still does, with fairly obvious empirical causes and desired effects: the machine-breakers knew what they were doing and they knew many of the reasons why they were doing it. Wordsworth's narrative persona, in its very efforts at ontological security, stages an indeterminate social identity that registers the presence of something sinister and invisible governing everyday life, something whose considerable powers cannot be readily apprehended or controlled: the dynamics of commodity form. We mistake Wordsworth's distinctive historical intelligence by attributing his condition of arrested concern – his awareness of problems he seems to be unable to handle – to some sort of moral inadequacy. We can learn more, I think, from regarding his stagings of narrative incapacity and detachment in the face of the needs or sufferings of others as materials for deciphering the secrets of commodity form. A major figure of its presence (or half-life) is the specter, the permanent–impermanent shape that comes and goes without obeying the ordinary categories of space and time. Commodities are hard to figure, especially when commodity form seems to threaten or even govern figuration itself. Marx, as we shall see, comes up with some fantastic and even indecipherable personifications (coats talking to linen, tables standing on their heads) in order to represent their bizarre ghostliness: Wordsworth has his daffodils, and ghosts of his own. His poetry hardly ever describes the exchange of commodities, which we might take as the index of his preference for residual subsistence and barter subcultures untouched by modern commercial society. But that same poetry is suffused with representations of commodity form.

Commodification is then not just about the status of particular objects and our particular attitudes to them; it is a process in time and a structured complex in space that is always more than the particular transaction before our eyes. Marx explains commodity form as that which governs the circulation of capital and its transformations from money to goods and back to money.[17] Commodity form was not new around 1800: "it makes its appearance at an early date, though not in the same predominant and therefore characteristic manner as nowadays."[18] As production increases more and more capital must take form as commodity; everything that is not being produced or consumed at any point in time exists as "stock" within the commodity form.[19] As such it is both hidden and labile; it will grow when raw materials cannot be rapidly conveyed to production sites, and shrink when there is a steady and reliable supply. It may linger in storage or be sold off quickly according to market trends. The bigger and more complex markets become, the more capital will be tied up in the form of commodity stock, where it is subject to decay and maintenance costs as well as to the ups and downs of the market. In other words commodity form is always economically kinetic, always on the move, even when it is standing still, for example when it languishes in a warehouse. It is the key to commodity circulation even when it seems not to be moving from its place of rest: it is in fact only "normal" when "apparent stagnation is a form of the flow itself." Even producers can be deceived by this hidden-away operation, fooling themselves, for example, that their stock is moving when it is actually stagnating in the hands of merchants. Similarly, stockpiling can take on the appearance of an increase in production, even if actual production is falling, "particularly if the real movement is mystified by the development of the credit system" (p. 225). Its potential as consumable goods is inseparable from its abstract mobility as money.

The power and paradigmatic status of commodity form expanded hugely because of other transitions occurring at the same time, each enabling the others. Chief among them were automation and machine labor, which is a broader category than "factory" labor and which radically refigured space–time coordinates, and mass warfare, which brutally emphasized the general equivalence of everyone to everyone else. One of Marx's key insights was that historical developments in the modern economy gathered up inherited paradigms, intensifying and combining them in quite new ways, imposing acceleration and crisis, and secrecy and substitutability, as normative and thereby refiguring the habits of daily life for an ever-increasing proportion of the population. Thus it was not only those directly engaged in factory work (relatively few by 1800) who felt the changes. Take the cotton industry. By the end of the eighteenth century it was expanding rapidly. For this it required capitalization and the relocation of working populations to the regional centers (in Lancashire especially). It also relied upon imported raw material, largely from the West Indies but also from North America and elsewhere. This in turn required a large merchant marine and British naval supremacy. There were probably many more engaged in "machine" labor in building and manning ships than there were in the cotton factories, even though they were not so much operating machines as playing out their lives as if they were themselves *parts* of machines. Without the movement of money and capital enabled by commodity form, none of this could have happened; and without the movement of raw materials on a global scale, commodity form would not have become as central to economic and social life as it did.

Marx thus understands commodity form as a singular plurality and a dynamic principle, not a simple mechanical component of a social whole but a circulatory structuring energy that changes the shape of everything it touches. It is a governing but not a transcendental agency and it includes within its operations an indefinite sequence of conflicts that are sensed but not always seen. Like the formal unity of capital itself to which it is the key, it disguises the conflicts generated by its own energies. We are dealing with what Wordsworth called "a multitude of causes unknown to former times" coming together into a new formation some of whose operative principles can be fully apparent only to theory even as others can be visually and empirically located.[20] The speeding up of change can be sensed and sometimes seen, but the increasing dominance of commodity form over labor, productivity and value has no single, visible form; it is apprehended as uncanny and thereafter can be accessed only by thought. It is not the only kind of secret ministry around 1800 – memory, sexuality, winds and waters are all sensed as operating in hidden ways – but it is a critical secret agent within and among those other secrecies, a force that makes them take shape and form as – to a historically unprecedented degree – deeply unknowable and mysterious. Content itself can be evacuated, as it is, for example, in "The Ancient Mariner," where no motive for the voyage is given, no cargo specified, and finally no crew remains on board a ship driven by occult forces beyond human knowledge in a passage retold as one of endless circulation. The slave trade may well be the primarily repressed referent of Coleridge's poem, but it is as such representative of the generically impersonal and global dispersal of commodification itself. Commodity form impinges on but is not limited to or the same as class conflict, divided labor and alienation, mass militarization, surplus value, machine labor, finance capital, fetishism (the investing of inert things with living powers) and reification (the figuring of living things as dead forms). Even today, when we somewhat take for granted that commodity form is everywhere and explains everything, its constitutively abstract operations remain enough of a mystery that very able economic historians, some of whom I will draw upon, must still work hard to describe it.

Partly for these reasons I have decided not to try to offer a lengthy freestanding account of commodity form as it took shape around 1800, but to take up the task a bit at a time (especially in chapters 1, 4, 5 and 6) and in the light of interpretive questions argued through particular poems. Only at the end will the reader gain a sense of the larger pattern. More than a century of writing about Marx has not settled either the formal intricacy of his arguments or their precise application to contemporary conditions, so it is no false modesty that makes me declare myself incapable of demystifying the functions of the commodity once and for all. If anything we are even more deeply implicated in its operations than Wordsworth was, and in chapter 5 I will hope to show that Marx himself, like Wordsworth, was very much aware of the rhetorical complexities generated by writing from within the very paradigm he was trying to describe. His own response often took the form of comic personification or of critical parasitism, an enormous laboring of the negative through the writings of his precursors (Smith, Ricardo, Say, Stirner, Bauer, Feuerbach, Proudhon, Hegel and others) whose mistakes and half-truths served to help him articulate his own ideas. It was never easy, and it still isn't, to follow him into the mysteries and secrets of commodity form.

Marx often reduces himself to parody as a way of dramatizing the unavailability of cool objectivism. So too does Wordsworth, and I hope that the juxtaposition of these two writers may restore some sense of surprise to Wordsworth's remarkable poetry, which was not yet attuned to the normality of commodity form as a general principle governing human culture and the human mind. He was able to register the shock of something newly intense and to explore its workings with a complexity that no one before him had managed because there had been no need for such exploration. Marjorie Levinson's pathbreaking study argued the case for Keats's poetry as an analysis of money and commodity form, an analysis which, she claimed, "does not stamp itself upon the face of the other Romantic canons."[21] She attributed Keats's distinction in this respect to his "unusually stressed, self-conscious, and fragile ideological image" (p. 293). But at around the same time Alan Liu published a major study of Wordsworth which, as we will see, began to work out a very similar reading of Wordsworth as responding to the pressures of commodity culture; his approach was taken up and further developed by Celeste Langan.[22] All of these studies have been formative for my argument, and indeed one might speculate that Keats himself sensed Wordsworth's prescience in his comments on the Chamber of Maiden-Thought, the second stage of maturation, where:

> we become intoxicated with the light and the atmosphere, we see nothing but pleasant wonders ... However among the effects this breathing is father of is that ... of convincing ones nerves that the World is full of Misery and Heartbreak, Pain, Sickness and oppression – whereby this Chamber of Maiden Thought becomes gradually darken'd and at the same time on all sides of it many doors are set open – but all dark – all leading to dark passages – We see not the ballance of good and evil. We are in a Mist – ... To this point was Wordsworth come ... and it seems to me that his Genius is explorative of those dark Passages ... Here I must think Wordsworth is deeper than Milton.[23]

Deeper than Milton, and in a mist, through which we glimpse a series of dark passages, an underworld of ghostly forms and shadowy powers: this is profound criticism and may take us further than Keats's more famous identification of a Wordsworthian egotistical sublime. Literature is full of ghosts and specters, but they are not like Wordsworth's nor do they portend the same aesthetic and moral consequences. The metaphysical, theological and psychological coordinates of Wordsworth's specters, which have been written about, require also a historical and sociological analysis that attempts to notice where these particular ghost-figures differ from others and how they express the conditions of their time, which is, in the case of the social concerns I here address, still our time and as far as we can see the time still to come.

Chapter 1, "At the limits of sympathy," begins by exploring the fascinating conjunctions between Jeffrey Sachs's bestselling *The End of Poverty* (2005) and Wordsworth's account of meeting a "hunger-bitten girl" in France in 1792 in an encounter that both stages and undermines the presumptive distance of political commentary while refusing to resolve the anxieties of human interaction by endorsing sympathy, either in its stoical-Smithian or its sentimental versions, as a founding principle of restorative social relations. He similarly refuses to place his hopes in dialogue and thus proleptically undermines the Habermasian model that has been so popular in recent theories of civil society. The poems work not so much to create or represent consensus as to dramatize the perpetuity of dissensus, and thus they preserve as a problem (dialogic interaction) what has all too often been presented as a solution. An extended reading of "The Ruined Cottage" describes the disturbing effects of ghostliness and of a purely spectral sociability that does not sustain a plausible human community, and relates the poem's virtual resolutions to the pervasive power of the commodification of modern life.

Chapter 2, "At home with homelessness," continues to explore the lineaments of a world where sympathy is absent or insufficient, juxtaposing recent theories of inevitable homelessness (Heidegger, Adorno, Derrida, Agamben) with Wordsworth's concerned presentations of homeless protagonists and correspondingly homeless narrators. I undertake a detailed reading of "The Old Cumberland Beggar," where the old man's ghostly, automaton-like movement is described as a poetic instance of machine time and of commodity circulation, a syndrome which includes the embedded but invisible narrator who is the panoptical sociologist of village life. Here it is the apparently idle beggar who does the work, an inversion symmetrically opposite to that of "Gipsies" where the narrator who declares himself active actually accomplishes nothing, casting himself into a fascinating literary orbit around planet Milton and planet Shakespeare that finally embodies the disembodied, ghostly functions of money and commodity.

Chapter 3, "Figures in the mist," groups together three protagonists who subsist in vaporous twilight, darkness and mist and embody the challenge of spectral forms to human understanding and exchange: Poor Susan, the discharged soldier of *The Prelude* and the ghostly fisherman who is the object of the narrator's misunderstandings and a compound figure of dispossession in the "Point Rash-Judgment" poem, where the mist that enfolds the old man also shrouds a landscape that is saturated with the signs of death and death-in-life. "Poor Susan" further implicates the writer of books, along with the objects of his poems, within the subculture described by Marx under the name of the *lumpenproletariat*, a group that also includes the objects of the other two encounters analyzed in this chapter. Marx's class which is not a class threatens to include everyone within a mobile population migrating between city and country and in and out of military service and sustainable employment: everyone is potentially exchangeable for anyone else.

Chapter 4, "Timing modernity: around 1800," seeks to explain further the relation of narratives of concern to the historical profile of commodification at the turn of the nineteenth century: why then, and in this way? I argue that a distinctively modern conflation and confusion of time and space informs the famous "spots-of-time" syndrome which is at once a resistance to the temporality of modernization and itself a reflection of the operations of value and commodity form. Wordsworth subjects the spots of time to an accounting that holds open three different possibilities: gain, loss and simple preservation of the wealth that they enshrine. The memory places of classical mnemonics are here transformed into a composite version of the modern value form governed by an absorptive present. The superimposition of gain upon loss that characterizes the memory paradox in *The Prelude* is symptomatic of a modern subjectivity founded in a psychoeconomics of insecurity. Wordsworth's compulsively reflexive narrative is not here an avoidance of historical reference but is itself the vehicle of an unresolved history we still inhabit.

Chapter 5, "The ghostliness of things," begins with the extraordinary recollected – and misrecollected – account of the young poet's visit to the convent of Chartreuse in the summer of 1790, wherein the narrator of *The Prelude* at once avows and disavows a desire for the preservation of a Carthusian monastery as an emblem of the "ghostliness of things." Spectral form is here the bringer of death and the recorder of an ongoing process of mortification in a figurative crescendo closely analogous to the famous image of a table standing on its head and having ideas in Marx's *Capital*, an example restored to its full (if comedic) uncanniness by Jacques Derrida's important reading. Marx's table does not dance, though Derrida thought it did; Wordsworth's daffodils do, or are said to have done. I here read the most famous and diligently recycled of all Romantic poems as a covert but coherent presentation of the spectral operations of commodity form.

Chapter 6, "Living images, still lives," explores Wordsworth's own declared ambivalence about poetic images, famously apparent in his discussion of the similes of "Resolution and Independence" and evident also in key passages of *The Excursion*, the longest poem published in his lifetime. If the "spot of time" was his most positive though still ambivalent attempt to resist the speeded-up temporality of modernization, then many of his other aesthetic explorations confront and confess to the replication of still life and deadened form. The proximity of reification and imagination is evident throughout the poetry and powerfully dramatized in *The Prelude*'s account of crossing Leven Sands and hearing the news of the death of Robespierre. Wordsworth's highly distinctive use of the word *still* speaks to a condition that is both desired and dreaded, applauded and critiqued. Neither modern, premodern nor primitive time affords the poet a steadily valued measure of life, since the life that is to be measured is already driven by motions it cannot hope to control. Wordsworth writes from within a modern lifeworld whose immanence he yet seeks both to analyze and to resist.

Chapter 7, "The scene of reading," offers an account of Book 5 of *The Prelude*, which can now be recognized as an extended and coherent account of books as not just the givers of life (for future generations) but the embodiments and analogues of death. Wordsworth's sense of the bookishness of experience (formed both by high literature and by cliché) has been traced in previous chapters, but his reputation as a nature poet has inhibited his readers and critics from thinking through this topic as a major preoccupation in his work. Wordsworth sensed the power of commodity form most immediately in the book trade; thus he presents literature, even when most alive (in the writings of Milton and Shakespeare), as a dead or dying form subsisting in a landscape always on the point of being enveloped in mist or drowned by water. The falling leaves of autumn and the decaying leaves of books enfold the narration in a world becoming ever darker and ever more constrained, a world that is visionary but spectral, a world that makes the would-be creative imagination more than ever aware of the obstacles that stand in the way of a fulfilling personal life and a positive historical future for the human species. The old idolatries whose return Wordsworth fears at the end of *The Prelude* come back refigured and intensified not just as isolated moral lapses but as forces threatening to pervade a whole way of seeing and a whole way of life. They thereby render the poetics of social concern an unfinished project in the world to come.

Two final introductory comments. First: I have written two other books on Wordsworth, and the appearance of a third risks the suspicion of repetition and even of obsessiveness. I once imagined gathering together in book form a number of published but uncollected essays; but on rereading them I found them dated and they appear now if at all as references in footnotes. All but one were written in the 1980s in and around the ferment of those two earlier books (which were published in 1982 and 1987). Since then much has changed and Wordsworth has become if anything more modern. The changes can be summarized by two dates: 1989 and 9/11/2001. The first marked the end of the Soviet empire and was greeted in the West by a heady triumphalism and in some quarters by confusion and concern, as the gap between wealth and poverty increased radically across a world now marked by fewer if any constraints on the expansion of the neoliberal economic order. These changes shocked Derrida into a brilliant reading of Marx. The second date, 9/11, both inspired and was deemed the result of "terror." It is also, in ways not yet widely or fully understood, implicated in the onset of a one-world system controlled by those who "won" in 1989. The increased pace and extent of commodification on a global scale may seem new again to us, and perhaps newly threatening, as it once did to Wordsworth.

Commodification breeds concern because its operations are too volatile and too abstract to generate precise insights and popular analytics, leaving us with a besetting sense of unease that we can ascribe exclusively neither to ourselves nor to others. Even positive estimates of the benefits of wealth and commerce that do not understand commodity form have acknowledged a downside. Here is John Millar, writing in 1803, seeing a world to come in which

> opulent families are quickly reduced to indigence; and their place is supplied by professional people from the lower orders; who, by the purchase of land, endeavour to procure that distinction which was the end of their labours. The descendants of these upstarts, in a generation or two, usually go through the same round of luxury and extravagance, and finally experience the same reverse of fortune. Property is thus commonly subjected to a constant rotation, which prevents it from conferring upon the owner the habitual respect and consideration, derived from a long continued intercourse between the poor and the rich.

Government and vested interest may work against this circulatory instability, but it is inherent in a commercial economy which affects not just "tradesmen or merchants" but "all orders and ranks ... and every member of the community."[24] In the world after 1989, we are again confronting a multitude of causes unknown to former times, and one symptom of them is a heightened awareness of the substitutability of self and other (rich and poor, defended and defenceless) at precisely the point of greatest material differentiation: 9/11 was widely taken to demonstrate that the box-cutter is mightier than the long-range ballistic missile. The developed world is haunted (and haunts itself) by figures it can hardly identify or imagine, vacillating between complete indifference and avowed panic. Representations of global diasporas, homelessness, permeable borders, terror and genocide take on a hallucinatory intensity that exceeds what can be contained by rational assessment. The most profound poetry I know of that shadows forth such figures and speculates about their origins and future destinies is written by Wordsworth.

Second: I have not found that this profundity is easy to understand and therefore to teach. Some of my undergraduate students particularly find Wordsworth largely irrelevant to their own lives. One or two identify with the nature poet, while others feel a kinship with the author of a major autobiographical poem who never quite seems to know what to do with his life. A few can appreciate the "doggerel poems" as intriguingly postmodern before their time, but many more agree with the student who wittily described Wordsworth's poetry as the "brussels sprouts" of literary history – you have to read it but you don't like it and you would never order it yourself. To discover Wordsworth's perceived remoteness from so many of the few natural hearts I had hoped to find in the modern university was a shock of not so mild surprise. Strategies that I suspected might seem embarrassingly obvious, like pitching "The Old Cumberland Beggar" as a poem about how you deal with meeting a homeless person, failed to work in the classroom. I found myself halted, enveloped in a mist. What is it that I do and why? Many thoughts and ideas came to mind – about the difficulty of the language and the obscurity of the poet's references to the poor law debates of the 1790s, about the possible embarrassment that students might feel at *not* having made a connection with the plight of the homeless in their own lives, about a plausible fear of speaking up in case they might say the wrong thing. (Some of course had not done the reading.) On reflection – and I am still reflecting – I think that some of the awkward silences in the classroom occurred because Wordsworth really is a difficult poet, and never more so than when he heads into the troubled and troubling territory of social concern. I think that he is, as Marx said of the commodity, full of "metaphysical subtleties and theological niceties" and that his writings hold "secrets" we have to work hard to decipher.[25] What seems at first obvious and even trivial holds many mysteries, some of which are close to the bone and resist simple articulation. In this he is a very modern poet and seems likely to remain so for the foreseeable future.

CHAPTER I

At the limits of sympathy

PROMISING THE WORLD

In the foreword to a bestselling book bravely titled *The End of Poverty*, world-famous rock star and human rights activist Bono declares that we are the first generation that can afford to end poverty, "that can unknot the whole tangle of bad trade, bad debt, and bad luck. The first generation that can end a corrupt relationship between the powerful and the weaker parts of the world which has been wrong for so long." The book's author, Jeffrey Sachs, begins with the same message: "currently, more than eight million people around the world die each year because they are too poor to stay alive. Our generation can choose to end that extreme poverty by the year 2025."[1] Sachs argues that the massive disparity between the wealthiest and poorest populations is a problem of relatively recent origin, dating from the take-off of modern economic growth "around 1800" (p. 27) – that is to say, at about the time William Wordsworth's poetic career was entering its most productive and enduring phase.

Sachs's argument becomes more modest and more subject to familiar qualifications as one reads on: it is only "extreme" poverty, not all poverty, that can or should be subject to relief (p. 289); it is the means toward self-help and not simple charity that is to be offered (p. 291); it is our own self-interest and not pure altruism that should encourage us to allocate resources to debt relief and direct assistance (pp. 288f.). As Sachs's rhetoric of compassionate problem-solving evolves by way of these restrictions, it becomes more and more reminiscent of those voluminous eighteenth-century debates about how to treat the poor, conveniently summarized in Sir Frederick Eden's *The State of the Poor* (1797), debates which evolved into the systematic social welfare schemes devised by so many during the nineteenth century. With almost all such schemes, the ending of poverty was partly intended to relieve the woes of those who were felt to deserve such relief, but also thereby to keep somebody else poor – the so-called "undeserving" poor whose neglect maintained the integrity of a disciplinary paradigm for the rest of us as well as shoring up a rhetoric of thrift whereby society could assure itself that it was not throwing good money after bad.

My aim here is not to undertake a balanced review of Sachs's book but to point to the strong conjunction of his concerns with those evident in a reading of Wordsworth's poetry – that same Wordsworth who records himself as seeing, while in France in 1792, a "hunger-bitten girl," hearing from his friend Michel Beaupuy that "'Tis against that / Which we are fighting" and then opining, though without Jeffrey Sachs's command of economic data, that

> I with him believed
> Devoutly that a spirit was abroad
> Which could not be withstood, that poverty,
> At least like this, would in a little time
> Be found no more, that we should see the earth
> Unthwarted in her wish to recompense
> The industrious and the lowly Child of Toil.[2]

Sense and syntax in this passage are complex and convoluted. What is poverty "at least like this"? Does Wordsworth mean to specify a particularly extreme poverty, especially desperate and abject "like this," or does he intend to identify a particular class of persons (young, female, rural, itinerant)? If the second, is that class composed of the "industrious" (i.e. the deserving) poor *and* innocent children, or is the "lowly Child of Toil" an appositional figure for those who are also industrious? Is the girl a true child or a youth of working age? Making decisions between these options is made all the harder because it is not absolutely clear that Wordsworth approves of himself here: he could be retrospectively casting himself as a rather pompous young man endorsing the views of a figure whom he admires while adding in his own limiting conditions drawn from the British poor law debates of the time. They were not quite the same as the French debates, to which Beaupuy might well have been responding.[3] What does it mean to be "lowly"? Does this simply mean near the bottom of the socioeconomic order, or does one have to demonstrate abjection as well? Is the girl/child working at all, allowing her to qualify as "industrious"? Her depiction is one that is familiar in other Wordsworth poems, one of near-animal insentience and mechanical motion:

> a hunger-bitten Girl
> Who crept along, fitting her languid self

> Unto a Heifer's motion, by a cord
> Tied to her arm, and picking thus from the lane
> Its sustenance, while the Girl with her two hands
> Was busy knitting, in a heartless mood
> Of solitude . . . (9: 512–18)

She is indeed "busy" but busy within a state of languor, guided by forces outside herself and converting the uneven progress of the cow into the mechanically regular motion of knitting. In this sense she is a figure of the machine worker whose "heartless" alienation from the labor process was already the subject of commentary by concerned political economists. She is alone with her work and detached from the world, tied by the arm to a creature that she, in the conventional hierarchy of species, ought to be leading, but which instead governs her motions and sets the pace of her progress.[4] And she is *knitting*, a young *tricoteuse* who may or may not be forecasting the famous rituals of the guillotine which would be staged as the orchestrated revenge for her own presently pitiable condition.[5] The image is a complex one, and if the girl is indeed a spectral form of what is to come – the detached observer of public executions whose hunger is both physiological and temperamental, caused by bodily needs and also expressive of a desire for justice or revenge – then Wordsworth's utopian wish can seem to be heading off not only poverty itself but the penalty yet to be exacted upon the perceived beneficiaries of the old regime whose culture of "chivalry" the narrator has already admitted as exercising a certain charm upon his youthful imagination (9: 502–3). But there seems to be no chivalrous incursion into the life of the hunger-bitten girl, who remains uncannily detached from her socially distanced observers and gives rise to no knightly boons or favors.

We have already moved well beyond the rhetorical limits of Jeffrey Sachs's argument; we have moved from a straightforward (but still unresolved) problem about who is and is not included in an imagined future benefit to a ghostly conflation of past and present in which the narrator's own point of view is itself unstable and perhaps undecidable. How can we be sure whether or not Wordsworth here opens himself to ironic attention, whether he is a solid advocate of limited social reform favoring only the working poor and perhaps children or is dramatically exposing his youthful self's limits in so proclaiming? The passage was barely revised for the published text of the poem: the girl's hands become "pallid" but otherwise things stay much the same, including the slippery syntax and the awkwardly dangling modifier ("picking thus from the lane") that wants to attribute the act of foraging to the girl herself, thereby creating a composite, foraging human-animal unit whose governing pronoun is *it*.[6] Girl and heifer are indeed a bipartite productive machine: the cow takes in food and the girl knits, but the cycle of nutrition is not complete, and she remains hunger-bitten. Man no longer has dominion over the beasts; the beast powers the machine that employs the man. Its motion sponsors activity but it does not feed its workers (we are to assume that it might produce milk, but we don't see that part of the process). She walks along a country lane but she might as well be in a factory, for she demonstrates exactly the symptoms that Marx would identify as typical of working with machines: "Factory work exhausts the system to the uppermost; at the same time, it does away with the many-sided play of the muscles, and confiscates every atom of freedom, both in bodily and in intellectual activity."[7]

The girl-heifer is not a machine, and there is no sense that surplus value is being generated. The heifer will probably never calve, and the girl knits languidly, not at machine speed. But she moves mechanically, like a machine in slow motion or moving at idling speed, waiting for a switch to be thrown; and the lack of apparent purpose or motive to her efforts suggests that she is the victim of exactly the disturbance of "the metabolic interaction between man and the earth" that Marx (p. 637) specifies as the effect of the dominance of urbanized industrial labor. No commodity is apparent, but she is nonetheless a victim of the operations of commodification, operations which we cannot see but which render her a specter. For it was in the textile industry above all that some of the earliest effects of machine manufacture were felt, and they were felt in rural locations where small-scale mechanization occurred before and separately from the development of a factory system.[8] In France as in England much of the labor in textile production was provided by women working part time and intermittently.[9] Riots against machinery were staged in England throughout the second half of the eighteenth century: the first spinning jenny was destroyed by hostile workers in 1767, and many other similar events were to follow.[10] The hand-loom weavers were especially hard hit, and they are the example Marx chooses to illustrate very simply how productivity, price and value relate in the new machine economy:

> The introduction of power-looms into England ... probably reduced by one half the labour required to convert a given quantity of yarn into woven fabric. In order to do this, the English hand-loom weaver in fact needed the same amount of labour-time as before; but the product of his individual hour of labour now only represented half an hour of social labour, and consequently fell to one half its former value. (*Capital One*, p. 129)

The hand-loom weaver does not work in a factory but is nonetheless radically affected by a production process that halves the value of his work by way of radically refiguring the prevailing time–space coordinates. If he is to keep up, he must work twice as fast – but he can never keep up because by the time he is up to speed, value will have been reset again to compensate for a fall in prices: more and more will have to be produced to maintain profit. The hunger-bitten girl is figuratively also impacted by a textile industry in which she herself is not working; even if she is knitting something for her own use, its value is decreasing by the minute and the value of her own work on the scale of social labor is eroded. In her apathy and languor, she thus images the last gasp of a domestic textile industry as much or as well as the negative impact of an aristocratic old regime. The vagrant, ungoverned progress of her heifer through an improvident landscape also indicates a disorder in another of the basic components of the rural economy, that of pasturage.

Who or what is then the enemy against which Beaupuy and his companions (endorsed by Wordsworth) are fighting? What is evoked by the *that* in Beaupuy's apparently simple but secretly vague apostrophe: "'Tis against that / Which we are fighting"? If *that* is a state of avoidable suffering caused by inherited wealth, then the aristocracy could be removed or diminished, as it was after 1789. If *that* is unequal access to basic resources caused by other forces, and avers that no one should ever go hungry, then the problem is larger. *That* might even, by a definite but not implausible prolepsis (which is already written as retrospection), come to identify the knitting girl as the figure of vengeance, thus marking out Beaupuy as the voice of a bourgeois revolution troubled by or even opposed to the emergence of a violent working-class interest that must threaten his own. She would then be "heartless" in the sense of *unpitying*, immune to any sympathy for those whose fates are about to be decided when "the People" come to have a "strong hand / In making their own Laws" (ll. 532–33).[11] He would then be fighting against the girl herself and not the hunger she is suffering. Or might *that* evoke the labor pattern that the girl's hapless knitting motions embody? If so, the prospects for redress were not good. The modern machine-driven economy could not be turned back, and it was not. Marx would claim that it was indeed only the achieved dominance of commodity form [*Warenform*] as "the universal form of the product of labour" that could have given the "concept of human equality" the "permanence of a fixed popular opinion" in the first place.[12] Popular democratic ideals, in other words, of exactly the sort that gave the French Revolution its rhetoric, are themselves only conceivable in a world where modern capitalist production has already implanted a sense of the equivalence of everything to everything else. Democracy in its modern form is a by-product of commodification. The Revolution did not then challenge modern economic conventions but rather reflected their procedures in the constitution of its own political ideals. These are then not just about liberty, equality and fraternity but carry the darker suggestion that everyone is in the same boat, that each is mechanically substitutable for others. Beaupuy's recognition of the impoverished girl as his equal in being worthy of human attention is made possible, according to Marx's logic, only by the very forces that will perpetuate the existence of an impoverished class. Liberal egalitarianism is founded upon radical and punitive division of labor under the governance of machine production and commodity form.

THE CONCERNS OF CIVIL SOCIETY

Whatever Beaupuy's attitude bespeaks, it is not a simple, uncomplicated sympathy, an outpouring of empathic identification with a fellow being. It suggests, indeed, that sympathy may be far from a simple thing. *The Prelude*'s reported meeting with the hunger-bitten girl does not describe any extended human warmth flowing between the observers and their subject. Beaupuy's " 'Tis against that / Which we are fighting" (9: 519–20) produces the girl as an emblem of poverty, a still-life figure or spectacle of grief. Her recounted failure to respond to or acknowledge the presence of the onlookers accords with their own seemingly comfortable, objective state of mind; her "heartless mood / Of solitude" (ll. 517–18) seems at first to allow them to remain unchallenged in their moralistic distance from apparent fellow feeling – though as we have seen the passage presents more than a few challenges. They do not speak to her and there is no dispensing of charity. They are fighting against *that*, not suffering with *her*. Beaupuy's rhetoric marks him out as more of a rational policymaker than a fellow sufferer. But Wordsworth's poetry is often no more confident of those who do claim fellow suffering, like the pedlar of "The Ruined Cottage" whose case will be discussed in the last section of this chapter. It seems that neither utilitarian or aristocratic condescension nor professed empathic sensibility is convincingly endorsed as a means for creating or maintaining a visibly functioning civil society. Matthew Arnold thought that poetry might manage this, and that Wordsworth's poetry in particular would "be found to have a power of forming, sustaining, and delighting us as nothing else can," so that we would be compelled to turn to it more and more often "to interpret life for us, to console us, to sustain us."¹³ Before taking up the evidence of "The Ruined Cottage" on this question, I will attempt to sketch out some of the connections between sympathy, civility and civil society that preoccupied those living around 1800 and that continue to recur as symptoms of and pseudo-solutions for those theorizing the state of the world after 1989. These are among the approved doctrines to which I take Wordsworth to be responding so critically.

First, the absence of any spoken exchange with the hunger-bitten girl asks radical questions of our contemporary commitment in the humanities and political and social sciences to the sacredness of dialogue, conversation, round tables and measured communicative interactions; these routines are not just assumed or appreciated but set forth at length and in detail as political goals and social goods.¹⁴ This strenuous appeal to self-monitoring habits and inclinations arguably entails a purposive overestimation of the capacity of civility and civil society to fill in the blanks left by the incremental pulling back of government support for the basic welfare and employment conditions that had formerly assured people of the rewards of good behavior. As social stability and individual well-being come to be less and less legislated and rendered less subject to state bureaucracies, we are expected to find in ourselves the resources to create and maintain them. Civility, itself premised on dialogic consensus, thus becomes more and more instrumentally coercive and disciplinary as alternative constraints are weakened or disappear. At the everyday level this comes across as nothing more than a constant assertion of the need for good manners; more loftily it can be offered as the precondition of a positive "mutual interrogation" and of a "cosmopolitan conversation of mankind."¹⁵ Interpersonal decency of the sort that everyone who lives in a safe neighborhood takes for granted has become a paradigm for the recognition and resolution of global conflict. There is nothing of this going on between Wordsworth's travelers and the girl they encounter, not even the beginning of a dialogue. Instead an uncanny distance accrues, not least because of the compression of time and history, the sensing of the future of the past, and the girl's commitment to a silence that is at once abject and accusatory. Any paradigm for a culture of civility that might emerge from this encounter would be at best a cold and watchful one.

By contrast, and to take just one example, let us look briefly at Alasdair MacIntyre's *After Virtue*, a book first published in 1981 during the build-up of democracy movements in the Soviet bloc but aimed principally at the perceived internal breakdown of the social fabric of the West. On the last page of his book, at that point where all authors are tempted to some sort of melodrama, MacIntyre says that we are risking a repeat of the Dark Ages unless we do what the Romans failed to do in sufficient numbers: find "new forms of community within which the moral life could be sustained so that both morality and civility might survive the coming age of barbarism and darkness."[16] Two sentences later, as if adopting Matthew Arnold's habit of saying over and over again what he most wants us to attend to, he says it again: "What matters at this stage is the construction of local forms of community within which civility and the intellectual and moral life can be sustained through the new dark ages which are already upon us." Civility, not poetry this time, is what can sustain us, but only if the forms of community are adequate to its preservation. MacIntyre's preface warns us that Marxism and liberalism have both failed under the pressure of a "modern and modernizing world," a "large part" of whose norms will have to be rejected if a rejuvenated moral and social life is to come about (p. x). Communities are going to have to be local. Put together enough of them, MacIntyre suggests, and you have a world. A world that sustains.

Wordsworth's poetry embodies a similar suspicion of modernity but also projects a thorough investigation of local communities and their problems and potentials. What does it have to say about civility and civil society (for the one invokes the other and each is the other's enabling condition)? About the viability of dialogue and conversation as the foundations of creative and adequate social and political relations? About the dynamics of niceness, its benefits and personal gratifications? About the possibilities for effective sympathy? What kinds of bonds do people form when left to themselves? What models of "local forms of community" can be derived from them? Will a reading of Wordsworth in the light of the contemporary obsession with civility sustain or disturb the aspirations of its advocates, also newly confident because of the perceived end of history that came with the assessment that what brought down the old Soviet order was precisely its overreliance on the state and its failure to invent and sustain a healthy culture of dialogue and a flourishing civil society? Can sympathy between unencumbered individuals (no longer disciplined by a bureaucratic calculus) do the positive work that coercive socialization and the welfare state have apparently ceased to do, if they ever did it at all?

Many of these concerns were explored exhaustively in the eighteenth century by Shaftesbury, Chesterfield, Smith and others; they formed part of the vocabulary that Wordsworth inherited.[17] I have written about Wordsworth's ideas and ideals of local community elsewhere, and so have others, and it is a familiar knowledge, I think, that the communities he found most likely to nurture positive human interactions were those most threatened historically at the time he wrote about them: owner-occupier or long-term leasehold farmers raising enough animals and crops to assure subsistence but not enough to tempt participation in the luxury economy that came with the availability of a significant surplus. The strains upon these small, locally organic societies are not just those of the external changes that were rendering them more and more untypical of the national life. They are undermined from within, and most of all by the figure of the poet himself, wanting to belong but never quite belonging, and bringing with him a sense of personal discomfort and an aura of concern that implacably refute any image of harmony and any prospect of exact description or judgment. What is here proleptically refuted is the fragile optimism that can be traced in so much of the current post-1989 civility talk. Where neither the self nor the other can be stabilized for clear representation and simple, direct discourse, there proves to be little or no basis for any grand model of dialogic democracy.

Wordsworth's imaging of the demise of modern subjectivity is marked by attention to personality, to individuation, to selfhood, and therefore at the same time to the obligation to account for oneself in the sphere of public life: Who are you? Or, more decorously, "How is it that you live, and what is it you do?"[18] This question, put by the poet-speaker to the old leech-gatherer (for the second time, since the poet wasn't listening to the answer the first time), is of the essence of modern democratic interaction, only slightly less aggressive than the famous Althusserian moment of interpellation, "hey you!" It says: identify yourself, explain yourself, account for yourself. The old man, again famously, is a model of civility, with his "courteous speech" and "demeanour kind." But the poet-speaker is tuned out, tripping, carried along by self-absorbed projections of the tragic lives of poets and the failures of the faculty of imagination. There is no celebration of dialogue or conversation and no mutual accommodation, and it is to Wordsworth's credit that he does not pretend that there is. This is not the standard picaresque or charitable interaction in which some bond is established between strangers that models or presages the initiation of a social contract. Instead, the poem presents an anatomy of how hard it can be to take that step. Lots of Wordsworth's best poems send this message – think of "The Old Cumberland Beggar" or "Old

Man Travelling" or "Simon Lee." These poems stick in the mind because they cannot be solved or slotted away; each reading repeats a primary undecidability and suspends the anticipated or desired relaxing of social tension that ideally accompanies a first encounter with strangers and promises the removal of the threat of violence and the onset of future sociability. Here, to the contrary, nothing makes us feel better, or feel good.

By way of contrast, think of the copious shedding of tears that so often concludes human exchanges in the sentimental novel. These shared and contagious experiences of weeping are misunderstood if they are taken to signify a loss of control. They can be just the opposite – a foundation of selfhood and of social bonding.[19] They tell us that a level of basic human nature has been tapped – tell us that there *is* a basic human nature – and they offer a guarantee of future relationship whereby those who weep together will stay together. When Augustus Harley, Henry Mackenzie's "man of feeling," meets a returning soldier on the road, the unfamiliar is progressively tamed to the point that the stranger turns out not to be a stranger at all but the kindly companion of Harley's youth. The passage is both presciently Wordsworthian and something quite different. At the moment of encounter, there is disturbance and embarrassment: "He looked at Harley with the appearance of some confusion; it was a pain the latter knew too well to think of causing in another; he turned and went on."[20] Again: "He had that steady look of sorrow, which indicates that its owner has gazed upon his griefs till he has forgotten to lament them" (p. 60). But the uncomfortable distance that Wordsworth so often maintains and explores is dissolved as the two men fall into conversation and discover that, after all, they know one another. The strange becomes the familiar, what was disturbing ends up providing the reassurance of social closure – as if the world were after all a patterned system within which there are no enduring forms of alienation. Hence the lines which cannot be specified in the narrative as belonging exclusively either to the narrator, or to Harley, or to the old soldier, for they belong to all of them, and therefore to us: "Father of mercies! I would also thank thee that not only hast thou assigned eternal rewards to virtue, but that, even in this bad world, the lines of our duty and our happiness are so frequently woven together" (p. 71).

Wordsworth knew the contrary: that duty does not assure happiness, and that duty can be hard to ascertain as well as hard to perform. He abandons the world of the eighteenth-century picaresque (which would live on in the novels of Dickens) where there are no strangers, where every chance meeting embodies the providence of a narrative as well as moral closure, where an unknown person met at a country inn in chapter 2 must reappear fully identified in chapter 40 as a long-lost family member or friend or at least a figure crucial to the proper development of the story. Wordsworth's strangers remain strangers, often ghostly strangers open only to minimal intimacies that dramatize alienation rather than community. In "Alice Fell," for example, we are left hanging at the end. The child has her new cloak, but only because the narrator has left *money* to be spent on her behalf, thus invoking a connection that Simmel would later make between the stranger and the money form. Wordsworth uses lyric economy to foreground difficult questions about the sufficiency of single acts of charity both for givers and receivers. Has the narrator done enough? Why does he not himself make the gift instead of delegating it to another? Is he on his way elsewhere and in a hurry? We find ourselves, as we so often do in reading Jane Austen, entering into the scene as interested participants, always aware of its fictionality and yet driven to find a tale in everything, to make up and test out explanations that might or might not be adequate and are always inconclusive. What is one's duty to the poor, the disabled, the bereft and bereaved? Many of Wordsworth's poems ask these questions even as they seem to be answering them and thereby stop short of offering the peace of mind that follows the narration of a job well done. Instead, one goes along one's way troubled and with a sense of powers not understood.

In this way Wordsworth offers what I take to be the first comprehensively modern formulation of the aporias of human interaction in a society of dispersed populations governed by the operations of commodity form, the first one in which the rhetoric of resolution is so fully withheld. This does not mean of course that he is having unique insights into a hitherto unsuspected element of the human condition: Pope's *Dunciad*, for one, attends passionately to the commodification of modern society and of print culture in particular. But Wordsworth almost completely abandons satire and the consolations of received genre in order to explore the dynamics of subject-formation in a language of ghosts and apparitions: in this respect he stands more fully than Pope within a history through which we are still living. This ongoing modernity projects a democratic imperative (whereby we are or should be all equal) awkwardly conjoined with persistent or increasing economic and other disparities which cry out for address (a man speaking to men) but seem impossible to redress. We thus enter a sort of charitable sublime, a relentless self-questioning about what is enough, too much or too little, and an epistemological uncanny, where the object of our attentions shifts and shimmers and becomes in its limit conditions a projection of the self.

Wordsworth may be the first English poet to perfect the expression of a historically insecure rhetoric whose components include the radically aporetic investigations of failed communication and unmade communities. This poet who thumps the tub for nature and sometimes even nation, in other words, gives considerable and I think greater weight to more indecisive voices, thereby adumbrating a syndrome still being urgently addressed at the turn of the twenty-first century. Marx's revision of Hegel took the existential drama out of the dynamics of recognition (for example in the master–slave relation) and saw there only the operation of commodity form whereby each selfhood is exchangeable for another under the form of the general equivalent.[21] Wordsworth comes to this point by way of the language of poetry, preserving the pathos of failed or inadequate human exchange. It will surely remain plausible for people to read him as Arnold read him, as thin on philosophy but a fine nature poet and as such a restorative for frayed sensibilities: above all a sustainer. But there are many important poems that maintain the problem of human interaction *as* a problem. They are the ones that obtrude the "feeling of labour" to which Coleridge objected, the ones that display the "anxiety of explanation and retrospect" he also thought inappropriate to great poetry.[22] For all his efforts at and hopes for the discovery of a basic human nature beyond the reach of the differences of doctrine, rank, and occupation, and for all the ingenuity of the case made in the preface to *Lyrical Ballads*, Wordsworth's poetry dwells most often with the sad perplexities of disappointment, and with what Coleridge described as the kinds of "intensity of feeling" that cannot be shared with "men in general" (p. 136). This is at once its utopian hope – that we might someday have such a world – and its historical resonance, then as now, that we do not have it yet. None of the contemporary techniques for imagining communities quite work out: not the sentimental contract sealed in the sharing of tears, nor its opposite, the stern respect for stoical self-control; not the act of individual charity that remains the keystone in much present-day social policy, not the panoptical eye that thinks it can dispense sympathies and resources in ways adequate either to deserving persons or to statistically desirable outcomes. Sympathy is impeded or ineffective, and dialogue is often stillborn, at best halting and at times completely misdirected. If these lacunae point to a history yet to happen, one would have to say that we are not there yet. So where are we?

RATIONAL SYMPATHY, VIRTUAL SYMPATHY

Civility tends to be a poorly defined or strategically vague attribute: it requires a large dose of nature and a measure of culture, a basic urge for company trained up and focused by a studied application of good manners and educated tolerance. It is not merely sympathy, a feeling for and with the other, nor is it a purely rational calculus according to which persons choose to moderate their more divisive needs and desires for the sake of a general social harmony. Wordsworth presents a challenge to the romance of a self-sustaining dialogism that has swept the liberal democratic "West" since 1989, and which places a huge emphasis on the open discussion of everyone with everyone else, though of course it can only ever sustain itself by remaining a highly selective, representative system wherein a very few persons get to speak *as if* for others. The ongoing dismissal of bad manners in the name of a culture of civility is justified by a rhetoric that claims universality (all can speak for themselves and from their own identity conditions) but functions by a highly selective process of representation.[23] A world in which everyone gets to speak would be deafening and chaotic, and there is a lot lacking in a political imaginary that has no recourse for the staging of radical conflict other than a round table or town meeting format governed above all by the obligation to speak, and thus to throw into the voice, into conversation, the entire weight of the needs, scarcities and inequities that not infrequently take their more natural form as silence or as a noise that is at best impolite or protosemantic. Ulrich Beck has thus broached the possibility that we are living within the "negotiation state, which arranges and stages conversation and directs the show" – a state which in other words preserves its controlling function precisely by obscuring it.[24] The dialogic ethic presupposes as already in existence an equivalence of confidence, habit, fluency and opportunity to a degree that would have already done away with (or have never experienced) those most intransigent forms of conflict that it purports to be resolving. In other words when dialogue works, most of the hard work has already been done.

I will now take three important examples of efforts to theorize the relations between dialogism, sympathy and civility: they appear in the writings of Jürgen Habermas, Adam Smith and Georg Simmel. All are distinctively modern, which is to say that despite the historical distance between them their insights and examples are mutually intelligible and still being worked through. All are helpful in specifying the ways in which Wordsworth does and does not fulfill the needs or desires of modern society for a transparent self-understanding. Of the three, it is Habermas who seems least interested in finding a foundational role for sympathy, which is for him displaced by the primacy of rational and dialogic models for conflict resolution. And although Habermas is often produced as the spokesman for a regnant western-style civility culture, he can be read against the grain of his own popularity in this respect as most doubtful of what he most assures.[25] Here, for example, are his first words on the importance of the *lifeworld* [*Lebenswelt*]:

Subjects acting communicatively always come to an understanding in the horizon of a lifeworld. Their lifeworld is formed from more or less diffuse, always unproblematic, background convictions. This lifeworld background serves as a source of situation definitions that are presupposed by participants as unproblematic ... The world-concepts and the corresponding validity claims provide the formal scaffolding with which those acting communicatively order problematic contexts of situations, that is, those requiring agreement, in their lifeworld, which is presupposed as unproblematic.[26]

In other words the resolution of disagreement or confusion requires reference to an assumed common set of attitudes and habits that can provide enough of an appearance of cohesion to allow what follows to appear rational or justifiable. Habermas's case for the importance of tradition – "the lifeworld also stores the interpretive work of preceding generations" (p. 70) – is not so far from Edmund Burke's case for the importance of habits, customs and traditions. Communication, conflict resolution and new consensus are more efficient if there is already a good deal that can be taken for granted. And the more the "worldview that furnishes the cultural stock of knowledge is decentered" (p. 70), the more exposed and urgent is the work of the interaction itself.

Habermas himself thinks that the less there is to rely on in terms of a received lifeworld, the more likely it is that "rational action orientations" (not outpourings of sympathy) will occur (p. 70). He supposes that faced with putting communication itself at risk, those to whom traditional resources are unavailable will (or should?) resort to reason rather than experience chaos or radical dissensus. But the outcome is not sure, unless the natural or educated commitment to rationality can be taken for granted. So there is a question about how "divergent situation definitions can be brought to coincide sufficiently" (p. 100) for agreement to be reached. And in fact "stability and absence of ambiguity are rather the exception in the communicative practice of everyday life. A more realistic picture is that drawn by ethnomethodologists – of a diffuse, fragile, continuously revised and only momentarily successful communication in which participants rely on problematic and unclarified presuppositions and feel their way from one occasional commonality to the next" (pp. 100–1). Habermas again: "under the microscope *every* understanding proves to be occasional and fragile" (p. 130).

Wordsworth's poems, which project the fragility of lifeworlds and the increasingly rapid transformation of habits and traditions, provide exactly such a microscope. The narrator of "Resolution and Independence" famously does not listen to the old leech-gatherer for most of the time they are engaged in what we might call conversation. The narrator of "The Old Cumberland Beggar" does not speak at all to the object of his story. The narrator of "Michael" tells us frankly at the start that his interest in the story is mediated only partly through human beings (the shepherds he knew in his youth) and rather more by the pleasures he took in the landscape they inhabited. Dialogue in "Beggars" produces pompous disbelief, while in "Old Man Travelling" it results in something like a rebuke. One could go on. Poems like "The Thorn," "We Are Seven," and even the "Tintern Abbey" poem all call into radical question the competence of speakers and narrators to tell straight stories, not least because stories themselves are never straight. Habermas's mention of ethnomethodology reminds us not only of Alan Bewell's persuasive case for Wordsworth the anthropologist (studying his neighbours as if they were members of remote societies) but again of Derrida's invocation of the moment of ethnology as itself the symptom of the decentering of the worldview of the western subject, the now threatened flag bearer for Johnsonian general nature or Coleridge's "men in general."[27] This moment is transcribed in the numerous volumes of exploration and classification that came after the great voyages of the eighteenth century – Bougainville, Anson, Cook, Banks, Forster and so forth, – volumes which at once transcribe and perform the impositions of an imperialist worldview and at the same time record the interactive challenges it cannot fully or adequately meet. The urgency of the appeal to a neutral and sustaining *nature* that is at the core of the common understanding of what Wordsworth's poetry is up to derives from the intuition that nature cannot be presupposed as an unproblematic part of the lifeworld. Romantic nature is invented precisely at the moment when it cannot subsist, when it is already as good as lost. It is articulated as what is threatened both by historical changes in the landscape and economy of the homeland, by the changes in habits of mind that accompany those physical transformations, and by the recognition that different cultures see and imagine different natures. This is what increasingly divided labor, urbanization, commodification and global conflict do to people. One no longer points to nature – "look, how beautiful" – with the expectation that others will nod agreeably or understand. One does so in the hope that they might, that there are a few natural hearts, or perhaps just Dorothy, left to make up a passable communicative interaction, a club of more than one.[28]

Wordsworth's sense of this crisis explains, I think, the panic and moral hyperbole of a poem like "Gipsies" (at which Coleridge and Hazlitt both took eloquent offence), where the poet-narrator simply cannot fathom what is going on for a group of people who seem to him (although he does not ask) utterly immune to the pleasures he himself has been taking in the spectacle of nature and the sense of movement. One way of reading the narrative bombast is to see it as a defense against the unbearable or unmanageable intuition that there might be *no* common assumptions about the natural world on which communicative interactions of the more difficult sort might be founded. The gypsies are immune to nature's charms because their lifeworld does not include that version of nature. Nor is there a shared foundation in a human sympathy or sociability that can include a narrator who casts himself as alien to it.

The field of concern informing Habermas's theory of communicative interaction – which devolves into a utopian rather than an empirically descriptive paradigm – is apparent also in a book closer in time to Wordsworth, a book indeed fundamental for an understanding of the late eighteenth-century address to questions of civil and social behavior: Adam Smith's *The Theory of Moral Sentiments* (1759). Here too the endorsement of sympathy is subject to critical redescription by rationalist criteria. As is well enough known, Smith's argument depends on the idea of sympathy as an imaginary gesture – we respond to the predicaments of others by thinking about what we would expect to feel in their place. What matters most is not the passion itself, which cannot be accessed, but our recreation of something in ourselves by way of an estimate of the "situation" that caused it.[29] In order to make this estimation, the spectator must pay maximum attention to the minuscule details and "bring home to himself every little circumstance of distress which can possibly occur to the sufferer. He must adopt the whole case of his companion with all its minutest incidents; and strive to render as perfectly as possible, that imaginary change of situation upon which his sympathy is founded" (p. 21). But even after this effort, says Smith, "the emotions of the spectator will still be very apt to fall short of the violence of what is felt by the sufferer" (p. 21). This prefigures a passage in Wordsworth's preface to *Lyrical Ballads* which admits that even the greatest poet's language "must often, in liveliness and truth, fall short of that which is uttered by men in real life, under the actual pressure of those passions, certain shadows of which the Poet thus produces, or feels to be produced, in himself."[30] Both Smith and Wordsworth are responding to the received materialist doctrine according to which no two persons are ever identically circumstanced however much they experience apparently common conditions. So no one can ever expect to enter fully into the "real life" of another: hence Wordsworth's qualification that the poet produces *shadows*, or *feels* them to be produced in himself.

Both Smith and Wordsworth thus admit that the sense of connection between one person and another comes at the expense of fidelity to the "actual" situations of both. What people really experience is *not* what connects them. Coleridge realized that this could imperil the very thing Smith supposed it to guarantee – sociability itself – when he pointed out an "occasional" defect in Wordsworth's poetry whereby a "minute adherence to *matter-of-fact* in character and incidence" threatens poetry's proper address to the condition of "men in general."[31] The matter-of-factness, according to Smith's argument, is crucial to the cultivation of sympathy because it is what gives us access to the details of the situation: Smith's "every little circumstance" and "minutest incidents" are what allow us to imagine the experience of the other. According to Coleridge these same items put pressure on any poetry of sympathy because poetry is not supposed to stimulate a "feeling of labor." It is supposed to be a medium giving access to universality rather than "accidentality," and if it is Wordsworth's poetry, it is supposed (according to its own mandate) to focus on the common elements of human nature and not on "those things on which man differs from man" (II: 126–27). Wordsworth's poetry, however, shows not only the aspiration to common feeling but also the sheer difficulty of imagining or experiencing it. How do you gain access to a common human nature if the minute circumstances of the situation are what you must use to construct it, while living in a world where the minute circumstances are themselves not completely recoverable (this is another legacy of eighteenth-century materialism), and where the passions that devolve from them may not be legible? This is why the poet's language is indeed likely always to fall short of what is produced by "the actual pressure of those passions, certain shadows of which the Poet thus produces, or feels to be produced, in himself."[32]

Smith's solution to this conundrum is to propose the existence of a compulsion to normalize experience deriving from a fundamental need for sympathy. We make our best effort to imagine ourselves in the actual situation of the other, and to the degree that we fail (or find the actuality unbearable), we then manufacture an imagined intermediary state of being which describes neither sufferer nor observer but establishes a virtual meeting point for exchange, an emotional money form. Thus *The Theory of Moral Sentiments* proposes that the person suffering pain "passionately desires a more complete sympathy," so much so that the sufferer is willing to misrepresent the degree and extent of his or her own emotion (even suffering) to make it more palatable to the spectator, "lowering his passion to that pitch, in which the spectators are capable of going along with him. He must flatten, if I may be allowed to say so, the sharpness of its natural tone, in order to reduce it to harmony and concord with the emotions of those who are about him" (p. 22). In other words, what we get is *neither* the original situation *nor* the original passion but something already worked upon in order to render it less threatening to the spectator than it would otherwise be. Wordsworth's poetry functions in just this way when it confesses that it is not able to replicate the power and force of original emotions, that it is always emotion recollected in tranquillity, that it makes use of metrical language both to assist in self-control and to maximize communicability. Sympathy, in Smith's schema, is not a direct identification of one person's predicament as another's but an imaginary intersubjective construct that mediates between what the sufferer first feels and what the spectator can deduce from the situation and imaginatively bear to find in him- or herself. It is true neither to exact circumstances nor to original passion, and there is no way in Smith's model that it could be. What saves it as worthwhile communication is the sufferer's own desire for sympathy, which is what helps him or her modify the violence of passion in order to allow others to see the situation as one within their own imaginative capacities, and the beholder's willingness to take a small step away from self-security in fulfilment of the same need for companionship. Sympathy is a function of the desire for sympathy, of the desire for consensus. It is a mediated formation whereby the subject seeks to produce itself into an exchangeable item: an emotional version of Marx's general equivalent. The quantity and quality of one's suffering is converted into a socially average emotion that others can be expected to cope with and thus to buy into according to a natural disposition for trucking, bartering and exchanging. What sustains sociability is a virtual construction that embodies neither the passions of the sufferer nor those of the beholder. It is the emotional money without which there would be, according to Smith, no emotional commerce.

But suppose that there are persons in whom the desire for sympathy is not there, or has broken down, so that the sufferer makes *no* effort to adjust his or her self-presentation in order to allow for a comfortably empathic reaction in the spectator? This is exactly what is described in some of Wordsworth's poems, either in the form of an excessive passion that refuses to see itself as if in the eyes of another – the mad mothers, abandoned women, even the child of "We are Seven" – or in the form of an intransigent silence that seems to defy any urge to decipher and identify – the hunger-bitten girl, the old beggar, the old man traveling. Here we are challenged either by an excess of passion that cannot be reduced to any social and sociable average, or by an even more baffling withholding of expressivity itself.[33] This second case opens up the possibility that a person might feel no passion or a low degree of passion in some or other situation – say bereavement or poverty – while we the spectators feel a great deal of it on our own imagined behalf, and thus feel a tendency to cast the actual sufferer as somehow incompletely human or even inhuman. Seeing an old beggar or an old man traveling, I have to imagine their situations in order to imagine their passions. In both cases, Wordsworth's poeticized observation is that these men hardly feel at all, and they thereby put into question what it is that the beholder feels or should feel when there is no evidence (in Smithian terms) of an effort to play by the rules of the emotional money system. The old beggar is not struggling with or trying to communicate the experience of dying but simply ceasing to live.

These figures are breaking the Smithian circle, for there is no way to tell the difference between a person who has decided on strategic stoicism, successfully normalizing his passion to the point of social acceptability, and one who does not feel at all (or who, in a third and very Wordsworthian variant, may be so fully in the habit of normalizing that he *has* effectively ceased to feel, or is so traumatized that he cannot speak). These distinctions do not matter if the import of the sympathetic instinct is located exclusively in the beholder, but this is to make the emotional transaction entirely one-way: all that matters is what the beholder thinks and feels. Wordsworth raises this possibility quite bluntly in, for example, "The Old Cumberland Beggar," a poem which refuses its readers the consumer satisfactions for which they think they are willing to pay, and for which some of its protagonists indeed do pay. Smith comments: "How amiable does he appear to be, whose sympathetic heart seems to reecho all the sentiments of those with whom he converses, who grieves for their calamities, who resents their injuries, and who rejoices at their good fortune ... And for a contrary reason, how disagreeable does he appear to be, whose hard and obdurate heart feels for himself only, but is altogether insensible to the happiness or misery of others" (*Moral Sentiments*, p. 24). This describes Mackenzie's world well enough, but Wordsworth refuses both of these positions and discovers a place where what is amiable and what is disagreeable are much harder to specify and to experience than Smith suggests, and where the self-approbation about which Smith also writes at length is very hard to come by or to maintain. Wordsworth's special genius is one that heightens and presents the acute discomfort of being somewhere between these positions, which is always nowhere. It is no accident that so many readers have had trouble acceding to the Wanderer's account of how happy he felt after experiencing the events of Margaret's life and death at the end of the first book of *The Excursion*.

Jeremy Bentham made an extreme case that aptly focuses the concern that Smith initiated and Wordsworth inherited. Bentham roundly dismissed sympathy both as an agent of effective sociability and as an object of respectable philosophical description. To him it looked like little more than caprice, needing no verifiable reference to the happiness of others, merely an index of whether or not one is disposed to certain beliefs. An endless variety of circumstances and predispositions goes into making up our individual sensibilities and thus our propensities to be sympathetic or unsympathetic to others.[34] The sources and effects of pleasure and pain are far too quixotic to be proposed as the foundations of any social policy, although Bentham does observe rather cynically that "the stronger and more numerous a man's connexions in the way of sympathy are, the stronger is the hold which the law has upon him. A wife and children are so many pledges a man gives to the world for his good behaviour" (p. 54n.). Sympathy is good for maintaining order, in other words, but less reliable for creating it spontaneously; sympathy can be exploited by those applying the laws but it does not of itself produce those laws or any equivalent informal organizational protocols. Or perhaps one might infer that it is more likely to bond together those who are already like one another than it is to breach significant differences in rank and disposition. The famous scene in Fielding's *Joseph Andrews*, where the sight of the unfortunate hero lying naked in a ditch inspires sympathetic action only from the coachman and not from his upper-middle-class passengers who all find an excuse to leave him where he is, could indeed be taken to indicate an ordinary man's expression of unperverted human nature, but it can also be read as evidence that identification with the other is only likely among those close enough in socioeconomic terms to be able to see themselves as similar victims. If so, it would be proof of the power of divided labor in forming minds and hearts rather than an instance of self-absorption being superseded by universal feeling.[35] The coachman comes to the rescue because he can imagine himself in the same situation more readily than can his passengers. He sees the logic of equivalence, they do not.

After Smith and Bentham but before Habermas, there is Simmel, whose 1910 essay "On Sociability" understands its object somewhat in the Smithian manner as a "sociological artifact" rather than as the emanation of a foundational human instinct.[36] Sociability creates an "ideal world" wherein the pleasure of each depends upon the pleasure of the other(s), and thus requires a "pure interaction" from which "both the objective and the purely personal features of the intensity and extensiveness of life" have been excluded (p. 133). Smith's sympathy-based paradigm preserved some place for the effort of the beholder to approach the "intensity and extensiveness of life" of the sufferer, even though that effort was constrained by both sensory and epistemological limits. Wordsworth too seemed to hold out at least the ideal of approaching the quality of real and substantial action and suffering. Simmel, on the other hand, fully accepts the artificiality of the social experience, which depends not on natural, unencumbered human nature but on the willed renunciation of empirical life into a "stylizing of the sociable man." It is not a lie because it was never real, but it becomes one as soon as it is mistaken for an expression of natural man rather than understood as the cultivated "play" of a Kantian disinterest analogous to the aesthetic response. So it is that "sociable converse" cannot produce or even subsist along with "serious argument" or the aspiration to "truth" (p. 136). It is not an ethical medium but its "shadow world, in which there is no friction, because shadows cannot impinge upon one another" (pp. 137–38). One might call it the ghost of ethics, except that it is entirely virtual, not representative of anything that has been and that might therefore return from the dead. Deep identification with the other, if it were all-possessing and thoroughgoing and not pretended, would threaten or contradict Simmel's model of efficient sociability because it would insist upon the very access to truth and reality that would rob his construct of its purely aesthetic status. Sociability here becomes less an assertion of human affiliations than a conscious curtailing of them, a willing suspension of connections and commitments.

Like Smith and Habermas, Simmel is responding to a longstanding modern interest in informal mechanisms for social bonding that lie beyond or outside what is prescribed by laws. The topic was laid out in great detail by Shaftesbury in the early eighteenth century. The recourse to politeness, conversation and conversability and the critique of that recourse were fundamental to eighteenth-century theorists as they have been to their modern successors.[37] The Chesterfield debate of the 1770s was a particularly intense confrontation with the problems of accepting an avowedly virtual foundation for the maintenance of civil interaction. If good manners are simply a convenient fiction rather than expressive of a sincere commitment to deeply held moral standards, how can we tell the impostors and hypocrites from the virtuous? Does it matter if we cannot tell them apart? If civility or sympathy are only abstractions designed to facilitate the exchange of mutual approbation and tolerance, are they any different from the money form, which is nothing in itself but only a means to enable exchange and to store labor in order to redistribute it more efficiently in the service of profit? Simmel's sociability principle lives in a spectral world where "shadows cannot impinge upon one another" (*On Individuality*, p. 138). His language, derived as it is from the Kantian model of the aesthetic judgment, suggests that even this most purposively uncommodified gesture – I only assume agreement in aesthetic judgments because I place myself outside the world of getting and spending – is imprinted by the ghost of commodity form: assumptions of shared response are premised on abstraction from particular objects of desire or exchange and relocated in a general equivalent (pure form) that has itself no content.[38] The form of an object is thought of as something apart from its material existence and isolated as the proper focus of aesthetic attention, and we think we can see it as such; we abstract form from function and from empirical presence. So for Marx the "relative value-form of a commodity . . . expresses its value-existence as something wholly different from its substance and properties."[39] The double life of commodities as "at the same time objects of utility and bearers of value" (p. 138) makes them at once familiar and mysterious. The abstract component is what we do not see: it must be produced by theory as an object of thought. Formalist aesthetics thinks we can see form and hence comprehend value. But Smith and Simmel seem to understand sympathy and sociability as abstractions in a dynamic process, shifting their locus as rolling averages with every human exchange and thus never themselves open to being seen.

All of these efforts to expound how the bonds of civil society can be strengthened, and which as such compose a sort of ethical long modernity, rely upon the work of an abstract general equivalent. Kant's aesthetic judgment, Habermas's dialogism, Smith's sympathy and Simmel's sociability may be thought of as variously ingenious ways in which one learns to live with the hegemony of commodity form by enjoying or making virtue of its symptoms. The systems they support only work because there is nothing (no thing) holding them together: they depend upon abstractions as the bearers of value. One might read this as a triumph for theory – or as the last and still secret laugh of commodity form. Wordsworth's poetic articulation of its operations will be the main topic of the rest of this chapter and this book. It will take us through dark and watery ways, through mists and vapors, but we will start out with a poem that begins on a burning plain at noon.

WHO CAN "AFFORD TO SUFFER"?

Habermas, Smith, Bentham and Simmel together exemplify some of the important received ideas about sympathy and sociability into and out of which Wordsworth projects his poetry of concern, a poetry that engages an enduring component of the communicative dynamic of modern life – life within modernity – that has not gone away under the historical umbrella we call the postmodern. Wordsworth's poetry insists that there is no comfortable place to stand and no easy way to feel good about oneself in the face of the social and material inequities that continue to perplex all efforts at justifying one's own place in the world. Some of these can be attributed to inexorable nature: old and near-death persons are always with us. But the poor, and the disturbed and disabled military veterans and industrial workers who have been more and more with us, cannot be consigned to the realm of unavoidable suffering. Wordsworth dramatizes a more or less constant uncertainty about what we can and should do to address both "natural" and social-historical afflictions and generates radical doubt over whether we can decide clearly which is which. These urgently confusing questions are explored in a major poem that went through various incarnations, published and unpublished, which ended up as the first book of *The Excursion* but was first fully organized into the manuscripts of "The Ruined Cottage." It is in the first book of *The Excursion* (1: 370–71) that the narrator makes a claim for the pedlar that, in the light of what we have seen of the sympathy debate, must seem controversial: "He could *afford* to suffer / With those whom he saw suffer."[40]

"The Ruined Cottage" is one of the most frequently discussed of Wordsworth's poems, and for good reasons. The poem touches on almost all of the issues I am exploring in this book as typifying Wordsworth's address to social concern in modern life: poverty, death, charity, homelessness, civility and civil society, haunting and spectrality. It is a tragedy, a ghost story, and both a staging and a study of the dynamics of commodification. Above all it raises questions about sympathy, a very difficult notion in Wordsworth which criticism has not yet at all settled.[41] It does so in a series of framing narratives that nest one within another and thereby ask questions about narration itself as the vehicle of differently motivated and overlapping histories. The relative ease with which the pedlar comes to terms with the human suffering he describes remains the poem's most disturbing topic, but there are others. The character Margaret is the primary but not the only sufferer: her husband Robert's misfortunes are major contributory causes of her tragedy, and her children are also implicated. But she is the principal object of the poem's attentions and has accordingly been at the center of critical efforts to make sense of Wordsworth's attitude to distressed women, familiar to his first readers from the Gothic and sentimental traditions from which he claimed to be keeping his distance.

The poem is also freighted with visibly literary allusions and thus imposes on its reader an almost vertiginous oscillation between coolly appreciating its bookishness and even its conventionality and feeling the pressures of a vividly reported first-hand but past experience.[42] Karen Swann finds that Wordsworth's description of the figure of Margaret "stems as much from literature as from life" and draws explicitly upon "the circulation of received ideas."[43] Even the landscape is literary, a Spenserian-Miltonic bower where sin, death and pleasure all compete for precedence. The grove of elm trees and its ruined house signal not only the supposed location of a recounted ordinary life but also the pleasant place of noontide repose familiar to the pastoral tradition that will be so radically disrupted by the tale of Margaret and her family. Even before he reaches the shade, the narrator has conjured up not only Virgil and Theocritus but Milton. He begins by noting that while the landscape might look good to one reposing beneath a "dewy shade" (of the sort that he will soon attain), the experience is quite different for one like him who is out in the middle of a "bare wide Common" on a hot summer's day when there is no respite from the heat or from the "insect host" that swarms around his face.⁴⁴ He dallies with gentle hyperbole in alluding to the first book of *Paradise Lost* and to the burning plain upon which the fallen angels find themselves disposed: so too the "insect host" recalls the cloud of locusts in Milton's simile (l. 340) and the beehive humming of the angels' deliberations (l. 768) that signals their own loss of epic scale, "now less than smallest dwarfs" (l. 779). Wordsworth's narrator is seriocomically pestered by bad angels as he makes his transit across the landscape of a fallen world whose climatological extremes mimic (albeit on a less punishing scale) the torments of Pandemonium and of the fallen human world to come. Subjected to an excess of light, not darkness, he also is an image of the fallen man who is prefigured by the fallen angels, now making his way across a "subjected plain" through "torrid heat" (*PL*, 12: 634, 640). The punishing modern wasteland is shrouded in a "pale stream" to the south and to the north reveals a vision of "embattled clouds" whose "determined and unmoved" shadows seem to signal that time itself has stopped (p. 43).

The fallen angels of *Paradise Lost* are afflicted by darkness rather than this excess of light, but Milton still inhabits this passage.⁴⁵ Nature has been touched by culture; or, to say it better, the human presence in and view of nature is already cultured. The story has not started but this *is* the story. Wordsworth's narratives are commonly crafted to allude to and emanate from literary precursors either too famous for it to be possible that he wants to efface them (Dante, Virgil, Shakespeare, Milton) or too clumsy for us to avoid suspicions of cliché. They thereby raise questions about the commodification of tradition as well as about the capacity of the modern subject to see simply what is in front of it, most critically when what is in front of it is extreme distress and suffering. Will fallen man make good, make partial amends, or just exemplify the limitations he has inherited from Adam and Eve? Will he remain an erring but redeemable human or show himself to be a Satanic figure, eternally a pained and punishing observer? Is salvation in the offing? What is the status of the ordinary life we are left with after the first disobedience? What does it mean to come at the world by way of written books?

This small and delicately intimated literary-theological drama prefigures the narrator's access to the "cool shade" shared by the pedlar and the ruin, and reminds us that this space too is prefigured, both as the umbrage to which Adam and Eve resorted to hide from the sight of God after their first disobedience (*PL*, 10: 100) and as the compensatory space provided for respite from the worst effects of the postlapsarian climate: the same "dewy shade" (p. 43) that Wordsworth's narrator has already found himself wanting. So many stories interpose themselves before we get to the story, so many possible modes of significance and possibilities for resolution: a change in the wind might help, or a metaphysical makeover, a new heaven on earth. The burning plain has also a historical life. The ascribed coincidence of bad harvests and war "some ten years gone" (p. 52) is a vague allusion to the American War, but one motivated by Wordsworth's own experiences of the more recent war against France and by the bad harvests of 1794–95 (see pp. 478–79). Only the pedlar would conclude that the affliction of war was sent by "heaven" (p. 53). Robert's fever is one cause of the family's impoverishment, but the implication is that it follows in some sense from the extreme "self-denials" made necessary by the dire economic situation. There is no relief from the parish for one in his condition: like the shepherd in "The Last of the Flock" he has to use his savings, which are "all consumed," in order to survive (p. 53). When the parish does intervene later in the story, it is to take away Margaret's oldest son to an apprenticeship. Robert's decision to join the army is driven by his predicament. In signing on he fulfills two needs at once: he earns money for the family and removes himself from their sight, so that he need no longer feel ashamed (in this dewy shade of his own) at having his decline witnessed by his loved ones. Natural and political causes combine to produce a circumscribed set of choices that are not absolutely unnegotiable but are yet strongly persuasive. Robert has a choice, but not much of one. He is not an individual who has a full range of options for redeeming the fall of man by good deeds or hard work. The poem transcribes in some detail the ways in which individuals respond to the challenges of empirical life, and it both inhibits any simple ascription of personal responsibility and questions the integrity of the prevailing welfare policy, which fails when it is most needed and only later does potential good (to the boy, perhaps) by doing an equivalent harm (to Margaret). What is *not* available here is any recourse to a sustaining civil society of friends, neighbors and concerned parties. Neither Robert nor Margaret is reported as receiving any concerned or sympathetic response from the neighbors, if they have any – it is a "stranger" who gives Margaret news of her husband, and another "stranger" who tells the pedlar of her life of grief and distraction (pp. 61, 63). The one glimpse of community afforded Margaret seems to consist in the irregular visits of the pedlar himself, which are few and far between and particularly scarce during her time of deepest need. While he offers short-term comfort and improves her morale when he is there, he provides no sustained support. The conditions of sociability as theorized by Simmel cannot prevail here – there is too traumatic an intrusion of empirical life for the game-playing abstractions of sociability to develop or survive, and the disparity between the pedlar's and Margaret's lives is too radical to be wished away. The situation requires an active and continual redress that seems not to be open to a wanderer, a man professionally engaged in roving "o'er many a hill and many a dale" (p. 61).

In *Paradise Regained* it is the Prince of Darkness who is "roving still / About the world" (1: 33–34). Wordsworth's rovers (preeminently the poet-narrator himself) often have Satanic qualities, expressing the pain of their own alienation from human communities or from individuals with whom they cannot bond. They are not figures who generate or display any of the simple forms of sympathy. The pedlar has chosen to come back to a site associated with memories of pain, which he finds pleasurable, indeed a source of avowed "happiness" (p. 75). Kames had taken up this topic (rather less systematically than Adam Smith) in describing sympathy as "the great cement of human society," a force so powerful as even to "overbalance" the "self-love" that would otherwise cause us to flee from scenes of distress.[46] Painful as it may be, sympathy is productive of a yet greater pleasure, thanks to the benevolent God who has not bestowed upon us a split personality but has "given us this noble principle entire, without a counterbalance, so as to have a vigorous and universal operation" (p. 20). Thus it is that we seek out distress in order to experience the pleasure of relieving it or, when it takes the form of tragic art, to "humanize the temper, by supplying feigned objects of pity, which have nearly the same effect to exercise the passion that real objects have" (p. 21). The pedlar's emotion recollected in tranquillity seems to stand between the two, neither present life (Margaret is dead) nor quite fiction (the events really did happen): it is an awkward icon of the bad faith latent in poetry itself. Wordsworth introduces a deliberately false note in distancing his narrator from the pedlar, who is touched with the spectatorial personality of both arch-fiend and practicing poet, and in playing up the nonuniversal particularity of the old man's habits and education.

While it would be going too far to limit the roving pedlar to a purely Satanic role (or indeed to cast the narrator as entirely a fallen angel), it is no accident that questions about his good faith and disposition have consistently arisen for readers of the poem.[47] In the midst of his recounted sympathy for Margaret, he evinces disengagement rather than anguish, and his detachment allows him to tell the story and to pass on to others the burden of making sense of this human tragedy. His storytelling raises powerful feelings in his listener, and as such functions to test out the limits and possibilities of sympathy for both the poem's narrator and the second-order listeners embodied in its readers. He is also himself a character of a distinctly literary bent, signaled not least when he denies the literariness of this "common tale" by differentiating it from the "moving accidents" of Othello's narratives (p. 59). He muses on the cottage "as on a picture" (p. 51), as if the reduction of a lived environment to a still-life ruin – "so still an image of tranquillity" (p. 75) – makes possible the time and space for meditation only after the lives that flourished here have passed away.[48] This "venerable Armytage" (p. 45), very much in the character of the rigorous Scottish or Cumbrian Protestant persona developed in other versions of the poem, mystifies the entirely secular events of war and famine by invoking God's violent punishment of Nineveh from Nahum 3: 17: "And of the poor did many cease to be / And their place knew them not" (p. 53). His puzzling specification of Margaret's being deprived of life till "he shall come again / For whom she suffered" (p. 67) – is it Christ or Robert who must come? – has an uncomfortably sanctimonious aura; and his placid invocation of "the hour of deepest noon" when even the "multitude of flies" is "chearful" (p. 57) seeks to convert to good the overdetermined moment in the day where critical things happen in *Paradise Lost* – Raphael's visit to Adam (5: 231) and the moment of Eve's fall (9: 410, 739) – which in turn prefigure the noon-to-three darkness of the crucifixion, also proleptic in *Samson Agonistes*'s "dark, dark, dark, amid the blaze of noon" (l. 80). The pedlar's diction is steeped in the interpretive fabric that religious literature provides; this is how he thinks, and what helps him both tell his story and fortify himself against the potentially disabling distress it arouses. But its allusions are disjunctive and disturbing, serving not to affirm his holy mandate but to implicate him in grandiose and self-protecting gestures. The very literature he cites works against him.

In its implacable tale of decline and death, the poem has the rhythm of a tragedy whose villain has yet to be decided. It is also a ghost story. The details of Margaret's life only emerge in the story that is the poem after she herself "sleeps in the calm earth" (p. 75). It is the vocabulary of haunting and spirit seeing that characterizes the pedlar's narration: "I see around me here / Things which you cannot see" (p. 49). His recollections of the dead woman make up a story "hardly clothed / In bodily form" (p. 59), one telling how Margaret becomes more and more ghostly as she wastes away with grief, "pale and thin," seemingly committed to an eternal wandering that is beyond the solace of death: "as if my body were not such / As others are, and I could never die." She is a spectral form pursuing another like herself, her vanished husband whom she seeks "but cannot find" (p. 65) and frantically hallucinates, "shaping things / Which made her heart beat quick" (p. 71). The pedlar's capacity finally to dismiss grief as an "idle dream" dissolved by "meditation" (p. 75) is not easily shared by the less theologically secure narrator who responds to the pedlar as to a conjuror – "the things of which he spake / Seemed present," – who succumbs to a "heartfelt chillness" in the veins (p. 57), and who experiences "the impotence of grief" (p. 73) much more fully than does the man telling him the story. This is not the frisson of Gothic fiction whose conventions Wordsworth has so carefully avoided in electing to allude instead to the canon of high poetry. The "impotence of grief" is only imperfectly assuaged if at all, and the haunting remains apparent. It stands alongside and offset from the rhetoric of wealth and money. The poem seems to offer a choice from the marketplace of ideas about suffering and how to handle it, but it is hard to stand with the pedlar who, in the expanded version of the poem that was eventually published as the first book of *The Excursion*, is described as one who "could *afford* to suffer / With those whom he saw suffer," and who thence becomes "rich" in "best experience" (1: 370–72).[49] Why should the pedlar's virtues, if that is what they are, be described in the language of commerce and wealth? Is it a virtue to live "unclouded by the cares / Of ordinary life" (1: 355–56), or does this privilege work in part to insulate us from sympathies with our kind? Could we experience sympathy at all if we were not thus paid off and protected from collapsing into traumatized inertia or from running a mile at the sight of the miseries of others? The pedlar does not need to "turn aside from wretchedness / With coward fears" (1: 369–70), but is the price of his ability to face adverse reality the loss of a self-involvement that might have proved more positive and made him more than a mere listener to Margaret's story? Is it the case that those who can afford to suffer with others are less willing or able to act decisively against the causes of distress because they live within a carapace of physiological and doctrinal indifference, evident both in the pedlar's ability to leave the scene of suffering at a critical time and by his recourse to self-righteously biblical rhetoric? The expense of Margaret's life seems to subsidize the pedlar's spiritual profit.

The weird intercession of commodity language specifying the pedlar's wealth, which allows him to *afford* to suffer, is not just a conventional figure of speech: it points toward a more extended commodification of the emotions. Alan Liu has offered a carefully documented and critically powerful reading of the congruence between peddling, weaving and making (and selling) poetry that can be deduced from the various revisions of the poem in relation to its complex framing narratives.[50] He finds in Wordsworth's biography a crisis in the "industry of writing parallel to that of weaving" (p. 341). Margaret's husband Robert was a weaver, and a member of the artisan class particularly associated with assiduous reading habits (p. 611 n. 26), as well as one under increasing economic stress. The time of the writing of the poem is at one with a historical crisis in the domestic textile industry, while Wordsworth himself is involved in "an expanding universe of debts" (p. 338) because he is lending out money at high but risky interest and is thus concerned about his future as potentially akin to that of the immiserated (and now dead) Margaret. Nor is the pedlar a fully comfortable figure for fantasy identification. The peddling life was under political inspection as a threat to the emergent retail trade, standing out as an emblem of premodern, unregulated commerce whose analogue is (Liu argues) poetic imagery itself (pp. 344–47).[51] This is resolved by an "economy of lyric" which provides "riches" out of "sublimated denials of normal economy" (p. 353) – the smaller the poem the greater the gain.[52]

Liu's reading is richer than anything I can here reduce to paraphrase, but I take up, for now, its major insight into the fundamentally economic nature of both the poem's topic and its coming into being (and therefore, inevitably, of its circulation). Liu proposes that this is "not a poem of humanity" but of "a capitalization upon inhumanity" (p. 325). We may add to this a second set of concerns set forth by Celeste Langan in her fine reading of the poem as an instance of the "split subject of liberalism" in its depiction of an encounter between "surplus and distress."[53] The pedlar has more than he needs both spiritually and economically, so he can "afford" to face up to the sufferings of others; but Margaret has much less than she needs. Here there is no meeting in the middle, no redistribution of goods such that each might have enough. The poem does not stage a utopian society that has undone excess and, more important, done away with the consequences of unequal sustenance, let alone wealth. Instead it offers an uneasy and visibly disturbed conclusion whereby no satisfactory state of mind can be assumed without painful knowledge of the limits of "happiness" and the alternatives to it. The sublimation of tragedy as moral uplift cannot be carried out without ignoring things that no good reader can ignore: we would have to be blind to the limits and conditioning circumstances of the pedlar's narration, which the second narrator refuses to allow us to take for granted.

What then is to be said about the poet's labor, and the implied expectations about its success or failure? The narrator proper is a somewhat colorless figure with no designated vocation: we are not told much about who it is that is toiling across the scorching plain and why he is doing so. Margaret, Robert and the pedlar (especially in the poem as published in 1814) are given lengthy biographical identities. Robert and Margaret are both described in some detail as falling out of work and out of the work–life balance that makes life worth living. Margaret in particular takes on the spectral form of the factory laborer whose profile we have already seen in the hunger-bitten French girl and will see again in other figures encountered on the public roads. Limited as she is to a single "path":

> There, to and fro she paced through many a day
> Of the warm summer, from a belt of flax
> That girt her waist spinning the long-drawn thread
> With backward steps. (*Ruined Cottage*, p. 70)

Although she lives and works in the middle of a bare wide common with endless opportunities for random peregrinations, this woman spends her days walking backwards, to and fro, spinning her own tether in a motion that mimics the movements of a machine and the automated motion of a ghost. She thus signals her unwilling affiliation with the very processes of industrial production that are putting her and her kind out of work.[54] Her physical wasting away is thereby echoed in and perhaps partly caused by the effects of her work discipline. Her emotional distress makes her ghostly, but so does her occupation. Both of these conditions inform her decline into apathy: "her eye-lids drooped, her eyes were downward cast; / And when she at her table gave me food / She did not look at me" (p. 66). The wandering she undertakes, further and further from home but always coming back to it, merely lengthens the string around her waist; there is no clear distinction between work time and leisure time. The remnant of free choice that is suggested by the narrative's refusal to spell out the terms of an absolute social-historical determination is undermined by the motif of the leash around her waist, upon which she performs her work life and replicates the spinning of the threads of fate. Here, in the middle of England, Wordsworth finds another distressed woman held in place by string.

The pedlar's motions are seemingly more random and certainly unpredictable, as befits the bearer of a more spasmodic economic order.

This "chosen son" who sees a "moral life" in everything is, I have suggested, limited in his ability to deviate from the religiose terms of his upbringing and personal inclination, so that describing his feelings being bound "as in a chain" (p. 48) seems like a negative judgment. The power of his conditioning is further played up in *The Excursion*, which has him reared according to a "strictness scarcely known on English ground" (1: 117) while enjoying an ideal Wordsworthian childhood amidst the great forms of nature, "with no one near / To whom he might confess the things he saw" (1: 130–31). The fruits of this social isolation are not quite as simple as the famous thesis about love of nature leading to love of man might suggest, since the nature of his love is so visibly complicated by his eagerness to make happiness out of tragedy. By the time of the encounter with the narrator, he has retired from peddling and become a kind of tourist, revisiting the places that were on his working circuit, "the scenes / That to his memory were most endeared" (1: 390–91). As such he is an icon of emotion recollected in tranquillity, with the ironic proviso that he was already tranquilized in his former life, enough so that Margaret's sufferings did not disable him. He may also be the figure of a poet whose ability to face the facts and tell his story is dependent upon an acquired insulation from the trauma of unmediated experience. As is common in Wordsworth's narratives, the power of the story being told is framed by a recognition of the human limits of its teller, as if we cannot have the one without the other. There are three options for identifying the persona of the poet in this poem: the tragic Margaret, the distressed and disturbed narrator who comes too late to assist her, and the perhaps all-too-capable pedlar. There is no simple mechanism for choosing between them.

The pedlar is hooked into a pattern of movement that is less restrictive than Margaret's but still programmed. He repeats in his retirement the perambulations of his working life, which were not absolutely regular but still governed by a routine: that of making a living by selling goods. He would always show up again, but his customers were never sure just when. He was not tied to the repetitious regularity of mechanized, proto-industrial labor, in the way that Margaret eventually is figured as being, and his role in the commodity economy did not conform to the standard of immediate reciprocity set by the fixed retail trade: instant exchangeability on demand. His situation mimics the desire of a poet who is notably anxious about the commodification of his own and all writing in that it exempts him from the aura of the most punishing production and the most tawdry consumerism though never from the economic cycle as such. To the same degree it embodies the fear of an emerging professional writer that he might not find any customers, that his products might appear too rarely and unpredictably to earn public esteem, that his own muse might wander afar and come home all too occasionally. Margaret's ghostliness inversely affirms the pedlar's real-life status in the story that is the poem, but his own spectral career – always having been, always to come again – is also apparent. The poet's hopes are inextricably bound up with the poet's fears. Sympathy and sociability are not fully enough developed to assuage them, and a wider civil society seems nonexistent. Above all, commerce does not create sympathy, as it was supposed to do according to the legions of Whig apologists of the benefits of trucking, bartering and exchanging. Margaret cannot afford very much, which may be why the pedlar comes around less often the more impoverished she becomes. He may remember himself as having been kindly, but his concern had its limits: business comes first. His failure to appear as she approaches the lowest point in her life marks him as an emblem of the inexorable logic of profit. His appearances become infrequent toward the end, when Margaret is dying not buying.

So the pedlar too is something of a ghost. He is now retired and on a tour of his former circuit. He is old, perhaps tending toward his own death. In his narration of the history of his various visits to Margaret, there is never a mention of her *ever* buying anything from him or of him giving or selling her anything she needed. Neither commerce nor charity, in other words, seem to have marked their interactions. She may not have had the money to purchase even the minimal wants and desires that itinerant salesmen habitually satisfied, but she clearly had radical needs which became more and more exigent as the pedlar's visits became less frequent. What he dispensed, it seems, was at best sympathy along with the tea she made him; there is no account of active charity of the material kind. His work as a salesman seems then to have been suspended during these stops at Margaret's cottage. What kind of society is it that subsists without either giving or selling? This absence of material transactions might be taken to emphasize the pedlar's role as proxy clergyman, spiritual counsel in a place where the established church seems not to figure. As such it might signal a purity of interaction. Or it might prompt some reflection on the pedlar's role as a poet-proxy, one who makes stories out of the demise of others and whose profit is deferred for a future while maintaining a detachment that can seem forbidding and even amoral. It might even suggest that the pedlar is an analogue of circulation itself, of the commodity or money form that enables everything while remaining in itself nothing.[55] Simmel made much of a traditional association between money and strangers, each seen as threatening while being necessary to the image of local solidarity and its wider relationships, and both in turn associated (as in the case of the Sophists) with an "uncanny power of the mind . . . neutral and heartless like money." Modern life, he conjectured, had diminished the power of the stranger only because "the money form of transactions has now been taken up by the whole economic community."[56] So the pedlar becomes a familiar stranger, circulating unpredictably and often not there when you need him most, but yet a recognized figure capable of supplying temporary comfort. He is abstraction itself, enabling exchange but not able to offer something for nothing. The more you have to spend, the more often he comes around. The comfort, whether free or purchased, cannot last – or lasts only as long as you hold it in your hand.

This is as true for those who hear or read Margaret's story as it was for Margaret herself. At the end of the poem, pedlar and narrator make their way to the inn where they will spend the night, but there is no invocation of sweet society to come, nothing to dispel the aura of melancholy introspection or at best tentative consolation. The poem's reported and twice reported dialogues are instances of the communication of more pain than solace, and such solace as there is seems to be bestowed introspectively and in a state of precarious solitude. Thoughts and feelings come with difficulty and bring with them identifications that threaten to collapse the boundaries between separate individuals; in so threatening, they do not project Kames's sympathy as the "cement of human society" but the "heartfelt chillness" of a more disabling response. If the pedlar administers a lesson in how to resist going under at the sight or hearing of the tragedies of others, then it does not bring with it much satisfaction or self-esteem – surely not the "happiness" that he himself professes (p. 75). The sight of pain elicits only false assurance or bewilderment.[57] There is no sustaining community in the world the story tells about, and no simple position of comfort for its hearers. The griefs that are related are not efficiently processed by the modifying instinct that Adam Smith imagines as operating upon sufferers who above all want to communicate with their fellow humans, and are prepared to diminish the intensity of what they project to serve that end. Here the image of human suffering is of a force that can take one altogether outside the social world into a timeless void populated by specters and hallucinations, from whence there is no return.

Wordsworth's poetic analysis of sympathy and sociability makes clear that Smith and Habermas are first and foremost theorists of the normative and of normalization, and thus utopian thinkers. Smith's argument depends upon the sufferer's desire for sympathy; he has nothing to say about what happens if this disappears or fails to exist. Habermas is exploring a model for rationally defensible interaction in an ideal democracy, of the sort that we have never yet had and, it seems, show few signs of ever having. Reading Wordsworth along with these theorists of sympathy and civility might suggest the degree to which his poetry engages with exceptional cases, but it also suggests that especially during times of national and international crisis exceptionality is itself the rule. The political iconography of the 1790s made much of the contrast between the well-tended and the ramshackle cottage, the first imaged as the dwelling of a contented, loyalist peasantry and the second housing morally improvident and often politically radical spirits who threatened to reduce everyone else to the same shabby circumstances as theirs.[58] The fashion for cottage life as the site of an escape from the cares of metropolitan life, whether in fact or fantasy, had already become widespread.[59] It was above all in cottage life that family bonds were supposed to stay firm and traditions remain intact, that loosely federated communities of owner-occupiers or long-term renters could subsist together as independent but still residually social: Mary Russell Mitford's *Our Village* (1824–32) sums up quite a few of the received wisdoms. Wordsworth's ruin fulfills none of the established and propagandist images of cottage life. It is haunted by figures conjured from the past by the pedlar's storytelling, persons who subsisted neither as bad nor good peasants but as ordinary people overcome by forces well beyond their control, and who suffered unassisted by either friendly neighbors or benevolent parish policies. There are no prospects for a better life for such people either in this world or the next. If there is a possible solution, it has yet to be articulated; the pedlar's accommodationist metaphysics helps him come to terms with the pain of others but does nothing to prevent it. Sympathy is aroused, but left to wander through a landscape that pays tribute only to its previous insufficiencies. The narrator's capacity to pass beyond the "impotence of grief" (p. 73) is never clearly announced, which leaves the poem's readers a choice about where and how to bestow their own emotions – with the pious pedlar, the distraught speaker, or in some other place.

If there is another place, it is not located in the poem: it remains a matter of unspecified concern. Wordsworth's embedded narration – a poet telling about a pedlar who tells about a dead woman – establishes enough commonality among its three protagonists to suggest the potential substitutability of each for the others. If substitution were to produce a fuller empathy, then it might seem morally desirable even as it would inevitably be subjectively devastating. The narrator could be the pedlar or Margaret, but isn't; the pedlar could be Margaret, but isn't. And the differences do not sustain any gestures of conclusive intervention. The narrator only hears the story after Margaret's death, and the pedlar, who knew her when she was alive, never did enough to make a radical difference. The "spec(tac)ular reversal" that Gary Harrison has found typical of Wordsworthian encounters, whereby "those who are not poor are confronted with a disturbing sign of their own economic precariousness and possible pauperization," works to some degree for the narrator (as a proxy of the apprentice poet) but not at all for the more self-satisfied pedlar.[60] But we cannot say that either of them fully shares the pain, a state of affairs that leaves open (while insisting on) the question of whether it should or can be shared. The young Marx's 1844 manuscripts described how the overseer experiences a version of the worker's alienation, but as a state of mind rather than as an activity: the overseer does not fully "do against himself what he does against the worker."[61] There is no equivalence of suffering, although the overseer does suffer in his way: we may suffer with those we see suffering, but it is not the same suffering. We do not share the pain, but we may want or feel we ought to suffer more, and we may sense (as the narrator does) that the same suffering might soon come our way. Unless you are a righteous pedlar, potential substitutability always looms.

So, in response to the claims made after 1989 for the end of history, for a cosmopolitan category of civility that is able to preempt the need for statist policy and for a saving power in human sympathy, reading Wordsworth produces the sense of a history that has by no means ended and might indeed have barely begun. He writes out of a radical uncertainty about what is changeable and what is not, but not in the service of an ideological obfuscation whereby politics calls itself nature. The pain that is witnessed and sometimes unwittingly enhanced by his narrators (how much Margaret must have wanted the pedlar to call more regularly than he did) and the pain in their own hearts and minds that these witnessings give rise to may not be fully containable by acts of sympathy or routines of civil behavior, but their absence from the poem is crucial. Similarly, the representation of human lives as ghostly and of the landscape as haunted by the living dead does not consign them to the supernatural but demands attention to their continued life in the history of the present as lived within the governing conditions of commodity form, machine labor and mass warfare. The exercises in unresolved moral and interpersonal problems that Wordsworth's poetry commonly represents thus remain not simply available to us; they deserve to be required reading against the simplifications in the rhetoric of social life that we still live with. Against the tendencies to give up hope altogether or to join in the self-applause of the neoliberal consensus about the end of history, reading Wordsworth offers a place of not knowing, a space of disturbance and concern. His poetic encounters with the poor, the homeless and the distraught function as demanding paradigms for understanding a history in which we are still entangled.

CHAPTER 2

At home with homelessness

And homeless near a thousand homes I stood,
And near a thousand tables pined and wanted food.[1]

IN THE PLACE OF THE OTHER

The author of the unpublished "Home at Grasmere", with its intensely expressed desire to be enfolded and nurtured by a protective natural and social space, was otherwise not much in the habit of describing himself as at home in his world. Even though he spent much time walking up and down in his garden or close by his house – not to speak of sitting around reading books or sleeping late – his poetic persona is that of a long-distance wanderer across the hills and along the public roads, a figure of exemplary loneliness whose isolation rendered meaningful and critical every human encounter he experienced. Here he is not a cosseted genius surrounded by adoring women ready to cook his dinner, wash his clothes, take down his every line and fragment and copy them over and over, but a compulsive and constant traveler through the world. He was indeed an intrepid walker capable of keeping going for hours and even days and of covering considerable distances: De Quincey seriocomically estimated that Wordsworth might have walked 180,000 miles during his lifetime and declared him to have found in walking the stimulus to the animal spirits that others sought in alcohol.[2] But the reality of a life spent fretting over the oscillation between manic activity and indolence, self-doubt and ill-health – not at all the "unclouded happiness" that De Quincey imagined – is transfigured in many of his poems into a series of heroic or Satanic peregrinations which he was habitually compelled to invent even where he did not make them. So it is that "Alice Fell" and "The Solitary Reaper," for example, are presented as if they are based on personal experiences, whereas they are in fact derived from, respectively, the travels of a friend of a friend and an encounter described in another friend's manuscript. "Resolution and Independence" describes meeting an old leech-gatherer on a "lonely moor," when in fact the meeting occurred (as he would tell Isabella Fenwick) "a few hundred yards from my cottage."[3]

The terms of this poetic metamorphosis of ordinary mooching and muddling into a steady, lonely circulation of near-planetary proportions involve much more than a petulant refusal to share the limelight and to remind us, for instance, that the figure who so famously "wandered lonely as a cloud" in fact enjoyed on that exact occasion the company of his devoted sister. Walking and wandering, as Anne Wallace has told us, were becoming fashionable, no longer (for the middle class) the sign of brute indigence but the consequence of a preference for the benefits of physical exercise, and perhaps the expression of a political solidarity with the common man: Rousseau and Thelwall had both publicized themselves as ramblers. The new enthusiasm for walking was also, Wallace suggests, the result of a transport revolution which made it possible for more and more people to move around, thus rendering the roads rather safer than they had been before: Wordsworth meets no highwaymen, whereas the heroes of earlier eighteenth-century novels could be guaranteed at least one.[4] Wanderers are omnipresent in literature from its early origins to Kerouac and beyond: it is "a rare work" that does not contain a variant of the chronotope of the road, as Bakhtin tells us.[5] But the function of this familiarity is to sponsor the unfamiliar, the uncanny. It is on the road that, as Bakhtin says, "people who are normally kept separate by social and spatial distance can accidentally meet," so that what is revealed is the "*sociological heterogeneity* of one's own country" (pp. 243, 245). The everyday experience – getting from here to there and back again – becomes a site for the incursion of adventure and surprise: you never know who is around the corner. Wordsworth is deeply interested in sociological heterogeneity and is of course famously committed to mitigating its effects by employing the language of ordinary men; it is one of the many ironies of his poetic situation that the differences he deplores were already being erased by forces far greater and less manageable than those of social rank and diction, leveling forces deriving from machine labor and commodification and producing a sameness not at all to be desired but one inseparable from the otherwise positive effects of a democratizing culture. This is one of the insights of his poetry, where the magical realism of first encounters is implacably revealed as hiding the sameness and reproducibility of a condition of death-in-life. The shock of the unexpected and the challenge of apparent otherness is constantly brought within an inclusive logic that governs both the object of encounter and the subject encountering it. The persons encountered are indeed strangers, but they and the narrators are reduced to a common condition rendering their individualities largely unimportant. What emerges is something darker and more dangerous than any merely democratic brotherhood of man: a solidarity of dispossession and displacement based not on elected but on imposed equalities that we might prefer to live without.

Sociological heterogeneity, the promise of the new or newly noticed, is thus deflated by the recognition of a commonality that is undesired and imposed, and one that threatens to overpower any working experience of the brotherhood of man. The spectrality of the Wordsworthian encounter signals not just the threat of the unknown other but a derealization of life itself, and for the self as well as for the other. Often the termini of the Wordsworthian narrator's journeys are not specified; we are not told where he is coming from or where he is going. While appearing to remove these poetic events from the sphere of a sociology of the real, this withholding of empirical information signals the reality of alienation itself. Franco Moretti's work on the formal geographies of literary sites has made newly significant the comings and goings of fictional protagonists in their described environments; he finds, for example, that the pattern of notable events in Mitford's *Our Village* describes a series of concentric circles, with the village always in the middle as the place of reference and return. In later installments of the collection, the circles get larger as the centripetal force of the village weakens in the face of new social and economic circumstances, so that the pattern eventually falls apart.[6] If one were to try to map the *actual* excursions on which Wordsworth based his poems, patterns would emerge readily enough: to and from Grasmere to Ambleside, to Scotland, to Italy. We can usually track the poet's movements quite accurately thanks to the copious records, diaries and letters that record them. But in the poetry these realities are conjured away. Motion itself becomes the governing principle, as if the narrator is in a constant state of circulation, a man without home or shelter and worldly destination, a figure of implacable homelessness.

Homelessness indeed haunts Wordsworth like a poem that cannot be finished, and many of his unfinishable poems themselves describe a condition of homelessness. He was, for example, famously unsure about what to do with the materials that composed the "Salisbury Plain" manuscript, which included the section published in 1798 as "The Female Vagrant" and the poem eventually appearing in 1842 as "Guilt and Sorrow." The incomplete manuscript drafts of 1793–94 (which provide the epigraph to this chapter) end with an appeal to the doctrinal "Heroes of Truth" who might end "Superstition's reign," but offer no solace to the wandering widow who has "no house in prospect but the tomb."[7] The poem published in 1798 as "The Female Vagrant" has its narrator say that what matters most to her is "that I have my inner self abused" but holds out no reward for such self-admonishment in the form of home or shelter: she remains as she began, a weeping wanderer upon the moors.[8] The longer, framing narrative completed by 1799, into which a version of "The Female Vagrant" was to be interposed, has two homeless persons, the discharged sailor and the widowed woman, as well as the sailor's displaced wife who dies on the road while being ferried by the "overseers" from her father's house back to the place she left behind.[9] This is a tale dominated by the powers of conscience and remorse in the old man whose death sentence ends the poem: he finally finds a home in death, hanging in the "iron case" that justice demands (p. 154). The fate of the female vagrant is unspecified; no restitution for her is mentioned. The poem's variants have a declared social-historical occasion, so that when "Guilt and Sorrow" appeared in 1842, it included a preface in which Wordsworth recalled and did not rescind his 1793 conviction that the war with France would produce "distress and misery beyond all calculation," especially for the "poor" (p. 217). As such it makes clear that the homelessness it describes is no mere metaphysical condition, but a feature of the world he saw around him. For such unfortunates the desire for home is only fully resolved in death, and being alive is a constant experience of transit and displacement.

The versions of this poem span almost the whole of Wordsworth's career, one throughout which the unsolved matter of homelessness is seldom far away from his attentions.[10] The early poems are obsessed with homeless people who encounter a narrator as visibly displaced as they are, one who always casts himself as alone even when Dorothy's journals and his own recollections tell us that he is walking the landscape in company or close to his own backyard. Even in the later poems, so often received as testimonies to smug self-composure and merely spent passions, there is a high incidence of writing about transit – the progress of rivers, tours of Scotland, of Europe, and journeys through British and European history. The narrator's peace of mind is less visibly disturbed than it was in the early work, but he is still habitually on the move. Then there is the massively hyperbolic homing rhetoric of the unpublished *Home at Grasmere*, whose excess undoes its own credibility; the continually worked-upon life-as-journey narrative called *The Prelude;* and *The Excursion*, whose title should be taken seriously but whose termini – the places from which and to which – are for its most important characters crucially vague. To be sure the melodramatic, Satanic roving and roaming that energizes poems like "Gipsies" seems in this poem to have been thoroughly domesticated: wandering across the face of an uncooperative earth turns at the end into a stroll around the lake. But *The Excursion* is an exercise in false closure and subtle retraction. The image of the "snow-white ram" that rewards the walking party in Book 9 (l. 441), for example, is meant to recall a similar image in *Aeneid* 8. Aeneas's vision tells him where to build his city, where to make a home. Wordsworth's protagonists see something different – no allegorical portent or metaphysical imperative but simply the reflection of this "most beautiful" ram's "imperial front" in the water, matched by its own image:

> as beautiful,
> Beneath him, showed his shadowy counterpart.
> Each had his glowing mountains, each his sky,
> And each seemed centre of his own fair world:
> Antipodes unconscious of each other,
> Yet, in partition, with their several spheres,
> Blended in perfect stillness, to our sight![11]

Such is empire, from homeland to antipodes, an image of an image that can be dissolved in "a breath" (l. 453). Instead of a divine imperative to the founding of a city, we have here the insubstantiality of an image, an icon of reflexivity itself as it includes both the real ram and its watery reflection united for a moment only and only from a particular perspective. The ram's message to its beholders is a refusal of messages and of the epic pretension to summarize the fate of nations and the course of history: the image is all there is. The "imperial front" is just that, a front. And there is no home to be had in images, which simply reflect back upon us and our own unhoused condition. The ram itself seems uninterested in any experience of the mirror stage; it is the watching narrator who combines the two images, "blended ... to our sight" in an achievement of "perfect stillness," but one that cannot last:

> "Ah! what a pity were it to disperse,
> Or to disturb, so fair a spectacle,
> And yet a breath can do it!" (ll. 452–54)

A good thing, surely, that this "twofold image" (for both the living ram and its reflection are images) can be dissolved in a breath; for without breath there is no life, and perfect stillness would be death. And an odd thing, just as surely, that the ramblers would regret its dissolution, as if wishing themselves dead and perfected in still life.

There is a paradox governing Wordsworth's place in literary history: that a poet who has become (and who made himself) one of the major figures in the British heritage industry's celebration of locality is in most of his poetry emphatically not at home, and neither are those he encounters on his wanderings. As such he is the harbinger of our contemporary ideas about postmodern nomadism, and of the thoroughly modern displacements that precede and perhaps constitute present-day claims for the normative nature of exile and mobility: he is an exemplary dromologist, to recall Paul Virilio's term.[12] His wanderers also have a markedly literary heritage, drawing upon Odysseus, Aeneas, the Wandering Jew and (above all) Milton's Satan in their images and allusions; they might thus seem to invite attributions of another familiar component of the postmodern condition, that of pastiche.[13] But they are above all historically embodied in the gypsies, beggars, discharged soldiers and abandoned women of the English countryside, so that literature here is the vehicle for history and not the other way around. These figures are proleptic, looking forward to a future in which questions of home and homelessness – and of home *as* homelessness – would become more and more urgent and obsessive. The massive human displacements of 1914–45 have seemed to many Europeans to stand as the signature events of the twentieth century, bringing home to the developed and familiar world the conditions that had formerly been ignorable because they were seen as pertaining only to faraway peoples speaking exotic languages. Adorno, responding to the coincidence of Auschwitz with the logic of commodification as symptomatic of modern life, declared that "dwelling, in the proper sense, is now impossible" and that residing within traditional houses has become intolerable, making "the enforced conditions of emigration a wisely-chosen norm."[14] One might as well consciously acknowledge the inadequacy of the approved "living-cases": henceforth, he goes on to say, "it is part of morality not to be at home in one's home" (p. 39). Heidegger, stimulated by but determined to surpass the empirical conditions of the postwar German housing crisis, pronounced the problem of dwelling [*Wohnen*] as primordial and implicit in the human condition, and not just the source of a short-term emergency – though of course it was from within those emergency conditions that he was writing.[15] More recent thinkers – Deleuze, Derrida – have followed through with an extended analysis of the *unheimlich* (the uncanny, unhomely) which Freud found to be at the heart of and at one with the *heimlich* (the homely), a thesis with profound ramifications for state-sponsored ideologies dependent upon setting clear and distinct boundaries between the domestic and the foreign, the natural and the unnatural, the acceptable and the rejected or punished. And Giorgio Agamben's continuing theorizations of the modern state as a state of exception in a posture of never-ending war have produced a model of normative citizenship coincident with the status of the refugee, and an image of the polis as the camp. In the state of exception, any one of us can be removed from wherever we are and anything can be done to us (Agamben thought this out well before Abu Ghraib, Guantánamo and the exposure of "extraordinary rendition"): political philosophy must now begin "from the one and only figure of the refugee" as the reference point for "the forms and limits of a coming political community."[16]

It would be easy enough to dismiss Agamben's paradigm, and perhaps Wordsworth's foreshadowing of it, as mere bourgeois fantasy. Is it not a spurious gesture of imaginary suffering that allows those of us in the affluent nations to describe ourselves as inhabitants of a camp? Does this not make it all too easy for us to ignore the world's real refugees because we imagine them as no worse off than we are ourselves? Similarly, is the Wordsworthian narrator's self-inscription as a lonely wanderer (when the poet himself can lay claim to ample home and shelter) not a cheap excuse for his failures of charity and imagination when faced with the genuinely homeless persons he encounters? Can there be an identity proposed between the haves and the have-nots that is not pure ideology and thus nothing more than a legitimation of laissez-faire social policies?

There is indeed something more than a little melodramatic and troubling in Agamben's stagings of normal life as refugee life, but we would be unwise to deny their power as indicators of a historically important tendency, and one that Wordsworth visibly prefigures. Both writers might be described as practitioners of a poetics of concern, with all the incipient bad faith that is latent in the term *concern* itself: an inclination to arrest practical response by recourse to a state of reflexive bewilderment. To be sure the narrator who sees himself "stepping westward" and salvaging a few scarce thoughts of "human sweetness" on his "endless way" is not being honest about the hot dinner he expects to find at the next cottage or inn, or cooked by loyal women awaiting him at home.[17] Such home truths may remain central to judgments about Wordsworth the man (and there have been a good many of those) without however circumscribing the ethical and informational possibilities implicit in his poems. One could indeed say that the posture of narrator as existentially isolated traveler through the world is a tired instance of the Romantic hero, gendered male, but one can also explore it as a synecdoche for a condition of modern alienation that does not know such straightforward limits and boundaries. Similarly Agamben's insight into the transient and vulnerable quality of all of us in the modern state of exception rings true as long as we preserve a sense of degree within the kind: the Romanian gypsy impounded while trying to cross the English Channel experiences a different degree of refugeedom from the middle-class American theoretically vulnerable to the vagaries of the Patriot Act. But if that same middle-class American happens to be of Arab descent or to have the same or almost the same name as someone on a "watch" list, then he might well find himself compelled to a much greater degree of refugeedom than he (and we) had previously thought possible. Agamben does suggest that the faceless masses of the rest of the world, previously known to us as the "Third World," have now become groups of which we can imagine becoming members; instead of us *and* them, which is of course still the chosen rhetoric of the defenders of the homeland as a homeland, we see increasing instances of us *as* them, moments at which we become what was formerly the other. There is a democratic-utopian potential as well as a brutal disorientation embodied in this condition, which the massive militant-nationalist response to 9/11 has done its best to negate and redirect but which it cannot completely erase. It too tells us (in Agamben's words written much earlier) that "what is most proper to every creature is . . . its substitutability, its being in any case in place of the other."[18]

Substitutability is a useful term for understanding the dynamics of Wordsworth's poetry. It is stronger and less negotiable than sympathy, and it does not require an effort to produce the social average in the way that Adam Smith's model of sociability depends upon. It is based on a simpler and much more threatening equivalence: it says that each of us could be in the place of the other without doing anything at all to assist in the exchange. It generates not so much a human bond as a state of panic, because identity itself becomes impersonal and subject only to the laws of exchange. What absolute substitutability portends is nothing less than the end of social and economic classes and of all such distinctions, which is exactly what the British conservatives of the 1790s saw as the threat of the French Revolution: the reduction to bare life that is one of the narratives we might discover in the meeting between Wordsworth, Beaupuy and the hunger-bitten girl. Whichever side one takes on the question of Wordsworth's responses to 1789 and its aftermath, it can be argued that those of his poetic narratives where the narrator is figured as on the same level of distress and insecurity as his subjects, or at least prone to such leveling, is indeed a figuring of the end of received distinctions. For Adorno and others like him, this leveling has taken the form of a universal commodification of human life, so that there is little that is progressive to be hoped for from its implementation. Agamben too wonders whether the universal standard with which humanity is "moving toward its own destruction" might be that of a "planetary petty bourgeoisie" (*Coming Community*, p. 64). For some others, most famously Michael Hardt and Antonio Negri, the "alternative global society" has positive democratic possibilities not preconditioned by the political forms it is displacing.[19] These alternative views indicate an ongoing and unsolved (because yet-to-come) set of possibilities not yet settled in our own time and just as unsettled in Wordsworth's: his poems may be taken to register varieties of both positions. The kind of substitutability that is enacted in Wordsworth's poetry has thus not been exhausted or rendered merely a historical curiosity. Its profile continues to shape the way we formulate our own experiences of concern for others and concern for our own being in the face of others.

One could bring up for inspection any number of instances in Wordsworth's poems, especially the early poems, where a dramatically unstable and problematic narrator transcribes an encounter with a person less fortunate than himself with whom he turns out to have a covert identification or shared predicament. In "Beggars," for example, it is a pointed literary allusion to a poem by Spenser that finally casts the narrator in precisely the position of insouciance and quixotic instability of which he first convicts (but also admires in) the young gypsy boys he meets and talks with. If the beggar woman is to him a "weed of glorious feature" then *he* is the butterfly attracted to the flowers that Spenser describes exactly thus in "Muiopotmos." This identification undermines the poet's self-consciously pompous claim to a bourgeois steadfastness in which he judges the beggars to be so deplorably lacking. In "Gipsies" there is a bewildering succession of attractions and repulsions to and from the vagrant life and its sexual and communal attributes that figures the narrator's own fallen condition in a world of work and isolation. In "The Thorn" the analysis of the gullible sea captain's imaginative and perceptual limitations shows that no one can assume that he or she has a true vision of things: *not* claiming to know exactly what one sees is the only humane alternative.[20] Wordsworth both in person and as poetic narrator often took tours of varying length and duration, but the spirit and ambition of his encounter poems is the opposite of touristic travel, if by that we understand "human circulation considered as consumption, a by-product of the circulation of commodities . . . nothing more than the leisure of going to see what has become banal."[21]

Commodification as Wordsworth represents it does not confirm leisure but disrupts the self by bringing on acute anxiety about the potential exchangeability of everyone with everything and everyone else. We can indeed discover here the pattern of the tour (and thus of tourism) as Alan Liu describes it: an attempt to make sense of a passage without "completion," to accommodate "simple seriality," and to maintain a position within which history becomes merely "ornamental."[22] But Wordsworth's peregrinations are not so comfortable. Seriality registers its own deep history, that of commodification itself: the leveling down of all experiences to a continuum whose pattern is not one of desired routines and common sympathies, which it implacably empties of content and creativity, but of automated repetition. The surprise encounters that are the matter of so many poems disrupt self-contemplation only to redraw the other as a figure of the self. Travel and encounter thus produce both the symptom and the antidote, the poison and the cure. Surprise comes upon the traveler as a creative disturbance of routine, as Geoffrey Hartman made clear in his influential discussion of the *siste viator* motif; but routine simultaneously digests and deflects surprise at its very moment of emergence.[23] Wordsworth explains this as the psychologically necessary normalizing of response whereby emotion is recollected in tranquillity, and he intends it as a defense against the dangerous powers (both aesthetic and political) of unmediated sensibility. But it also erodes the revisionary potential of the truly unforeseen, the absolutely unexpected, and thereby reincorporates novelty into habit. When the spectral figure of the other comes to be reduced to common shape, then it is only by way of the reciprocal spectralization of the self. So too the reading of books enables us to process experiences we might not otherwise be able to cope with, while it also blocks us from the arguable benefits of trying to so do and renders our lifeworld implicitly virtual. This paradox should not be reduced, for it is the form of Wordsworth's sensed implication in the very commodification culture he himself critiques. Instead of putting him outside history, it records the features of a history we have not yet exhausted.

MOVING PARTS

In what remains of this chapter, I will discuss an important and indeed notorious Wordsworthian address to a topic and object of social concern: "The Old Cumberland Beggar." Critics seeking to estimate Wordsworth's probity as a political radical or simply as a minimally decent human being have found it a challenging poem, not least for its recourse, a third of the way through, to a startling and hyperbolic apostrophe. Carl Woodring sets out the problems in a few powerful pages of his book on Wordsworth, noting that the poem is "incontinently given to preachment."[24] James Chandler sees in it a critical early instance of the poet's embrace of Burkean arguments against active welfare policies.[25] Other accounts have shown how the poem addresses a wide range of contemporary debates about vagrancy and the poor laws, and how it makes specific reference to Pitt's proposed 1796 bill aimed at making the poor industrious, and to Bentham's response recommending workhouses, which he called "industry houses."[26] The recent consensus seems to be that Wordsworth's attitude to charity and homelessness is seldom less than complicated. Toby Benis, for example, offers intelligent speculation about the ways in which the story of the old beggar is after all covertly Pittite, not on the literal matter of workhouses but in the larger sphere of the scarcity problem, because it images the marginal poor as still being *able* to distribute charity, and therefore as living above the starvation point, however minimally. At the same time Benis senses the image of the freely wandering beggar as an anti-government icon, to the extent that all mobility of populations was held by the conservatives (after 1789) to be a risk to ordered civilization and a challenge to the logic of what we have come to think of, after Foucault, as the great confinement.[27] The poem puts into play various of the available positions on charity and outdoor relief, and despite its preacherly crescendo, it does not by any means end the debate. What looks like pure charity in this poem, for example, is not quite so since there is a tangible benefit to the givers in terms of immediate self-respect, whether purely secular (meeting the demands of sociability, or briefly assuring themselves that they are not yet in absolute want) or residually religious (performing a duty to God). The poem undermines the notions of pure charity and pure gift: nothing here is without self-interest, even if not all forms of self-interest are the same. The idle beggar is actually at work constantly, performing a good for the community, so that the poem's initially apparent dualism of employed and unemployed persons is turned around. The able and employed citizens need the beggar as much or more than he needs them.[28]

Gift giving, of which the charity represented in "The Old Cumberland Beggar" is an example, was associated with premodern societies held together by personal relations not yet dissolved by a dominance of the commodity form. Such societies were, around 1800, encountered or imagined in the pursuit of global discovery and dominion as primitive others (like the natives of North America), or figured in the national past (like the Highland clans) as the feudal or pre-commercial precursors of the modern British economy. Gifts typically involve obligations for both givers and receivers. The person bestowing a gift or giving charity makes a claim on the recipient, whether of loyalty, future reciprocity, or just plain gratitude. James Cook, according to Jonathan Lamb, was distinctly uncomfortable with the unclear and unpredictable limits of gift exchange in the South Seas, which he sought to redefine as more controllable commodity transactions.[29] Wordsworth's poem makes gift giving metaphysically beneficial to the givers but only materially so to the receiver. His depiction of charity as residually important to the social health of the homeland is thereby flattened and its general paradigmatic function as anything other than residual is almost eviscerated. The beggar is not visibly grateful, and there is no vertical hierarchy of middle- and upper-class persons maintaining a string of dependents through a comprehensive trickle-down process. The cycle of obligations is curtailed as the homeless man is helped only by those who are themselves at best the marginal poor. (Where the beggar might sleep at night goes unmentioned.) No one above the subsistence class is involved; the feudal order no longer exists, and the middle class is out of the picture. The beggar's life is not one of leisured retirement from a life of service, nor is his dependency a source of pleasure or pride. Thus he cannot be made to stand for the wider virtues of the economy in which he subsists. The poem may well perform a conservative, even Burkean function in presenting the poor who have or rent houses as stakeholders in propertied society, made happier with their lot because there are others worse off than they are. But Wordsworth eschews key aspects of Burke's vision: for Wordsworth there is no real organic solidarity, no worshipful commendation of a supportive national culture. The givers give and go back to their hearths and homes, and nothing changes.

The poem performs an interesting switch between idleness and work, making the apparently unproductive beggar the provider of a social good that deserves to be called work; his maintenance is payment for the labor of moral education he performs. So too there is a bizarre inversion whereby the beggar's homelessness is what guarantees the homes of others in the community. The *unheimlich* is at the core of the *heimlich*; without the unhomed, the uncanny, there would be no home. The site of domestic security, of roof, hearth and table, could not subsist as even minimally sociable were it not for the monitoring presence of routinized homelessness. Bentham's argument was ironically the opposite – that social benefits would flow from giving the beggar a fixed abode, which Wordsworth called a "House, misnamed of industry";[30] Wordsworth proposes that giving him such a house would unhouse everyone else. Instead of being a threat to property, homelessness is here its guarantee. What Bentham calls industry will according to Wordsworth produce idleness; what seems like idleness in the beggar – his "idle computation" of his food stocks (p. 229) – is in fact productive work, a computation nonetheless implicitly governed by principles of accountability. He is monitoring the accounts as if he were the village bookkeeper or banker, and the narrator is his teller.

To see the beggar as a worker precisely to the degree that his behavior seems a complete negation of work is to recognize the degree to which work habits and work theories have permeated even this remote and residual rural enclave. In his 1844 manuscripts Marx laments the experience of the modern machine laborer as one that "mortifies his body and ruins his mind." Since the laborer is alienated from his work, he cannot find himself there; he "only feels himself outside his work," in a space that becomes and presumably includes the space of the home: "He feels at home [*zu Hause ist er*] when he is not working, and when he is working he does not feel at home [*ist er nicht zu Haus*]."[31] Marx does not say that he has to go home in the literal sense, but that any place that is not the workplace can give the feeling of being at home – at home with oneself. The old beggar's workplace is the whole landscape: there is then no place he can feel *at* home, just as there is no physical shelter of the sort others call *the* home. He is thus (in Marx's terms) alienated from himself wherever he is. His whole life is for others; there is no distinction between work and leisure, concentration and relaxation, or between one place and another. The person who appears to be doing nothing is in fact working full time, but for others.

What I have just described is a powerful instance of Wordsworth's understanding of the process Agamben calls substitutability, whereby the interchange between preferred and disapproved terms like home and homeless, work and idleness, gift and commodity, images the imminent transference of human subjects across similar class-sanctioned boundaries. It is not just a matter of seeing ourselves in the other in some morally approvable way but of recognizing the incumbent historical logic that pressures each to become the other: we don't have a choice. One of Bentham's contributions to the welfare debate (this one unpublished in its time and so unread by Wordsworth) seems unwittingly to articulate a similarly radical inversion effect. Attempting to justify why the construction of industry houses (as he called them) was financially as well as humanely rational, he wrote a long account of the other attendant uses to which the buildings could be put: hospitals, community centers, concert halls and meeting rooms, hostels for travelers (felons as well as citizens), shelters for shipwrecked sailors, and a host of other ingenious cases itemized at the length of fifty pages.[32] In other words it is as if the entirety of a community's social *and* administrative functions might come to be performed in this single place – all under the rationale of making it pay its way – so that its primary designation as a place aside from society, a place of incarceration, has been overturned, rendering *it* the locus of essential community and the world outside an array of mere empty spaces. The home for the homeless becomes the home for us all, and the homes we think we possess wither into uncanny vacancy. Sociability is to be experienced not in the home but in the multipurpose site of the poorhouse. Wordsworth's poem similarly inscribes the beggar, who circulates as if on the periphery of propertied or domiciled society, as the only thing holding it together. The gratifications experienced by the givers do not extend beyond their own domestic spaces; their donations remain one-on-one transactions that only unknowingly add up to a larger system. Insofar as this is a system at all, it relies upon a hidden hand that leaves its members alienated from one another except through the virtual medium of an aged itinerant who does not talk.

Bentham for one thought that the poor would always give more charity than the rich because they were the more likely to sense the probability of becoming objects of need themselves.[33] That is one reason why he thought that reliance on charity as a public policy was unfair. Wordsworth's poem does not suggest this and might indeed be taken to suggest the opposite. But the sustaining self-congratulation felt by the poor who give charity is built around an emptiness, and despite its strenuous appearance of rhetorical closure, the poem does not exhaust itself in a straightforward sociometric analysis. It has, for one thing, a narrator, who is more interesting and complex than just the bombastic persona who interrupts the story with an address to misguided politicians. Frederick Garber comments on the poem's deployment of a narrative point of view "so disorganized that it skirts the borders of absurdity," and Kenneth Johnston goes even further in sensing the onset of a "comic grotesquerie" as the old beggar's eyes seem to take on an independence from their bodily housing: "and as he moves along, / *They* move along the ground." Toby Benis notes the beggar's depiction as "an imbecile collection of purely physical responses."[34] I think that these are subtle and telling observations; they align, for example, with the description of the old man's spastic hand movements as he tries but fails to hold on to his food (a famous instance of an inadvertent trickle-down economy – he does not *want* to feed the birds), and with the narrator's insistence throughout on the man's sheer insensibility.[35] These attributes render the old man quite literally disorganized, his body dismembered into body parts. They reinforce the claim that the old man is scarcely human, perhaps not human in any way that makes sense to others. Such display of the point where life is passing into death can have a salutary humanizing effect on its beholders, making them sensitive and caring, or it can generate the syndrome of the *Muselmann* whom Agamben, following Primo Levi, figures as ignored and despised because already beyond help, beyond identification as human.[36] Nothing in the poem specifies the beggar as a military veteran, but his grotesquely figured body parts do align him with the distorted physiologies of *Tristram Shandy* that result from war (in the case of Toby) or (according to Walter Shandy) from the disproportioning effects of commerce.[37] War and industry indeed go hand in hand in requiring for their successful pursuit a highly divided labor system. The fact that we cannot be sure whether the beggar "really" looks like a disassembled body or is merely seen that way by a motivated narrator only emphasizes the syndrome of substitutability; no one is free from implication in the refashioned physicalities of the military–industrial complex.

Wordsworth's villagers clearly care up to a point, but mostly for themselves. It is hard to attribute anything of stoic virtue to the beggar's refusal to complain about his own physical decline; the poem makes more sense as a comment on the simple, amoral materiality of the passage from life to death which has robbed the old man of speech itself. Wordsworth might have taken such a message from Rousseau, who proposed that among the aged in primitive cultures "the need for food diminishes with the faculty of providing for it; and since ... old age is, of all ills, the one that human assistance can least relieve, they finally die without it being perceived that they cease to be, and almost without perceiving it themselves."[38] The beggar still eats, but barely, with no apparent sense of enjoyment and completely outside the circle of human sociability that is normally associated with the sharing of food.[39] The poem can be and has been read as endorsing a stoic ontology; but the endorsement comes from a narrator whose view of things can seem startlingly idiosyncratic. The old man's feelings are the product of the narrator's surmise since there is no dialogue nor any sense that the beggar even has the power of speech. The "hope whose vital anxiousness / Gives the last human interest to his heart" (ll. 170–71) is the narrator's supposition on the beggar's behalf. This is one of the few benefits the narrator assumes for the man himself, as opposed to those accruing for the rest of the community from his continued existence: the faint flicker of energy that goes with avoiding death.

As he is between life and death, so the old man is between the animal, the protohuman and the human, and as such he prompts some of the same perplexities as arise in the current debates about stem-cell research, life support systems, abortion and animal rights: where does life begin and end, where does the human begin and how much of what we call life is limited to meaningful or satisfying life? What is the relation between being and *knowing* being, or meaning? And who is to speak for those who cannot speak? If "vital anxiousness" is what we share with animals, is the old man now an animal as much as or rather than a human form? The little birds about to benefit from his physical incapacities represent an economy of circulation that crosses the boundary between humans and other species, and not a little of the old man's ghostliness comes from his withholding of the signals of a conventional humanity. To the degree that he shares the condition of Primo Levi's *Muselmann*, "an emaciated man, with head dropped and shoulders curved, on whose face and in whose eyes not a trace of thought is to be seen," he also inhabits the sphere of the merely animal, the realm of "creaturely life."[40] The man–animal interface seems to be another of those eighteenth-century concerns that has not been superseded by the progress of technological reason.[41] Technological reason might indeed be among the means of its perpetuation. Thus Marx saw the modern worker as "freely active" only in his "animal functions," and resorted to one of his habitual chiasmic locutions to make the point: "what is animal becomes human and what is human becomes animal."[42] These animal functions include not just eating, drinking and procreating but dwelling [*Wohnung*] and adorning oneself [*Schmuck*].

Marx's worker here has a lot more left to him in his animality than does Wordsworth's old beggar, who is beyond procreation, has no shelter and no interest in dressing up. The narrator is motivated to imagine him as relatively indifferent even to protective clothing: "let his blood / Struggle with frosty air and winter snows, / And let the charter'd wind that sweeps the heath / Beat his grey locks against his wither'd face" (ll. 165–69). The same exposure to harsh weather rendered William Cowper's waggoner all the *more* human, insensible to the pains acquired from a refined sensibility and finding "wholesome air" and happiness where others might see only hardship.[43] A varied and active life for Cowper kept the laborer content and healthy even in old age, bestowing "A sparkling eye beneath a wrinkled front" (II: 22). The "same repeated joys" (II: 25) of the urban sitting room offer only a facsimile of pleasure, making it the site of a debilitation and alienation never produced by rural labor. But Wordsworth's beggar conflates the languid and lifeless habit of mind with the primitive inertia of mere motion, refusing the contrast that ennobles the rural poor while upbraiding polite society. If modernity has in effect increased the pressure of conditions identifying man and animal, each open to being substituted for the other, then the consigning of the old beggar to animal status in no way limits or solves the question of what we might or might not owe him: it just realigns the elements of discussion.

The narrator's description of the beggar's body as an assembly of body parts is bizarre; so too is his admission that he has known him since he was a child, and that he has *always* seemed old: "and then / He was so old, he seems not older now" (ll. 22–23). We can certainly choose to read this admission naturalistically. All adults seem old to children and seem to be at a point beyond which they do not change: thus the old man *seems* to be no older now because of the memory of the child's perception in the past. We can, however, pursue a different train of thought, one that recognizes the beggar's supernatural, ghostly status as one of the walking dead, a not wholly benign specter who always shows up in the same form and at the same time each week. A sense of the supernatural is supported by the eeriness of the old man's presence, by the slowed-down homage and "sidelong and half-reverted" look (l. 32) he attracts from persons otherwise in a hurry, by the way the spinning wheel stops and the dogs cease to bark. If indeed he is a reminder of the death to come for us all, then there is nothing odd in the caution with which he is treated by those who meet him and support him. What they are exposed to is their own being toward death. The plea to "let him pass, a blessing on his head!" (l. 155) thus has about it something of an exorcism, a desire that he be removed from sight as the reminder of an implacable future fate. In this context his "weary journey"(l. 53) is that of life itself, and the "little span of earth" that is "all his prospect" (ll. 50–51) is nothing other than the grave, the common prospect of us all. The quality of stillness that marks everything about him is at once adverbial and adjectival, each becoming the other. While he is engaged in time – "still attempting to prevent the waste" (l. 17) – he is also still, both in the artifice of the poem and in his nearness to death: "so still / In look and motion" (ll. 60–61). Here death is stealing upon life and reducing it to still life. His feet scarcely disturb the summer dust (l. 60) because he is already half a ghost. Death-in-life is not here a figure of the Gothic supernatural (as it is in "The Ancient Mariner") but a component of common life, one with which we live all the time, as is readily apparent to those who witness the slow decline of friends and relatives in extreme old age. The old man is a figure of the supernatural precisely to the degree that he is natural: there is no boundary. This is another example of substitutability. The aged man becomes a proleptic figure of ourselves, what is normal becomes paranormal and life turns toward death, both conditions reconciled in "the natural silence of old age" (l. 175).

It seems apt, then, that this man's fixed ambulatory circuit of near-Newtonian regularity should sponsor the idea that he has always been the same: "he seems not older now." Like the stars and planets he does not change; the computation of his progress is not idle but exact, the same houses on the same day, so that the world to come is the world we have and have had already. The sameness of the old man's age and routine makes the community he maintains seem suspended in time as well as cut off spatially from the wider world. There is no incursion from outer space and no exit from the local field of gravity that he both obeys and recenters upon himself: the apparently circumferential old man holds in place the lives of the dwellers in homes who thus themselves move, figuratively, to the circumference. The self-sufficiency of the system marks the socio-political fantasy of a world wherein nothing changes, a world of predictability and stability, but it is thereby also a metaphysical figuring of a space in which death has already arrived and walks the highways and byways. The one is the price of the other, and if the beggar is not quite frozen into the finished image or stilled life that fully betokens death, then he is and has always been poised at that point, in Wordsworth's twenty-eighth year as in his childhood. The slowing down of time that the beggar imposes upon the lives and routines of others – the arrested horseman and spinning wheel, the slowing post-boy – is matched by an involuted sense of space and place, creating a sleeping-beauty castle or happy valley into which no one comes and from which no one departs. What is threatened by its full evolution is the end of social as well as of individual life.

The care and attention that the beggar inspires is inseparable from fear, and the commitment to his ongoing life is haunted by a sense that he is already dead, so that he is, for the community he maintains, something between a poison and a cure, a classic *pharmakon* figure like his great precursor in the third of Sophocles's Oedipus plays. If the local working poor cannot express this for themselves, then the narrator certainly says it for them. In arousing this conflation of pity and terror, the beggar is not so much a figure of tragedy as an incarnation of the automaton, the machine human who will go on and on doing the same thing, seeming never to change, as long as his parts continue to function, after which he will simply slow down and stop without any metaphysical or ontological consequences. La Mettrie's *Man a Machine* famously explained the soul as an "enlightened machine" (p. 128) and proposed that all thought – the faculty supposedly distinguishing man from animal – was only a product of animal sensation. Man as automaton promises well for a developing machine-labor economy eager to extract more and faster work from its labor force but threatens to refigure human nature itself as a primitive computer program. Automated travel is indeed inscribed in the roadways which the old beggar follows, but he does not see them:

> Thus, from day to day,
> Bowbent, his eyes for ever on the ground,
> He plies his weary journey, seeing still
> And never knowing that he sees, some straw,
> Some scatter'd leaf, or marks which, in one track,
> The nails of cart or chariot wheel have left
> Impress'd on the white road, in the same line,
> At distance still the same. (ll. 51–58)

Here is Levi's *Muselmann* with his drooping head and thoughtless mien,[44] and here again is the stillness on which the narrator focuses so often: "seeing still" and "still the same." What he sees he does not see, but we see it on his behalf and thus see it for ourselves and as if we were him. We see a straight line punctuated at regular intervals by the tracks of nails in wheels – almost a proleptic image of the railways against which Wordsworth himself would fulminate later in life, and certainly an image of automation, of the conversion of inconstant energy to a constant, measured motion: clockwork perhaps, or the steam engine. The beggar moves slowly – "Him even the slow-pac'd waggon leaves behind" (l. 66) – but seems to be without evident or critical fatigue: that same human and mechanical fatigue that was becoming the major challenge and concern of coming generations of scientists and engineers who saw it as the crucial impediment to dreams of perpetual motion and ceaseless profit.[45] He is no railway engine in his speed but is figuratively allied with the engine in his indifference to obstacles and distractions. Thus James Adamson, in 1826, would celebrate the locomotive for its ability to move "regularly and progressively along the smooth tracks of the way, wholly unimpeded by the speed of its own motions"; and W. B. Adams, in 1837, would describe steam as "a drudge who performs his work without speech or sign, with dogged perseverance but without emotion."[46] The locomotive is like a ghost, passing across the earth without leaving any traces, unopposable in its progress and supernatural in its speed and regularity of motion. And in these senses it is also like the old beggar, and like the Sandman in E. T. A. Hoffman's story of that name published in 1816 and invoked by Freud as the primary exhibit in his essay on the uncanny – for it was the uncertainty about whether something was a human being or an automaton, according to Jentsch on whom Freud also draws, that was one of the most successful devices for creating uncanny effects.

We have seen such automation before, in the knitting of the hunger-bitten girl and in Margaret's backward spinning routine. Marx, following Dugald Stewart, finds that modern manufacture "converts the worker into a crippled monstrosity ... the individual himself is divided up, and transformed into the automatic motor of a detail operation."[47] Deidre Lynch has plotted analogous representations of automated behavior in the novels of Burney and Austen.[48] In this too Wordsworth was of his time. One of the earliest modern examples of the positive effects of having complex tasks "divided and subdivided into a great Variety of different Labours" was Mandeville's account of building and sailing a ship.[49] But rather than making this into a hymn to the happy exercise of the human imagination, Mandeville's protagonist suggests that the benefits come from habit and hands-on experience applied to the parts rather than from any rational prevision of wholes. The successful operation of a modern ship comes from passive learning and "nature" and can be exercised in a state of near-insensibility, as when a boy takes the helm: "his Knowledge in sailing, and Capacity of steering his Vessel become so habitual to him, that he guides her as he does his own Body, by Instinct, tho' he is half a-sleep, or thinking on Quite another thing" (II: 144). The boy is not so much operating a machine as becoming himself a part of a larger unit that is itself a machine and requires only his passive cooperation. This is very different from Adam Smith's sprightly lad figuring out how to automate his steam valve so that he can be "at liberty to divert himself with his play-fellows."[50] Mandeville's labor-attuned worker is in a state of insentience, like the old beggar, and is as such all the more prophetic of the world that Marx and many others would observe.

Surely it is no accident that the one line that Wordsworth himself acknowledged in a letter to John Thelwall in 1804 as "the most dislocated line I know in my writing," one that "taken by itself has not the sound of a verse," occurs in the passage cited above from "The Old Cumberland Beggar"?⁵¹ The line thus noted is line 57, "Impress'd on the white road, in the same line." Any such dislocation, he there opines, can be justified "by some passion or other," and in this case the words distinguished by passion are "white road same line and the verse dislocates [for the] sake of these." Dislocation, or prosodic surprise, comes at a point describing repetition and automation, whose mimetic equivalent ought to be prosodic monotony. Two pairs of strong stresses (white road, same line) preempt any such mimicking of sense by sound, as poetic craft itself bears witness against the subject of its own description – routine progress – and interpellates an element of the cacophonic uncanny into the poem's predominantly stately rhythm and diction. The uncanny here almost promises to take over and to establish a new metrical norm, as if introducing a new setting for the machine: "on̆ the whīte rōad in̆ the sāme līne." In a poetry of minimal statement almost completely free of melodrama, the effect is – quietly – stunning; the doggedly natural features of a modern highway and its automatically spaced records of passing vehicles are made by this passionate dislocation almost supernatural: the same line on the white road.⁵²

The case for a Romantic interest in a naturally self-generating energy independent of individual will and indifferent to idiosyncratic form – an automatic system of work and exchange called (using Rabinbach's term) "productivism" – has been persuasively argued by Ted Underwood as being a rhetorical capture of the terminology (and dignity) of labor for the legitimation of middle-class professional lives: the more natural energy one can lay claim to, the less deliberate diligence one has to exercise, so that poets and proletarians can be made equivalent within a "general philosophy of production" governed by theories of solar power.⁵³ If human effort is thus linked to the productive forces of nature, then humans become vehicles of impersonal processes and indistinct both from each other and from other life forms: birds, animals, trees and plants. They become creaturely on the grandest of scales. The quantification of sunlight promised to bring about in the domain of physics an analogue of what the general equivalent or money form did for Marx in the domain of economics: it provided a single standard of measurement for all exchanges and transformations. In Underwood's words, "it became possible to measure nature's contribution to production in the same units that were used to measure the contribution of human laborers" (p. 159). "The Old Cumberland Beggar" can be read as evoking just such a process of energy transmission now tending to near inertia and to the end of life. According to Underwood's account the paradigm proposes that "all living creatures participate in vital power drawn from the sun" (p. 156). The old beggar's exposure to the elements, of which the narrator seems to approve almost to the point of cruelty, would then be the source of his perpetual motion, his uncanny automation: as such it is a principle relatively indifferent to his humanity. But Wordsworth interpolates a new metrical pattern – "on the white road, in the same line" – that can be associated not only with natural forces but also with the regularity of the machine.

Underwood offers a serious argument (see, for example, pp. 85–88) against the possibility that any such endorsement of universally available natural energy can ever come up with a theory or description of alienation. As soon as all energies are rendered mutually equivalent among all life forms, then no energy is wasted or displaced or turned inward as a form of self-destruction: everyone and everything is integrated into the circuit. Applying this to *The Excursion*, he then finds it necessary to read the Wanderer as delivering poetically authenticated doctrine in his admiration for the achievements of industrial technology. This goes, I think, too far: the Wanderer begins and remains a highly questionable figure, just as he was when standing at the site of the ruined cottage. Nonetheless, Underwood is convincing in his case for a certain congruence, complicated and confused, between Wordsworth's rhetoric of placelessness and constant circulation and the terms in which the forces driving industrialization were imagined and described. He finds an ideology and therefore a self-deception here, whereby the middle-class writer can assure himself of possessing powers not circumscribed by land or inherited wealth; I am arguing the other side of the case, proposing that this same ideological option is so thoroughly laid open and haunted by darker forces as to undermine its own sustainability.

A DANCE OF DEATH

We have traveled some distance from Wordsworth's poetic addresses to the poor law debates of the 1790s. But there is, I suggest, an implicit connection between his effort to oppose the coming modernity, the not-so-idle computations of Benthamite policymakers and the formal effects of a narrative that plays around issues having to do with slowing down and almost stopping time. "Him from my childhood have I known . . . he seems not older now" movingly encapsulates the empirical impossibility and mythic desirability of a narrator and a community that never grows old and never changes. The speeding up of everything that Wordsworth saw as symptomatic of the world to come – the mail coaches, the increasing accumulation of persons in cities, the speed of communication and of events themselves – is here outfaced in poetic story. But the counterexample, seemingly intended to be positive, is itself mechanical and mechanized, both in the motions of the old man and in the anatomical separation of his downcast eyes and shaking hands from bodily and intellectual wholeness and control. The homeless man and the dwellers in homes dance with and around one another in an ongoing movement, each center and circumference to the other. If it is not a fixed image, dead to all fluency, it is yet something like a carnival ride, always in motion but always the same. To this extent it is a dance of death. The price paid for absolute familiarity – the always known sameness of the beggar – is a certain degree of liveliness. The slow motion inspired by the beggar is at once the desired aesthetic of the rural way of life – people in daily contact with the great unchanging forms of nature – and a tendency to extinction that may figure the imminent historical dominance of urban and metropolitan time, which moves faster and which will render the beggar's world a backwater slowly dying into complete still life. That speeding up of time is reported in the opening of Book 3 of *The Prelude* as having begun at the moment the young Wordsworth was careening in a post chaise down Castle Hill and across Magdalene Bridge into Cambridge, sucked in as with an eddy's force. Before this all his experiences of speeding up had been induced voluntarily: ice skating on the lake, galloping horses across the sands. In Cambridge, London and the greater world, he would no longer be master of the speed at which time passes.

So we have a paradox: a poem that seems to recommend the slowing down of time as a desired alternative to the quickening tempo of modern life, but which also invites an association between slow and regulated time and the passage toward mechanical inertia and death. The beggar is a "silent monitor" in all senses of the word: a figure who gives warning and admonishes and one who keeps order and maintains discipline, like the senior schoolboy (also called a "monitor") or factory overseer. In this he is complicit with the very work discipline of factory labor he is described as avoiding. A similarly automated movement is mimicked by the Wordsworth family itself walking back and forth among the trees they knew as "John's grove."[54] The image of preindustrial, primitive integrity and charitable giving that is embodied in the rural ritual maintained by the old beggar is countered by the repetitive nature of his circulation, which monitors the passing of time with clockwork regularity and brings with it the specter of death-in-life. Marx would note that "dead capital always keeps the same pace and is indifferent to *real* individual activity."[55] The "continued repetition" of habitual work activity teaches the worker "how to attain the desired effect with the minimum of exertion," a process that finally "disturbs the intensity and flow of a man's vital forces."[56] Continued repetition marks the beggar, Margaret and the "hunger-bitten girl" of *The Prelude* "who crept along, fitting her languid self / Unto a heifer's motion, by a cord / Tied to her arm ... knitting, in a heartless mood / Of solitude" (9: 513–18). Giving charity is also tending to the machine.

This is of course to read against the grain of a poem which seems to propose the beggar as the antitype of the modern factory worker compelled to repetitive machine labor. He indeed has something of the "irregular habits" that Marx (p. 607) described as anathema to the employers and which Adam Smith before him had noted as one of the unproductive effects of undivided rural labor. He comes and goes as he wishes, and is not subject to regulated mealtimes: "and let him, *where* and *when* he will, sit down" (l. 184). In this respect he might seem to be an icon of the "self-regulation" that Otto Mayr argues to be popular in the mechanical discourse of the late eighteenth century, where it was "splendidly matched" with the then current ideas of political liberty: human lives, like dynamic systems, are "capable of ... maintaining themselves in equilibrium by their own resources without the need of outside help."[57] But the beggar does need help, and the result of his ability to make up his own schedule seems to be near-complete regularity in the eyes of others, a "stated round" enacted on "fixed days" (p. 228) that indeed depends upon its very predictability to achieve the approved moral outcome. We might then propose a connection between Wordsworth's automaton figures and the inhuman mechanisms of the new machines as well as the circulation of money and commodities they supply, though it will need the rest of this study to develop the case and accumulate the evidence. Celeste Langan has discussed images of walking in *Lyrical Ballads* as allegories of the circulation of money, with which Wordsworth (as Alan Liu also reminds us in his discussion of "The Ruined Cottage") was famously preoccupied in his personal and professional life.[58] Like the pedlar on his rounds through rural Britain, providing for the needs and wants of his customers (although only in a limited sense for Margaret's needs), the beggar circulates through the community. Both of them provide for those they encounter, the one with goods and good cheer, the other with silent stores of self-esteem. But the beggar's apathetic demeanor is not the result of a nurtured, stoical self-discipline or rigid religious conviction, as it is for the pedlar (and even more so for the Wanderer he becomes in the poem's published form). It is seemingly empty of all feeling, as it is for Margaret and for the hunger-bitten girl, and indeed for the modern factory worker who is described by the Wanderer himself as a ruined "organic frame . . . / Dull, to the joy of her own motions dead."[59] These are figures who seem to be worn down by toil and suffering. The beggar may indeed be experiencing the consequences of sheer old age, but the others are prematurely aged, like the factory workers whose truncated lives and thwarted physical development Marx and Engels would point out (though they were not the first to do so).[60]

The beggar's automatic motions preempt any distinctions between the deserving and undeserving poor, of the sort that public debate and private morality liked to make: there is nothing of the "paroxysm of sorrow" that Godwin found so suspicious in the mendicant class, no material for the extended speculations about one's duties to the poor that Rousseau published.[61] His existence allows the villagers to exemplify the positive values of habit. At the same time the habituated behavior of both beggar and donors, in being stripped of any personal interaction and rendered automatic, hints that the old man's escape from the "house misnamed of industry" has not prevented him from falling into a network that is more generally governed by the routines of industrial time, even though they are benevolently slowed down almost to a standstill. This paradox does not disable the poem or hopelessly confuse its message: it is itself the message. The regularity of machine production is maintained, but it is rendered almost completely unrecognizable as such because things move so slowly. Wordsworth approved of slowing down as an entry point for the meditative reading called forth by good poetry, in contrast to the commonly rapid response to billboards and newspapers. But here, the story seems to be about suppressing as much as creating the shocks of mild surprise that so often serve to register Wordsworth's dissent from the commodification of reading, just as the shock of the beggar's spectrally disjointed body is assimilated to the regularity of its reappearances. The disembodied narrator, who gives no charity, confesses to no home and participates in no conversation hovers over the scene in a ghostly replication of the beggar's own virtuality. He has been monitoring this ancient monitor since his own childhood, and yet he describes no exchange with or embodied relation to him.

Beggar and narrator both are in this way eerie incarnations of *urbs in rure*, persons displaying the impersonality of city dwellers though they in fact inhabit the country. The city for Wordsworth was a place full of strangers passing each other by in a bewildering array of differences and degrees, a world where any moment of recognition or respite is hard to find – a man with his ailing child, a blind beggar. In postrevolutionary France this speeding up of encounter and exchange was briefly held to be a positive and exciting experience, buoyed up by political hope, though always more so in the countryside than in Paris. But for the most part, Wordsworth was wary of the incrementally compressed sense of time and space produced by the modernization process visible at its maximum intensity in London. The *Prelude*'s "little space of intermediate time" (7: 65) that is first described as sending the young poet to the metropolis is rapidly filled up with more and more rapidly passing sights and shows which seem to frustrate the measured pace of poetic description itself. Wordsworth had to get up early to find the peace and quiet registered in the famous "Westminster Bridge" sonnet. The Cumberland beggar and his donors are clearly not city types because their lives move slowly and they exist to each other as known quantities, not strangers. But the incursion of remoteness into their interactions does suggest the manners of the metropolis, as well as the pattern of machine labor; the familiar is rendered unfamiliar, uncanny, by the complete absence of expressive response on both sides. They are strangers in their very familiarity. The poem declares an obvious resistance to and yet visibly embodies the modernizing forces it presents for inspection. This is not a mere logical impasse or trivial contradiction; it is the index of Wordsworth's profound reflection on a historical predicament. The narrator who has "known" the beggar since his childhood remains a stranger, everywhere and nowhere in the poem, a ghost telling stories of another ghostly form, a ghost and a machine, always about to return.

Everywhere and nowhere. We might conclude that because the old beggar is always walking, then the narrator has no need to do so. He does not have to set forth in search of an encounter because the encounter regularly and predictably comes to him. But any such simple self-placement is undermined by his failing or refusing to interpellate himself as one among those who give out charity, those who enjoy home and shelter. He does *not* write himself in as part of the group of static villagers. To resort to a filmic analogy: the narrator is behind the moving camera, in charge of the tracking shots, the zoom lens and the editorial montage. We do not see him but see as if through his eyes. He is disembodied and socially remote from his subjects and sees what he sees as always the same. It is not only the beggar who might be taken to reflect and represent the circulation of money (as Celeste Langan argues), but the narrator as well, as the overseer of exchange and the operator of the general equivalent. Perhaps he does not give money because he *is* money.

There is another notoriously pontifical poem in which money impinges on the narrator's relations to those he subjects to observation and moral identification, though this time it is the narrator who is on the move while those he writes about stay still: "Gipsies." I have written on this poem before and found in it a decisive citation of Milton, one placing the narrator in the role of Satan, a figure in anguished exile from all social and sexual satisfaction and envying the gypsies just as Satan envied Adam and Eve in paradise.[62] He claims to disapprove, then, of what he wants but cannot have. But Milton is not the only literary Titan written into this poem. Reading Derrida on Marx reminds us of the place of Shakespeare's play about money, *Timon of Athens*.[63] Marx was famously invested in the passage from Act 4 in which gold is described as subverting all human civilization. The exiled Timon has turned his back upon "all feats, societies, and throngs of men" (IV.iii.21) and is digging up his gold, the "yellow slave" that can "knit and break religions" (ll. 34–35), privilege "willing misery" over "incertan pomp" (ll. 242–43) and defile "Hymen's purest bed" (l. 383). Gold is the "visible god" that "sold'rest close impossibilities / And mak'st them kiss" (ll. 386–88). I shall have more to say later about Marx's implied conjunction of poetry and money as agents soldering together impossibilities. Let us focus for now on the attribution Wordsworth's narrator bestows upon the evening star, "outshining like a visible God / The glorious path in which he trod."[64] The Luciferic allusion (Satan falling through the heavens) is supplemented by Timon's invocation of gold as a "visible god" which is indeed, in the eternal time of literary history, conjoined with and fulfilled by Milton's description in *Paradise Lost* (1: 670ff.) of the rebel angels as the first discoverers of the precious metals and thereby of so many of our human woes. Wordsworth (as both Satan and Timon) looks upon the "still unbroken knot" of gypsies as an intact social state which he, like gold, can choose to "knit" or "break" by his own intervention, his own moralizing ascription. In his doubly coded knotting, there is both a constant sexual union of persons forever knotted together and an as yet unbroken virginal state – "Hymen's purest bed" – that he himself (as Satan) can never deflower but which (as gold) he will defile.[65] Constant sexual union and anticipated but forever suspended defloration are both outside of time and change, like the endlessly circulating sun, moon and stars whose supervision is invoked by the narrator, and like the narrator himself who has traveled a twelve-hour cycle across the landscape and returned exactly to his starting point. Wordsworth's "weary sun" and "mighty moon" whose emblematic functions as productive workers ("The weary Sun betook himself to rest") are disregarded by the gypsies are also specified by Timon as agents of pestilence (IV.iii.1–6) and as thieves who cooperate with earth and sea to render the world a "composture stol'n / From general excrement" (ll. 441–42): in other words, a world of shit.

General excrement and general equivalent? The gypsies' disregard for sun and moon is then, in reference to the Shakespearean precursor, a determined ignoring of the powers *corrupting* human society. They ignore thereby the Wordsworthian narrator whose self-ascribed alliance with the heavenly bodies undermines his assumption of moral superiority and renders him doubly demonic, as both Satan and the figure of money that Satan himself helped to invent. Timon wished upon Athens a dismal descent into "confounding contraries" (IV.i.20). These contraries are written into Wordsworth's poem and tellingly enumerated: too much society or none at all, too much sex or none at all, too much motion or none at all. The one thing which narrator and gypsies share, in which they are not contraries, is their negation of work. The poet figure, despite his claims to self-righteous effort and activity, is not doing anything except walking for its own sake. The claim to "bounteous hours" is never substantiated. Here he fulfills the circulatory logic of money as always on the move, never at home, never hospitable, performing nothing in itself. No wonder, then, that the gypsies seem to him a "spectacle," a fixed installation immune to the passage of time and thus also spectral, always in the past and present and always still to come. It is the narrator who moves, but moves in a regular pattern (like the Cumberland beggar), so that his ghostliness is just as striking in its embodied form as it was in the disembodied voice of the earlier poem. Here is Derrida: "As is well known, Marx always described money, and more precisely the monetary sign, in the figure of appearance or simulacrum, more exactly of the ghost."[66] That which holds together other forms has only virtual form. The poet is a figure of want: he desires and he lacks. He is also a figure of death, bringing with him the power of consigning living things to fixed form, "the frame / Of the whole Spectacle the same." The gypsies are gathered within the same frame of sameness that governs the old beggar, who seemed always to have been the same age. If the poet has just given over the reins of Apollo's chariot, allowing the "weary Sun" to go to its rest, then all he has created is an image of uncreation. Gypsies, traditionally poeticized as figures of motion, coming and going unpredictably (though semiresident bands were not uncommon) and roaming near and far, are here stilled into inertia and made to participate in the aesthetics of the painting or panorama. They are presented as betraying the obligation to honest toil that is one fruit of man's fall, and the natural order of day and night that signals the passage from labor to leisure. Their punishment is death by poetry.

CHAPTER 3

Figures in the mist

BRIGHT VOLUMES OF VAPORS

"The Old Cumberland Beggar" depends upon a narrator who occludes his own presence from the landscape in order to record the details of his story, whereas "Gipsies" obtrudes upon its readers a distinctly sanctimonious poet-figure who dominates the tale with his confident moral judgments. In neither case is the teller of the tales comfortably at home in the poem; in both cases he bears an aura of the uncanny, of a spectral death-in-life. One narrator implacably records the progress toward death of an aged man, while the other freezes his subjects into a hyperbolic immobility within a still-life scene which they can never escape, imaging thereby his own demonic eternity-in-time as a figure of Satan or of the Wandering Jew. Both the overbearing and the self-effacing narrator, the one too much present and the other too remote, demonstrate a condition of alienation that governs many of Wordsworth's best-known encounter poems. They share also a ghostly identity and a rhetoric of machine-like motion that describes both what they see and how they themselves behave: they have become what they behold. Other extremes also meet: the city comes to the country, mechanical regularity to rural routine, repetitive rhythm to freedom of action. This chapter will focus on two more poems and an important fragment which further articulate the strange constellation of concerns at work in "The Ruined Cottage" and "The Old Cumberland Beggar." All of them explore figures of death-in-life, and variously involve the tellers of the tales in a cycle of incremental reification. All of them can assist us in developing a deeper sense of the complex extent of Wordsworth's analysis of the function of machine labor habits and of the comprehensive influence of commodity form.

I begin with one of the 1800 *Lyrical Ballads* that is especially interesting for its representation of metropolitan time–space and in its conjunction of a homeless or distressed person with an ambiguously concerned narrator: "Poor Susan." Here is the poem in its first published version of 1800:

> At the corner of Wood Street, when daylight appears,
> There's a thrush that sings loud, it has sung for three years:
> Poor Susan has pass'd by the spot and has heard
> In the silence of morning the song of the bird.
>
> 'Tis a note of enchantment: what ails her? She sees
> A mountain ascending, a vision of trees;
> Bright volumes of vapour through Lothbury glide,
> And a river flows on through the vale of Cheapside.
>
> Green pastures she views in the midst of the dale,
> Down which she so often has tripp'd with her pail,
> And a single small cottage, a nest like a dove's,
> The only one dwelling on earth that she loves.
>
> She looks, and her heart is in heaven: but they fade,
> The mist and the river, the hill and the shade;
> The stream will not flow, and the hill will not rise,
> And the colours have all pass'd away from her eyes.
>
> Poor Outcast! return – to receive thee once more
> The house of thy father will open its door,
> And thou once again, in thy plain russet gown,
> May'st hear the thrush sing from a tree of its own.
> (*Lyrical Ballads*, pp. 178–79)

I have elsewhere expounded in some detail the nexus of historical circumstances that positions Susan in an unstable role as servant girl and/or prostitute: girls coming to the city from the country found themselves in a very precarious position whereby even if they had employment as domestic servants they were prone to lose their jobs and to find themselves thrown onto the streets. The specific parts of London mentioned in the poem were associated with commerce and low life, and there is every sign that Susan's status as an "outcast" indicates that she has been cast out into homelessness and prostitution – Charles Lamb certainly drew that conclusion.[1] The thrush (which the 1820 revision describes as caged) stays in one spot – Susan is peripatetic, she passes by (or *has* passed by), she is one among the constantly mobile city dwellers who do not, in an extended sense, dwell at all. The poem's first four stanzas (which after 1802 made up the complete poem) move from present perfect to present tenses and then to a suspended past–present whereby what is occurring is described by way of what has been: the colors have (now) passed away from her eyes. The narrator's turn to apostrophe in stanza five of the 1800 text – "Poor Outcast! return" – is akin to the pontifical turn taken in "The Old Cumberland Beggar" and not wholly remote from the histrionic address of "Gipsies." Here as there it is a peculiarly remote address, for this is not a poem of encounter but one of distanced description. Here again the narrator views his object of concern from a panoptical position; Susan is a feature of his landscape rather than a sharer in dialogue or exchange. This attitude is less common in Wordsworth's rural poems, where there tends to be some sort of physical proximity or conversational event, however minimal, but it is more typical of his city experiences, where the narrator tends to be an embedded observer of whom his subject is unaware. When it appears in both rural and urban poems, then it speaks to a shared condition and a coming together of the two environments Wordsworth spent so much energy trying to keep apart.

Neither the narrator nor any of the neighbors appear to talk to the old beggar, who is imaged as being anyway beyond speech. But his regular appearance stimulates at least a brief interruption of the self-absorption of the silent villagers. In Susan's case it is unclear whether she passes by the spot frequently or only once; we cannot tell whether the poem reports a still continuing habit, a past habit now ceased, or just a single event in the past, either recent or long gone. The narrator claims habitual knowledge, telling us that the thrush has been singing in the same place for three years, but we don't know whether Susan's vision is habitual or a one-time event. This uncertainty about the repeatability of Susan's experience, about whether she passes by *every* morning or just happens to pass by once, is heightened by the narrator's silence about his own location or state of mind. He does not tell us that this is how things seemed to *him*, as so much of Wordsworth's poetry does, but that this is what happened. We do not know with the usual Wordsworthian specificity (famously drawn out with great complexity in "The Thorn") just whose story this is, and after 1802 (when the fifth stanza is dropped), we do not know whether Susan is still alive and has a future or has herself passed away. She might just have lost any memory of her past life, or she might be dead: "the colours have all pass'd away from her eyes" can describe either the outward details of her fantasy, the colors of the landscape, or the signs of life itself, the light of her living eyes. It could be both: like Falstaff's hallucinations of green fields, her vision would then mark the moment of her death, making the silence of morning into that of mourning. Even the 1800 poem's mention of "the house of thy father" seems to invoke an eternal afterlife in the middle of its timely good advice.

Susan's mobility is then more than a little ghostly – she has been seen, but we are not sure whether she will be seen again, or when. This spectral presence and "note of enchantment" she has in common with the Cumberland beggar and with the discharged soldier and fragile fisherman whom we will soon be discussing. She is as ephemeral as the features of her vision, and as insubstantial: death-in-life. In 1815 Wordsworth decided to resolve the puzzle somewhat by calling the poem "The Reverie of Poor Susan," but even this specification does not entirely preclude the possibility that she is dying, that "what ails her" is mortality itself, or, given the ambiguity of the genitive, that the reverie is the poet's and not hers. The omniscient narration that becomes all the more emphatic after 1802 is itself a figure of death, because the passing of time makes no difference to a speaker who is not here vulnerable to the admonitions of others or to changes of mind or heart, as so many Wordsworthian speakers are. Only in the fifth stanza of the 1800 poem does the narrator suggest (though not without ambiguity) a future that may be different and thus signal that the passing of earthly time might still be critical. But Susan remains formally a stranger to the speaker even as he seems to claim (unless the "reverie" is indeed his own) to know all about her.

It is not even clear that we can trust him to know her name: "Susan" was a generic term for servant girls, and figures as such in, for example, Swift's "Description of a City Shower."[2] Most such girls were Susans or Bettys in the eyes of employers, outsiders, or poets and novelists. For all the proposed particularization of this one girl in this one place, the narrator's attitude obeys the prescription Wordsworth offers in *The Prelude* for an impersonal urban experience where people live "Even next-door neighbours, as we say, yet still / Strangers, and knowing not each other's names" (7: 120). Susan is accorded no physical features of the sort that figure in, say, "Beggars" or "The Sailor's Mother" and numbers of other poems. Even the "plain russet gown" that is (in 1800) perhaps to come, and which opens (without solving) the question of what she might be wearing now, is a literary motif borrowed from Milton and Goldsmith. She is a generic name and the vehicle of a vision that may or may not intend an imminent afterlife ("her heart is in heaven"). This empirical vacancy allows Wordsworth to avoid the stereotyped images of female virtue and vice, eroticized and abjected, that populated popular prints and ballads.[3] It also allows more scope for us to imagine the missing details and to project Susan as servant or prostitute (and, I have argued, to understand their mutual coexistence in the vicious economy of immigrant female labor). Above all it renders her disembodied and spectral, haunting the places where her honor might have died and even life itself have ended. Early death was indeed the all-too-common fate of country girls who entered into the worlds of commodified domestic and sexual service, so that the poem's ambiguities about time can be read as registering the full cycle of being toward death that so many of these unfortunate persons passed through so quickly. The instability of the temporal grammar is then the figure of an inevitable passage toward a past historic which is already happening before it happens. In the 1800 poem the father's house may or may not already be in heaven; in the poem of 1802 and after, there are fewer hints of escape.

What about the narrator, self-distanced as he seems to be from the street-level details of the empirical world? The streets mentioned in the poem are, as I have said, those associated with commercial and low-life London, not the smart sectors inhabited by fashionable people. According to Franco Moretti, early nineteenth-century maps disagree about exactly how these streets connect up, whereas they are quite reliable (or at least in agreement) about the geography of the West End.[4] But the streets and districts were real enough to those who lived there, and specific enough in their associations among those who did not. Wood Street, Lothbury and Cheapside are on the borders of the old city, not so far from the old Fleet Ditch made famous in Pope's *Dunciad*. Wood Street not only functions mock-allegorically as the signifier of a wood that is not there: it is (or was) close to Grub Street, the infamous workplace and infernal demise of the hack writer whom Wordsworth had not yet (I am surmising) convinced himself that he might not yet become. Pat Rogers has described the eighteenth-century attributes of Grub Street as those of "crime, poverty, martial ardour, sexual misbehaviour, low literary commerce and much else."[5] We have here, in other words, another conjunction of homelessness, poverty, protocriminality and the life of the writer, whose identity as just another kind of prostitute was becoming a standard trope.[6] Additionally, according to Deidre Lynch, the analogies between "legible faces, minted money, and imprinted texts" were being more and more strongly drawn by the end of the eighteenth century.[7]

Kenneth Johnston, responding to the clues in the Wordsworth archive for the year 1791 when the young poet was living in the city, has concluded that "a likely address for Wordsworth would be Wood Street at its intersection with Maiden Lane and Lad Lane, just below Love Lane."[8] Here penury and shabby gentility were mixed in with sex for money (Love Lane was a renaming of Gropecuntlane) and writing for money: newspapers, bookshops and print shops were concentrated in this area of the city, which was also home to the Royal Exchange and the Bank of England. Johnston has noted that "by far the greatest number of Wordsworth's urban references fall within the compass of less than a square mile around this central point" (p. 241). Does this conjunction of sex, print and money explain the striking reflexivity of the line describing Susan's vision: "Bright volumes of vapour through Lothbury glide"? This is one of the most distinctive lines in the poem, the one most vigorously distant from the clichés describing pastures, pails, cottages and doves' nests. Is it just a poetic incarnation of the London smog, or is the narrator (not Susan) here hallucinating a tide of airborne books, bright volumes that are virtually weightless, passing through the streets? Are the contents of such books weightless, without substance, mere vapors – not just bright mists but disruptive humors of the sort that inspire querulous publications? And are those publications ephemeral, like vapors and like Susan herself as well as her vision? A fanciful association perhaps, but one not implausible in a poet who was very concerned about making his way in the world of professional writing, and who according to Alan Liu, we recall, was overwriting even the tale of Margaret and the pedlar with his own life story of peddling poems and proleptically ruined prospects.[9]

Literary overproduction (and its attendant temptation to vicarious consumption, economically a lowering of prices and aesthetically a corruption of taste) conventionally characterized for Wordsworth as for many others the wrong sort of literature: the "frantic novels" and the "deluge of idle and extravagant stories in verse" as well as the "files of ballads" that "dangle from dead walls" and that sit together with and seem indistinguishable from "advertisements of giant-size" on the streets of London. Wordsworth would recall tradesmen's advertisements that made the "fronts of houses" look like the title pages of books, with "Letters huge inscribed from top to toe."[10] The English newspapers had been heavily involved in advertising since the later seventeenth century, and by the middle of the eighteenth century a significant majority of advertisements were for books, though real estate later took over the lead.[11] Books themselves, even as they came forth in their variously splendid isolations, often also advertised other books. The end pages of the first edition of Southey's *Thalaba* (1801) listed and priced others of Longman's available titles by Wordsworth, Coleridge, Cottle, Mary Robinson and others. As one's career progressed, one might hope that the other books advertised would be one's own, as they were for Southey in the second edition of this same poem in 1809. But even under the imprint of singularity, there was no way to ignore the importance of printed books as commodities in a competitive market. And almost all eighteenth-century books were published in London, not very far from Wood Street, though they did not as yet use wood pulp. Vic Gatrell cites a 1785 source listing 600 print shops and booksellers in the Covent Garden area; meanwhile book prices fell by half in the 1780s and fell again in the 1790s.[12] There was a sea of print, and one with its own ephemeral tides. After William Lane had set going his notorious Minerva Press, James Lackington initiated (in the 1790s) a trade in remaindered books; when Wordsworth wrote his poem he would have been aware of more books, cheaper books and more disposable books, as well as bad books.

The superimposition of an implacably urban literary commerce made up of books produced by the vapors and with vapid contents upon the residual integrity of Susan's rural vision implicates the narrator in Susan's predicament, and even suggests that the vision itself is of questionable origin. Perhaps the clichés are deliberate – they often are in Wordsworth – and signal the second-hand, derivative nature of the tropes of country life (pails, cottages, doves' nests) in a sentimental pastoral vocabulary that is all that is available to an alienated urban experience fed by bad books. If so, then protagonist and narrator are brought together in his imagining of her vision, diminishing (though without fully collapsing) the distinction between well-being and suffering that seems to keep apart the girl on the street and the writer in his narrow room. The poem then reads as the story of a narrator whose recourse to vapid poetic diction seems only to distance him from the incontrovertibly harsher reality of life on the street. If Susan's vision of country life were to be taken in good faith, then she might (in the 1800 text) have a brighter future than the writer himself, who even as he produces the poem interpellates himself as engulfed by mass-produced print. (Susan, in other words, would not be expected to appreciate the pun on "volumes of vapour" which readers are supposed to attribute to disillusioned but clever poets.) If, on the other hand, the whole poem is the projection of a conjuring narrator, then it would be wholly Grub Street that sings at the corner of Wood Street.[13] The moment of quiet, privileged time, between day and night, which (as on Westminster Bridge) allows the narrator the sensory collectedness to see and think anything coherent at all – one bird, one girl only before him – collapses before a vision of a street drowning in words. The distinction between the poet figure and his Susan also collapses; he can be substituted for the sufferer; he too experiences the inflictions of a world of commerce and commodity. The implied security of a dwelling from which he observes a homeless girl is purely virtual, without clear location.

The temporal ambiguities that describe Susan's comings and goings also govern his own identity as death-in-life, another ghost.

Like the Cumberland beggar Susan seems to belong to the familiar homeless: she has a name (though it may be generic) and is sorted from the crowd that swallows up most of the rest of the inhabitants of cities. But as with the beggar her familiarity is tinged by estrangement, by an aura that is uncanny, *unheimlich*, and which inhabits the border between night and day that belongs not only to meditative poets but also to ghosts and other things of darkness. Once again the familiar turns into the unfamiliar, the comforting into the unsettling. The account of the homeless girl projects at first a stable, resident narrator looking from afar or above who then turns out to be himself virtual, dislocated and threatened. The sentimental poetry (poetic diction) that may at first sight seem to seek to frame the experience (country cottages, brown robes and doves' nests) and that will likely offend the fastidious reader as just *too* vaporous comes to signal instead the imminence of a narrator out of control, collapsing into the fog of bad poetry that invades his own walls and windows. A similar dynamic informs the poem about the old beggar, whose ghostly demarcations of the landscape are echoed in a narrative voice that seems to have no bodily form, no feet upon the ground. The power of a commodification cycle that levels and empties out everything, evident in the presentation of work time and charity-as-work in "The Old Cumberland Beggar," is apparent also in "Poor Susan," which literally addresses the demise of woman's domestic and sex work but covertly inscribes and assimilates a similar predicament for the producers of books (though not, it must be said, an equivalence of suffering).

Ghostly vapors emanate from both poems and suggest a commonality between economic, bodily and other-worldly circulation that we will next explore in the famous encounter with the discharged soldier reported in *The Prelude*. But before doing so I want to recall the creative specter of Milton haunting not only Wordsworth's language and imagination but also his geographical habitation. Milton, as Johnston reports, had been born in nearby Bread Street and lived at the end of Wood Street "near the turning to Grub Street, the hack writers' slum."[14] He had been in the news in 1790 because his body had been disinterred and parts of the skeleton were stolen and sold off: another blunt conjunction of literary celebrity with making money. But Wordsworth did not need the breaking news to remember Milton; and vapors, in Milton's work, are almost always negative, as is the "noxious vapour" of the lower depths and the "Vapour, and mist, and exhalation hot" accompanying the change of climate consequent upon the Fall in *Paradise Lost* (2: 216; 10: 694). Most saliently of all, these vapours appear in the description of the flood that drowns the corrupted earth:

> all the clouds together drove
> From under heaven: the hills to their supply
> Vapour, and exhalation dusk and moist,
> Sent up amain: and now the thickened sky
> Like a dark ceiling stood; down rushed the rain
> Impetuous, and continued till the earth
> No more was seen. (11: 739–45)

The vapors that the arguably dying Susan is no longer seeing are not just the mists of her native region but those of a world gone wrong, smothered in print and drowning in water – an allusive conglomerate that dramatically undercuts the sunny-minded pedlar's effort in *The Excursion* to compare the "smoke of unremitting fires" that signals the urbanization of the countryside – "abodes of men irregularly massed / Like trees in forests" – with "vapour glittering in the morning sun."[15] Cowper's *Task* had borrowed from Milton for its own mock heroic account of manuring a greenhouse whose "pestilent and most corrosive steam" requires the opening of a window, whereupon "the overcharg'd / And drench'd conservatory breathes abroad, / In volumes wheeling slow, the vapor dank, / And purified, rejoices to have lost/ Its foul inhabitant."[16] But it is a false nurture embodied in the excremental matter from Pope's Fleet Ditch that remains available to Wordsworth on Wood Street, who is not growing cucumbers but writing books.

WHEN LEGS FORGET THEIR BODIES

Wordsworth's reported encounter with the discharged soldier introduces another watery realm and engages explicitly with the melodrama of spectrality and of absolute and avowed uncanniness. These lines were written in 1798 and conceived as part of the original schema for *The Recluse,* though they were actually to be published in *The Prelude*.[17] The figure of the soldier is fully exorbitant, coming from nowhere on a dark night, more like a comet than a planet. His appearance is unpredicted and his fate unknown. The episode is well known and has been often written about.[18] In Book 4 of *The Prelude*, the events are embedded in an account of the first summer vacation from college, with the young poet experiencing a lighthearted interval of pleasures and social activities and being sobered up by the meeting with the soldier. In the 1798 fragment which I will here take as my text, there is no context given except the narrator's predilection for nighttime rambles on the public roads in pursuit of a "deeper quietness" than is available during the day.¹⁹ The road has a "watry surface" and seems to be a "stream" flowing down to join the one running in the valley: like poor Susan and/or the speaker of her poem, this narrator sees a vision of water (her "river" and "volume of vapours") where there is only land. His state of "peace and solitude" produces further "beauteous pictures" composed of "harmonious images," a seeming countertype to Satan's progress toward the temptation scene in *Paradise Lost*, "wrapped in mist of midnight vapour . . . Like a black mist low creeping" (9: 158–59, 180). Wordsworth as narrator, unlike Satan, is happy enough, though perhaps rather like a mist himself – "Thus did I steal along the silent road" (l. 21). His body *drinks* the "stillness" (l. 22) and his visions, like Susan's, are "like dreams" from "some distant region of my soul" (ll. 30–31). But this "self-possession" (l. 34) is interrupted by the sight of an "uncouth shape" (l. 38). What follows is a reprise (or anticipation) of the Cumberland beggar and of various other figures in the Wordsworth canon:

> [He was in stature tall,]
> A foot above man's common measure tall,
> And lank, and upright. There was in his form
> A meagre stiffness. You might almost think
> That his bones wounded him. His legs were long,
> So long and shapeless that I looked at them
> Forgetful of the body they sustained.
> His arms were long and lean; his hands were bare;
> [His visage, wasted though it seem'd, was large
> In feature, his cheeks sunken, and his mouth]
> Shewed ghastly in the moonlight . . . (ll. 41–51)

The narrator's "animal delight" (l. 33) is countered by this vision of animal insensibility, as his self-possessed silence is displaced by the soldier's "murmuring sounds" (l. 69). This eerie presence is a familiar ghost compounded out of other Wordsworthian protagonists. His body is deformed, whether in fact or in the narrator's excited vision, to the point that it barely seems to hold together the sum of its parts. He is between life and death and seems to register already the agony of passing into death and thenceforth into skeletal form. He is uncannily tall and uncannily thin, full of ghostly attributes. He seems not to seek "any living object" and to be "more than half detached from his own nature," whatever that might be; and he is scarcely "akin to man" (ll. 57–59). He does have a shadow (good news for the startled narrator) but the noise he makes is alinguistic, merely a "groan scarce audible" (l. 79). The narrator asks him for his story and learns that he is a discharged soldier returning from the tropics and now journeying toward his "native home" (l. 103). The narrator persuades him to board at a nearby cottage for the night and goes along his way.

Like many of Wordsworth's liminal old men the soldier eventually speaks with a "stately air of mild indifference" (l. 97) and lapses into silence – or rather the conversation runs dry – as they walk through "shades gloomy and dark" (l. 147) as if descending into the underworld. If they are so doing, then Wordsworth himself is the infernal guide: a Virgil to this Dante, or Anchises to Aeneas, in another substitution whereby the poet becomes the leader (in the search for shelter) and not the led. The soldier's "murmuring sounds" serve, as Langan notes, to identify him with the murmuring poet himself: Wordsworth was well known for his habit of composing out loud while walking the public roads.[20] Their epic destiny turns out to be only a neighbor's cottage, a comic icon of ordinary life above ground. Along the way there is another inversion, or moment of substitutability, when what looks like complete decrepitude in the motionless man transforms itself into supernatural mobility as soon as he starts to walk:

> He appeared
> To travel without pain, and I beheld
> With ill-suppress'd astonishment his tall
> And ghostly figure moving at my side. (ll. 121–24)

His aptitude seems to be for a sort of perpetual motion, which gives his tired body life; is it at odds or in accord with the "strange half-absence" and the "tone of weakness and indifference" (ll. 141–42) that marks his diction? If this is a man between death and life, a *Muselmann*, what is the meaning of his capacity to put aside his pain by walking, and by walking like a ghost? His transition is like that of a machine, able to pass from inertia to astonishingly regular motion without any hesitation: an automaton. In this he performs as another icon of the new labor discipline, with the poet cast as the bewildered operative trying to keep up. While remaining a real soldier returning from the wars, the ghostly figure is richly freighted with literary antecedents and analogues: Odysseus, Aeneas, the Wandering Jew, the wandering and desolate Satan, the ancient mariner and, above all, as Bewell has noticed, a figure adorned in the imagery of Dante's *Divine Comedy*.²¹ But the bookishness of the scenario does not dissolve the strangeness of the scene; the narrator's effort to convert the soldier's uncanniness into familiar behavior is rebuked. When advised to make known his situation and go begging as others do "at the door of cottage or of inn," he responds: "My trust is in the God of Heaven / And in the eye of him that passes me" (ll. 162–63). He invokes, in other words, the same treatment that the Cumberland beggar receives, but with just a hint of the animal magnetism that casts a spell on those accosted by the ancient mariner's glittering eye, and perhaps even with a nod to the fate of Polyphemus, whose single eye undergoes an agonizing punishment for seeking to limit the mobility of Odysseus. The determination to remain at large and thus to impose the same shock of encounter upon other travelers as the narrator has just experienced preserves the soldier's radical unfamiliarity, his refusal to be domesticated.²² Despite accepting shelter for the night, he promises to continue to reside in the uncanny. The 1798 fragment ends abruptly with the parting of narrator from soldier: in *The Prelude* the episode is sealed off with the narrator's seeking "with quiet heart my distant home" (4: 504).

This sealing off resolves one question: why the narrator did not himself offer hospitality instead of waking up a sleeping laborer. That question remains open in the fragment version and enhances the sense of the soldier's threatening and admonitory demeanor. Both versions include reference to a dawning sociability in the soldier, who thanks his guide "with a reviving interest / Till then unfelt" (ll. 167–68) for finding him a bed. This exchange rounds off the visionary component of the event – remember the watery road and dreamlike images – with a transition into ordinary life, of the kind that the old Cumberland beggar never invites or achieves. The soldier now looks less like a ghost and more like a conventional fellow traveler. Perhaps it is this final concession to familiarity that allows Wordsworth to claim a quiet heart, the reward of a charitable act now completed. The identification of narrator with the veteran that is always incipient but never fully established is at the end averted by the poet going to his own home, though it is a distant one: his nocturnal experiences are not yet over. Johnston has noted that the narrator's "mingled sense / Of fear and sorrow" echoes Aristotle's prescription of the proper response to tragedy, suggesting not only that this adventure has a disjunctive potential but that the soldier is a spectacle to which the narrator is the audience, affected by what he sees but finally insulated from real and substantial acting and suffering of his own.²³ The danger, then, passes by, but the figure of the discharged soldier remains a haunting one, just as Margaret continues to possess the reader after the narrator describes his own and the pedlar's access to their "evening resting-place."[24]

There is, once again, more to say. Alan Bewell, in one of the most important contributions to Romantic studies in many a year, has made it very clear that to contemporary readers the image of a discharged soldier would have been inseparable from an awareness of the massive mortality rates suffered by soldiers and sailors going overseas, especially those who went to Africa and above all to the West Indies.[25] The "simple fact" that Wordsworth's discharged soldier "to the tropic isles had gone, / Whence he had landed now some ten days past" (ll. 99–100) would have recalled a knowledge of the massive predominance of disease over military encounters as the primary cause of death and debility.[26] The soldier's ghostly demeanor is, in other words, not to be taken as a mere instance of poetic license, the product of an excited perception in a young man taken by surprise, but as an empirical description of a suffering body. Some of these diseases, moreover, were or were held to be contagious, so that the return of the natives risked the importation of alien infections into the heart of the homeland. There is then a simple, physiological sense in which healthy young Englishmen might have feared encountering the returning veterans of foreign wars; they might also have identified, across the barriers of class and education, with those thus afflicted. The soldier, as Bewell says, not only evokes "the colonial tropics as a haunted burial ground" but "brings the hunger, malnutrition, and disease of the colonial world home" (p. 117). The slave-owning economy whose interests the soldier would have been defending, so important to the British treasury, sends back its signature upon his body, if not as equivalent suffering then as suffering nonetheless. The watery visions that the narrator has of the landscape before the encounter may thus foretell an ensuing recognition that the flotsam of foreign oceans really might be lapping at his feet.

As indeed it is when Wordsworth has himself narrate another encounter, that with the fisherman in the mist in the fourth of the "Poems on the Naming of Places" published in the second edition of *Lyrical Ballads*. I have proposed that there is in this poem a complicated and comic allusion to the widely read accounts of Cook's voyages to the South Pacific, evident in both the naming of places and the misnaming of the royal fern, *osmundia regalis*.[27] This is another poem in which there is a figure of the anthropological other, as Bewell has observed and others have confirmed.[28] The poem suggests that we do not need to go to the ends of the earth in order to experience strangeness, and that the mistakes we tend to make in identifying exotic others and defining our differences from them can be shown to occur just outside our own front doors. The local is the exotic, not just because of the power of imagination to transfigure humdrum experience into significant surprise, but because the local scene is, as the discharged soldier makes clear, already populated by those who have been the followers and servants of empire and foreign wars. You never know who you will run into or where they have been. So when the idle ramblers offer a pompous sermon on the evils of idleness in others, as they do in this poem, we can almost be assured of the rebuke which duly follows. The figure they see behind a "thin veil of glittering haze" is not a malingerer opting out of working the harvest but a figure of complete emaciation, another *Muselmann:*

> We saw a Man worn down
> By sickness, gaunt and lean, with sunken cheeks
> And wasted limbs, his legs so long and lean
> That for my single self I looked at them
> Forgetful of the body they sustained.[29]

These are the same lines Wordsworth had used in the as-yet unpublished tale of meeting the discharged soldier; here, the "tall and upright figure of a man" has diminished on closer inspection to that of a broken shadow of a man "too weak to labour" (ll. 50, 69). To commemorate their error, the ramblers liken themselves to Cook's crewmen and name the place "Point Rash-Judgment," a name just as "uncouth" as anything devised by mariners "on a new-discover'd coast" (l. 85). In their seriocomic misjudgment, they also invoke a lively contemporary debate about the rumor that the inhabitants of Patagonia were giants, a possibility sustained by Cook's editor, Hawkesworth, and by Commodore Byron's claiming eyewitness authority even though Joseph Banks himself measured the Fuegians and found no evidence for it.[30] So the problems of seeing straight in the wilder regions of the Southern Hemisphere are no greater than those attending the most ordinary encounters among the English lakes.

Being a long way from London, the expected location of exotic visitors, does not guarantee one's protective isolation; Wordsworth has his discharged soldiers and gypsies as De Quincey's Grasmere had its visiting Malay. At best one's remoteness allows for the time and space needed to process the implications of one's misunderstandings. It is the possibility that the fisherman in the mist could be all sorts of persons, including the discharged veteran of foreign wars whom Wordsworth encounters elsewhere, that renders imperialism a local, domestic issue requiring moral vigilance even in the most apparently sequestered places. That the fisherman is a local man reinforces a connection between agricultural and military labor, between the *lumpenproletariat* and the army and navy which were according to Marx involved in a cycle of mutual supplementation and substitution, one rendering all encounters unpredictable and potentially implicated in global politics. Reading the old man as a comic incarnation of the Patagonian giant, and Grasmere's local topography as a hyperbolic *terra incognita*, brings together the close at hand and the far-flung, the local and the global, as subject not only to the same observational distortions but to a similarly exigent moral obligation. Botanical curiosity and incipient or actual spoliation add a further dimension to the situation, suggesting that taxonomical incompetence or ambiguity and not scientific truth might be the result of gathering specimens in northwest England as well as in Botany Bay. The self-accusation of Wordsworth's speaker works to disarm readerly outrage by having him do justice upon himself, while laughing very softly at the self-importance of doing just that. Wordsworth has been packaged by a heritage industry that seeks to shore up a fortified local environment as *the* critically precious and protected place; his reputation has also endured the animadversions of politically attuned critics who have presented him as a defender of reactionary ideals. His own poetic understanding of his home in the world was, I am arguing, a more complex and demanding one.

For although the ramblers tell themselves that they have learned to "temper all our thoughts with charity" (l. 79), no actual charity occurs. They are thus just as instrumentally indifferent to the fisherman's wants as is the "dead unfeeling lake" (l. 71) by which he fishes. There is no exchange or conversation: their determination to be "reserv'd in speech" (l. 78) is for the future; they say nothing at all to the man on the shore, so that their self-correction seems to perpetuate the initial failure of sympathy and charity. The ramblers' response is the opposite of that prescribed by Wordsworth's radical acquaintance John Thelwall as normative, and as guaranteeing a connection between the local symptom and the larger political system: "the subject of our political abuses is so interwoven with the scenes of distress so perpetually recurring to the feeling observer, that it were impossible to be silent in this respect, without suppressing almost every reflection that ought to awaken the tender sympathies of the soul."[31] Wordsworth makes silence the subject of his poem and thereby inhibits any easy identification either with tender feelings or with transparently clear political positions. It makes sense that the ramblers' embarrassment might cause them to pass by in silence but that silence also functions to specify the lesson learned as a purely selfish one, with no apparent prospect of positive interventions in the lives of others. They may feel better about themselves by recalling the moral of the tale but not necessarily do anything to change their world. Wordsworth once again calls attention to some of the troubling invocations of charity by using the word for a purely mental experience: they will temper their *thoughts*, and nothing more, with charity. They learn humility but extend no active assistance. The encounter thus embodies not only the positive potential but also the bad-faith component of the experience of concern as that which enables us to avoid an obligation to act by invoking a mood of pending resolution and reflexive ambiguity: we do not or cannot decide how to apportion a practical policy, we *remain* concerned. The imperialist swagger of hasty moral judgments is deflated but the consciousness that regards the world principally as a site for self-development remains subtly imperious. The narrative claims to come to know the man for what he really is, and in this way the ramblers seem to be doing better with him than they were with the Queen Osmunda plant misnamed beforehand in the poem. But we have only their own word that they are here recording an accurately enlightened fact about another person. Can we assume that they succeed as social anthropologists even as they fail as botanists and as charitable givers? Has the mist, the "veil of glittering haze" that surrounds the fisherman, really been dispersed and replaced by the clear light of reason?

It seems convincing to construe the glittering haze as the mist of misunderstanding and oblivion.[32] Is it then incipiently supernatural, like the mist that befuddles Homer's heroes at those moments when the gods seek to make them blind and disable them from self-preservation? What of Milton, who claims in *Paradise Lost* to want to have the mists of mortal existence purged so that he may "see and tell / Of things invisible to mortal sight" (3: 54–55)? Milton's mists mattered as much as his vapors to his attentive successor. Satan is a creature of false light, hiding himself "involved in rising mist" (9: 75, and again at ll. 158, 180). The mist that hides the fisherman from the ramblers also hides them from him, so that they too appear from his perspective as involved in haze. And they remain mysterious, since they do not speak: no response to his greeting is recorded. Miltonic mist is a positive force at the creation, when it waters the ground at a time before rain has been produced (7: 333), though it is also inevitably proleptic of other functions yet to come in a world about to fall. At the end of the poem, the assembling cherubim appear ambiguously "as evening mist" (12: 629). Mist here is the means by which the sight of paradise is withheld from Eve and Adam, obscuring perhaps mercifully the sight of what is lost; but it is also, as a remembered figure of Satan, hurrying them along on their path into a nebulous world. It is the mist of Eve herself and one that evens (despite Michael's orthodox gender system) man with woman; it hurries the laborer toward home but also threatens him with being misled, as were his first ancestors, in the gathering gloom (ll. 631–32). Mist is mysterious and spooky. Wordsworth elsewhere speaks of the character of the beloved dead as properly seen "through a tender haze or luminous mist, that spiritualises and beautifies it; that takes away, indeed, but only to the end that the parts which are not abstracted may appear more dignified and lovely."[33] To see better, we must take away – one of the most profound insights of Wordsworth's aesthetic and a topic to be discussed in a later chapter. What we see is accurate – it is (or was) really there – but also inaccurate – it is a part standing for the whole. Wordsworthian mists are both enabling and concealing, sensuously gratifying and physically threatening; they pun upon what is missed (like a path across the Alps) and proffer imaginatively powerful substitutes (like the sea of mist below Snowdon). The poem we have just been attending to begins in the haze, "ere the mist / Had altogether yielded to the sun" (ll. 7–8), and may well end there. Mist is water turned to atmosphere, an instance of all that is liquid evaporating into air. In "Poor Susan" it is one of the attributes of the protagonist's vision, but that vision is ambiguously positioned between life and death and between the woman observed and the poet observing. In Book 5 of *The Prelude*, which is supposedly about the solid world of books, Wordsworth is, as we will see in chapter 7, obsessed with the liquefactions wrought by water.

Or is this mist a miasma? Not or not only a metaphysical trope but an empirical embodiment of disease and putrefaction? As so often with this poet, one wants to say *both/and*, both metaphysical *and* material. We have noted the overlap between the description of the fisherman in the mist and that of the discharged soldier encountered on the narrator's watery way. The fisherman too imports and imposes what Bewell has called a "pathogenic space" corrupted by the airborne agents of tropical disease and providing an "epidemiological contact zone" for the dissemination of infection.[34] Tropical threats were anyway already close to home: malaria and cholera were domestic and European diseases, so that the ill-fated Walcheren expedition of 1809 would be marked by the death from malaria of 4,000 of the 39,000 troops involved, with another 10,000 returning home sick (p. 97). The ghostly forms of Wordsworth's broken men need not be read as simply the creations of an excitable narrator but can also be taken to register the blunt existences of damaged and displaced human beings. The damage to others in foreign places was also reciprocal with self-damage in arguably psychological as well as physiological senses, and in contexts beyond strictly military ones. "The Ancient Mariner," for example, can plausibly be read as the story of a sailor who has served in the slave trade and has been afflicted with a hallucinatory sense of guilt. Anyone casting himself as a mariner might then sense some affinity not just with the heroic explorers of unknown lands and those achieving famous victories but with the workers who kept going the business of slavery. There is a brief invocation of the slave trade in "The Brothers," another of the *Lyrical Ballads* in which the narrator, a "homely Priest of Ennerdale," fails to recognize a returning seaman as the beloved brother of a dead parishioner.[35] The vicar claims to know his dead but fails to identify the living, thinking of Leonard Ewbank as nothing more than a stranger and a "moping son of Idleness" (l. 11). But it is with some poetic justice (albeit at the expense of any natural heart) that he construes the older brother as already dead. For Leonard has returned "with some small wealth / Acquired by traffic in the Indian Isles" (ll. 63–64), perhaps not itself the slave trade or plantation profit (where fortunes tended to be larger) but possibly so, and certainly tainted money insofar as the entire West Indian economy was dependent upon slavery. Such money comes from death, and death is what it deals out.

The narrator of the "Point Rash-Judgment" poem places himself in the role of overseer and comes to regret it, but he too has already dealt out death and read it out of the landscape of his dead and unfeeling native lake. Here, as in "Poor Susan" and "The Old Cumberland Beggar," there is no dialogue at all between the narrator and his (primary) human subject. In the discharged soldier fragment, where there was a conversation, it was never easeful or spontaneous. The shock of the man's appearance caused the narrator to hide in the bushes until he became embarrassed at his own "specious cowardice" (l. 84) and initiated an exchange that proved, until the very end, acutely awkward and difficult. Sociability is impacted, sympathy cannot circulate freely and charity is both mediated (through the sleeping laborer) and critiqued (by the soldier himself refusing to beg). In the case of the fisherman, the aura of ghostliness and the explicit handing down of "admonishment" (l. 82) are further enhanced by the absence of spoken exchanges (so too with the Cumberland beggar as "silent monitor"). Behind his "veil of glittering haze" (l. 48), he remains a figure from another world, an icon of death-in-life. The natural world, which is actually the world outside Wordsworth's front door, has already been figured as lifeless even *before* the sighting of the fisherman. The narrator goes into some detail about the dead objects left by the waves, the "dry wreck" along the shore (l. 16). The seeds that skim along the water seem "lifeless half, and half impell'd / By some internal feeling" (ll. 19–20), and thus between death and life; and the lake itself is "dead calm" – the phrase is used twice in two lines (ll. 22–23). Again, the fisherman who seems half dead fishes in a "dead unfeeling lake" (l. 71). Despite the narrator's assertion of the "happy idleness" (l. 74) that marks the mood of the ramblers, they see death and dead things all around them from the first, and in picking flowers they are also bringing more death and conforming the living landscape to the unfeeling stillness of the lake and to the desiccated pages of the botanical album. If this is not a beneficent and sustaining nature but a cold, ungiving medium that does not minister to human wants, then its human inhabitants are doing nothing to make it better. As John Beer notes, both man and nature stand as a reminder of the "death-principle that is always in the universe."[36]

What do we make of this? Is the whole poem the dramatic projection of a melancholic narrator whose exclusion from the work cycle imaged in the "busy mirth / Of reapers" (ll. 42–43) makes him unable to envisage an enlivened nature or human nature and renders him prey to an uneasy gaiety of mood that is in fact founded in alienation and can reproduce only reification, causing him to find fault both in an improvident landscape and in a ghostly fisherman? Can reliable scientific knowledge, of the sort that botanical description seems to promise, be produced under such conditions, or must this too remain only the mechanical reproduction of prefigured forms? Rousseau had made the point, one very apt for Wordsworth's narrators, that the entire enlightenment aspiration toward the gathering of new knowledge from distant places could never succeed because "under the pompous name of the study of man everyone does hardly anything except study the men of his country. In vain do individuals come and go; it seems that Philosophy does not travel." Thus it is that people go to the ends of the earth and come back with the "fine adage of morality" that "men are everywhere the same." They discover what they could have noticed "without leaving their street" because in their mind's eye they have not really left it.[37] Wordsworth's poems are full of analyses of these projections of the self as descriptions of the other. Here, it is death that is projected: the dead lake and death-in-life figure of the fisherman, the botanical enthusiasts picking flowers and even the "reapers" who are happily cutting the wheat are all images of life vanished or vanishing. The narrator claims it as his *occupation*, his work, to "observe / Such objects as the waves had toss'd ashore" (ll. 12–13), thus projecting a self-designated role as beachcombing mortician and heightening the irony attending his misjudgment of the fisherman. But his observations are more than merely passive when it comes to plucking flowers. In both cases the acts of disengaged inspection making up the scientific gaze require the production of dead objects.

It is not just the ramblers' place (or non-place) in the work cycle and their compulsive taxonomizing that constitute the poem's affiliation with death. The cyclic exchange of exhausted labor between city and country, and between both and the army and navy, made it highly likely in the empirical sense that a physically decrepit man seen fishing might indeed have served in the wars and come home with a radical affliction. The work cycle that produces reification and physical disability is also the mechanism of empire, which brings death or mutilation by disease, sword and cannon. Wordsworth's working out of the motifs of ghostliness and mortality includes not just a metaphysical but a historical referent, both domestic and imperial, each in the other, and one that arguably produces the metaphysical dimension itself and makes it matter. Derrida's *Specters of Marx* insists that the anxiety attached to ghosts is not just about what they evoke in the past but about their claim to be always about to return, to be the eerie companions of what is to come. What is to come threatens to be chillingly like what has been, at least in terms of our expectations of the massive disposition of death and destruction by modern nation-states and other political and natural agents. The dead nature projected by Wordsworth's narrator is all too predictable for those of us living with the threat of silent springs and melting ice caps, just as the specter of disfigured human bodies is routine (and is routinely repressed) in a world marked by continuous war with no promised end. The idle stroller who speaks the poem about Point Rash-Judgment can see his own fate in the ghostly fisherman, and we can too. The death that will and must close all is not just and not simply a natural one; it is intensified and overdetermined by the historical conditions we inhabit and which render it a topic of radical concern and perhaps despair – since so many forms of death really could, in a different world, be avoided or delayed.

Derrida's assessment of the legacy of Marx was itself not just an abstract, metaphysical tour de force about life and death and death-in-life but an engagement with a moment in history: the "fall" of the Soviet empire in 1989 and the hyperbolic and therefore insecure celebrations in the West that proclaimed a final victory in the Cold War. His insistence on the specter – and on Marx's insistence on the specter – as that which disorders time and projects the past as the form of the future while critically disturbing any sense of a present in a radical "disadjustment of the contemporary" was a challenge to the vociferous neoliberal chorus that sought to consign not only Marx but significant historical change itself to the vanished past.[38] In the face of this triumphalism, he insisted that to conjure away the specter that was haunting Europe and the world is also to conjure it up anew (p. 47): exorcism itself is ongoing and subject to history. It was (and is) the newly charged global-capitalist hegemony that voiced the desire to bury Marx, and with him the exigent kind of social concern he articulated. But "haunting belongs to the structure of every hegemony," says Derrida (p. 37), and this particular haunting is rendered all the more insistent because of the historical record of the recent past and present, with its "massive exclusion of homeless citizens from any participation in the democratic life of States, the expulsion or deportation of so many exiles, stateless persons and immigrants" (p. 81) and its overwhelming evidence that "never have violence, inequality, exclusion, famine, and thus economic oppression affected as many human beings in the history of the earth and of humanity," that "never before, in absolute figures, never have so many men, women, and children been subjugated, starved, or exterminated on the earth" (p. 85).

Wordsworth's poetics of social concern remains modern and continues to compel attention for these same reasons: it too posits from the past a world always returning and about to return, and returning now on perhaps a grander scale than ever before. The ontology that critics have found (or founded) in Wordsworth's constructions of the self could thus be renominated a *hauntology*, taking over Derrida's telescopic term for the instance and insistence of spectrality in attributions of substance and essence: "ontology is a conjuration" (p. 161), so that "I am" must mean "I am haunted" (p. 133).[39] The haunting is reflexive: one makes oneself not only through beauty but through fear, and projects spectrality out into the world as the source of that fear (as Wordsworth does with his discharged soldier among others), so that all things other to oneself become capable of generating that fear: "The subject that haunts is not identifiable, one cannot see, localize, fix any form, one cannot decide between hallucination and perception, there are only displacements, one feels oneself looked at by what one cannot see" (p. 136). So too does Wordsworth when stealing a boat, hearing low breathings, and conjuring up the living dead on Salisbury Plain. This is not purely a disabling condition, either for Wordsworth or for Derrida, who indeed sees in the obsession with ghosts one of the generative conditions of ethics, a responsibility to the specters of the past and to the lives of those yet to come (p. xix). But we cannot dispel anxiety by claiming to know the form of this ethics. The kinds of responsibility that Wordsworth's ghostly encounters give rise to cannot even be clearly specified: they remain matters of concern.

Such concern is only potentially a generative condition and not at all an achieved ethics. That has yet to be produced, and the task is as daunting now as it was in the years around 1800. Wordsworth's opening up and openness to a problem of concern that we ourselves are far from solving articulates an aporetic paradigm at the heart of our shared modernity. Take the case of hospitality, another syndrome to which the work of Derrida has directed recent critical attention. The visible lack of hospitality shown by Wordsworth's narrators – recall that it is the nearby laborer who is roused from sleep to give the discharged soldier a bed for the night, the narrator's own home being "distant" – and the limiting of charitable behavior to giving on the open road rather than sheltering in the home, speaks not only to their compulsive self-imaging as homeless wanderers but also to an intuition about the assumptions of hospitality itself. To cast oneself as homeless is more than romantic Satanism; it is a staging of an imminent symmetry between the haves and the have-nots. Derrida, Heidegger and Adorno have all claimed that no one in the modern world should ever feel entitled to claim to be at home. With so many homeless, complete hospitality becomes impossible and possession itself embarrassing. Moreover, for Derrida, to possess home and shelter is to claim kinship with the dead upon whose remains the would-be permanent features of dwellings are erected. It is not an escape from threat but a constant reminder of it: "hospitality therefore presupposes waiting, the horizon of awaiting and the preparation of welcoming [*accueil*]: *from life to death*."[40] Out in the open or safe at home, there is no safety. Man's home is eventually always in the earth.

Thinking through the conditions governing hospitality, Derrida has called for an inspection and questioning not only of the boundary between life and death but also of any "possibility of a rigorous delimitation of thresholds or frontiers: between the familial and the non-familial, between the foreign and the non-foreign, between the citizen and the non-citizen, but first of all between the private and the public."[41] Hospitality is only purely such when it tolerates and welcomes the absolutely unanticipated and is given with no expectation of return, including that form of return embodied in the onset of good feelings about one's own virtuous behavior. Wordsworth was taken by surprise in meeting the discharged soldier, and he neither walked on by or delivered hospitality: it is the sleeping laborer roused from his bed who is called upon to extend an unforeseen welcome. Absolute hospitality is perhaps impossible, a goal to be thought rather than a gesture that can be enacted. Wordsworth does not ignore the soldier, threatening as he is to both person and conscience. But the demand he makes of the laborer is not the demand he makes of himself. His own commitment to more time on the road, with all its visual shiftings and inversions, puts him back into an openness to further surprises that is not necessarily at one with the "quiet heart" that the publication of this episode at the end of Book 4 of *The Prelude* tags on to the narrative. It puts him into a position to write more poetry about more encounters but only by casting him as insufficient, unable or unwilling to respond *adequately*. One senses both the metaphysical message that home is always distant, always to be sought but never fully occupied, and the empirical or ethical failure to make amends. At least since Hazlitt (in a response to "Gipsies") described Wordsworth as the "prince of poetical idlers," he has been a target for moral disapproval.[42] And indeed it is hard to resist the idea that a shilling here and there might have helped. Such charities, which indeed Wordsworth the man, like many of his class and kind, did often actually distribute, would have made for less challenging poetry. They would have located him outside or above the order of necessity to which he clearly felt he also belonged. Wordsworth could have written about giving out charity and hospitality in a mood of moral wholeheartedness; the fact that he mostly did not opens up much deeper channels of moral and historical concern. A further understanding of the historical circumstances of this concern can be gained by considering the uncanny aptness of Marx's infamous characterization of the *lumpenproletariat* for a reading of Wordsworth's poetry.

THE CLASS WHICH IS NOT ONE

The most extended account of the *lumpenproletariat* occurs in *The 18th Brumaire of Louis Bonaparte*, where it is described in parodic terms as the foundation of the charlatan emperor-politician's support. Here is Marx's memorable passage:

Alongside decayed *roués* with dubious means of subsistence and of dubious origin, alongside ruined and adventurous offshoots of the bourgeoisie, were vagabonds, discharged soldiers, discharged jail-birds, escaped galley slaves, swindlers, mountebanks, *lazzaroni*, pickpockets, tricksters, gamblers, *maquereaus*, brothel-keepers, porters, *literati*, organ-grinders, rag-pickers, knife-grinders, tinkers, beggars – in short, the whole indefinite, disintegrated mass, thrown hither and thither, which the French term *la bohème*.[43]

Here are the beggar and the discharged soldier (though perhaps not Poor Susan), as well as the human odds and ends that Wordsworth found earning various sorts of livings in and around Bartholomew Fair. Foreigners and nationals, those clawing themselves up from the bottom of society and those slipping down from the top or middle, ordinary tradesmen (knife grinders) and criminals, the dwellers and the homeless, all come together in a potpourri of turbulent and inchoate humanity. Adam Smith's *Wealth of Nations* had listed some of the same subcultures as "unproductive of any value" even when "respectable": "In the same class must be ranked, some both of the gravest and most important, and some of the most frivolous professions: churchmen, lawyers, physicians, men of letters of all kinds; players, buffoons, musicians, opera-singers, opera-dancers etc" (p. 331). These are the laborers whose efforts cannot be fixed or realized "in any permanent subject, or vendible commodity, which endures after that labour is past . . . the work of them all perishes in the very instant of its production." But Smith seems unsure, and says that their work "has a certain value" (p. 330–31). The specification of this class or order of workers is ambivalent; they have a certain value but are also "unproductive of any value." They do some good, though the value thus indicated is not the value of the economist, that which can be redeemed.

Similar instabilities govern Marx's account of the *lumpenproletariat*, though unlike Smith he does not ascribe to them any value at all. They are not fully a class – Marx is clear about this – and yet they are players in the history of their times because they are the natural constituency of Louis Bonaparte, who is making the history. So they, the "scum, offal, refuse of all classes," function as if they were a class – "the only class upon which he [Bonaparte] can base himself unconditionally."[44] Perhaps the *lumpenproletariat* is a class that is not a class because all classes elide themselves into it? Peter Stallybrass has brilliantly explored the inversions and displacements that appear in Marx and Engels and others on this question: Marx attributes to the *lumpenproletariat* the same conditions of chaotic anomie that others saw in the *proletariat* itself, and that various commentators assigned to the aristocracy as a society of unproductive laborers.[45] Jacques Rancière has indeed proposed that Marx's almost hysterical enumeration of the various segments of the *lumpen* population asks to be read as "the myth of a bad history that comes to parasitize the good," one seeking to occlude the recognition that among them are "the parasites and castoffs of the German revolution in exile" including the good Karl himself and his closest comrades.[46] For Rancière the secret is that there *is* no authentic proletariat with which the *lumpen* can be historically contrasted: "the conquering class seems to be decomposing between the backwardness of its past and the fear of its future" (p. 95). What occurs is not just a dynamic of inversion but of total confusion, where everyone becomes or risks becoming everyone else. Classes dissolve into a gathering of types and figures where all differences are idiosyncratic and without meaning. Substitutability runs riot.

It will not then be surprising that here too are the men of letters, the literati whose British equivalents send their volumes of vapors to and from the Grub Street traders. And here are the ragpickers whose trade made possible the manufacture of the paper upon which vapid books could be printed. They indeed give their name to the whole collective: *Lumpen* in German means *rags*. Marx's catalogue offers resounding evidence of the precarious status of the writer in relation to both minimal well-being and definite class identity, and he himself would show how all writers tend in the modern world to the condition of wage-laborers and all books to the status of commodities.[47] But it is the miserable demise of the ragpickers that most fully and brutally brings together the craft of writing with the immiseration of women and children and provides a haunting mediation between the disembodied poet and the girl on the street near Grub Street whose fate he attempts (in 1800) to remedy by poetic apostrophe before giving up altogether (in 1802) on the rhetoric of positive advice. Here is Marx:

Owing to the excessive labour performed by their workers ... certain London firms where newspapers and books are printed have gained for themselves the honourable name of "slaughter-houses". Similar excesses occur in book-binding, where the victims are chiefly women, girls and children ... One of the most shameful, dirtiest and worst paid jobs, a kind of labour on which women and young girls are by preference employed, is the sorting of rags. It is well known that Great Britain, apart from its own immense store of rags, is the emporium for the rag trade of the whole world ... The rag-sorters are carriers for the spread of small-pox and other infectious diseases, and they themselves are the first victims. (*Capital One*, pp. 592–93)

The connection between young homeless girls and writers may then be based on something more than figurative equivalence in the general money and commodity economy, powerful as that equivalence certainly was for those conscious of selling their best selves for cash. If what Marx describes in the 1860s was at all a feature of the London of 1800, then its image as the assembly point for rags flowing in from all across the world, only some of which go to make paper (others go for "manure" or "bed flocks") lends another kinetic element to the "vale of Cheapside" that Susan inhabits and hallucinates. The ghostliness of the girl on the street may well be again linked to the incursion of alien diseases and the experience of brutalizing work regimes, just as it was for the soldier returning from the West Indies.

Both social and literary history seem to be oddly silent about the lives of the ragpickers who must have been unignorable on the streets of London, the center of the book trade and of the warehouses often attached to stationers companies where rags and paper were stored. Old-clothes gatherers were typically Jewish: one such figure plays an important role in Maria Edgeworth's *Harrington* (1817), and in 1810 James Peller Malcolm visited the Jewish district of London and found the stereotypical clothes dealer himself to be little more than "an upright bundle of rags."[48] The popular image of the Ashkenazi Jew was that of a "ragged old-clothes man."[49] These were the low-end brokers who bought or collected clothes for repair and resale at Rag Fair on Rosemary Lane, and there were an estimated two thousand of them in London in the 1790s.[50] I have been unable to find any comparable figures for the true ragpickers who were lower down the economic and social ladder than the clothes gatherers, though they must have been very numerous indeed, especially during the French wars when the supply of imported rags fell below what the industry required, a situation which at least one scholar has invoked to explain a boom in poetry (which made for shorter books) during the years of the blockade.[51] The quantity of imported rags had risen twenty-fold in the years between 1700 and 1800, supplying the sea of print that was by the 1790s seen to be drowning the population in words. In the domestic sphere, stationers were often also rag merchants, middle-men who took in the findings of the pickers and passed them to the paper factories.[52] Henry Mayhew's *London Labour and the London Poor* did not begin to appear until 1851, but there we find an account of the ragpickers as urban wanderers of classic Wordsworthian proportions, leading a "wandering, unsettled sort of life, being compelled to be continually on foot, and to travel many miles every day in search of the articles in which they deal. They seldom have any fixed place of abode" and, Mayhew goes on, they are often victims of downward mobility, "who from some failing or mishap have been reduced to such a state of distress that they were obliged to take to their present occupation, and have never after been able to get away from it."⁵³

The apparent non-appearance of the ragpickers in the fictional and historical accounts of both the book and paper trades and of London street life at large is an eerie phenomenon, one that seems to render them specters haunting an industry that could not have carried on without them. Walter Benjamin's much later account of Baudelaire's Paris makes much of them and makes them famous in literary history, though not systematically enough for Adorno, who wished to see some further theorization of the "capitalist function of the ragpicker – namely, to subject even rubbish to exchange value."⁵⁴ Poor Susan is probably no ragpicker, though such persons might well have been starting out on their rounds along Wood Street at dawn. But the cycle of substitutability governing actual or potential immiseration gathers together not only writers, prostitutes and servant girls but ragpickers too, the foot soldiers of the publishing industry and thus members of the *lumpenproletariat* to whom they gave their name: the class typified by the sorters and wearers of rags. Or rather the non-class. Marx later goes on to associate Bonaparte with what seems to be a class, that of the "small-holding peasant." But this class too is not a class, because it is unable to become any sort of collective. It is a residual and withering social group whose members are cut off from one another by their very mode of production: "their field of production, the small holding, admits of no division of labor in its cultivation, no application of science and, therefore, no diversity of development, no variety of talent, no wealth of social relationships."⁵⁵

The very conditions and the very subculture that Wordsworth celebrates, in other words, as the last best hope for social and aesthetic satisfaction – the world of "Michael" and of the Lakeland owner-occupiers with their frugal subsistence economy and their openness to the great natural objects around them – is here specified by Marx not only as expiring and redundant but also as the base of support for the new facsimile of empire in mid-century France. It is, as it were, coming and going at the same time, disappearing in the long term but momentarily invented and resuscitated as the pastiche core of a political movement: Bonapartism. Here is Marx describing exactly what Wordsworth most approved of around 1800: "Each individual peasant family is almost self-sufficient; it itself directly produces the major parts of its consumption and thus acquires its means of life more through exchange with nature than in intercourse with society" (p. 478). But for Marx this set of persons no longer forms a whole, if it ever did: its members are related "much as potatoes in a sack form a sack of potatoes" (pp. 478–79). A few more or less makes no difference, mere contiguity is all that each has in common with others, there is "no community, no national bond and no political organization" (p. 479). They *are* a class insofar as they have a common identity in relation to other classes, but they are *not* a class because they cannot organize or represent themselves. Thus their fantasies are raw material for others to exploit in authoritarian ways for their own interests. The deepest aspiration of the peasant smallholders is to hold on to what they have, to "consolidate" (as Wordsworth's Michael had done), and it is the promise of this that attracts them to "the ghost of empire" (pp. 479–80). But the capitalization of the land in the hands of the "urban usurers" is converting them into "troglodytes" who "dwell in hovels" (p. 481). Feudal-aristocratic traditions are collapsing owing to the "vampire" (p. 482) of bourgeois capital (again, as in "Michael").

The historical tendency Marx articulates here is one that is increasing the numbers of the homeless and vagabond poor: "To the four million (including children, etc.) officially recognized paupers, vagabonds, criminals and prostitutes in France must be added five million who hover on the margin of existence and either have their haunts in the countryside itself or, with their rags [*Lumpen*] and their children, continually desert the countryside for the towns and the towns for the countryside" (p. 482). There is continual circulation between the two, so that no strict distinctions between town and country can subsist. We have seen the same distinctions breaking down in the poetic versions of rural life staged in Wordsworth's poetry. Even if poor Susan were able to leave the streets of London and put on once again her plain russet gown, there is no guarantee that what she sees in her vision will still be there when she returns. The old beggar embodies precisely the emptiness of social relations Marx describes among the smallholders: he is the mobile principle of a sociability that never otherwise exits the dwellings of the rural poor, and he himself neither speaks nor is spoken to. The discharged soldier is even more fully the icon of strangeness, the unfamiliar and unpredicted bearer of a world elsewhere that can only be reassimilated uneasily if at all into the rituals of local life. For Marx the French army is one of the main repositories of the displaced smallholding class that is no class, functioning as the recourse of "substitutes" and as the "swamp-flower of the peasant *lumpenproletariat*" (p. 483) which increasingly turns upon itself in being paid to perform police actions within the nation-state. The presence of the discharged soldiers [*entlassene Soldaten*] in that memorable description of the *lumpenproletariat* already cited thus indicates a temporal circularity whereby this class which is no class is being constantly reinforced by the return of soldiers it has previously provided as it is still providing to the army. There is a continual toing and froing between army and navy, the vagabond class, the pool of factory and farm labor, the country and the city, with every person passing potentially through some or all parts of the cycle for as long as he or she can stay alive. The human fate of each member of this desperate aggregate is entropic or devolutionary even as its numbers increase, although for Marx the forward motion of history is preserved in the hypothesis that the same process must eventually lead to the collapse of a state that is founded only on Louis Napoleon's abilities as a "conjurer" [*Taschenspieler*] commanding a rhetoric that masks the "death struggle" of the smallholders who appear as "spirits transformed into ghosts" (pp. 487, 484).

During the French wars the numbers in military service were huge: by one estimate some 800,000 men out of a population of around 9 million were serving in Britain's army and navy by 1813, and some 200,000 of these were demobilized between 1814 and 1817.[56] This was a massive increase in the proportion of combatants over all previous conflicts. The French army, raised by conscription, was even larger, perhaps 1.5 million by 1794. Add in the Russians, Austrians, Prussians and other combatants, and the whole of Europe can be imagined as the scene of a circulating *lumpenproletariat*. Primitive or primary [*ursprüngliche*] accumulation had been typical of the modern economy for some time, and had led to much concern about migrant and vagrant populations as early as the sixteenth century.[57] In the early 1800s the numbers were simply greater and the coincidence of militarization, demobilization and regional redistributions of labor made the "relative surplus population" more apparent than ever.[58] During the "great fear" in late 1789 in France, when several local migrations among the poor all happened at the same time and gave the appearance of being coordinated, there had even been rumors that the vagrant classes were allied with the aristocracy against the revolution.[59] In England, in the form of the "Church and King" mobs, they often were, although the establishment propaganda was aimed more commonly against the "people."

In Wordsworth's *The Excursion*, the Wanderer has a more focused concern. While he admits that the transport revolution and the pace of urbanization have changed the face of the countryside, he sees an even more radical transformation in the introduction of factory shift work that renders night indistinguishable from day and compels the workers – men, women and children – to enact a "perpetual sacrifice" to "Gain, the master-idol of the realm" (8: 184–85). The factory system levels everyone to the same function, "with appetite as keen / As that of war, which rests not night or day, / Industrious to destroy" (8: 94–95). The conflation here made of war and factory labor (and Marx would make it again himself) is one that goes to the heart of the social experience embodied in the *lumpenproletariat*, since conditions in the armed services were very much like those in the industrial workplace. Cobbett's pamphlet of 1792, *The Soldier's Friend*, protested that enlisted men were not receiving their contractual three shillings a week, but were being constantly underpaid, with the missing sums embezzled by their officers and provisioners.[60] They too were a labor force being employed at the cheapest possible rate for the maximum amount of work. Conditions in the navy were even harsher, although opportunities for prize money did exist there for some of the officers and crew. Running a ship involved a highly divided system of labor enforced by a discipline perhaps even more severe than that of factory labor. Sailors returning from the sea then arrived at the port cities, when they temporarily assimilated into the rootless, mobile population, often driving up the crime rate.[61] Going back to sea meant going back to a carceral society and an industrial routine: even John Wordsworth developed compulsive behavior on board ship which he could not abandon when on land, wearing a path through the trees "In that habitual restlessness of foot / With which the sailor measures o'er and o'er / His short domain upon the vessel's deck."[62] Staying on land, if that were possible without falling foul of the law, offered for many poorer sailors only incorporation into the reserve army of the poor which eventually again fed back into the military services for those able enough to keep the cycle going.

There is one striking and important difference between Marx's representation of the *lumpenproletariat* and Wordsworth's of his protagonists. Marx always portrays a crowd, a "noisy, disreputable, rapacious bohème," whereas Wordsworth encounters people singly, a choice that renders them both more and less threatening.[63] Their singleness means that they do not project any violent revolutionary potential of the sort that crowds represented for so many after 1789; they are always one on one with the narrator, and their sex (poor Susan) and age (the beggar) often render them physically unchallenging even when they are metaphysically threatening and strange. But the discharged soldier, remember, is capable of surprising and preternatural quickness, and is a head taller than ordinary men. Carrying his staff and more than keeping up the pace as he does, he is a scary figure, all the more so given his reluctance to appease the narrator's urge for conversation. The beggar too has something of the aura of the aged Oedipus, a presence to be handled carefully lest his supernatural powers be provoked. Beggar and soldier are at once deprived of and endowed with energy. Above all they possess the power to disturb; energy is transposed from the natural to the preternatural, making them spooky. It is a matter of interpretation exactly why Wordsworth thus registers the alienation of the poor and the homeless – whether by describing them singly he transcribes a fantasy of control against the tide of the history supposed by Marx to be bringing in more and more crowds of such people, or whether he thereby embodies in powerful poetic form the inclination to death that they both embody in themselves (as does Susan) and threaten in those they meet on the roads. If there is no image of the massing of the dispossessed in Wordsworth, there is also seldom any of the compensatory ambiguity of the carnivalesque, which is oddly appealing even in Marx's descriptions (as it does sometimes appeal to Wordsworth in London). Wordsworth's vagrant spirits are more often possessed by an apathy that can sometimes seem stoical (as in the poem "Old Man Travelling") but can also appear to be the result of exhaustion and despair. In *The Condition of the Working Class in England*, Engels attributed a similar apathy both to the working conditions of the factory and to the social conditions of the city, which produced "the unfeeling isolation of each in his private interest" and a "dissolution of mankind into monads."[64] This was further compounded by the homeless population – 50, 000 in London alone, Engels estimated (p. 336) – who contributed to the "reserve army" (p. 384) that Marx would later call the *lumpenproletariat*.

Wordsworth's concern with homelessness is a preoccupation that is simultaneously personal and historical, and all the more personal because it is historical. A positively endorsed collective homelessness does crop up in *The Prelude*, where the poet recalls relishing his trip through France and converting the mental vagrancy of his Cambridge experiences into a facsimile of the gypsy life:

> Unhoused, beneath the Evening Star we saw
> Dances of Liberty, and, in late hours
> Of darkness, dances in the open air. (6: 380–82)

But this does not last beyond a few months after July 1789. The projected wanderings of the typical Wordsworthian narrator are mostly solitary, the encounters one on one, monad to monad. The various complexities and failures of these encounters do not confront directly the phenomenon of the disheveled masses that Marx saw to be on the increase, but they do preserve a sense of threat associated with the denial of ordinary sociability or sympathy and with the projection of the aura of death. They are thus, in their way, powerful instances of an alienation both singular and social, both psychological and socioeconomic. Above all, in their dramatized uncertainties about judgments and obligations, in their concerns about boundaries, they image the breaking down of barriers between the classes and professions that Marx saw in the *lumpenproletariat*. The same prospect is there in the *Communist Manifesto*, which indeed begins by proposing a historical conflict between the workers and the bourgeoisie as "two great classes directly facing each other," but goes on to explore all the ways in which each is becoming identified with the other. So it is that the members of the professional class, "the priest, the poet, the man of science," have also become "paid wage-labourers," while the "lower strata of the middle class ... sink gradually into the proletariat" which is thus "recruited from all classes of the population."[65] By a similar logic, as we have seen, both classes then stand threatened with slipping into the *lumpenproletariat*, the human mass providing the fund of primitive accumulation from which the capitalist economy selects and discards according to its needs.

These prospects can, I think, be traced through Wordsworth's poetic encounters with beggars, soldiers and abandoned women, encounters which always reflect back upon his own narratively privileged position as itself threatened and unstable. The fully dialogic narrator of "The Discharged Soldier" fragment gets a scare; the embedded but uninvolved, invisible narrator of "The Old Cumberland Beggar" is himself something of a specter; the fully detached speaker of "Poor Susan" is yet more so, as is the young woman he writes about. Far from making the poems inefficient or unsatisfying, these moments record the history of the years around 1800 with extraordinary precision and analytical power, and without any loss of urgency about the claims and aspirations of human feeling. The ghosts are images of human alienation: of persons from persons, of children from parents, of workers from products circulating as commodities for the profit of others. They instance the virtuality that affects everyone's experience of a death-in-life enforced by specific historical conditions. As such these ghosts threaten the sunny common sense of the new man far more than anything enshrined in the genre of the Gothic, because they are resolutely part of everyday life: you can meet them on the road. They are compelling emanations of the dilemmas and dynamics of concern, and they should be as immediate to today's reader still at home among the homeless as they were to those who saw them when they were first published, because the conditions they illuminate have yet to be historically superseded.

CHAPTER 4

Timing modernity: around 1800

A MULTITUDE OF CAUSES UNKNOWN TO FORMER TIMES

In chapter 1 I explored both the conjunctions and the distinctions between Jeffrey Sachs's recent argument for abolishing poverty and the issues raised in Wordsworth's reported encounter with that starving girl on the roads of France. The conjunctions are to be attributed to an enduring component of modernization that renders the unsolved questions raised by a brilliantly sensitive poet around 1800 still urgent for us today. The distinctions have to do with the poet's commitment to an arresting and haunting personification of the problem of poverty that cannot be boiled down to an unambiguous propositional statement, whether positive or pessimistic. Wordsworth's poetry of social concern remains current because the modern address to poverty and welfare, which Sachs finds to have been indeed inaugurated by the massive economic growth and radical differentiation of wealth around 1800, remains as unsolved now as it was two hundred years ago. Much else has of course changed. Around 1800 there was no Internet, no space shuttle, no knowledge of the DNA model. But the population was on the point of rapidly increasing, the beginnings of modern transport and communications systems were in place (to the extent that Wordsworth could complain about them in terms that we still find familiar), modern mass warfare was occurring for the first time, and the factory economy that would transform the workplace so publicly and profoundly had established itself in Britain, assisted by modern banking and financing institutions. Rural labor too was undergoing visible modernization: small-scale machine labor appeared first in the countryside. Many important elements in the world that we in the mature capitalist democracies know today were taking on exemplary form and substance around 1800. My focus on the secret ministries of commodity form in relation to social concern is not meant to suggest that this and this alone is the key to all understandings of the transitions then occurring: there was at work, as Wordsworth himself wrote, "a multitude of causes unknown to former times,"[1] and they range from the visibly empirical, the things that could be seen – the experience of machine labor, the huge increase in the size of the army and navy during the French wars – to the invisible forces whose impact was equally empirical but whose workings could not be seen – valorization and the credit economy. Many of these causes really were "unknown to former times," others took on newly intense forms. *All* of these determinations are significant in making commodity form what it was becoming then and remains today: a formative paradigm governing more of the operations of social and personal life and thought than ever before.

By the early twentieth century, it seemed that no good case could be made for Wordsworth's contemporaneity, which had been affirmed by John Stuart Mill and Matthew Arnold as therapeutically urgent for the anguished doubters of the mid-nineteenth century but appeared to have been nixed once and for all by the likes of Pound and Eliot in their preference for a retooled anti-Romantic ethos of objectivist description, one calling for a negation of the personal perspective rather than a Wordsworthian exploration of its lineaments and consequences. With hindsight, however, it is the Modernist moment that looks like a deviation from a larger historical trajectory which has since affirmed over and over again the importance of the personal for the adequate articulation of all sorts of ethical and epistemological inquiries. The return to a perspectivist aesthetics may be explained as in part a response to the powerful pressure of a society whose work patterns and living habits have been more and more decided by the division of labor and the accompanying diversification of lifestyles. Among the causes unknown to former times, Wordsworth picked out as especially important "the encreasing accumulation of men in cities," where they were exposed to monotonous work disciplines, rapidly disseminated news items and purely sensationalist leisure options (*Prose Works*, I, p. 128). The coming together of urbanization, an intensifying divided labor system and a culture of spectacle available for speedy mass distribution through the modern media is one of the major formations underpinning the continuity between Wordsworth's modernity and our own. Not for nothing do Frank Lentricchia and Jody McAuliffe see in his work the seeds of a "literary terrorism" whose outrage at the conditions of modern life reappears in the fictions of Don DeLillo and the manifesto of Theodore Kaczynski, the Unabomber.[2] Certainly the coincidence between Wordsworth's famous analysis of the deteriorating conditions for the production and appreciation of serious literature and Horkheimer and Adorno's critique of postwar capitalist culture is so remarkable as to seem uncanny were it not for the continuity of a historical syndrome whose latest incarnations often claim to have turned the corner from modernity to postmodernity while still repeating the terms of an earlier critique. Thus Horkheimer and Adorno:

> Amusement under late capitalism is the prolongation of work. It is sought after as an escape from the mechanized work process, and to recruit strength in order to be able to cope with it again. But at the same time mechanization has such power over a man's leisure and happiness, and so profoundly determines the manufacture of amusement goods, that his experiences are inevitable after-images of the work process itself . . . Pleasure hardens into boredom because, if it is to remain pleasure, it must not demand any effort and therefore moves rigorously in the worn grooves of association.[3]

Written a century and a half later, this passage stands as an updated form of Wordsworth's argument about the dominance of those "gross and violent stimulants" which "blunt the discriminating powers of the mind . . . unfitting it for all voluntary exertion" and reduce it to "almost savage torpor." For Horkheimer and Adorno there is an absolute continuity between work and leisure, with leisure reproducing mere "after-images of the work process." Wordsworth made a different point, arguing that the torpor thus produced led to a "craving for extraordinary incident" as a compensation for the "uniformity" of men's occupations.[4] But they agree that the corruption of leisure by work is complete; the thirst for extravagant stimulation is just as mechanical as the listless replication of work habits. That indeed is what Horkheimer and Adorno would themselves argue in their explanation of the popularity of cinema and television.

The Frankfurt School exiles wrote in the aftermath of two catastrophic world wars and from within the perceived hegemony of the monopoly phase of capitalism within which "all mass culture is identical" and almost all forms of art have become mass culture: "what is new is not that it [art] is a commodity, but that today it deliberately admits it is one; . . . art renounces its own autonomy and proudly takes its place among consumption goods."[5] Wordsworth's world had not fallen quite so far or so fully, but all the signs of such a future were there to be read. He too was living through a world war in which the reduction of individual life to impersonal labor or military routines of life and death promised an equivalence between persons that was far from democratic and hardly to be desired.[6] And he too was acutely aware of the increasing pressure on would-be serious literature from a popular market serving up books offering only "gaudiness and inane phraseology."[7] The shock of the new that his own poetry registers – that "sudden shock of *recognition*" that Raymond Williams says is central to the "structure of feeling"[8] – indicates a historical moment at which the modern world according to Horkheimer and Adorno was beginning to take on a recognizable profile but was not yet fully formed. It was most advanced in London, and is described as such in Book 7 of *The Prelude*, but it was not confined to the great cities, notwithstanding Wordsworth's efforts to maintain nature and the rural life as uncontaminated spaces. The appearance of the patterns and dispositions of machine-driven labor and its ghostly emanations in remote rural areas seemingly governed by the forms and rhythms of untamed nature reflects not only an incursion of alien habits but draws upon the already existing mechanical fieldwork routines described in the poetry of Stephen Duck and in other versified accounts of working in the countryside.[9] The population movements that became more visible with the expansion of the *lumpenproletariat* also meant that the same worker might see service as a reaper, a sailor or soldier and a factory hand, and perhaps even as a small-time man of letters. This blurring of boundaries – or perhaps the increased pace of an already-incipient conflation of town and country – helps explain why Wordsworth's narrators are so error-prone, so uncomfortable and so alienated from their fellow human beings, and why they demonstrate and perpetuate a besetting condition of concern. Unable to settle upon an attitude, caught between distance and involvement, and unable to experience distance as other than alienation and involvement as other than misjudgment, they haunt the afterlife of printed poems as unrealized but also disappointed energies.

Many of the conditions that the London sections of Wordsworth's *Prelude* had set out – the culture of the panorama, the tyranny of the eye, the anonymity of strangers passing close by without any knowing another's name – are rediscovered in Baudelaire as famously read by Walter Benjamin, who renders him the archetypal poet of high capitalist culture.[10] Wordsworth's narrators are seldom members of a city crowd, but their minds often work as if they were. They do not know what to say or how to say it. They misperceive and misjudge as if they are immersed in a masquerade, in a world of strangers, or of ghosts. The formal lineaments of Wordsworth's poems reflect the aesthetics of an urbanized imagination which their avowed topics and locations seem to deny; this is apparent even in the seemingly intimate form of the lyric, the same form that would dominate for Baudelaire and for Benjamin's reading of him. The most private and supposedly spontaneous of all poetic forms is suffused with the lineaments of a prefigured world. Wordsworth's frequent use of the term *spectacle*, even in rural locations, captures some of the dynamics of the newly intensified and dispersing urban aesthetic. The word *spectacle*, like the word *concern*, has a reflexive dimension: to invoke a spectacle is to refer not just to what is seen but, by virtue of its being staged and put up for display, to the person seeing, the spectator, the very figure who underpins so much of the aesthetics of modernity from Addison to Debord. To observe a spectacle is to make a spectacle of oneself. One sees, but tries to hold back from full absorption in what is seen, to hold on to a securing sense of the framing of the scene by conventions and time limits. One sees oneself seeing. Thus it is an apt association that affiliates the spectacle with the commodity, the thing put out for consumption, the object one knows to be embedded in an economic cycle before which one is an outsider (its makers having forgotten their contribution of living labor). In each case there is anxiety about control and self-control: I do not want the commodity or the spectacle to speak for me or dominate my senses but sense its tendency to do so.[11]

Wordsworth's uneasy preoccupation with the language of the spectacle encapsulates once more the deep reflexivity of his poetics, his extraordinary commitment to self-inspection as he inspects the world around him. It signals also his interest in exploring the lineaments of such key experiences as seem to stand outside historical time and to concentrate its tendencies into emblematic or essential expression. Benjamin tried to formulate a critical aesthetics capable of both representing and challenging its own historical inheritances, bringing its past into a critical formative moment wherein knowledge comes "only in lightning flashes [*nur blitzhaft*]" and where "actualization [*Aktualisierung*]" displaces the idea of progress as governing the modern subject's gathering up and incarnation of its received legacies.[12] The lineaments of Benjamin's "now-time [*Jetztzeit*]" have proved both obscure and appealing for those searching for alternatives to both traditional historicisms and disabling hermeneutic circles. Declaring the notion of historical objectivity (how things really were) as "the strongest narcotic of the century," Benjamin offers the image [*Bild*] as "that wherein what has been comes together in a flash with the now [*mit dem Jetzt blitzhaft*] to form a constellation" (p. 463). As if to dampen the radical hopes for social transformation that readers have tended to imagine in this paradigm, he elsewhere associates it with "a moment of danger ... the danger of becoming a tool of the ruling classes."[13] And indeed it remains very much an open question whether this experience of "constellation" which is described in various ways in

Benjamin's writings offers an empirically transformative or a merely aesthetic possibility, and whether it leaves open the potential that the one might under certain conditions also become the other. There is an intriguing symmetry between Benjamin's "constellation," wherein the past explodes into the present, and the "spots of time" through which Wordsworth claims to draw a sustenance that is both self-disciplinary and an assurance of personal identity through time. Both are seeking an alternative to the powerful pressure of a commodification culture that produces shock itself as familiar, as itself some or other genre (the Gothic, the action movie), wherein commodification has taken over and displaced surprise while being disguised as itself surprising.[14] Benjamin was aware of this problem and so was Wordsworth, whose "spots of time" were part of a carefully worked effort to insist on the possibility of surprise by withdrawing critical memory experience both from the control of the conscious will and from the sphere of a public life increasingly subject to the circulation of commodities. But they were not, as we shall see, immune to a deeper companionship with the formal dynamics of commodification and the value form itself.

VALUING THE SPOTS OF TIME

A radical conflation of time and space is at the heart of the spots-of-time episodes which formed a key component of *The Prelude* from its first manuscript inception in the two-book poem of 1799 and remained central not only to the evolving and finished poem but, as Johnston among others has suggested, to the organizing principles of a whole range of Wordsworthian experiences.[15] They have also, and not without reason, remained exemplary for literary criticism and for generations of readers of Wordsworth, and they have been widely understood as key motifs in the poet's conversion of both personal and political-historical distress to a positive spiritual restitution. The value of Wordsworth for Mill and Arnold was his unchanging restorative power to correct the deviations of a modernizing world by reference to a persisting natural order of objects and feelings – as if Wordsworth's poems themselves exemplified the sort of stability whose impossibility is one of the premises of their own staging. The spots of time have been conventionally implicated in this narrative as the signatures of a unified self, an achieved personal identity and psychological synthesis. James Chandler made an important modification of the received wisdoms in proposing that the spots of time should not simply be read in "private psychological terms," arguing instead that their rhetoric of self-discipline draws upon a Burkean model of "national character" and "native tradition" and as such refashions Burke's positive evaluation of "prejudice" into poetic form.[16] Alan Liu subsequently made the psychological motif itself historical in seeing here a process of "supervision of time by selfhood" culminating in the account of climbing Mount Snowdon, where he finds evidence, at the very moment of this apparently most private achievement, of Wordsworth's borrowing from newspaper reports of Napoleon's 1799 triumphal proclamation.[17] There is still more to say about the historicality of the spots of time, whose claims for a masterful self are unsettled by the very model of valorization that seems to sustain them. There is indeed an effort at the successful supervision of time by selfhood, but the poet's apparent refusal of the commodification of the past and of the self is secretly structured by the lineaments of commodity form.

The historical form of the spots of time has thus to be read through their own refusal and apparent subsumption of historical time itself. For they do project a timeless, existential dimension, one that has a formal precursor in the syndrome of the "halted traveler" isolated at the beginning of Geoffrey Hartman's great book on Wordsworth and there associated with death and death-in-life. The figure of the halted traveler, Hartman notes, is adapted from classical apostrophes inscribed on gravestones and directed at passing persons, bidding them pause to remember the dead and thus imagine their own deaths.[18] Experiencing a halt in time endows space with the attributes of time passed and passing: time meets space in being displaced as the place of death. Such moments of suspended animation amidst life's passage are also what makes Wordsworth's encounters memorable and productive of what Hartman calls "liberty and expansiveness of spirit" (p. 9). But the price of such expansiveness is still the recognition of death, and while Wordsworth did write poems in which the balance between the two effects is maintained and even tilted toward the positive liberties thus afforded, he was also aware of and articulate about the deathly and death-dealing attributes of stopping in one's tracks to contemplate a set of images or the materials out of which images might be made. Turning time into space, or stopping time to contemplate space, is touching upon death, all the more so when it is allied with that prosopopoeia about which Paul de Man found Wordsworth to be so anxious: "making the dead speak . . . implies, by the same token, that the living are struck dumb, frozen in their own death. The surmise of the 'Pause, Traveller!' thus acquires a sinister connotation that is not only the prefiguration of one's own mortality but our actual entry into the frozen world of the dead."¹⁹ The price of a potentially transformative moment is the loss of a little bit of confidence in the continuing expectation of life. This in turn raises the prospect that one might be permanently arrested, turned to stone, forever thingified. Time then would be meaningless, monumental space alone would count, and then only for others passing in their turn to be reminded of the ghostliness of things, and of their own being toward death.

The conjunction between halting, or *being* halted, and death is made baldly clear in the opening lines of the unpublished "Home at Grasmere," when the narrator (who in the later manuscript casts himself in the third person) finds himself "with a sudden influx overcome" at the sight of Grasmere Vale and avows that it would a good place to live and also to die. The extinction of life is adumbrated again later in the poem as he imagines being embedded in his chosen space and entering a state of suspended animation, "Without desire in full complacency, / Contemplating perfection absolute / And entertained as in a placid sleep."²⁰ It is then notable that the two well-known instances offered in *The Prelude* of the power of "spots of time" are both saturated with intimations of mortality: the first (11: 279f.) records the six-year-old boy's losing his way and coming upon a gibbet, while the second (11: 345f.) tells of an experience just before his father's untimely death. And yet in the 1799 manuscript, these spots of time are said to generate a "fructifying virtue"; in 1805 their positive potential is further played up by having them generate a "deepest feeling that the mind / Is lord and master, and that outward sense / Is but the obedient servant of her will"; and in the published poem of 1850 this confirmation is made yet more emphatic when "deepest feeling" is revised to "profoundest knowledge."²¹ Why these experiences of mortality and self-admonishment should convince the mind that it is lord and master is something of a puzzle, only partly resolved by the other 1805 additions that describe the narrator going back to the gibbet in adult life and remembering his first visit with at least some sense of acquired self-control: he is not as shocked by it now as he was at first. In the second example the connection between waiting impatiently for the horses that will take him home and the subsequent death of the father is that between wishing that time would speed up and being reminded that it is implacable and prone to pass all too quickly when you don't want it to. Lordship and mastery here seem to have the function of inviting self-rebuke. The felt triumph over outward sense carries with it a warning against any attempt at coercive manipulations of the flow of things: one does not in fact control time, nor one's obligations to it and within it, even though it sometimes helps to think that one does. Feeling like or knowing oneself a "lord and master" is then not just the positive result of a spot-of-time experience but its cautionary attribute and one we may expect to find subsequently complicated.

These existential puzzles do not, however, dwell alike in all times and places; they have a historical profile, one shared by the philosophers to whom one might most readily turn to elucidate them (Freud, Heidegger and Marx). We might dwell a little (halted and surmising) on the strangeness whereby Wordsworth figures time as space, as a *spot* of time. A spot may be punctilious, an abstract point in a geometric model, minimal to begin with and imaginable as dwindling to the point of invisibility; or it may be extended, an envisioned (and bounded) place with form and feature. The filled-out descriptions strongly suggest the second sense, that of embodied local places.[22] At the same time the common idea of spots as minimally defined locations (spots of color, spots of dirt) implies that the phrase may be temporal, indicating something prone to disappearance or transformation, with the spots acting as spacing devices (spots as stops) in ongoing time. Wordsworth's use touches on both senses. Time may be stopped, or feel as if it is being stopped, while the enlivened imagination summons up or re-encounters the features of a special place. But lordship over time is offset by re-encountering something threatening and disciplinary. For Kant time is a more comprehensive pure intuition than space since it is not limited to outer intuitions but governs also our experience of our inner selves.[23] In the critical philosophy he is not interested in pursuing the implications of nonconsensual space–time configurations: time and space are separately described and do not seem to interact in deviant or unpredictable ways. But he does say that time needs space in order to see itself represented: the temporality of "all inner perceptions" can only be derived from "the changes which are exhibited to us in outer things" (p. 168).[24] Time needs spots of space to see itself as time.

Wordsworth's poetry is suffused with such mutualities, mostly those which describe time as if it were space, often in the pursuit of that very sense of personal identity which Hume's *Treatise* described as having become "so great a question of philosophy, especially of late years in *England*" (p. 259), and thus a very modern concern. *Time*, Herbert Lindenberger tells us, is one of Wordsworth's ten most commonly used words, "as it was not, for instance, with Shakespeare, Milton or Pope."[25] The spot-of-time trope is central not just to Wordsworth's moral and structural imagination but to his entire rhetoric of temporal specification.

Let me give some examples. In the *Prelude*'s telling of the discharged soldier episode, the narrator "lingered near the door a little space" before heading home (4: 503). This is time construed as space: he means a short time (perhaps with a secondary sense of being close to the doorway). Later in the poem his visit to London is undertaken to fill up "a little space of intermediate time" (7: 65). Time as space again: he means that he has some spare or uncommitted time. In the Cave of Yordas, the shifting shapes start to settle down "after a short space" (8: 724). Again, time as space: he means after a short time. A glance at the concordance will show that the phrase "a moment's space" was a Wordsworthian favorite, occurring five times in different poems.[26] Time is figured as space on numerous occasions in similar phrases – there is no need to list them all. The "spot of time" is exactly such a phrase. Idiomatic convention (spot of trouble, spot of lunch) perhaps assists us in understanding the sense as "bit of time" without initially pondering the locational gesture – spot as place – as the significant one. But the spot of time *is* a place – a gibbet on the moors, a rock near the public road – made significant by the time in which it was experienced and in which it is recollected, as well as by the process of time passing (mortality) it evokes. Time is primary, then, as it was for Kant, because time governs our procedures for monitoring the inner self as well as outward things: to have a moment's space means to be able to rest from motion, in a place, as time passes, but not fully to escape temporality. The spot of time is thus a clever or canny (and therefore uncanny) inversion whereby place is not taken out of time but rendered always available *in* time, for timely utterance. It is a moment of time lodged in the memory and associated with a physical place but it is not a purely spatial entity. It begins as a place punctiliously defined (the first event) but becomes a resource more and more mobile in the time of recollection. Time masters space by relocating place.

This compulsive figuring of time as space – "a moment's space" – is a Wordsworthian signature and not a cliché of poetry in general. (By my count the figuring of time as space occurs only six times in Shakespeare and three times in Milton.) Is time taking over space, becoming its lord and master, or is it just that space is needed to make sense of time, in the way that Kant proposed? Despite revealing himself elsewhere as an inveterate namer of places, Wordsworth does not name the sites where the spots of time originate, and he thus attempts to avoid or displace the authoritarian gestures that conventionally accompany the bestowing of names upon places. What is "monumental," indeed, about the site of the gibbet is the *writing* on the ground that explains its history, but that writing is maintained as "fresh and visible" by the "superstition of the neighbourhood" and not by the intrusion of a passing poet (11: 297–99). The physical effort required in order to maintain this written record through time contrasts with the mobility of memory in the poet's ongoing life. He fails to mention the gibbet at all in his first recorded memorization (ll. 312f.) and redescribes the "girl" ten lines later as a "woman," as if mediating past and present sensations. The virtuality of memory here serves to dislocate spatial sites through time, even when it is the same place that is being contemplated: things are the same but not the same.

The classical and medieval mnemonic systems that used spatial locations to remember things were premised on the desire for and possibility of exact recall: remembering the features of a room and the rooms of a house, for example, was supposed to assist in remembering the things or ideas for which these features had been made to stand. By this means everything important "is diligently imprinted on the mind, in order that thought may be able to run through all the parts without let or hindrance."[27] Wordsworth does not picture himself as in a position to make choices about what to represent and how – things impose themselves on him – nor does he claim perfect recall. What was a convenience for earlier memory teachers came to him as an imposition from outside, and the impressions made upon his mind are not those of predictably recoverable text. We can sense here, I think, a revolt against the mnemonic associations of a certain kind of writing as exact record keeping, and a turn to something more volatile and productive of surprise, something that stimulates the "workings of my spirit" (11: 389) while not predisposing exactly what it is that will emerge from that process. In this way the spots of time become one more instance of the protest against the commodification of print culture and of the desire to fashion a more valuable resource in deep subjectivity. Mary Carruthers has argued that classical and medieval authorities did not make any distinctions between writing on papyrus or clay and imprinting on the brain, so that for them a good memory was like a library of texts.[28] Wordsworth, in contesting the hegemony of fallen forms of print, interrupts this identification and takes memory out of the sphere of textuality into something more mysterious and ungovernable.

Does he nonetheless still instantiate the triumph of time over space and the reconstitution of space as time that has been seen as symptomatic of a modern life wherein machine labor and industrial capitalism have taken over? Is the suppressed polemic against modern print culture undermined by an affiliation with the broader conditions of capitalist time itself? The question is not easy to resolve since different constructions of time and space govern debates about modernity and postmodernity, although there has been common agreement that time ruled modernity while space has made a comeback with the postmodern. In the late sonnet "Steamboats, Viaducts, and Railways," Wordsworth claims that steam power has made it possible for time to triumph "o'er his brother Space."[29] He is willing to accept the steam engine as one more instance of man's creative use of natural forces and of the power of mind itself but finds that the visual obtrusiveness of the railways and their capacity for shrinking distances between places are altering our ability to dwell upon the "loveliness of Nature." The management of natural forces here preempts a response to nature as a spatial complex. The increasing speed of travel and its mechanically regular motion (like that of the old Cumberland beggar) reduce space to a continuum which recognizes no qualitative distinctions between one moment and another, one place and the next. The steam engine's contributions to industrial manufacture were felt to have the same effect, both in the case of the individual machine punching out its products at mathematically regulated intervals and in the more intricate timing required for the meshing of each machine's output with that of other machines sharing the same integrated circuit, the whole performing "uninterruptedly, simultaneously, and side by side."[30]

Lukács saw the dominance of machine labor as transforming man's entire being in the world, not only driving him to a purely "contemplative [*kontemplative*]" relation to his work (machines need supervision but not creative action) but also flattening out the space–time complex to a "common denominator." The qualitative content of time is degraded as it becomes space; it loses its "variable, flowing nature" and "freezes into an exactly delimited, quantifiable continuum filled with quantifiable 'things' . . . time is transformed into abstract, exactly measurable, physical space."[31] Lukács calls this the degrading of time *into* space (p. 89), while Wordsworth writes of the power of time *over* space, but they are describing the same process: the coming together of the two categories into a punctilious sequence of regularly spaced products and attendant sense-perceptions wherein timing is spatially registered and there is no need or room for "individual 'caprice'" (p. 98). This kind of regularity seems to be what is resisted and outwitted by the operation of Wordsworth's spots of time, which come unbidden both as first experienced and as henceforth recollected. But the spots of time also have the effect of a psychological flywheel, regularizing the self's sense of itself by assisting in the conversion of shock to continuity, threat and fear to familiar and companionable routine, even to the point of authorizing notions of lordship and mastery. As such they both resist and reflect the profile of modern machine time, providing the subject with a fund of reliably expendable resources as well as an experience of surprise – but only mild surprise. Exploring this conjunction or apparent disjunction takes us into another dark and secret passage leading out from the already darkening chamber of maiden thought, and through yet another perplexing mist where specters loom. This place goes by a disarmingly simple phrase: the theory of value.

According to one commentator, "Marx's concept of value is arguably the most controversial in the corpus of his thought."[32] Given the already-encountered mysteries of the commodity, this is not promising, but luckily the two go together: the function of value is at the heart of the operation of modern commodity form. Just as the commodity conceals its origins in social relations, so too does the value form which adjudicates the relation between commodities: both commodity form and value form efface the evidence of any connection to human labor. Marx's first, apparently basic though still difficult, explanation of value comes in the early sections of *Capital One*, where it is firmly dissociated from material objects and located as a strictly "social relation between commodity and commodity" (p. 139), for example between coats and linen. Human labor creates value but is not itself value, whose objective form is virtual; this is the sphere in which the linen relates to the coat in a language we cannot speak, "a language with which it alone is familiar" (p. 143). Different kinds of concrete labor are translated into abstract labor in the value form; this is the point at which common human language finds itself superseded and excluded from the conversation between commodities, one wherein the linen recognizes in the coat "a splendid kindred soul, the soul of value" (p. 143). In chapter 5 we will encounter the problem of gaining access to the sight of tables standing on their heads and having ideas: only those outside the society of commodities can see this as an inversion, while to those within (most of us) things seem completely normal and right-side up. Any commodity can stand as a measure of the equivalent form of value toward any other in an "indefinitely expandable series" (p. 154) open to "the whole world of commodities" (p. 155), although the "crude bourgeois vision" acknowledges only one money form at work (p. 149). Money as the general equivalent in its simplest, primitive form already leads to the separation of value (and space) from *place*, as David Harvey explains: "The exchange process is . . . perpetually abstracting from the specifics of location through price formation. This paves the way for conceptualizing values in place-free terms. The abstract labour embodied at particular locations under specific concrete conditions is a social average taken across all locations and conditions."[33] Neither time nor place is represented as or in itself but they are reformatted as a space-in-time where neither particular place nor familiar time (clock time or concrete labor time) need be recognized as important.[34] The spots of time are also the result of realizing value in place-free terms; they can obtrude themselves anywhere and synthesize all past perceptions into an urgently present experience.

Marx's second and fullest account of valorization comes well into *Capital One*, after commodity, exchange and money have all been discussed. Value attends even the simplest and most fundamental economic exchanges of the sort we might imagine to have taken place in primitive societies, but in the modern economy it becomes, like the commodity itself, much more complex and effectively invisible as it adjusts the balance between actual labor-power costs, stored expense (in raw materials and precommodified product parts yet to make up wholes), and exchange and surplus value by way of a socially necessary standard set to assure the production of absolute surplus. Again, value is the objectification of *abstract* labor and as such has no directly reflective relation either to concrete labor or to particular commodities: it is the result of the continually transforming *relations* between an indefinite series of commodities, an abstract form which nevertheless has real consequences (as when price falls with an increase in productivity). It is a "general social mediation" which subsumes concrete labor into a social average and local production into a general norm.[35] Along with this there goes a flattening of the historical record, a subsumption of past time (the time of production) into an always present entity (just as the yarn "stores" the labor that went into it). The past is "a matter of no importance" and the technical particularity of what is now to hand is reduced to the common category of value according to the demands of "socially-necessary labour-time."[36] As capital evolves, value becomes less and less dependent on concrete productivity: the labor of the past comes to be "stored" and realized in a continually transforming structural formation such that, as Postone puts it, "*value is an expression of time as the present*" (p. 296). Again: "the accumulation of historical time occurs in an alienated form that reconstitutes the necessity of the present" (p. 360). All that matters is a present that contains transformed and hidden elements of its past. Like a spot of time "capitalism . . . is characterized by the constant translation of historical time into the framework of the present, thereby reinforcing that present." Again, like a spot of time, "both temporal dimensions lie beyond the control of, and exert dominion over, the constituting actors" (p. 300). Postone again: "value is reconstituted as a perpetual present, although it is moved historically in time" (p. 346). Concrete (familiar) time comes to be subsumed within abstract time, and is "hidden" within it (p. 295), never to be recovered again in its original form.

All of this is just what Wordsworth's spots of time seem to resist by reinscribing the critical claims of past places within present time and refusing the full abstraction that characterizes the operations of the value form. They do indeed refuse full abstraction, but they make critical strides toward it. Richard Terdiman has very shrewdly noticed the place of commodity fetishism in a historical memory crisis: because we forget our role as providers of labor in the face of the finished commodity, "*the enigma of the commodity is a memory disorder.*"[37] Wordsworth wants to counter such forgetting, but his acts of memory cannot include a full restitution or conservation of place and space and the items within them. Absolute recall would be delirium – Frances Yates reports on a certain Peter of Ravenna who claimed (perhaps just to advertise his method) to have *begun* as a young man with a hundred thousand memorized places, and to have added to them since.[38] But Wordsworth laments the loss of significant memories, not just of circumstantial details. To lose such information is to lose evidence of the making of the self, the entity that must never become a finished product or commodity but which, in its sorrowing for the losses accruing with the passage of time, sets itself the goal of being just that. Predictable time and space are both unsettled. Does one have to be back *at* the place for its effects to be felt, or can one experience them anywhere, by way of memory and association, just as the dancing daffodils in one of Wordsworth's most famous poems can be conjured up in the privacy of one's sitting room? In putting memories of the past back into *place*, the spots of time would work as an apparent countertendency to the hegemony of time over space that was identified with the modern world in "Steamboats, Viaducts, and Railways."

The first of Wordsworth's examples indeed has him sensing the power of his past by revisiting the exact location of the gibbet and the pond (11: 316f.), so that the memories and the present experience occupy the same place. But the memories are selective from the very start: beacon, girl and crag overpower the gibbet and the writing on the ground. The second example is different: he reenacts the memory of his "anxiety of hope" (l. 372) from a distance, whenever and wherever mist and rain lead his thoughts that way. This suggests that the spot of time is transferable across space as well as through time: it becomes virtual and works to reinvest a presently occupied place with the powers associated with another place. Such capacity to apply or experience the feelings attached to one location while being in another is a feasible translation of what it might mean to call the mind a "lord and master": it can defy the geographical and temporal limits governing the world of objects and assure itself of its own transcendental identity – something like what Liu called "the supervision of time by selfhood" extended also to space.[39] But is this not then also akin to the profile of the value form as it makes present, in and for only the present, everything that happened before, every "history" that is brought to bear within it? "*Value is an expression of time as the present.*"[40]

Marx's theory of value is yet another of his cunning rewrites of the Hegelian legacy, in this case of the mechanics of recollection [*Erinnerung*], in ways that directly illuminate the architectonics of the spots of time. At the very end of *The Phenomenology of Spirit*, Hegel has the self realizing itself as spirit by gathering up and working through the "gallery of images" that is its past; these are embraced as the true "wealth [*Reichtum*] of its substance" at the threshold of the passage into "Absolute Knowing."[41] Here there is a change of state that still preserves within it all previous states, a transformation of quantity into quality without any loss of value, an end to time with nothing temporal left behind: this is "wealth" indeed, and as such the analogue of one of Wordsworth's desires about his own past.[42] Marx rewrites this whole sequence as the history of the commodity and its passage through valorization: instead of absolute retention we have absolute forgetting, so that the subject loses instead of finds itself and is projected (for it does not project itself) into a world to which it cannot ever belong, the world of commodity form. Marx's rewriting of Hegel has the quality of neat antithesis; Wordsworth is in between, or all over the place. But if there is in the spots of time a dark analogy or kinship with the operation of valorization in modern commodity culture, might this be why Wordsworth's rhetoric is not simply triumphal, a happy (Hegelian) indulgence in the "beneficent influence" (11: 278) that the spots of time are said to provide? For between the two exemplary spots of time as they are reported in Book 11 of *The Prelude* there is a confession of limits and of strained desire:

> the hiding-places of my power
> Seem open; I approach, and then they close;

> I see by glimpses now; when age comes on
> May scarcely see at all, and I would give,
> While yet we may, as far as words can give,
> A substance and a life to what I feel:
> I would enshrine the spirit of the past
> For future restoration. (ll. 336–43)

The experience of recollecting is *not* then under the narrator's control, and despite his previous claim that this same experience offers a sense of the mind as lord and master, whatever it is that is earned is here adumbrated by a devastating sense of loss and prospective future losses. An interesting paradox: the sense of mastery comes only unpredictably, incompletely ("by glimpses"), and is likely to diminish ("soon may not see at all"). We are not then so far from the subject position that Postone identifies as typifying the operations of the value form: a continual present into which past history is compressed and reformatted without offering us as "constituting actors" any sense of decision or control (p. 300). The mind that feels (in 1805) or knows (in 1850) itself lord and master is then in a posture we will see again: it is standing on its head.[43] In a radical shift from the mechanics of the classical memory *loci*, the self cannot know itself because it cannot remember what it needs to know to be a self at all.

Everything is brought into the present, but there is no present. Lindenberger notices that the poem has only one celebration of a pure present, right at the beginning, and points out also that the *carpe diem* motif is missing throughout.[44] It is as if the present is desired but never open to occupation, to being fully lived in the moment, while the loss of past intensities is also and to the same degree lamented. There is at work here an obvious analogy with the method of psychoanalysis that I shall not pursue, although it is helpful in confirming (as it is historically companionable with) the relation between the value form and the spots of time: the associating subject is shocked into recollection of a trauma which it repeats but also recovers from (as in mourning), but the recovery happens in the simultaneous knowledge of an irretrievable loss of both event and intensity that will keep recurring, always to come (as in melancholia). The labors of the past are not recoverable in their original form or intensity; they have been changed by being accumulated into the space of an ongoing present ("emotion recollected in tranquillity"). Their value ("beneficent influence") cannot be cashed in for anything under the self's control, or for anything that is visible to or exchangeable with others. The spot of time feeds into an economy internal to the self, but it does not assure even the self of any predictable recollection or continued life ("soon may not see at all").

But Marx based his theory of value on the understanding that nothing in the world of commodities *can* be exchanged for itself, it "cannot make its own physical shape into the expression of its own value" and thus it is an essentially social relation.[45] Nothing *has* value in and for itself. The spot-of-time syndrome compresses the (social) value form into the single subject that is the self, which hopes to spend its accumulated capital (its past) on its own present (which is that same past in and as present) as if it were indeed exchanging itself with itself. It is as if Wordsworth withdraws the product that is his self from circulation and still wants all the benefits of profitable exchange – with himself. So in order to perform valorization, the self must split into two, past self and present self. What is regretted as a loss is what makes possible a gain. Earlier in *The Prelude*, Wordsworth articulates the split as follows:

> so wide appears
> The vacancy between me and those days,
> Which yet have such self-presence in my mind
> That, sometimes, when I think of them, I seem
> Two consciousnesses, conscious of myself
> And of some other Being. (2: 28–33)

If this were not so then no value could accrue: exchange of the self with the same self (or absorption of the one by the other in a process of accumulation) would be the tautology that Marx specifies as impossible. The lordship and mastery that Wordsworth claims is thus that of the present self at the expense of the past self: it is not a social relation in Marx's sense, and its internalization bespeaks a loss of conventional sociability, a state of alienation. In becoming a stranger to himself, he replicates the estrangement of city life where men are neighbors but still strangers "knowing not each other's names" (7: 120). Wordsworth wants two incompatible things: the preservation of his investment (the same self through time whose loss he regrets) *and* the payoff that comes with risk, the "beneficent influence" (11: 278) of capital accumulation. Only the loss of control he otherwise regrets can make this happen, and it brings with it the possibility of loss as well as gain; but he also wants the intensities of youth preserved as always worth what they were originally worth. Their loss offsets the gain in psychological surplus value that enables an enhanced quality of life, an experience of "radiance more divine / From these remembrances" (11: 324–25). The internal memory market of the self, just like the stock market, has its ups and downs, and Wordsworth monitors them carefully and with concern. Unlike Hume he does not solve his personal identity problem (albeit temporarily) by recourse to sociability, by dining, conversing, playing a game of backgammon and forgetting about it. On the contrary, he declares that "Here must thou be, O Man! / Strength to thyself; no Helper hast thou here" (13: 188–89). Nor can Wordsworth live cheerily in the moment, as Hume says he himself does, yielding to a propensity to be "positive and certain" at each time and place, and knowing that this is a false certainty even as he experiences it.[46] Wordsworth regrets every lost item of memory and sensation even though no present life could be maintained without such losses. He laments his loss of access to Hegelian confirmations while reflecting his residence in the world better described by Marx: the world of commodity form and capitalist valorization.

Wordsworth wants to *enshrine* the *spirit* of the *past* for *future* restoration, to seal up or bury the ghost so that it may be later disinterred and come again, to bury something of himself for later resurrection, as if fearful of facing the possibility that "what speaks in autobiography is a dead man."[47] But what will return is at best a spirit, and what it brings back in both of the spots of time is an encounter with death. The formal analogy I have been pursuing between the spots of time and the valorization process is quite broadly delineated; it is tempting to wonder whether quite different or more familiar paradigms might prove equally illuminating. Don't we all experience memory and anxiety about losing it, all the more so now that we have a name for acute amnesia: Alzheimer's disease? But the ghostliness of this spirit of the past locked up in its shrine for future conjurations bespeaks a history and not an existential universality. Such concern about the economy of continuous selfhood is not universal, and the historical record suggests that it is relatively recent. The use of memory places or sites was, as we have seen, traditional in classical and medieval mnemonics; it is summarized, for example, in Book II of Quintilian's *Institutio Oratoria*. These sites were described as collected together in treasuries [*thesauri*], storage chests [*arca*] and even money pouches [*sacculi*]: economic metaphors for one's memories seem to have existed among the earliest theorists.[48] But there are few if any instances of a radical instability in the value of one's fund; one expects to withdraw exactly what was deposited in the first place. In Book 10 of Augustine's *Confessions*, there are hints of the unpredictability of what will be recalled and forgotten, but it is John Locke who begins to build up a more visibly modern model of memory as an unstable economy. Once again memory is a "Repository" in which the mind can store things it has no room for and dig them out as they are needed.[49] But the use-value of ideas thus deposited in the memory bank cannot be guaranteed to remain what it was. If they are not regularly recirculated then "the Print wears out, and at last there is nothing to be seen" (p. 151). Like old books and papers, they perish with the passing of time, for "*The Pictures drawn in our Minds, are laid in fading Colours*; and if not sometimes refreshed, vanish and disappear" (p. 152).[50] Past ideas bear interest in unbidden and unpredicted ways, appearing "of their own accord ... roused and tumbled out of their dark Cells, into open Day-light, by some turbulent and tempestuous passion."[51] These ghostly emanations drummed out from their dark cells are very like Wordsworth's spirits of the past: both defy any notion of steady, uninterrupted accumulation and predictable wealth. You cannot be sure what is left in the memory bank nor what it will be worth when you cash it out.

Wordsworth's ghosts are welcomed and their failure to appear is lamented; even recollected grief, guilt and terror are pronounced to be somehow inevitably nourishing. But they are ghosts nonetheless; they are not always accessible and are never gathered within what Althusser called a Hegelian present – an "ideological present in which temporal presence coincides with the presence of the essence with its phenomena."[52] As such they offer no support for experiences of wholeness or transparency. For Althusser there is no single time called "history" but rather an assembly of specific temporalities latent in the unevenly developing (structural) components of a present that cannot be *seen* in its totality and which does not *reveal* itself to the critical gaze: there is no *coupe d'essence* or "essential section" of the sort that is "the basis of all historicism" (p. 138). The time of economic production is instead, like that of the value form, an "invisible time, essentially illegible" (p. 101) and requires construction in and by theory. Analogously the Wordsworthian spot of time is a bio-imaginative production whose accumulated past temporalities cannot be seen in essential section, whose symptoms remain always unevenly developing, and whose presentness may or may not be attached to the place of their initial figuration. One could say then that they too, while being indeed historical, do not belong to any governing historicism, any paradigm within which the part could stand for and reveal a personal totality or essence of the self.[53]

Wordsworth's embrace of opacity and psychological disaggregation is indeed a challenge to the monotony and regularity of a machine-like history which offers itself as one possible manifestation of modern temporality, and which makes each moment (and each person) equivalent to all others according to the logics of substitutability and automation. But we should not romanticize it because it is at the same time an instance of the deeper profile of capitalist time itself as invisible and secret, its component rhythms evolving unevenly and jostling against other parts of the totality (not a "whole"), its present at once promising a future restoration and embodying a past that is both lamented as not recoverable and, inasmuch as it is recovered, recalled as traumatic. *The Prelude* presents childhood as the time when there was only positive accumulation and no loss, "When every hour brings palpable access / Of knowledge" (2: 304–5). That is what Wordsworth wants for his creative adult life, hoping to either "lay up new stores" or "rescue from decay the old / By timely interference" (1: 126–27), whether in themselves or by way of value added to "collateral objects" (1: 622). These economic terms and others like them – growth, riches, wealth, value, gains, losses – do not negate the more familiar organic analogues of the poem, but they do form a coherent rhetorical cluster that signals an affiliation with the mechanisms of getting and spending that Wordsworth felt were all too much with us. The spot of time indeed resists the influence of those who "would confine us down / Like engines" (5: 382–83) and seeks to interrupt them, but neither even nor uneven time is offered as purely pleasurable or unambiguously creative: it is the incoherent and uncontrollable interaction of the two (which we might call the Romantic imagination) that most fully reflects the pattern of life around 1800 and its array of causes unknown to former times. Abstraction alone is not the issue. What is new around 1800 is the proliferation of machines that work faster and faster and radically upset relations between value and productivity, a financial system working to facilitate the circulation of commodities, money and credit in ways and at speeds invisible to human sight, and a threatening accumulation of evidence for the substitutability of everyone by anyone, as seen in the dead and disabled soldiers and sailors and industrial workers and perhaps as known about in the plantation economies of the empire. The spots of time obtrude themselves upon the present as both interest and debt, and one cannot exist without the other. The spirit of the past is another instance of the ghostliness of things.

Sohn-Rethel identified the emergence of abstract time and space with the "exchange abstraction" intrinsic to the money form introduced in classical Greece; its "full growth" brought with it the separation of man from nature now seen as incompatible with and impervious to any of man's "anthropomorphisms."⁵⁴ He is vague about exactly when that full growth occurred, but we can see in Romantic aesthetics exactly such a crisis in relation to a nature now defined within a relentlessly antinomic logic: it must be preserved, it cannot be preserved. The fully developed exposition of a syndrome that begins in classical Greece thus happens around 1800. Wordsworth is well known for lamenting the increasing distancing of man from nature, but he is also the astute analyst of the inevitability of just this process. The spots of time do seek to resist objectification and the homogeneous emptiness of modern time, but in allowing the mind the sense that it is lord and master, they reintroduce a separation of mind from nature (and perhaps of the mind from its own body) that is no more than an inverted form (turned upside down as in a camera obscura) of commodity fetishism itself. Now it is the maker and not the thing made that is objectified and imaged in the very social role of lordship [*Herrschaft*] that Hegel so famously described as the vulnerable (and substitutable) position of feudal aristocracy on the point of its painful transition to modern democracy.⁵⁵ The mind's mastery, like Hegelian lordship, dispenses death but also confronts its own debt to mortality. It puts itself at risk, but not in the same way as the real subject of bondage who is motivated toward an active insertion into history. Conversely, the history made by mental lordship is passive and neither visible nor open to control. The world does not change because of the mind's "feeling" or its "knowledge"; it is only the memory bank of the self that is involved in these transactions. Mental lordship is in fact an illusion, the product of our standing on our heads, and for both Hegel and Wordsworth can only be accessed by sensing actual and imminent loss. Wordsworth's excited uncertainty about time and memory is the symptom of a disorientation that works within the terms of the commodification it also seeks to resist. It is not insignificant that his occupation as a poet commits him to making a living out of making memory's ideas come back to life before their print wears out, and thereby to a constant anxiety, at every level from the philosophical to the vocational, about whether this can be done. The murderer on the moors has a troop of superstitious villagers working to "clear" his name so that it can remain on show as "monumental writing" (*Prelude*, 11: 295); the poet can expect neither such notoriety nor such assistance.

Wordsworth's Burkean affinities thus extend beyond the traditionalism described by James Chandler. He is not only (if at all) invoking a preferred culture of habit that can be preserved as beyond time's ravages but responding to the ambiguities of an emergent credit economy that destabilizes all values and expectations such that, as Burke himself put it, what a person "receives in the morning will not have the same value at night." It is in the light of this condition, Burke writes, that our "sullen resistance to innovation, thanks to the cold sluggishness of our national character," while hardly a fully admired personality trait, offers some limited hope.[56] J. G. A. Pocock's important reading of Burke's *Reflections* emphasizes not its well-known case for cherishing prejudice but its reactive obsession with runaway paper credit as a threat to property, which "has ceased to be real and has become not merely mobile but imaginary."[57] In other words it is not just that what one can *see* is going to ruin: the manners and social relations that many eighteenth-century writers claimed as the unsettling results of a burgeoning commercial economy. Much more threatening is what one *cannot* see: the operations of finance capital, and of the value form and commodity form, which are invisible and move with increasing speed in a credit system where no one need take actual possession of anything before it is moved on, reinvested or spent somewhere else by someone else. If the "cold sluggishness" of the national character is our best or only defense, could one turn to Wordsworth for its exemplification? Burke's irony, or sardonic ventriloquism – he is surely making fun of what a Jacobin radical might say about British conservatism – undoes its own apparent project in offering a model of behavior that around 1800 was coming to be seen as no longer an enduring or inherited national personality trait (if it ever was that) but the death-in-life demeanor of persons whose work rhythms are governed by machines, turning them into the automatons described by a number of writers from Adam Ferguson to Karl Marx and Friedrich Engels and poetically embodied by William Wordsworth.

The spots of time, I am suggesting, are both a protest against and a formal embodiment of the mechanics of commodity form. They refuse, in their commitment to opacity and surprise, ever to become fully self-identical through time and space, and thus to render every instance equal to every other in an abstract universality: time expressed as and conquering space by way of mechanical regularity. Their spasmodic incidence works against the monotony of machine time. But it also images the unpredicted and uncontrollable making-present of all the past that characterizes the process of valorization. The sites of memory are no longer safe in the storehouse of the mind, ready to be cashed in on demand with no loss of value. They are "spectacles and sounds" (11: 383) that feed the "spirit" (l. 389) but are also seen by glimpses, spectral shapes that come and go. Debord declared the function of the modern spectacle, as commodity, to be nothing other than "*to make history forgotten within culture.*"⁵⁸ Wordsworth absorbs both history and culture into himself and registers the passing of time as a series of personal failures and opportunities: the forgetting of history is regretted and thereby displayed.

Debord also found that "because history itself haunts modern society like a specter, pseudo-histories are constructed at every level of consumption of life in order to preserve the threatened equilibrium of present *frozen time*"(#200). It is indeed the case that the social-historical cycle of both intersubjective relations and world events is displaced in Wordsworth's spots of time by a visibly subjective accounting, what Debord calls a pseudo-history, as many have pointed out. And in the lament for what is lost and never to be regained, the poet does seem to aspire to frozen time, to what will always stay the same. Something like this appears in the image of the beggar who seems as old now as he always was, and no older; more fully still in the spectacle of the gypsies who are at the end of the day exactly as they were in its beginning. But Wordsworth knows that the aspiration to frozen time can only be satisfied by intimations of death or death-in-life, and by the admission of a Satanic precursor whose claim to "a mind not to be changed by place or time" can never be simply admired even when it is desired.⁵⁹ Empathy with the dead form of the commodity is empathy with Satan's "We know no time when we were not as now" (*PL*, 5: 859), an effort to make stoic virtue out of a bitter necessity that is imminent and thereafter immanent: Wordsworth too is of the devil's party, and he knows it. He faces and even welcomes the specters, which are the signature of the commodity as a form of frozen time whose human origins have disappeared and an eerie reminder of those origins as formerly alive. Things come to life as their makers forget their past labors: the tendency to commodification in and of the self is as much subjectively desired as it is objectively enforced. A resistance to this tendency is dialectically embedded in that same self as it comes to terms with its losses and markets them (to itself and its public) as gains. Life articulates itself as a death wish, and death impels the growth of the mind. The double reflection is exactly the profile of valorization and commodification as unpredictable and secret, hiding their histories in fixed forms always of the present (commodity) and yet always reconstituted by critical change while seeming the same (valorization).

The spots of time, which *The Prelude* says are "scatter'd everywhere" (11: 275), are Wordsworth's best effort to make virtue out of the secrecy of selfhood's operations. That the two major examples he gives both engage with death is not an accident nor the expression of a universal psychological disposition. The whole case for preserving (and perhaps destroying) the buildings of the convent of Chartreuse, as we will see in the next chapter, depended on their capacity to remind us of death, of "the ghostliness of things."[60] Being alive demands not only thinking about death but becoming deadened, not all alive nor dead, feeling one's way into the society of commodities where we might overhear, at last, the coat chatting to the linen, and sense the tables being animated by ideas. Commodities stop time as they reify into fixed forms; they are made to move again – to dance, to stand on their heads – only in the non-human exercise of the value form. The repeating present of the spot of time is spectral and disjunctive, responding to a power of haunting wherein the present is overwritten (and underwritten) by a personal sublime whose terms reflect a more general division within the self (through time) and between different selves (in space). What is emphatically no longer available to the poetic mind is any appeal to completely ordinary and habitual place–time coordinates: habit, Burkean or not, can no longer be trusted to embody purely sustaining rituals even as it continues to be figured as the last best hope of marginal communities like the one that maintains the old beggar but maintains him only in a state of almost savage torpor, one whose cold sluggishness seems to reflect the same routines of machine labor that govern the lives of the industrial workers and workhouse dwellers to whom the beggar stands in contrast. Habit pure and simple won't work, but neither will relentless innovation, the constant newness of everything. Habit is infected by the routine of machine time and novelty by the outrageous stimulations of mass culture. But mass culture is not alone in expressing the dynamics of commodification. They are everywhere: in books, in convent walls and in the mind of man.

So the spots of time, for all their declared particularity within the private memory bank of one William Wordsworth, are in their formal mechanisms both historically constructed and socially referential: they belong to the years around 1800 as a shared condition. They generate a personal interest that Wordsworth draws upon to maintain himself psychologically as a coherent self through time, and they are the raw materials and stored labor essential to the production and the value of the published poems through which Wordsworth sought to make a living. So central was the memory bank to this second obligation that wherever the poet had no memories of his own he would borrow from others – most famously from his sister Dorothy – and announce them as his. In all cases the value of the past is reproduced as a constant present that is first the making of the poem and thereafter its reading and rereading, which always happens "now." The private self is publically deployed as a surrogate trust fund for similarly self-imagining persons. The effort to know oneself and to have scientific control of one's memories is in fact staged with the covert aim of not succeeding: failure is itself success. *The Prelude*'s assertion that "each man is a memory to himself" (3: 189) describes what is simultaneously a possession and a dispossession. Reflexivity – the compulsion to reference oneself constantly, to make a spectacle of oneself going about one's business (for Wordsworth the business of poetry) – then seems to aspire to a self-knowledge (I know where I stand) which bears with it an underlying desperation (I have no idea where I stand or where I might stand next). The triumph of singularity, or of memory achieved, is also memory lost, and the signature of alienation.

The poetry that enshrines this attitude is a poetry of concern, comfortable neither in the rhetoric of subjectivism nor in an assumption of objectivity; it is permanently engaged in an encounter with the world wherein either kind of resolution is proven inept and insufficient. It is always in and out of place, in and out of time. Lukács saw the antinomic core of bourgeois thought embodied in Kant and his successors as consisting similarly in the avowed desire for a system that could not be fulfilled and for a rationalism that could not shake off the irrational.[61] Being preoccupied or obsessed with making the attempt blinds the bourgeois subject to the terms and conditions of historical-material life, one primary agent within which is the commodity. The rhetoric of self-making is shadowed by a paranoia that intuits everything as evanescent, about to slip away into a forgetting that is a psychological reflection of the formation of economic value as relentlessly unstable. What is then enshrined for future restoration is an ongoing compulsion towards concern, whereby relations between selves and others cannot be settled as either those of identity or distinction. One is neither one with nor fully distinct from the beggars, war widows, serving girls, leech-gatherers and fishermen, and the more stridently Wordsworth's narrators make the effort to stand aside or indeed to identify sympathetically, the more confused they become and the more subjectivity itself breaks down in the face of an invisible and uncontrollable but distinctly sensed common condition. The commonality is not that of simple humanity, the same for all times and places, but of brute substitutability, the effect of threatening historical conditions. One does not, or not only, claim to feel with and for the other ("I share your pain"); one also senses that being in the other's position is not a matter of choice, and that time and tide are enforcing an abstract substitutability in ways that can neither be controlled nor fully disclosed. Wordsworth resists presenting his anxieties as equivalent to the real and substantial sufferings of others but at the same time works to narrow the gap between actors and observers or overseers, protagonists and narrators: theoretical oversight cannot be maintained at a comforting distance from the active labor (or inertia) being observed. This has something to do with the instability of class and economic barriers in an environment undergoing changes that were more radical than usual, and perhaps with the particularly acute insecurity that comes from setting out as an apprentice poet in a literary marketplace governed by the early phases of a mass (non-elite) readership. The recognition that one is always available as a substitute for those one inspects or encounters, and that the position of mastery is inseparable from the prospect of slavery, is not only the working assumption of democracy but also of commodity circulation, as Marx observed in a pointed redescription of the Hegelian process of subjectification: "a man is in the same situation as a commodity ... Peter only relates to himself as a man through his relation to another man, Paul, in whom he recognizes his likeness."[62] What looks like a radical rejection of the commodification of the self – a painstaking dramatization of individuality by a narrator who constantly tells us that it is him and not another who tells the tale – is thus underpinned by a powerful intuition of the potentially irresistible equivalence of each to all. The good news is that this is democracy, and accords as such with some traditional theological incentives. The not so good news is that it reproduces the equivalence of commodity circulation and commodity form which is powered by agencies that are neither human nor divine. They are invisible to the empirical eye, but their presence can be surmised by ghostly forms like that of the hunger-bitten girl whose mechanical knitting routine, led by the cow she should be leading, bespeaks not any willed, Stoic *apatheia* but the death-in-life of what we come to recognize as an endlessly circulating *lumpenproletariat*.

CHAPTER 5

The ghostliness of things

SILENCE VISIBLE AND PERPETUAL CALM

After the end of the Soviet empire in 1989, Jacques Derrida responded to the near-hysterical victory songs of many in the neoliberal West with a proclamation of radical historical changes potentially still to come. Many reservations have now been lodged and circulated about Derrida's long-awaited encounter with Marx (adumbrated as long ago as 1971 in *Positions* but still declared there as yet to happen).[1] Nonetheless *Specters of Marx* remains spellbinding, and I find myself, like many others, haunted by its analysis of haunting and hauntology, not least because for a student of Romanticism the ghosts Derrida writes about are vividly apparent in the texts recording the condition of England around 1800. They have not always been so visible, although they have always been there. David Ferry and Geoffrey Hartman described Wordsworth's compulsive invocations of a liminal zone between life and death, but it is Derrida's return to Marx that opens up the potential for a historical understanding of the spectral figures in the Wordsworthian landscape, and construes them as still living among us. The haunted present that is contemporary life can then look to Romanticism as an exemplary form of its own preexistence. The ghosts and ghostly forms inhabiting Wordsworth's poetry bespeak a historical condition whose determinations we have not yet supplanted or displaced. This does not mean that nothing has changed, or that everything written around the year 1800 matters to the twenty-first century in the same way and to the same degree. It is rather the sign of a specific and particularly powerful formation whose limits we are not yet in a position to project. The light that is not yet to be glimpsed would only appear at the end of the historical tunnel of commodity form, which took on unprecedented importance for culture and consciousness around 1800 and has remained critically formative ever since.

Twenty-five years ago I wrote about fetishism and reification as central and contested obsessions in Romantic aesthetics, but it is only since reading Derrida that I have learned to pay attention to the ghosts, and thus to reconsider the force of Marx's metaphors (and their literary analogues) as they describe or emanate from the achieved hegemony of commodity form.[2] Literature to be sure has been comfortable enough with ghosts. There were the ghosts of the Gothic novel, and of the English ballads and wild German poems that fed into and came out of it, along with those of the Shakespearean stage. But these ghosts were either offered as "real" ghosts, emanations of the supernatural, or they were demystified as projections of troubled or excited minds, perhaps of minds intoxicated with too much reading of the wrong sort. Either Enlightenment thought conjured ghosts away in order to bring us to our senses, or Counter-Enlightenment reinstated them as fully and grotesquely real. Occasionally Gothic artifice leaves us hanging about which is which and how to tell the difference (this is what Todorov calls "the fantastic"); even more occasionally, as in the spectacular case of *The Monk* (1796), mystery and demystification tumble over one another from page to page in a hurly-burly so apparently indiscriminate and devoid of metaphysical or methodological charge that one might suspect the impersonal operations of the logic of commodification itself to be the governing energy behind the story, the force propelling one arresting moment into the next in a celebration of sheer contiguity, a narrative vindication of the general equivalent masquerading as a surprise which is always the same surprise.[3]

But the Gothic was what Wordsworth said he sought to exorcize from the national literary culture; its ghosts were therefore not to be taken seriously as worth being haunted by. The supernatural part of the job, if it had to be done, was to have been done by Coleridge. The famous division of labor set out in *Biographia Literaria* recalls Coleridge assigning himself that role and conversely nominating Wordsworth as the poet of real men and ordinary nature, the one who was to "give the charm of novelty to things of every day" and focus the mind on "the wonders of the world before us." He was to excite feelings "analogous to the supernatural" but not of them (II: 7). In the 1800 preface to *Lyrical Ballads*, Wordsworth himself claimed to be turning aside from "gross and violent stimulants," avoiding even "personifications or abstract ideas," in the worthy cause of showing that "the power of the human imagination is sufficient to produce such changes even in our physical nature as might almost appear miraculous."[4] This last admission is all too easily read as an encomium to the revivifying and creative powers of the mind, to the received idea of the imagination, and of course it is often exactly that. But it is then all too easy to miss the other side of the coin, the shadow of the substance, the "real" ghostliness of things that the imagination wants to attribute to itself, to its singular figurative operations, but which (insofar as it is a shared imagination) might be more convincingly assigned to a general condition. Wordsworth's interest in poetically staging figures who are between death and life, not dead but never fully alive, either animated things or deanimated persons, ghosts who are not fully of the present yet seem bereft of accessible pasts – haunting the present *from* the present itself – does not self-evidently lead to the absent presence that is commodity form, but that is the path I have been following. It is Derrida who has insisted on Marx's deep understanding of "the ghosts that are commodities," commodities that "transform human producers into ghosts" by way of a "becoming-social" that is enacted through "spectralization."[5] Derrida is here, as so often, a guide to the underworld of common sense, and the master of its unraveling.

He is also a guide to Wordsworth. There is a striking passage in Wordsworth's account, in the later drafts of *The Prelude*, of his visit to the "sacred Mansion" that is the convent of Chartreuse in the summer of 1790.[6] On the approach to the convent, he claims to recall seeing

> Arms flashing, and a military glare
> Of riotous men commissioned to expel
> The blameless Inmates; and belike subvert
> That frame of social being, which so long
> Had bodied forth the ghostliness of things
> In silence visible, and perpetual calm. (6: 425–30)

The figure of "Nature" is wheeled in to bid them halt, instructing them to leave unmolested "this one Temple ... this one spot / Of earth devoted to eternity" (ll. 435–36). Here the poet is throwing his voice and leaving us hanging about whether this could really be a performative injunction lodged by forces not to be disobeyed (by way of the enthused Romantic prophet) or a wishful request from a relatively powerless visiting poet. (Earlier drafts staged the apostrophe as the poet's own.) There are other puzzles. We know that Wordsworth could not have thrown himself or nature in front of the flashing swords and spears of the soldiers because in the summer of 1790 they were, as Mary Moorman points out, not there: only in 1792 were the monks expelled.[7] A slip of memory perhaps, since Wordsworth did not start writing this part of the poem until some time between 1818 and 1820, the records of which Mark Reed has published as the C-Stage reading text in his reconstruction of the immensely complicated manuscript history of Wordsworth's mid-career drafts of his autobiographical epic.[8] But slips of memory are often the bearers of significant interpretive energies.

What is most arresting about this passage is its invocation of the ghostliness of things. What kinds of things are ghostly? If these are matters spiritual, metaphysical things, then one would not expect to see them described as ghostly, as if they were legacies of a deceased material life still lingering in the world in spectral form. Protestant-Christian spiritual truths, if they are conventionally held, are formless and out of this world but not spectral. If, on the other hand, these are the ghostly forms of things that were formerly but are no longer in the world, then what happened to them, and what is the purpose of having them "bodied forth" again? Or if they are things still in the world, then why are they ghostly? The poem suggests that without the "social frame" that is the convent, or perhaps the objectified inmates themselves, ghostliness could not take on embodied form. The decisive Kantian formulation of the domain of *Verstand* (understanding) had insisted that noumena (things in themselves) are what must be assumed to exist in order to explain experience, but they are never to be deemed as bodied forth. Kant thus remained observant of a strict distinction between the realm of sense and that of spirit: no border crossings. Most commonly it is our ideas *about* things that are described as insubstantial and shape-shifting, with things in themselves remaining as virtual or imagined figures of continuous presence: Wordsworth's poems elsewhere fully investigate the varieties of phenomenal figuration as always refigurative. But here what is embodied in the walls of the convent, and perhaps in the inmates who have become part of the "frame" that contains them, is ghostliness in itself, a nothing or half-thing that is somehow visible as a thing.

The phrase is not comfortably deciphered by what follows, which tells us that what is here empirically instantiated is "silence visible and perpetual calm." How is a quality marked by absence, the absence of sound, made visible? How and when is calmness perpetual? Is this not the *caput mortuum*, the death's head? Who or what but the figure of death can be made visible by its silence, can claim (because already dead) devotion to eternity? But that which here is deathly has been made by man, has been as it were put to death: men have built the convent to remind themselves of death. This is a Carthusian convent, inhabited by men who have taken a vow of silence; they can be seen but do not speak, like ghosts. They have chosen to stage themselves as dead to living speech: both the building and the persons who occupy it are death's heads, a composite memento mori. We know that Wordsworth spent two days staying at this still unviolated place and thus had plenty of time to dwell with and upon the sight of silent men hovering in attendance upon their guests (although some inmates were in fact designated to converse with visitors). It is a conventional enough response, in such a place, to think upon death, as one is indeed bidden to do, and perhaps to remember Milton, as Wordsworth does so often and as he does here in the ghostly form of Samson, who defeated armies of riotous men, who was punished with blindness for being *unable* to keep silent, who heard "the tread of many feet steering this way" (l. 111), and who himself destroyed a "temple" as Wordsworth claims the revolutionary army is about to do.[9] Is Wordsworth too then somehow wishing to bring down this temple upon his own head? If so, who are his enemies and what ideals does he preserve? This is after all a Catholic convent, and thus a site for accepting or rejecting the purgatorial half-world in which ghosts do walk while waiting for a future (eternal) life. Is Wordsworth a Protestant Samson? Is the destruction of the temple desired even as it is resisted? The poet claims to be a preserver, a defender of Christian traditions against a secular incursion whose onset he conjures up here against the historical record. Milton's blind Samson also invoked a synaesthetic deprivation – the sun now "silent as the moon" (l. 87) – which in its metonymic compression (sun, daytime, time of human action and sound) also makes us work to decipher how it is that what is already silent (the sun) can be more silent, or made to be as silent as another heavenly body that is literally no more or less silent than is the sun itself. A man already blind can now no longer hear anything; Wordsworth's "silence visible" has him seeing sound's absence, besting Samson twice over. The phrase of course also mimics the well-known "darkness visible" of *Paradise Lost* (1: 63). All of these Miltonisms (and more than Milton) are gathered up a few lines later in the mention of "Vallombre's groves" (l. 481) – Vallombre just happening to be the name of one of the valleys of the Chartreuse while embodying also an entire epic tradition, pagan and Christian (Virgil, Dante, Milton and beyond) of falling leaves, and of that shady site visited also at the opening of "The Ruined Cottage." These groves are where the poet and his companion "fed the Soul with darkness" (l. 482) after passing through forests declared to be "unapproachable by death" (l. 467). How so? Even conifers gradually shed their needles, and as such were included in Horace's recognition of the deep affinity between falling leaves and the transient words of poets: "we are doomed to death – we and all things ours."[10] What does the darkness denote if not the death that is everywhere in this episode? Does being unapproachable by death mean being dead already?

So it is possible that Wordsworth's lapse of memory is not simple, that the superimposition of the (unseen) events of 1792 upon the recollections of 1790 has to do with a confusion of desires about the preserving and destroying of the convent, and about the acknowledged immanence but desired deniability of death-in-life. Samson is the iconoclastic hero of Milton's poem but is here allied with the disavowed destroyers of a temple Wordsworth claims to want to preserve, but which in its preserved form actually images the reign of death-in-life. This passage in the poem is full of death, and while it is good Christian doctrine to recall our promised end in the spirit of resignation and active faith, one can also discern a resistance, a longing for what is "unapproachable by death" (which is not quite the same as eternal life). The convent deserves to be indestructible (though most of the twelfth-century buildings had burned down and what Wordsworth saw dated mostly from the late seventeenth century) because what it figures is death itself, the ghostliness of things. It makes silence visible and so gives form to nothingness, unlike the pines that whisper in the wind and which are "not silent" (l. 438). Also audible are the "Sister Streams of Life and Death" (l. 440) whose murmurs are heard from below. Do these twin streams represent a choice, as of life over death, or a conflation of life *with* death, as its unavoidable end? Is death just a future destiny, or is there death in and with life already and at all times? Can nature be sustained as a form of life unapproachable by death or must it too, as Horace said, contribute to a cycle of decay in order to uphold renewal? It is in the hearing of these sister streams that Wordsworth describes himself as torn between approving and disapproving of the new republic, "by conflicting passions pressed" (l. 441). The life of the new order requires the death of the old regime, although what this part of the old regime projects is itself the lordship of death over life. But the death of death at least in the secular realm is not new life: Wordsworth is uneasy with the "undiscriminating sweep / And rage" of the "State-whirlwind" (ll. 488–89). There seems to be no place to go. Similarly the natural world proposed by a personified "Nature" as untouchable by death works to feed the soul with darkness. This scrambled figuration of life as death corresponds with the epistemology of the commodity.

In fact the poet need not have worried that the revolutionary enlightenment would do away with

> These courts mysterious, where a step advanced
> Between the portals of the shadowy rocks
> Leaves far behind life's treacherous vanities. (ll. 452–54)

He certainly could not have fooled himself, by 1850 or even by 1818, that state-supported religion was about to disappear from the face of the earth. Thomas Paine had indeed looked forward to a world that would have "no place for mystery," and William Godwin thought that it was "injustice that stands most in need of superstition and mystery."[11] Wordsworth famously had his moment of agreeing with them, and just as famously later found them wanting. The narrative of *The Prelude* is most often in between the two positions, endorsing the best values of the new cult of liberty but wanting to set limits. At Chartreuse we can suspect a wish, articulated even as it is denied, that this temple might indeed be destroyed, and there is the hint of a narrative affiliation with Samson, the heroic destroyer who brought about his own death. Wordsworth's declared negation of the revolutionary claim of equality on earth seems to be compromised by a wish that it might prove true. The convent never was destroyed, although the monks and their books were later moved out. It is destroyed before its time in the poet's memory of proximate witnessing: he thought he was there when it was about to happen.

Notably absent from the ongoing argument here is any sustained embodiment of Christian faith. Instead the narrative specifies that the preservation of positive mystery has more to do with the afterlife of history than of any enlivened faith in potentially resurrected bodies:

> But oh! If past and future be the wings
> On whose support harmoniously conjoined
> Moves the great Spirit of human Knowledge, spare
> These courts mysterious . . . (ll. 449–52)

Wordsworth here rehearses a recognizably Burkean commitment to the past as the necessary condition of a psychologically bearable and modestly reformist future, but he does so in a quite secular way, without any eagerness to set his sights on personal salvation outside of some Hegelian, metaphysical engine powering historical time. The convent's "votaries" represent "conquest over sense" (l. 459), but the spirit that they embody is spectral, as if it were a relic of the sensory world they have not quite left behind. The function of these buildings in future time will be to signify ghostliness, not substance.[12] If they once signified the prospect of eternal life, that function now seems to be but a memory for all except the monks within. What the buildings do for those caught up in "life's treacherous vanities" (l. 454) is to remind them not of a glorious life beyond but of death in this life, and of things haunted by their own supernatural selves: the ghostliness of things.

TABLES THAT THINK AND DO TRICKS

Wordsworth's account of the visit to the convent of Chartreuse enacts a strangely flattened version of the ideology cycle as Marx described it. Marx thought that Hegel had turned things on their head, making power flow from heaven to earth, while Marx himself saw earth as the only origin of ideas and heaven as a fiction, one of the "phantoms formed in the human brain."[13] Wordsworth preserves a rhetoric of spirituality but, notwithstanding his invocation of "God's pure sight" (l. 456), ties it firmly to the earth: metaphysics becomes physical in the ghostliness of *things*. The convent that subsists is remembered as having been destroyed because it was already dead, a visible silence, an eternity in time that persuaded even nature to feed the soul with darkness. The vow of silence that the Carthusians elected is told in poetry as a chronicle of silence and displacement detached from any human forms whatsoever; the embodied things are ghostly and the living forms that populate them are as if already dead. These inversions correspond to a long list of Wordsworthian protagonists who project the features of the living dead, who move but do not speak (the old Cumberland beggar), who appear like ghosts (the discharged soldier, the fisherman), who cannot be located unambiguously in either the past or the continuing present (Poor Susan), who speak as if from another world (the leech-gatherer). It can seem at times as if Wordsworth's poems amount collectively to one long spirit show. And what is shown, I suggest, is an encounter with what Derrida calls "the ghosts that are commodities," the commodities that "transform human producers into ghosts."[14]

Marx argued that the commodity form functioned by way of a "secret" [*Geheimnis*], one enabling the social relations between men to assume "the fantastic [*phantasmagorische*] form of a relation between things." To understand this – but only by way of *analogy* – we have to "take flight into the misty realm [*Nebelregion*] of religion."[15] Wordsworth at Chartreuse does take flight but keeps his feet on the ground; he is unentranced enough to make clear that the ghosts do not lift the burden of mortality but reenact and restore it. The gesture toward transcendence remains rooted to the spot. But Wordsworth's is not a confident, critical demystification of the sort that Marx seems to propose in standing Hegel on his head in order to set him back on his feet. Wordsworth finds the ghostliness of things appealing and laments the imminent clearing of the mists. Nor is Marx always so sure of himself. He makes clear that fetishism of the commodity is not like primitive fetishism, where the human agent fabricates the image it worships but feels able to toss it aside at the first sign of its inefficiency in an act of decisive rationality. To glimpse the secrets of commodity fetishism is to sense that there is no ready and easy way back to primary creativity and self-determination: one thinks and speaks from *within* the sphere of commodity form, where ghostly things circulate in a world of their own and have no need to appease human needs and desires. They are beyond all human fears and indifferent to human tears. And they seem to take over the figurative faculties that have traditionally been located in the human imagination. The agency of commodity form, with its hidden springs and secret operations, takes over the acts of comparing and contrasting that have been thought of as the province of poetry. Here it is not the crucible of the imagination but the abstract relations of value and the general equivalent that compare things together, or take parts from wholes and attach them to other parts. Rhetorical theory at least since Aristotle had concerned itself with the tendency of all metaphoric language toward catachresis and a threatened collapse of intelligibility: limits had thus to be set and observed. In the modern economy of around 1800, the capacity of individuals to place limits on acts of comparison and exchange threatens to be taken over or overpowered by abstractions that are not under human control even as humans have enabled their creation. The commodity does not speak, says Marx: it is silence visible, a death's head, but one nonetheless prone to take form as a fantastic and phantasmagoric liveliness.

Perhaps the most famous form of liveliness that Marx invokes is the animated table of *Capital*, which we will come to in a moment. First, some further remarks about commodities in general and in particular in the years around 1800. Commodities are congealed forms of human labor and are as such arguably immanent in all human production; but they are "phantom-like" [*gespenstige*][16] not so much in the primary detachment of each from the minds and hands of the persons who made them but more critically when they come to exist within the virtual, structured paradigm of a dispersed and intensified commodity *form* whose secondary abstraction (single product into invisible, extended system of exchange) commits each single artifact to an intangible and mysterious network not open to ocular proof or physical embodiment. The secondary abstraction thus becomes primary; it seems to come after production but is in fact *before* it in that the production of new items is itself driven by the dispersed economy of exchange already in place much more than by simple conditions pertaining to the transition from certain raw materials to individual made objects. The anomaly is that what we can see (the commodity as a thing) matters less than what we cannot see (the abstract power of developed commodity form). Although Marx's order of description can give the impression that the simple commodity is historically prior and thus somehow more important, his argument requires that we understand ourselves as already within the sphere of an evolved, structural determination (governing all exchange) that can only be thought but not seen.[17] This represents an inversion of the apparent order in which things are made. Raw material *seems* to go through a process of production from which something emerges as a potential commodity, but even here, insofar as machines are involved, its transformation is enabled only by the reserves of dead labor that the machines contain. There is no "thing in itself" even at the start of the modern production process, although we think that there is. The things with which we begin are already haunted by the ghosts of expired life. They take on further spectral attributes as they pass into the invisible, systemic network dominating the process of exchange.

This paradigm is historically specific. It is brought into being by the conditions of modern industrial capitalism as they were evolving around 1800. If it were just a matter of the invention of money, or of the creation of objects for exchange, then the terms of human alienation would not differ between, say, classical Greece and the modern world.[18] What changes in the course of the eighteenth century is the whole spectrum of circumstances that we call, rather loosely, social conditions and/or modes of production. The invention of modern banking, of mechanised, large-scale industrial production (and rapid increases in rates of productivity), "the encreasing accumulation of men in cities,"[19] and other related (though not simply consequent) developments – a huge increase in the circulation of print, various debt crises and increased dependency upon paper money and paper credit, the "massification" of warfare, the social and demographic results of empire – are among the primary components of a world that according to Marx (and Wordsworth too) was taking on a very new and terrifying shape. Some of the conditions of this world (for instance money and exchange) had been in place for a long time but others had not. Thus Marx's sense of modern history was indeed marked by what, in *Specters*, Derrida calls a "*finite delirium*," something that could be imagined as "coming to an end" (p. 163) because it had a historical beginning, albeit not at a single moment or in a single, simple form but as a coming together of critical conditions in a way that changed the whole, quantity into quality. Derrida's own motives for suggesting that the delirium is an immanent rather than a historical condition may have to do with his desire to affirm a permanently messianic potential in Marx (whereby what is to come is always to come and thus can never come). But "the possibility of dissipating the phantom" need not be premised on an "ontology of presence" (p. 170), as if the disappearance of the ghosts is the beginning of the real. For Marx what would then begin is not the "real" but a different form of historical life.

I do not read the Marx of *Capital* as a universalist apostle of a presence to come, although some of his rhetoric does tend toward the form of what Derrida calls a "relatively stabilized knowledge" (p. 170). We cannot stand outside history and assess the immanence or not of certain universally spectral dimensions to objectification itself, incumbent everywhere upon everyone, but we can see that the ghosts are different and differently intense in the critical phases of capitalist modernization in the later eighteenth century and thereafter. This is apparent in the extraordinary obtrusion of ghostly hauntings in Wordsworth's poetry, quite different and differently weighted than in the earlier Gothic conventions and more akin to the about-to-come intense interest in apparitional figures in Carlyle's work or in Dickens's *A Tale of Two Cities* or indeed in the writings of Marx himself. I have made some comments about the timing of mature industrial capitalism in chapter 4, though without laying claim to a full rehearsal of the issues of periodization raised by its formation. Something more must now be said about the coming together around 1800 of the various ingredients of a modern commodity culture.

Marx himself, in a passage already mentioned but not fully cited, has a trenchant if elliptical formulation of the order of events in the discovery of the secret of modern life:

The secret of the expression of value, namely the equality and equivalence of all kinds of labour because and in so far as they are human labour in general, could not be deciphered until the concept of human equality had already acquired the permanence of a fixed popular opinion. This, however, becomes possible only in a society where the commodity-form is the universal form of the product of labour, hence the dominant social relation is the relation between men as possessors of commodities.[20]

The existence of modern democracy as a commonplace idea makes possible discoveries in the realm of the intellect, but the idea itself can take form only in a world where the commodity form is already dominant. Thus Aristotle, brilliant as he was, was subject to the "historical limitation" (p. 152) of his own society, could get only part of the way toward an articulation of the role of commodification in mature capitalist economies, and could thus only imagine a restrictive democracy. He could understand money well enough, but he could not apprehend the profile of a developed commodification culture that had as yet no historical existence. Money itself was in the course of the eighteenth century increasingly understood as part of a rapidly evolving crisis in the health of nations. Early stockmarket disasters and failed foreign ventures combined with the remarkable growth of the national debt to create an atmosphere of both fiscal and rhetorical panic. Peter de Bolla has brilliantly described the analogies between developments in rhetorical theory (the sublime) and theories of personal identity (the subject) in the middle of the eighteenth century and the financial history of the Seven Years War and the American War.[21] The government borrowed money to finance war and thus rendered further warfare necessary to shore up its own creditworthiness. The national debt doubled between 1755 and 1763, and doubled again between 1775 and 1783. The wars of the 1790s produced more of the same runaway statistics.[22] This debt was in turn financed by taxes and by further investment of capital. In earlier years it had been luxury that was deemed guilty of ruining the health of the body of the nation: now it was the uncontrollable outflow of money. Soon it would become also the vampiric effects of industrialization and machine labor.

Money, in other words, was becoming itself more and more ghostly, more and more invisible or apparent only by glimpses. Bills of exchange meant that wealth and commodity stock could pass from hand to hand without ever being realized. By around 1800 a major debate about the mortifying effects of machine-governed and factory labor was also emerging.[23] So too there was a much-intensified moral inspection of the effects of consumerism, no longer seen as the bad habit or inadvertent gift of a favored elite but increasingly perceived as affecting the entire social order from top to bottom.[24] In the late eighteenth century, there was also an unprecedented degree of concern about the relation of paper money to "real" wealth, as the national debt was again manipulated to finance the huge borrowing need driven by the war with France. Writers as otherwise antagonistic as Paine and Burke agreed on the scope of the problem if not always on the best ways to resolve it.[25] Add in the visible dynamics of primitive accumulation, the increased mobility of the population and its passage in and out of the *lumpenproletariat*, the brute conditions of mass warfare, and the incidence of both tropical and industrial diseases among both military and civilian persons, and we might think it remarkable if a poet like Wordsworth had not registered the consequences of such transitions to a modern economy and lifeworld.

Thus it is that the poems of around 1800 and thereafter reveal a more thorough penetration of the ordinary world by spectral shapes than anything that could be contained within the genre of the Gothic, although the Gothic provided a vocabulary for them to work with. These poems do not just signal their status as part of the commodity culture of the literary marketplace, and they are not simply cries of lamentation that man has lost control of the products of his labor. They register something much more pervasive and baffling, a general condition of commodification as the secret agent threatening to govern all perception and expression and all forms of life. This is not to be discovered in the literature of 1600 or 1700, even though shared concerns (over luxury or money and even division of labor, for example) may be found well before 1800. Marx's analysis of the commodity begins with general observations about transhistorical constituents of the modern economy, for example with the argument that nothing of matter [*Naturstoff*] enters into commodities as values, and with an analysis of the "mystery of money," but it does not end there.[26] Some measure of spectrality may be there from the start, but it attains its maximum and critical potency only in relation to the vampirism of the modern world. What matters most is what you cannot see clearly or see at all, those powers whose origins and futures you cannot trace.[27] Commodity form is invisible but visible in its effects: draining life from persons and embodying life in things. The blood-sucking principle for one economist writing in 1753 was public debt, "which will suck the blood from the whole body ... and will never quit hold while there is a drop left."[28] When we get to *Capital*, vampirism is pervasive, manifested not just by money or by the capitalist in person but by capital at large, which is as evident in the "dead labour" embodied in the machines that further draw blood from a still-living labor force as it is in the money markets that finance them and in the owners who keep them running. The "vampire thirst for the living blood of labour" is then quite impersonal and cannot be adequately figured as a single or simple entity: a man, a machine.[29] But it is empirically deadly, as when it takes the form of the straw that cuts the mouths of children who literally bleed in the service of hat-making and straw-plaiting (p. 598).

The creation of specters is not then a clean and tidy theoretical business wherein the spirit subjugates itself to the forms its has itself made and finds them – and itself – forever haunted each by the other. The living dead are the product of a very physical putting to death that is intrinsic to the operations of modern capitalism, just as Wordsworth's ghostly soldier is a sufferer from real wars and real diseases. The rhetoric of attribution itself, as always within the syndrome it attempts either to represent or to critique, is staged in both Marx and Wordsworth as given to the ungainly, the melodramatic and the monstrous, always more or less than the obligation to any "proper" meaning might seem to warrant. There are no proper meanings in a world governed by spectral forms and vampiric forces. The old beggar's detached eyeballs and quivering hands and the old fisherman's and leech-gatherer's apparently virtual long lean legs are the poetic analogues of the broken bodies and minds more literally evident in the groans of the discharged soldier and the heartless knitting of the hunger-bitten girl. All in turn are relatives of the disfigured forms that populate the more descriptive pages of *Capital*, those which quote from government reports and fill in the empirical content to what Marx describes at the very opening of the book as an "immense collection of commodities" (I: 125). "Immense" here [*ungeheuere*] also and perhaps better translates as "monstrous," as Thomas Keenan has pointed out and made central to a reading of these opening pages as preoccupied with monstrosity itself.[30] What is true to life in this world must also be disfiguring, true to death and death-dealing. But there is some grim fun to be had in the dance of death – which brings us to Marx's table.

Remember: what you cannot see is what matters most. So somehow you have to see it, or think that you do. At the beginning of his discussion of the fetishism of commodities, Marx explains how a wooden table, in becoming a commodity, "changes into a thing which transcends sensuousness while remaining sensible [*verwandelt er sich in ein sinnlich übersinnliches Ding*]."[31] What is striking about this passage is Marx's comic eagerness to personify the table as already having mind and agency of its own, whereby "it changes itself [*verwandelt er sich*]" – changes *itself* – into a "sensible-supersensible" thing. There is here no human agency: what is said is that the table enacts this transition upon itself. The table already has agency – we do not see it being given agency. Marx goes on: "It not only stands with its feet on the ground, but, in relation to all other commodities, it stands on its head, and evolves out of its wooden brain [*Holzkopf*] grotesque ideas, far more wonderful than if it were to begin dancing of its own free will [*aus freien Stücken*]." The table, in fact, does *not* dance but behaves in a way even more wonderful than it would if it *were* [*als wenn er*] dancing.³² It thinks itself into possible agency, but it does not move; and in so thinking it does something even more miraculous than dancing.

We do not see anything, we are blind to these thought-events. Derrida's *Specters* brilliantly reads the paradox: "one must see, at first sight, what does not let itself be seen. And this is invisibility itself. For what first sight misses is the invisible." This is the "ghostly schema ... a thing in flight that surpasses the senses" (p. 149). Derrida is fascinated with the directness and apparent absurdity of Marx's prosopopoeia. For Marx does not say that the image is hypothetical or mere projection; he says that the table really stands on its head while remaining on its feet and invents ideas more wonderful than if it were actually to dance. *We* have not produced this prosopopoeia; it is already there. The work is done before we arrive on the scene. Could this table possibly be the property of Hegel; could it *be* Hegel? Marx deprives us of sight to make us think. The table is silence visible, but there is a lot going on. How are we supposed to know it is standing on its head if we cannot see it as other than right-side up?

This must indeed be one of the famous "metaphysical subtleties and theological niceties" (*Capital One*, p. 163) that comes with the commodity. If it is a joke is it *just* a joke, and who is the butt of such a joke? Marx's footnote offers a jocular (apparent) analogy which is another riddle: "One may recall that China and the tables began to dance when the rest of the world appeared to be standing still – *pour encourager les autres*" (p. 164). *These* dancing tables seem to be those of the nineteenth-century spiritualists who sat in dark rooms waiting for the furniture to move, and perhaps for the *china* to tremble on the shelves. Meanwhile the traditionally inert (according to Hegel) country of China is beginning to move at last, even to dance (with the Taiping revolution). Those spiritualists who see dancing tables are surely mad; but we who cannot see tables having ideas (which is more wonderful than dancing) are also disabled. To follow the latent (German, not Rhenish) sense that has the table actually dance is then to become a spiritualist, a poor man's Hegel desperate for some sort of presence. To refuse the trap and to stick with the Rhenish reading – Marx's reading – is to interpose oneself into the realm of theory, which in this case is the right place to be, but from which there is to be derived no clear finding. Marx says that the table stands on its head in relation to other commodities. Again the sense is active: the table puts itself or sets itself up [*er stellt sich*] on its head in relation to or against or in the face of [*gegenüber*] all other commodities.³³ Do all commodities do the same thing, or is the table in a uniquely antagonistic attitude? If the whole world is upside down, as it was once said to be in the famous early definition or illustration of the effects of ideology as akin to the effects of a camera obscura, then won't everything just look normal? Are all commodities standing on their heads in relation to each other and thus all orienting themselves in the same direction? Who then could see the topsy-turvy nature of this arrangement, who could stand outside the frame? Marx accused Hegel and others of turning things upside down, standing them on their heads. Are we with Hegel or against him, and can we tell the difference if there is nothing left right-side up with which to compare ourselves? Whether at home or in the antipodes, we always feel that we have our feet on the ground, thanks to the invisible secret of gravity. The invisible secret of commodity form is to make us all think we are upright when it is the inverted world of sociable (but not really sociable) commodities that really sets the pace and makes things happen. We are bystanders who cannot see or hear what the commodities are saying.

Again: what is most wonderful is the thing we do not see, the table generating ideas (or rather *Grillen*: whims, fancies, fads). What we can see does not matter, but this table at least does not give us the sight of a dance that would place us among the mystics and spirit seers whose currency in the nineteenth century was the mark of a certain unreason. A dancing table, if it were to appear, would be like a specter, and this is the trail that Derrida follows – I will come back to this – by imagining a dance that is not there, one obeying "the technical rigidity of a program" (*Specters*, p. 153). Derrida attributes not seeing what we are told is there (the upside down and thinking table) to the mirror that does not reflect, that shows us nothing, or "does not return the right reflection" (p. 156), just as the ghost or vampire can neither be clearly seen nor see itself in a mirror. The commodity dazzles us, puts out our eyes (p. 165). To see only an ordinary upright table embodying the fiction of a mere use-value is to misrecognize the operation of our commodity-saturated world. Getting beyond this depends not upon sight but upon thought. The elaborate figure that Marx devises here weirdly inverts, turns on its head or plays around with, ideology and its critique. The sign of our first entrapment within the fetishism of the commodity is the attribution of living energy to inert things; but in the more developed stages of commodity form, we lose control of acts of attribution, and things seem to function in a world of their own, neither dead nor alive. A table standing upright in its place, as tables do, seems dead but is actually (historically) alive, with a "supersensible or social" component that remains invisible and that is not human: it bestows movement but has no flesh and blood. Commonplace personification – giving tables legs to stand on – only misunderstands who (or what) is in charge, because commodity form and value relations have "absolutely no connection with the physical nature of the commodity," not even that of apt analogy.[34] To see a table standing still seems an innocent perception claiming a common-sense immunity to the operation of fetishism: we are not attributing to it any living powers. But it is the opposite, the result of our ignorance of the operations of this bizarrely animated world whose functions are not accessible to sight.

Marx's abrupt and unexplained attribution of thought and upside-downness to the table invites us into the society of the fetish, into the world in which we are in fact already living, where dead things have come to life and have taken over all the conventions and routines of human interaction and expression. We have to be willing to imagine that *tables* imagine – as if we were poets. We must also imagine the abdication of our own faculty for imagining and thereby understand our own uncreativeness. To acknowledge and accept the comically spectral posturings of rival commodities as something to be considered seriously is to accept the power over what we merely see, of what we can apprehend only through a massive effort of thought: tables having whims and fancies. This is also the power of theory: the evidence of things unseen. But it is theory from within: to think of the table as thinking is to think against ocular evidence, and to position oneself within the society of commodities, where the real action is. The way out is the way in. We are able to approach these secrets not in the spirit of pure, disinterested critique but only as one of the gang. Anthropomorphic projection to the point of seeming absurdity – radical catachresis – is the means whereby the historically dominant abdication and loss of creative opportunity itself can begin to be apprehended – but never fully seen. The figure is cut loose from the human origins and locations to which it has usually been thought to belong as instance or ornament. It has taken on autonomous life.

This is not the first occasion in *Capital One* where things that are to our normal (precritical) senses quite inert take on the attributes of thought or intention. In a little joke that now perhaps looks more serious, Marx describes how the coat is regarded by the linen: "Despite its buttoned-up appearance, the linen recognizes in it a splendid kindred soul, the soul of value" (p. 143).[35] The linen speaks a language of commodities

[*Warensprache*] understood only by itself (not, apparently, by the coat), although Marx notes (with a purpose I cannot yet fathom) that human languages retain "more or less correct dialects [*Mundarten*]" of that language (p. 144). Again the personification is pushed to the limit and perhaps beyond. The linen sees the coat as "a splendid kindred soul, the soul of value" (p. 143), but there is no kinship and no soul. The linen is talking to itself, and if the coat were to reply the fantasy would disintegrate. Because a commodity cannot "be related to itself as equivalent," it "must [itself] make [*muss sie sich ... machen*] the physical shape of another commodity into its own value-form."[36] These are playful passages – the "soul of value" [*Wertseele*] here surely jests at the *Weltseele* dear to Idealist metaphysics – but they forecast the more dramatic throwing of the voice (and skewing of the eye) that informs the description of the table that thinks up its own capricious notions. Here too we are invited to imagine the shadow play and pseudo-dialogue between things – coats and bolts of linen – as carrying out (and thus exhausting, preempting) all the rituals of social life (meeting and greeting one another, saying hello) in a prescient prefiguring of the world of animated cartoons, the world of Disney, where knives and forks fight battles and dishes serve themselves. Derrida relates all of this to the operations of automatons, figures that look alive but are moving only mechanically, and thus to apparitions. We have seen these figures looming on the roads of France and England in Wordsworth's poems. In Marx's narrative they take form as the last worst instance of complex machines operated by an automated center: "here we have, in place of the isolated machine, a mechanical monster [*Ungeheuer*] whose body fills whole factories, and whose demonic power, at first hidden by slow and measured motions of its gigantic members, finally bursts forth in the fast and feverish whirl of its countless working organs" (p. 503).

This imagined seeing of what cannot be seen – a mentally active table which seems to us only to stand lifeless and upright, or a piece of linen nodding at a coat – is, again, not to be construed simply as a projection of human qualities into inanimate things (primitive fetishism). It is something more and something more strange: the delineation of a world where there is no foundation in anything *proper*, in which it is impossible to distinguish the figurative from the literal, in which anything can be exchanged or substituted for anything else, and in which what connects things up is *not* the human imagination. This is a world governed by the unconstrained metaphorization that comes with commodity form. The sphere in which we are most accustomed to approve "the willing suspension of disbelief for the moment" about distinctions between proper and figurative senses is of course that of "poetic faith," as Coleridge so memorably proposed.[37] But here there is no willing. The capacity to entertain the image of a table turning itself on its head may smack more of fancy than of imagination in the highest degree (as the Romantics liked to think of it), but it definitely belongs to the same sector of the mind that is required for the understanding of and delight in good poetry. Is this what Derrida himself is exercising in his insistence, on more than one occasion in the last sections of *Specters of Marx*, that the wooden table really does dance even though Marx says clearly that – except for the spiritualists – it does not? Derrida wants commodities to do a dance, a "ghost dance," a habit that comes from the fact that commodities "have commerce amongst themselves. That is what makes them dance" (pp. 160, 155). But they don't, Marx says: we (and they) only think that they might. We think of them that way in order to get some figurative purchase on a society of commodities, imagining them as if they were human. But they are not; their relation is one of pure equivalence, substitutability, which has no analogue in the familiar human world except as the deadness and emptiness that commodification itself has already produced. They are not truly sociable, because they are related only by an abstract sequence. So their dance would be the dancing of automatons, which for Derrida casts the table as "a puppet, a stiff mechanical doll whose dance obeys the technical rigidity of a program" (p. 153). Derrida puts himself at a distance from both the complete inertia seen by common sense (tables standing still and upright) and the joyous sociability of human dance. He speaks from another place, one governed by "technical rigidity," the place of the machine and the automaton, of the *es spukt* that, Derrida finds, "invisibly occupies places belonging neither to us nor to it" (p. 172). This phrase will come back to haunt us.

Here again are our master tropes: automation, ghosts, money, endless circulation. Or, in their poetic incarnations, old beggar, fisherman in the mist, girl on the corner, gypsy, pedlar, narrator. The society that Guy Debord saw in the 1960s as dominated by the commodity as spectacle and by the "*hallucinatory social fact*" is already there around 1800: "in a society where no one can any longer be recognized by others, every individual becomes unable to recognize his own reality."[38] The negation of excessive buying and selling that lends Wordsworth's poetry its moral imprimatur as a polemic against surplus production and in favor of the merest subsistence also (and antithetically) expresses the ghostly performance of a commodity circulation that cannot be seen and which, therefore, matters.

The pedlar, by the time he tells his story to the narrator of "The Ruined Cottage" and *The Excursion*, has retired from buying and selling, but he continues to circulate. Recall that even in his telling of the past, there is no mention of Margaret ever buying anything from him. The poem does not spare an uncomfortable apprehension of the fungibility of human tragedy for the production of metaphysical wealth as well as of profit in the poetry trade. Margaret, again, is not buying but dying. She too has the "phantom-like [*gespenstige*] objectivity" that Marx attributes to the commodity once it has entered the cycle of exchange in which "all its sensuous characteristics are extinguished."[39] In the time of telling she is already dead, brought back to life only in the story. The Cumberland beggar also engages in no apparent buying and selling; we see him receive the odd coin in charity, but we do not see what he gives back, earthly self-esteem and other-worldly hope, metaphysical speculations allowing him to subsist as an icon of money itself circulating (says Marx) in a "constant and monotonous repetition of the same process" (p. 210). The magic of automation, the detached eyeballs moving along the ground, like the fisherman's and discharged soldier's separated body parts, have the aura of the uncanny that Freud found in the sight of "feet which dance by themselves" and which we can also think we see (but do not *see*) in the table that stands on its head and has ideas, a more wondrous thing than if it were to dance on its feet.[40]

Marx, as Derrida makes clear, always invests his accounts of the commodity with the vocabulary of the uncanny and supernatural: "magic and necromancy" [*Zauber und Spuk*], queer or strange [*vertracktes*], "mist" [*Schein*], "mystical veil" [*mystische Nebelschleier*] and so on.[41] The same vocabulary governs Wordsworth's spectral encounters. Paul de Man found a tendency to excess in all figurative language: "Something monstrous lurks in the most innocent of catachreses: when one speaks of the legs of the table or the face of the mountain, catachresis is already turning into prosopopoeia, and one begins to perceive a world of potential ghosts and monsters."[42] In so saying he reveals his own formation not just in rhetoric but in the rhetoric of Romanticism, in the historical moment when this tendency became unignorable and aesthetically disruptive on a grand scale, both in the spectral figurations of commodity form and in the more literal dismemberings that came with machine labor and military service in a time of global war. Mutilated, misfitting or ill-coordinated body parts are the visible signatures of a new world order. The leech-gatherer's work-trained ability to touch his head to his feet is at once an occupational skill and an affliction. The physical decline that comes with old age is redirected further toward the grotesque by the specific conditions of labor. Ghostly figures are made more ghostly by the work that they do, work that dismembers and reorganizes the body.[43]

In *Capital One*, Marx's disfigured figures also have an empirical life in a world where potters are "stunted in growth, ill-shaped, and frequently ill-formed in the chest; they are prematurely old ... phlegmatic and bloodless" (p. 355). Factory work injures "every sense organ" and reliably "produces its list of those killed and wounded in the industrial battle" (p. 552); labor comes more and more to approximate to "perpetual motion" (p. 526). Women and children suffer especially: children in wallpaper factories are fed while standing at their machines (p. 357), and milliner girls die from overwork in unventilated rooms (p. 364). Adam Smith, in a passage Marx quotes (p. 483), had commented on the physical constraints imposed by a strenuously divided labor system, but most of the concerned political economists of the eighteenth century focused on its psychological effects, which rendered workers unable to become or remain functioning citizens with minds of their own and independent powers of judgment. Smith thought that repetitious work would make the laborer "as stupid and ignorant as it is possible for a human creature to become": only an aggressive education policy could hope to offset the otherwise devolutionary effects of a factory economy.[44] Adam Ferguson similarly argued that all persons trained to highly specialized tasks must be "made, like the parts of an engine, to concur to a purpose, without any concert of their own," so that "manufactures, accordingly, prosper most, when the mind is least consulted, and where the workshop may, without any great effort of imagination, be considered as an engine, the parts of which are men."[45] Engels's *The Condition of the Working Class in England* (1845) shifts the emphasis to the physical damage done to the bodies of the men, women and children making up the parts of the engine, the "pale, lank, narrow-chested, hollow-eyed ghosts" and maimed persons who make us feel that we are living "in the midst of an army just returned from a campaign."[46] Many of these reports of premature aging, permanent lassitude, spinal deformities and deformed knees and ankles are drawn straight from the published reports of concerned health inspectors. The same rhetoric informs *Capital*, which uses many of the same sources.[47]

Wordsworth's awareness of the deformed body as the incumbent condition of more and more persons around 1800 might well have been partly gathered from seeing the effects of the pottery and textile industries in the Lake District, or from seeing the injuries sustained in mining and quarrying. He certainly witnessed the lost limbs and ravaged frames of returning soldiers and sailors suffering from war wounds and tropical diseases.[48] And he witnessed the critical phases of the processes of primitive accumulation that made possible the new machine economy and the psychological and empirical hegemony of commodity form, the movements of substitutable people in and out of agricultural, industrial and military work by way of temporary or permanent unemployment and vagrancy: the "reserve army" of the poor, as Engels called them, an image taken up again by Marx in describing the same increasingly large sector of the population as "the light infantry of capital, thrown from one point to another according to its present needs."[49]

This surplus population is, as we have seen, more or less indistinguishable from what Marx calls the *lumpenproletariat*, a class which is no class and which Jacques Rancière argued to be itself the substance of the party and the true identity of the communist movement at the time, and also thereby of Marx himself, the vagrant journalist not exempt from membership within the sociological category that had followed the call of the fake emperor of France. To say this is neither to diminish the power of Marx's mind and theory nor to make light of his radical critique. There is indeed a distinguished tradition of commentary that finds his work to be conventionally scientific, that is to say not implicated in any staging of personal or local-historical circumstances. But Marx's recourse to complex figurative language wherein one can find no simple place to stand and no "proper" order of significations against which to calibrate simple shifts between the figurative and the literal certainly supports the idea that he is writing from within the syndrome he sets out to critique, working not just to deliver a doctrine but to involve his reader in difficult engagements with the mechanics of representation within a culture that is already pervasively commodified, one where things stand on their heads but still look right-side up. Such a view is also consistent with the challenging narrative organization of *Capital*, which begins with the commodity but requires that we already know the end of the story: its completed coming-into-being in the modern world.

Thus to propose that *Capital* both describes and deploys a narrative persona whose being in the world is unstable is to extend rather than discredit the power of its analysis; such theory now references not only the state of the world but the language of the agent of critique in distinctively modern ways. In this one sense at least, Marx is to *Capital* as Wordsworth is to *The Prelude*. We have to think ourselves into the society of commodities in order to see the table standing on its head, and then at once move on to understanding that we do not see it but *think* it.

Knowing that we are really thinking what we might otherwise imagine that we see signals the moment of potential critique emerging from participation in a world of phantasms, but one has to take the risk of being arrested by the power of the sight, which is also the power of the image. In reporting his recollected visit to the convent of Chartreuse, Wordsworth makes the buildings a figure of death, of the ghostliness of things, acceding thereby to the logic of the commodity as Marx and Derrida after him describe it: what we see is silence visible, a thing which is no thing, something we cannot in fact "see" but can only think. Inert matter is given spiritual life, but it does not really move. The slippage or hesitation between inertia and movement allows for the entrance of ghostliness. Wordsworth will remain haunted by Chartreuse, imagining a violence that had not happened and would in fact never occur in the way he projected, and which is thus forever still to come. This is a hauntology, but not an "ontology of presence" of the sort Derrida (*Specters*, p. 170) claims to find (and I do not find) in Marx: a covert foundationalism rooted in use-value and a too-ready belief that the specters can be restricted to the imaginations of the bad or stupid guys.

Why does Derrida resist the possibility that Marx or his text knows what he or it is doing, finding instead a "predeconstructive" Marx alongside the more prescient one who is "among the first thinkers of technics" (p. 170)? Or, to be more exact, why does he find that Marx proceeds "as if he did not want to know" what he or his text apparently does know (p. 172)? It is Derrida, not Marx, who sees that table dancing. Even in the early *The German Ideology*, Derrida found in Marx's *es spukt* (it spooks, it haunts) an impersonal something that refuses categorization as predeconstructive, a ghostly power figure that is "undecidable, neither active nor passive ... that ... invisibly occupies places belonging finally neither to us nor to it" (p. 172). So Marx/the text is here willing to avow that he/it knows that things have gone well beyond and outside the inherited ontologies? A place that belongs neither to us nor to it – here comes that phrase again – aptly specifies the place of the table that thinks, that might have the option of dancing, and the linen ackowledging the coat. Derrida first seems to give the table a presence in seeing it as dancing when it isn't, but then says that it is mere technics, the dancing of automatons. The figure is first projected as under our control, as having human traits, but they are then whisked away as the dance is rendered independent of human agency. Derrida performs a rhetorical delight at seeing the dance, a delight that speaks for the joy of anthropomorphic projection itself, the joy of poetry; but he then tells us that it is a dance of death. The commodities are having even more fun than they were in *Capital*: they are dancing with Derrida, who puts himself into the ghost dance that is real enough but empty of weight and matter, a merry-go-round routine, as if he understands himself as sharing that place belonging "neither to us nor to it." If there is here a "definite social relation between men themselves," then it is one in which nothing of what is conventionally "social" remains.[50] With this lively dance of death in mind, we might now look again at the most famous of all of Wordsworth's poems, perhaps the most famous *Romantic* poem in English, the one about the daffodils. It is a poem about dancing while standing still.

SPENDING IN PRIVATE

Reading "I wandered lonely as a Cloud" again after reading Derrida and Marx at once brings up the narrator's opening self-image in which he is – or *makes himself* – a sort of ghost. In claiming to wander "lonely as a cloud," he gives himself vaporous form and also abstracts himself from the living company of his sister whom we know to have accompanied him on this particular walk.[51] If "as a cloud" means *in the form of* a cloud (like some latterday Zeus), then he is putting himself above the earth, surveying it but not of it; if he is simply *as lonely as* a cloud while keeping his feet on the ground, then he is still detached from human society, as if he were floating on high. This bizarre, gravity-defying self-location is a version of the trope of being left "hanging" that Paul de Man has identified as typical of Wordsworth: "instead of being centered on the earth, we are suddenly related to a sky that has its own movements, alien to those of earth and its creatures."[52] Two examples occur in the Winander Boy passage in Book 5 of *The Prelude*, where the boy hung listening and the churchyard hangs upon the hillside, both suspended between earth and sky, both contributing to a "curiously barren, dead-obsessed emptiness of non-being" (p. 84). The boy, the churchyard and the wanderer lonely as a cloud all occupy that place where Derrida found Marx's *es spukt*, one belonging "neither to us nor to it." So too they take on the weightlessness of puppets, which de Man finds again in Kleist's story of 1810, *Über das Marionettentheater*, where the puppets furthermore can "rightly be said to be dead, hanging and suspended like dead bodies," this being exactly the source of their gracefulness.[53] Perhaps the avowed loneliness of the living bespeaks its placement within a community of the lifeless?

Certainly there is no human community on offer. Wordsworth's poetry is full of narrators who project themselves and those they encounter into lonely circuits of near-planetary proportions. Here the prospect of society is reinvented and transposed onto the "crowd" or "host" of daffodils with which the poet can commune in solitary and silent pleasure. But why both "crowd" and "host"? Is this an opposition or an apposition, a choice between a distinctly earthly and predominantly urban crowd and a biblical or angelic host? Is the one converted into the other by way of the heightened imagination of a hindsight we have not yet had explained but which retroactively governs the whole event of the poem (for here too we are asked to read backwards)? Or is there perhaps an uncertainty about whether the line between material crowd and metaphysical host can be drawn at all? Must the poet take his chances with the crowd, or will the host welcome the ghost? The flowers do not of course dance but are animated *as if* dancing (though always on the spot, like the table turning on its head). But Wordsworth suppresses the simile in favor of an unembarrassed personification: "A crowd / A host of dancing Daffodils...Ten thousand dancing in the breeze."[54] He thereby asks us to imagine what did occur (the breeze making the crowd of flowers sway) as a movement that could not have occurred (flowers dancing on the spot or picking up their roots, a moving crowd). Modern readers are assisted in this imagining by the currency of the figure as something of a cliché in the common language, although it was not so in 1807. No more do the waves dance or laugh, as they are said to do, but the personifications are almost unnoticed now because of their sheer familiarity: dancing and laughing waves and flowers have come to belong to the common stock of poetic diction.[55] So we might miss the extravagant delight in absurdity whereby waves and flowers compete, by dancing, for the honor of being most gleeful: "The waves beside them danced, but they / Outdid the sparkling waves in glee." These are the images that compose the "wealth" (l. 12) that the poet is unconsciously storing up, allowing him to activate his own inert domestic loneliness ("In vacant or in pensive mood") with an after-image of delight. Like an automaton or a cistern, the poet's "heart with pleasure fills," and when the fill reaches the right level it "dances with the Daffodils."

And what sort of dance is this? One kind of dancing is a highly formalized expression of human sociability wherein what is potentially surprising or ungovernable is contained by an element of ritual; this is mostly what goes on in Jane Austen novels. Another, wilder kind of dance – typified around 1800 by the *carmagnole* and the *allemain* – was felt to threaten a political or sexual self-abandon. Wordsworth's daffodils are very formal: they sway while standing on the spot, perhaps not even touching one another. They cannot pick themselves up by the roots; they are an immobile crowd and a stationary host. They are a collective made up of individuals who are all the same, like the products of an assembly line – so many of them that they can only be described by way of synecdoche or hyperbole (for the poet has not really counted "ten thousand"). De Man notices a letter in which Schiller commends the English dance for its resemblance to an automated system in which each part fits elegantly into a whole, evolving pattern "rigorous enough to be patterned on the model of a mathematical language."[56] And in Kleist's story, de Man finds confirmation of the sense that the artificial motion of the puppet is even more graceful than human dance because open to being programmed yet more thoroughly and without glitches. Thus it is that the "loss of hermeneutic control is itself staged as hermeneutic persuasion" (p. 269); we are, says de Man, more pleased by the machine forms, so lifelike but lifeless, than with the living persons they imitate.

Kleist himself goes further in his remarkable story. The puppet dancer seems to have a soul, so perfect is its motion. His protagonist "doubted if this could be found unless the operator can transpose himself into the centre of gravity of the marionette. In other words, the operator *dances*."[57] And as he dances he loses his soul, gives it over through his fingers to the figure of the puppet. Human dancers seem clumsy compared to this, as they are mostly incapable of such perfect incorporation of spirit into matter. The puppets are also "weightless ... the force which raises them into the air is greater than the one which draws them to the ground." They are like ghosts, unimpeded by "the inertia of matter" (p. 16). Like Wordsworth, they float above the ground. Coleridge thought that Wordsworth might have lost his soul to the daffodils, or to his poem about them. He saw in it the beguiling appeal of a pantheism that bypassed the self's moral identity in favor of aesthetic gratification. Here he expressed the familiarly understood sense of this poem as describing the transference of energy from wind to flowers and waves to the heart of the poet who accepts it as a vindication of the power of correspondent breezes and of the shared receptivity of human and nonhuman objects to animating but invisible forces. The poem has mostly been received as a standard expression of Romantic pantheism of the sort that Coleridge found worryingly out of control when he compared it to "Gipsies" as an instance of Wordsworth's tendency to employ "thoughts and images too great for the subject" in "an approximation to what might be called *mental* bombast . . . a disproportion of thought to the circumstance and occasion."[58] Coleridge wanted the "inward eye" to be reserved for the moral conscience, the only proper "bliss of solitude" which should dwell not upon a transitory aesthetic pleasure but upon "the images and virtuous actions of a whole well-spent life." Two of Wordsworth's best modern critics, David Ferry and Geoffrey Hartman, also take up the poem and Coleridge's critique of it. Hartman suggests that what offended Coleridge – as well as Anna Seward – was the projection of the self as inseparable from the landscape, which becomes the figure of an overbearing "self-acquired revelation"; Ferry, following Coleridge's connection of this poem with "Gipsies," suggests that the poet, unlike the daffodils, begins as "what the gipsies were, emblem of that which does not participate in the eternal."[59]

But wandering lonely as a cloud is in one way about as eternal as things get, alluding to a vapor cycle proceeding through its course without human notice or interference: all that is solid turns into vapor. In this sense the poet is not like the gypsies but like the *narrator* of "Gipsies," the disembodied specter roving across the landscape for a full twelve hours while reporting nothing seen, touched or achieved. Nor is his death-like automation so different from the assembly-line form of the daffodils themselves, which only seem to move together while each is always rooted to the spot. At the end of the daffodils poem, Wordsworth has made a big deposit into the pleasure bank and made it available for future withdrawal. He is cashing in his accumulated "wealth." Astute critic that he is, Ferry notices the image of gold appearing in the poem – the image that also, I have argued, haunts the allusive language and situation of "Gipsies." For him the "goldenness of the daffodils . . . tells us that they are charming," but this is not the quality of real gold so much as the result of an alchemical transformation of "petty substance into gold." In this way the flowers become as valuable to Wordsworth *as if* they were real gold, but they provide a wealth that is metaphysical and not material; "he is like most alchemists in that the splendor of his achievement depends on the pettiness of what he begins with" (p. 11).

The daffodils do indeed invoke gold, and not just by way of their color. Ferry's reading prompts us not to accede too readily to an uplifting doctrinal (albeit somewhat pagan) reading of the poem. To do so would be to miss the near-comic ungainliness of the figures, the odd invocation of "wealth," the staging of the narrator as a spectral presence, and the elision of human society that makes the whole cycle available only to one enjoying the "bliss of solitude" (l. 16). Wordsworth goes to the bank to cash in accumulated wealth to provide an enjoyment that fills a vacancy, but he is himself the bank, the banker and the payee. Such spending did not for Coleridge amount to a well-spent life. The rhetoric of pantheism articulates itself as (and as at one with) the rhetoric of commodification: they come together. The prospect of seeing "into the life of things" invoked in the "Tintern Abbey" poem can reveal that things have a ghostly life which is maintained at the expense of those looking into them.[60] A long tradition of explicit associations between solitary imagining and masturbation also makes its appearance in Wordsworth's purposively heightened rhetoric of self-satisfaction, his bliss of solitude. Self-gratification was especially imagined (and depicted) as the outcome of novel-reading, that is of indulging oneself in the less exalted sectors of the literary marketplace.[61] A sexual motif can be traced in the scene of a poet reclining on his couch and remembering past experiences, just as it can in "Gipsies" where it is (among other things) the endless knotting of the reposing vagrants that exercises the poet's vigorously abstinent imagination, and does so in the light of miserly dreams of gold and rich rewards from his own "bounteous hours." One of the precursors of Wordsworth's motif is the scene in Spenser's *Faerie Queene* where Calidore, himself "unespyde," sees naked maidens "dauncing in delight" (VI.x.11.9). To say that the daffodils poem is "about" masturbation might shock some readers; but it is "about" masturbation in the specific sense that it is also about solitary consumption within an economy of commodity form, and perhaps about insipient poetic cliché, ready-to-hand words and images. In each of these spheres, it is a parody of or antitype to exchange, suggesting (against the logic of commodity circulation) that things really might be exchanged with themselves in a world of complete privacy where nothing really circulates. No social turbulence or even engagement ensues from this interior circulation of wealth, no passage of persons from riches to poverty or in and out of the *lumpenproletariat*. That so many have received this as a favorite poem asks serious questions about the function of the aesthetic in the modern world.

For the daffodils poem has paid off handsomely, and regularly reappears as an anthology favorite; but the integrity of its fantasy depends upon having internalized the movement of the commodity to the point of invisibility. All we see in our readerly mind's eye is the silence visible of a reclining poet. Without the poem's telling us, the expenditure would be a secret. It is easy enough to acquiesce in the images of dancing waves and flowers, but perhaps harder to imagine the poet's heart dancing with the daffodils. We cannot see this, we can only think it: the poet is lying on his couch and the movement is all internal. His enjoyment of his wealth is hidden from sight. The dancing heart is like Marx's dancing table, unnoticed except by those for whom it performs and with whom it competes. When looking at the flowers, the poet recalls himself as not thinking, as being entranced by the image as sheer spectacle: "I gaz'd – and gaz'd – but little thought." Without the later after-image on the "inward eye," the heart is unactivated, and when it is activated we still cannot see it. The inward eye is another dismembering whose oddity is hidden from us by its status as a cliché: it is the inward eye *itself* which is "the bliss of solitude," and not the things it happens to conjure up. The inward *I* that Coleridge wanted to preserve as the analogue of the conscience is here only an *eye*, and one all too prone to merely gazing and not thinking. As when the linen speaks (or thinks it speaks?) to the coat, the social life of the poem is entirely among things, with the poet reduced to or figured as an automaton responding in private to the unanticipated stimulus (directly deposited) that is his wealth. The image is reproducible and exchangeable (flowers to heart to published poem) without enabling any society that is other than virtual or imaginary.

Kleist's story goes on to report other directions taken by the conversation between the characters, telling the tale of a handsome youth who sees himself in a mirror in exactly the posture of the famous classical sculpture of the boy removing a thorn from his foot. The narrator tries to distract him, saying that he "must be imagining things" ("Marionette Theatre," p. 17): the German says *er sähe wohl Geister*, that he is seeing ghosts or spirits (p. 478). Indeed he does. So possessed is he by the desire to replicate this sight that he "began to spend whole days before the mirror," completely losing the "free play of his gestures" and all of the "lovely grace" with which he was originally endowed. He loses the qualities of liveliness in the cause of making himself a perfect figure, seeking to market himself – to himself – as a finished work of art. He becomes the ghost of himself. He becomes also a modern Narcissus, who is not only a famous figure in classical myth but the source of the name of the genus of flowers to which belongs the English daffodil.[62] All daffodils, including Wordsworth's, are species of narcissi. If they too are dancing for themselves and in search of their own perfect form, then the poet's mimic self-regard turns out to be oddly appropriate. For Wordsworth has here made himself alone again, as he did at the convent of Chartreuse, a ghost figure enjoying his own apparitions. His wealth comes from a "shew," a word which already by around 1800 had a long history (apparent indeed all over Wordsworth's poetry) of antithetical uses: on the one hand a revelation, a showing forth of something real and true, on the other hand a false or superficial appearance, a mere show, or even a popular entertainment in the modern sense (first recorded in the 1760s). He only seems to be lying still and unenlivened; in reality his heart is dancing with the flowers. Or, more precisely, he is spending the wealth he gathered (did he really earn it?) at a private show. We can only believe, we cannot see. Is Wordsworth still fully human, or has he turned into the "sort of automaton" Derrida saw in the wooden table, "a stiff and mechanical doll whose dance obeys the technical rigidity of a program"?[63] In Wordsworth's passive activity there is neither a conscience nor a consciously figurative faculty, but something invisible to us and therefore not a means to sociability except with the self, as solitary repetition. Contact can only be made in the virtual domain of the reading experience, through being *told*, not shown, which Michael specified in the last book of *Paradise Lost* (12: 9–11) as the fate of fallen man: we have to imagine what we cannot see. This too is the means of and medium for poetry and the mechanism of personification: dancing daffodils. It is also the means of and medium for the presentation and possible critique (by way of theory) of the fetishism of commodities: dancing tables. Marx immerses us in a seemingly impossible series of subject positions (commodity and not commodity, seeing and not seeing, in a place that belongs neither to us nor to it) to alert us to a crisis that seems at this point in his exposition best approached comically. Wordsworth does something similar without declaring any breach of faith in the power of imagination – indeed while declaring the opposite – in his careful employment of naturalized figures and pleasurable absurdity: waves competing with flowers to be (not seem) most gleeful. The ghostliness of things is at once the signature of the power of commodity form (which has itself embraced the afterlife of this most famous poem), the power of the imagination and of poetry, and the power of death-in-life that haunts both in these years around 1800. The daffodils are planted in the soil of the commodity: they are all the same, all made to seem moving while rooted in place, each deprived of choice or sociability with others, moving according to a technical program, and making up a show that generates wealth, one that finally (though Wordsworth could not have known this) could be cashed in as a bestseller. Like the table standing on its head and the *es spukt*, they occupy a place belonging neither to them nor to us. They disrupt the cycle of figuration that conventionally produces ontological presence by way of the facsimile or organic connection, life with living form.

In 1815 Wordsworth brilliantly revises the poem by adding in a comparison of the daffodils to stars "that twinkle on the milky way" in a "never-ending line," reinstating by grand cosmic analogy what Derrida might call the "technical rigidity of a program," stilling them in their very movement as dancing flowers: another figurative tour de force that dramatizes the act of figuration itself. He also upgraded the poem from its 1807 categorization as one of the "Moods of My Own Mind" by placing it among the "Poems of the Imagination." The highest poetic faculty, in other words, is claimed as on display here, which makes the poem's location in the commodity cycle all the more meaningful. Wordsworth writing for his reader is not quite linen talking to a coat, but there is a notable irony in his inserting himself into a cycle of natural energy he has himself figured (dancing flowers), even as he hopes that the figure does not exhaust the animating force whose effects led him to invoke it. At the convent of Chartreuse, the ghostliness of things is imagined as bodied forth, but what is embodied is death; under the spell of commodity fetishism, the liveliness of things is also ghostly and apparitional, depriving humans of the energies they can no longer locate precisely either in things (primitive fetishism) or in themselves, and can only sense as in that place belonging to neither. A poet's invisible and silent heart dances along with the flowers he has himself memorialized as figures in a dance before an audience of one. One of the poster-poems of our Romantic ideology cannot resist beginning to undo itself, cannot disentangle the showing forth of something real and vital from the mere show of apparitions and entertainments, and this is to Wordsworth's considerable credit. He thus joins Marx and Derrida and a few others in the crowd or host of those who have left us to continue this effort, not in the light of a promised end, but in hopes of a clearer beginning. What took on definitive historical form around 1800 might also at some point change shape or come to a close. But until it does the delight conveyed to generations of readers by the daffodils poem seems likely to suffice as a governing model of the most desired form of available satisfaction: a spectral rehearsal of internal expenditure where a high rate of interest is assured and no one else can drive down prices because they cannot get into the market.

CHAPTER 6

Living images, still lives

NOT ALL ALIVE, NOR DEAD

We have seen in chapter 4 that Wordsworth confesses a desire for frozen time, for memories that are always the same and always recoverable as fixed values, at the same time as he opposes the reification of the imagination (and of life itself) that such fixedness must bring with it. In chapter 5 we saw him standing in awe of the "ghostliness of things" and complicating a conventional antimaterialist metaphysics by invoking a rhetoric of death-in-life, whereby things take life only as specters, incarnations of the already dead. Marx confronted similar aesthetic questions in staging the figuration of the culture of the commodity, devising the fantastic forms of linen talking to coats and tables standing on their heads, bringing apparently inanimate things to life in order to signal the deadness of what we take to be our own lived experiences. Life and death interact in these images of death-in-life and life-in-death; in the spots-of-time experiences, life wishes for the full remembering that could come only in standing outside time and accepts its timeliness only by way of a rhetoric of loss.

In the daffodils poem Wordsworth has found a way of staging a figure of natural life that seems so obviously credible – who could contest the aptness of dancing flowers? – that we might miss completely the steady invocation of economic terms that assimilates incipient poetic cliché to an analysis of private (pseudo)circulation and commodification. I say incipient, since the commonplace status of nature poetry was not as well established in 1807 as it has since become. Coleridge found the poem overwrought and lacking in narrative self-control; perhaps this sense of excess is what gives the "host of dancing daffodils" the aura of a cliché at the very moment of its invention as an original image. Shakespeare and Milton produced dancing stars and planets, but not to the best of my knowledge any flowers, nor have I discovered any in any of Wordsworth's precursors (though my search has been far from complete). The bold personifications of *Paradise Lost* are explicit about confessing the place of simile: "last / Rose *as* in dance the stately tree" (7: 323–24, my italics). In the first book of *The Task*, Cowper's willows similarly "dip / Their pendent boughs, stooping as if to drink," although his ash tree does come to life by "far-stretching his umbrageous arm."[1] A rhetorical stretch, perhaps, as well. Wordsworth revisited the image of dancing forms in a strange little poem published in 1835, "This Lawn, a carpet all alive," in which his earliest draft specifies the dancing shadows of leaves as "a simile / For strenuous idleness," while his published text makes it an "apt emblem."[2] In both versions of the poem, he acknowledges the stretch of figuration itself rather than asserting the ontological integrity of dancing as a property of nature. Here, "genuine life" belongs to what is "mute" and "unheeded," the grass and flowers that remain unnoticed and thereby immune to the poet's figurative activities (p. 186). The apparent comfort with which the daffodils were seen to dance (too comfortably to appease Coleridge's moral vigilance) disappears in the later poem, which seems compelled to call attention to the artificiality or awkwardness of personification (though again it is idleness that is at stake). The daffodils do not speak, as flowers do in Blake's pantheistic *Book of Thel*; but many inanimate objects did appear in eighteenth-century literature as the masters of their own narratives, as is apparent in the fashion for novels retailing the life stories of coins, banknotes, hackney coaches, pins, shoes and feathers, and several more of the items in the fetishist's handbook. Such precursors of Disney's talking teacups have been taken as symptomatic of an intensifying commodity culture and of what Jonathan Lamb calls "troubled connections between the human and the non-human" whereby things are "alive and dead at once."[3] So indeed they are. Fictional license and overt dramatic irony can serve to keep things in their place, so that we are never really expected to believe that a guinea or a rupee can actually speak. But on occasions the hyperbole of prosopopoeia can take over, as it does at the beginning of Cowper's *Task* where the poet describes the importing of cane chairs from India:

> But restless was the chair; the back erect
> Distress'd the weary loins that felt no ease;
> The slipp'ry seat betray'd the sliding part
> That press'd it, and the feet hung dangling down,
> Anxious in vain to find the distant floor.
> These for the rich: the rest, whom fate had plac'd
> In modest mediocrity, content

> With base materials, sat on well-tann'd hides
> Obdurate and unyielding, glassy smooth . . .   (*Poems*, II: 3–4)

So persuasive is the syntactic inscription of the "restless" chair as itself the owner of the weary loins and dangling feet that we are unsure whether to sympathize with the reposing human being or the thing being sat upon. If a chair can have a back then why not loins and feet? Thus ensues the schoolboy humor of the well-tanned hides as describing not just the chairs but the backsides of their occupants who have, by virtue of their lowly upbringing, presumably also had their share of schoolroom discipline.

Cowper's humor is not so far from Marx's in its topsy-turvy logic, which pressures the figurative and the literal to change places so that the imported luxury chair can suffer the fate of being out of place and unappreciated by the very persons whose desire for display led to its passage across the world. This is a chair that might go dancing or even have ideas. Marx's 1844 manuscripts dallied with the image of money doing all the things that human beings might have done if the political economists had not turned upside down the relation between desire and capacity: "all the things which you cannot do, your money can do. It can eat and drink, go to the dance hall and the theatre."[4] Marx's 1844 manuscripts cited Timon of Athens describing gold as that which "solder'st close impossibilities" and "mak'st them kiss." Marx's own more plainly spoken summary of Shakespeare's view of money was twofold: that it "effects the transformation of all human and natural properties into their contraries," so that "impossibilities are soldered together by it"; and that it is "the common whore, the common procurer of people and nations" (p. 324). Writing for money, in this formulation, would look like dirty work. But Marx also describes money as the "*truly creative* power." In the modern economy more and more relations are mediated through and by money, which breaks social bonds even as it seems to create them by "turning an *image into reality* and *reality into a mere image.*" The person without money is unable to realize his desires and thus remains unrecognized, "*unreal* and *objectless*," while the person who does have money becomes equally inauthentic because his "*real essential powers*" are displaced by "abstract notions" and "tormenting chimeras": he buys things instead of making them himself (p. 325). Consequently we inhabit a "world upside-down" marked by "the confounding and confusing of all natural and human qualities" and by the "fraternisation of impossibilities" where "contradictions embrace" (p. 326).

The solution to this world turned upside down (now not just the table, but the world) would be a truly human reciprocity wherein "you can exchange love only for love, trust for trust, etc." (p. 326). This would be a world without commodification and commodity form, a world that Marx's later work finds harder and harder to imagine. What would be the place, in such a world, of the figurative language we call poetry? That which yokes together heterogeneous things, whether by violence (of which Samuel Johnson accused the metaphysical poets) or by love (according to Shelley's more positive estimate), is metaphor, and metaphor is the life of poetry. Soldering things together into unpredicted unities, making opposites kiss, embracing contradictions, turning images into realities: these are variously commonplace descriptions of what metaphor does. And metaphor has always been received as at once the best and worst of devices – splendidly original when it works but maddeningly incoherent when it doesn't. Marx's human reciprocity seems to propose nothing less than a utopian supersession of the entire problem of distinguishing between the proper and improper senses of words, one that had absorbed and perplexed rhetoricians from Plato, Aristotle and Quintilian onwards as they sought to identify the point where the pleasure of apt comparison or coinage collapsed into the delirium of uncontrolled catachresis. The poetics of specification without mediation, suppressing both simile and metaphor, would come later as one element in the aesthetics of Modernism: it would tell us that a rose is a rose is a rose.[5] But this is tautology, not reciprocity. It is not an apt comparison but a refusal of comparison itself, an assertion of intransigent identity, the thing in itself as it really is, or perhaps the shimmering of sheer language. It keeps us from slipping into the "world of potential ghosts and monsters" that Paul de Man saw as latent in the "most innocent of catachreses," like the "legs of the table," but only by way of avoiding any of the risks one takes in comparing one thing with another.[6]

De Man's important essay identifies a besetting eighteenth-century concern about telling "the figurative from the proper" (p. 16), and about relating the linguistic notion of the proper (which can mean simply what is conventionally accepted) to an ontological notion of essence (p. 17). His conclusion is that these problems far exceed the limits of a finite delirium of the sort that might be resolved by historical change, and that they are intrinsic to an aporetic condition that literature only pretends that it can resolve: "contrary to common belief, literature is not the place where the unstable epistemology of metaphor is suspended by aesthetic pleasure, although this attempt is a constitutive moment of its system. It is rather the place where the possible convergence of rigor and pleasure is shown to be a delusion" (p. 28). Coleridge, whom de Man has in mind here, spoke famously of the "willing suspension of disbelief for the moment, which constitutes poetic faith," and his words have mostly been taken as the mission statement for an affirmative view of poetry of the sort that de Man has just questioned.[7] But we should notice the momentary nature of the experience Coleridge describes, as well as its reliance upon faith: it does not last and it cannot be rationally justified. Wordsworth too explores, over and over again, the effects and implications of simile and metaphor, but not in any simply affirmative spirit. The glow of creative synthesis is often darkened by the sense of misattribution. Coleridge opines that one of the major tasks of the poet is to unify things into properly ordered patterns and to involve and appease thereby "the whole soul of man" (II: 15–16); Wordsworth makes some of the same claims but also consistently sees the poet as one prone to mess around with whatever is given to him, serially adding and subtracting without necessarily producing the experience of organic completion, someone "pleased with his own passions and volitions . . . delighting to contemplate similar volitions and passions as manifested in the goings-on of the Universe, and habitually impelled to create them where he does not find them."[8] Wordsworth's primary loyalty is to the human passions and their effects, however deviant they may seem and however much dissensus they produce; Coleridge wants a psychologically satisfying completeness, a conformity of parts to wholes that is also in the last analysis a social and political harmony by way of an observed and agreed-upon precedence of wholes over parts. This difference of emphasis is behind his criticisms of Wordsworth as too idiosyncratic, tonally incoherent, out of proportion, too much given to bombast and bathos and sometimes out of line with ordinary feelings.

To tell the difference between the figurative and the proper, or to discriminate between apt and excessive metaphor, might indeed be to establish for oneself a comfortable place in the world, but Wordsworth's narrators do not manage this either when they are made invisible (as in "Poor Susan" and "The Old Cumberland Beggar") or when they are dramatically implicated (as in "The Ruined Cottage" and the "Point Rash-Judgment" poem). At his most confident moments in *The Prelude*, Wordsworth could claim that his upbringing among the lakes and mountains provided

> forms distinct
> To steady me: these thoughts did oft revolve

> About some centre palpable which at once
> Incited them to motion and control'd. (8: 598–601)

But the declared access to such a "real solid world / Of images" (ll. 604–5) almost gives itself away. Images are only solid when they are fetish forms, and things are most real when they are not images. Wordsworth did indeed allow himself to hope for and imagine a condition in which words might be "things, active and efficient," but he knew too their propensity to become dead letters, so that the poetic image for him was never a simple liberation into the realm of freedom but a confrontation with the dynamics of reification.[9] Fixed value and controlled circulation are indeed attributed to what becomes in the published *Prelude* a "substantial centre" (8: 431), a projection of foundational integrity surviving intact through time and dependent here for its credibility upon a contrast with Coleridge's predicament in the city, "disjoining, joining things / Without the light of knowledge" (ll. 609–10). But Wordsworth's rural forms were often also far from solid, positively apparitional and not at all steadying: even the mountains could come striding after him.

Marx's later writings about commodity form and Wordsworth's poetic personifications project a world in which there are few if any substantial centers. What governs circulation and perception is virtual and abstract. The device of hypotyposis that de Man borrows from Kant describes what Marx does with his figure of the table standing on its head and having ideas: "hypotyposis makes present to the senses something which is not within their reach, not just because it does not happen to be there but because it consists, in whole or in part, of elements too abstract for sensory representation" ("Epistemology of Metaphor," p. 24). We can't see it, we have to think it. The leg of the table is a bit more visible since we can see it working in the same way that a leg works. So too the dancing daffodils. But the reliability of such figures for ready recognition depends upon cliché, which only preempts considerations of impropriety by resorting to utter familiarity. They work as good coin only because they are already debased coin, because they have been handled to the point where the evidence of any act of imprinting has worn down almost to nothing: not living images but dead metaphors, stilled lives. Where the cliché is noticed for what it is, as I think it is in much of the language of "Poor Susan," then it risks being discarded as simply worn out, as too tired for poetic employment, by readers who are not willing to believe (as I do) that Wordsworth's clunky locutions might have a dramatic purpose, that they are there to signal a profound and purposive qualification of the values they appear to endorse. In the "Daffodils" poem, the effect of cliché is achieved (and was felt by the early reviewers) even as the image of dancing flowers may well have been quite new: not a restrike of old poetic metal but a fresh figure.[10]

Wordsworth frequently makes poetic drama out of giving dead things life and taking life away from the living, and in this way he makes a drama out of poetics itself. The best-known instance of this is probably in "Resolution and Independence," where the leech-gatherer strikes the poet as "not all alive nor dead." He is death-in-life and is embedded in a complex set of similes that Wordsworth himself would later (in 1815) defend and expound as a prime instance of the operations of the imagination working "either by conferring additional properties upon an object, or abstracting from it some of those it actually possesses."[11] The passage is well known but is worth citing once again:

> The stone is endowed with something of the power of life to approximate it to the sea-beast; and the sea-beast stripped of some of its vital qualities to assimilate it to the stone; which intermediate image is thus treated for the purpose of bringing the original image, that of the stone, to a nearer resemblance of the figure and condition of the aged Man; who is divested of so much of the indications of life and motion as to bring him to the point where the two objects unite and coalesce in just comparison. (*Prose Works*, III: 33)

Living and dead things, the sea-beast and the stone, are first compounded to present the stone as "endued with sense," so that the compound image can serve to explain the appearance of the old man. Here is the passage upon which Wordsworth is commenting:

> As a huge Stone is sometimes seen to lie
> Couch'd on the bald top of an eminence;
> Wonder to all who do the same espy
> By what means it could thither come, and whence;
> So that it seems a thing endued with sense:
> Like a Sea-Beast crawl'd forth, which on a shelf
> Of rock or sand reposeth, there to sun itself.
>
> Such seem'd this man, not all alive nor dead,
> Nor all asleep; in his extreme old age:
> His body was bent double, feet and head
> Coming together in their pilgrimage;
> As if some dire constraint of pain, or rage
> Of sickness felt by him in times long past,
> A more than human weight upon his frame had cast.
> (*Poems 1807*, p. 126)

The "original image" is of the stone, and the primary figuration goes on between stone and sea-beast; the old man is constructed out of the coming together of these "two objects" in "just comparison." Without him there would be no point to the two images, but it is striking that he appears last, as the product of a poeticizing mind that wants to make him the point of exchange between two otherwise heterogeneous things, stone and sea-beast. Does he underwrite their value, or they his? The poet giveth, the poet taketh away, dispensing life and death, stillness and motion, for the purposes of making a striking record of how things seemed to him at the time, given his own mood and the particular slant of light. The dramatized fallibility of the poem's narrator is fully rendered and is indeed the primary moral of the tale. We can never know whether we would have seen the old man in this same way, as a *Muselmann*, bent so fully double that the feet touch the head, an implausible and almost supernatural deformation in one so old and frail, or whether the poet is hallucinating. And yet this is a vocational distortion, fully credible as the empirical result of the labor of constant bending. All that is solid melts into air; or, to try to come a bit closer to what Marx and Engels wrote, all that is hierarchical and able to measure anything [*alles Ständische*] and all that stands upright [*und Stehende*] turns into vapor, evaporates [*verdampft*].[12]

Or perhaps turns into print. Richard Onorato has noticed the poet's allusion to the fourth book of *The Odyssey* (ll. 382f.) in making the old man look like a sea-beast.[13] Homer's Menelaus is telling Telemachus how he escaped from Pharos by capturing Proteus – he of many forms – as he comes out of the ocean and lies down among the seals. Proteus does indeed turn himself into all sorts of things in an effort to escape. But Menelaus holds fast as he changes shape and is rewarded with advice about how to leave the island. It is not just his immediate peace of mind that is thus assured; he is also promised a final, painless passage to eternal life in the happy isles. No one could hope for better news. Is it something like this that Wordsworth hopes for in latching on to another shape-shifting old man, also like a sea-beast, and in insisting on hearing his story as a means of making himself more resolute? The former leech-gatherer was as we have seen actually encountered on the public road on his way to Carlisle to buy books for reselling. He is poetically relocated to the lonely moor, situated in a landscape once again reverting to water – so that a "little pond" becomes a "moorish flood" and his voice "like a stream" (as was the dark road where the discharged soldier is encountered), – and he is projected into a future existence as a specter, pacing "About the weary moors continually / Wandering about alone and silently" (ll. 81, 114, 138).

This imagined constant circulation likens the leech-gatherer to the old Cumberland beggar and the pedlar, and thus to the money form; but the narrator himself is (as in "Gipsies") yet more closely assimilated to money as Marx described it, converting things into persons and persons into things, performing his task over and over again, repetitively and without progress, and never finally changing in himself. We should not be fooled by the rhetorical finality of the moral lessons such poems declare: the same things happen again and again, whether with the leech-gatherer, the old man traveling, the discharged soldier, the ghostly fisherman, or the gypsies. Every walk can and often does produce its Point Rash-Judgment. If these narrators and protagonists are (as Celeste Langan has argued) circulating constantly as analogues of the money form, then they do not much exemplify the liberal model of circulation made famous by Adam Smith, smoothing the wheels of commerce and disseminating positive sociability; rather, in disposing of the powers of life and death and producing death-in-life and life-in-death, they fulfill Marx's understanding of the functions of the commodity form in general.

Wordsworth's "just comparison," then, cannot repress a tendency toward the unjust: proper and improper senses tend toward each other. How can a stone have life, and how can an old man be like a stone, except in the world of fairy tale or of poetic visits to the underworld? Proteus will never stop changing because, being a god, he cannot die. Menelaus's reward for holding him fast for a moment is receiving the good news about his own eternal life. The similes deployed around the leech-gatherer suggest that poetic images are instances of death-in-life in the only world we have. If they serve in the first instance to deaden what is living, to put to death in order to effect a memorable preservation, so they also provide the matter for after-recollection and attention, in other words an afterlife for generations yet to come. Such afterlife is positive in its availability for adverting minds as yet unborn, providing not only potential personal gratifications of the sort that enable a few natural hearts to get through their days but also historical provocations that can continue to prompt general debates and forms of attention that remain empirically urgent. It is in this sense that Wordsworth's images haunt our present and our imagined future. And because poetic images live only in language, in a virtual form that must always be read and reread, they are not prone to the sorts of negative instrumentalisms that govern great buildings or political institutions. A persuasive case can be made that we exaggerate the culpability of literary forms in associating them with or even making them responsible for moral lapses and historical cruelties past and present;

it has been said that poetry's virtual existence makes it antithetical to such negative embodiment, rendering it a force antithetical to all idolatries.[14] Poetry, in this light, may by its very nature be resistant to the final reification to which its own techniques inevitably tend. But if good poetry is to escape identification with the misfiguring functions of money, turning the world upside down and robbing us of our reason, then it can only be by way of our refusal to cash in on disposable meanings and to hold back from making it fully fungible. It must as such remain irreducible to the readings generated from it and finally refuse to uphold the desire for a "substantial center."[15] If Wordsworth achieves this end, then it is not by avoidance but by immersion in the destructive element.

The radical uncertainty of Wordsworth's poetry oscillates between claims for pure aesthetic pleasure and the experience of pure bewilderment, halting the critical eye and impeding its progress to further reflection. It does not come to rest at either extreme. Adorno complained that Benjamin's account of nineteenth-century Paris was devoid of "conclusive theoretical answers" because it had fallen under the spell of the "phantasmagoria" of commodification itself, leaving Benjamin staring wide-eyed and "bewitched" at objects that conspire in "almost demonic fashion" against the possibility of their own interpretation.[16] Wordsworth knows himself to be on the edge of being bewitched, and when he falls under the spell he shows himself falling, thereby making sure that the reported events remain open to a theorization that can never be conclusive but is also because of this very openness resistant to simple buying and selling, to the computation of spiritual price and the giving of intellectual change. Wordsworthian isolation is not a matter of achieved theoretical detachment and pure critique, nor is his immersion in the encounter purely a giving way to what Benjamin describes as "empathy with the soul of the commodity" (p. 135) of the sort that Derrida also perhaps invites in making Marx's table dance when Marx himself says that it doesn't. It locates its narrator and reader in that space of the *es spukt* that Derrida described as belonging neither to us nor to it.

So, when aesthetic immersion in the world does characterize Wordsworth's poetically reported experience, it is always adjusted or admonished; the immediate spell is broken but without releasing the narrator into any space that is free of other unpredictable ghosts. To experience aesthetic detachment is to project oneself outside of space and time and to mimic a death-in-life whose social correlative is alienation, a separation from one's kind, from those who are implacably within decisive space and time. Whatever is self-protecting or assuring about this comes at the price of a corresponding reification: one cannot be touched, but neither can one come to life. In the hands of later writers and indeed some Romantics, the preoccupation with the perfectly achieved image could take the form of an aestheti*cism* that was also explicitly cast in death's likeness. Wordsworth does not commonly rest, or rest for long, in such raptures; he more often transcribes image-making as a constant process, setting out the gains and losses (as he does in his account of "Resolution and Independence") over and over again, embodied in the strenuous self-positioning of a rhetoric of "so it seemed to me" or "as I stood and gazed."[17] Here there is no peace of mind. His images are staged as always in trouble, assembled in localized sites of time and place, such that they cannot be assumed transferable to others differently localized, or indeed to the same speaker at different times. The difficulty of their generation and preservation is part of their capacity to haunt; they are never quite there, or there for very long, rendering them always about to come again, if properly conjured up. All careful reading is like this, one might say: "a masterpiece always moves, by definition, in the manner of a ghost."[18] When the formal compulsion to repeated reading is matched by a content which is itself ghostly, the masterpiece becomes symptomatically modern. The ghostliness that is always to return both reflects and seems to resist the circuits of commodity form: it confirms acts of reading as at once the critique of commodity culture (because nothing is finally consumed or cashed in) and at the same time a reinscription of the logic of commodity form as itself interminable and virtual circulation. We read from within what we behold. Wordsworth's private daffodil show proved by spooky coincidence to be one of the hottest commodities in the poetry market.

As indeed is "Resolution and Independence," where figuration again runs riot. Rousseau, in a luminous passage in the "Essay on the Origins of Language," describes how the "proper" sense of words is generated out of powerful passions that can be recognized as figurative only with the passage of time and the onset of further experience:

Upon encountering others, a savage man will at first be afraid. His fright will make him see those men as taller and stronger than himself. He will give them the name *Giants*. After many experiences he will recognize that these supposed Giants are neither taller nor stronger than himself, their stature does not agree with the idea that he had first attached to the word Giant. He will therefore invent another name common to them and to him, such as the name *man* for example, and will leave that of *Giant* for the false object that had struck him during his illusion. That is how the figurative word arises before the proper word, when passion fascinates our eyes and the first idea it offers up is not the true one.[19]

Wordsworth too, as we have seen, deals in giants – the preternaturally tall discharged soldier, the grotesquely elongated fisherman in the mist. Sometimes he is governed by fear, sometimes by excessive self-confidence, but in both instances he is operating figuratively. The soldier turns out actually to be very tall, while the fisherman may only have seemed so, but the exact relation of the attributed physical reality (the thing in itself, outside of the narrator's imagination) to the figured form is never (and cannot be) fully stated. Rousseau traffics in "false" objects and true ideas; the passage from the one to the other is nothing less than a microcosm of Enlightenment itself. Once we understand that we have been using figurative and not proper terms, a certain idea of progress comes into play. Wordsworthian narrators tend not to depart the scene with any such comforting claims to thus disenchanting the world or restraining their own wandering imaginations. Wordsworth begins with the stone and sea beast as his original and intermediary images and only then comes around to the old man who has no "proper" shape, nothing that can be held in focus for very long before it is displaced by other figures. The proper may be a worthy object for science, but it is not the stuff of a poetics of concern, which finds itself unable to call a halt to a succession of attitudes and impressions whose fluid instability is at once aesthetically stimulating and ontologically hallucinatory.

Although "Resolution and Independence" does not deal in giants – the old man first appears bent double, more like a contortionist – it certainly plays fast and loose with the interplay of living and dead images not only in its famous similes of stone and sea-beast but throughout its narrative. The poem begins by risking accusations of dealing in base coinage, both in its first stanza's slant and half rhymes (floods/woods/broods, chatters/waters – there are only four of these clashes in the whole poem, including the one that ends it) and in its recourse to platitudinous descriptions, as if to make us suspicious of the rhetorical ease with which its narrator escapes from the roaring of the wind and rain into earshot of the "pleasant noise of waters" (l. 7). This is another of Wordsworth's watery landscapes, where water seems to be out of control or beyond sure definition. The old man stands beside a "little pond or moorish flood" (l. 81), but which is it? (We will look again later in this chapter and in the next at this strange conjuration of biblical, Shakespearean and Miltonic references.) After passing through a rapid cycle of pleasure, dejection and melancholy meditation upon the fate of recently dead poets, the narrator meets his admonitory icon of death-in-life, looking like a stone that looks like a sea-beast, "not all alive nor dead," "motionless as a Cloud," and compressed into a foetal-cum-burial position, "feet and head / Coming together in their pilgrimage," which seems to mark the end of the pilgrimage of life itself (ll. 73–74). Motionless as a cloud? Clouds are not motionless, nor are they usually so figured by a poet who so famously described himself as *wandering* like a cloud. The narrator qualifies his own hyperbole by adding that a cloud does not hear the winds that move it, and moves "altogether, if it move at all," as if to assign solid and unchanging form to what is vaporous and inevitably shifting. All that turns to vapor [*verdampft*] then stands upright [*Stehende*]? He seems to want to make nature a stiller, more permanent thing than it is, but only in order to body forth, once again, the ghostliness of things, a sense only enhanced by the closer appearance of the man with "a fire about his eyes" (l. 98). Even as the old man speaks, the narrator renders him silent in his "mind's eye," seeing him "pace / About the weary moors continually, / Wandering about alone and silently" (l. 138); Wordsworth upgrades him into a Satan or Wandering Jew figure even as he performs the remarkable hypotyposis, so subtle in its ordinariness, that renders the moors themselves capable of weariness.

The narrator "could have" laughed himself to scorn, but did he? The sequence Rousseau suggests whereby primitive figuration gives way to rational taxonomy with the passage of civilizing time is not what Wordsworth represents even on those occasions where he declares himself enlightened. For him the figuring is recurrent and indeed the mechanism of enlivening an ordinary world which would otherwise remain all too ordinary, unmarked by anything of the freshness of a dream. But the dream is not distinguishable from the nightmare; what is newly seen or imagined gives rise also to a primitive fear of the unknown and unpredicted, even as the unpredicted offers the most promising material for radical thought. This is indeed the poet described in *The Prelude* as "fostered alike by beauty and by fear" (1: 306). While the shocks of not-so-mild surprise work against reification by jolting us out of the sphere of received images and ideas, they themselves, by creating more images, set going a new cycle of objectification whereby what begins as new and original ends up by virtue of its very convincingness as "dead" metaphor. Wordsworth, like Shelley, has much to say about this in his critical-theoretical voice, and it is one of the primary energies behind the poetry. In ideal situations neither function can be detached from the other: death and life interact and interchange constantly in a nonprogressive metamorphosis embodying the passage of time and the rhythm of being alive, a process without resolution. But much of the time the new images are themselves already images of death or death-in-life: their novelty takes on the quality of repetition, of seeing in the present what has emerged from the past and can only haunt the future. The task is always both to conjure life out of death and to temper the overambitious claims of pure life by tracing in it the signatures of mortality, to preserve for life the image of death, the ghostliness of things. This is, I have been arguing, no merely metaphysical insight of the sort that Heidegger would describe as man's condition "in the issuelessness of death" so that his "being-there is the happening of strangeness."[20] It is the historically exacerbated awareness of the ubiquitous deathliness of the commodity form and of the physical lives of those who work to maintain it, so that even the old leech-gatherer embodies, in the middle of a rural wilderness, something akin to a punitive labor discipline:

> As if some dire constraint of pain, or rage,
> Of sickness felt by him in times long past,
> A more than human weight upon his frame had cast (ll. 75–77)

The ghostly forms of Wordsworth's wanderers, those who tell the stories as well as those whom they are told about – "and the whole Body of the man did seem / Like one that I had met with in a dream" (ll. 115–16) – are also what Derrida called, following Marx, "the ghosts that are commodities" which only enable socialization through "spectralization."[21] The commodity does not speak, and by not hearing what the leech-gatherer says when he does speak, the narrator speeds up and contributes to the process of commodification in the pursuit of a poetry that thus calls into question its own integrity.

A SPECTACLE TO WHICH THERE IS NO END?

Wordsworth both performs and resists reproducing the deadening forces of the modern world around 1800 in a cycle of energy and entropy that never settles into a narrative of either progress or regress but that also never collapses into simple repetition. He finds himself surprised by the recurring cycle and by mortification itself, surprised enough to deem the process notable and worth recording. Around 1800 he did not yet confront the "final form" of capitalism, as Agamben (paraphrasing Debord) describes it: "an immense accumulation of spectacles, in which all that was directly lived is distanced in representation."[22] The attitude of concern does not resolve itself into definitive action (which is shown in "Simon Lee" as just another form of evasion), but neither does it commit the events by which it is aroused to a historical past, allowing them ever to be left behind. Such openness to the dynamics of non-resolution is distinctively Wordsworthian, and it allows his poems to engage with what is uncomfortable without flattening out the discomfort or effacing the history that marks the condition of concern. Perhaps surprisingly, given what I have been arguing, Wordsworth's uses of the word *spectacle* – and there are many – are often positive, and here he departs from his beloved Milton, who uses the word rarely and without any hint of approval or appreciation. The spectacle, like the "shew" of daffodils, has an inevitable association with the idea of a contrived entertainment of the sort that no good Hebraist ought to find pleasing; but as long as things keep moving, Wordsworth seems to accept it. The narrator of "Gipsies" complains that there is no change – "yea, the frame / Of the whole Spectacle the same" – but he is shown as the one who imposes fixity upon the scene. Conversely, the poet who descends into the underworld of the cavern is able to tolerate and approve both sights "like Spectres" and the ensuing "Spectacle to which there is no end."[23] He thereby distances himself from Hegel's judgment against all images and against the ancient mnemonic tradition of turning names into images for remembering as if by "shallow, silly and utterly accidental links," a verdict allied with the denigration of childhood memory as intense only because "the stage of reflection" has not yet been attained.[24] The intensity of childhood is desired even while known to be lost, and the integrity of the eye is upheld even as its tyranny is resisted.

What subsists is a conflation of movement and stillness, still enough for distinct perception to be possible and mobile enough to preempt deadened metaphor. This works against achieved idolatry and allows for something like the primitive fetishism that Marx found to be disappearing from the modern world. In primitive fetishism the subject chooses to worship an inanimate object but retains enough self-control to throw it away as soon as it fails to satisfy. Where one personification or projection gives way to another, where there is no final form or sequence set up as immune from time itself (not even that of Christianity's eternal life), then creativity has not been fully stifled; but when those different forms become simply equivalent to one another, when differences cease to be noticed or to matter, then we have passed into a world fully governed by the routines of modern commodity form. In the Platonic tradition that Derrida finds Marx inheriting, there was a conflation of *eidola* with *phantasma*, image with specter, both "determined only against the background of death."²⁵ Premodern idol worship might then have bestowed upon its icons at least the dignity of ancestor worship, a recognition of one's place in a somewhat personalized, even if mortifying, tradition: one dies in the company of kin. Wordsworth's walking death-in-life figures are strangers. They still command an intimate attention and insist on being intimate and unignorable, but they do not invite worship. England in 1800 is very different from classical Greece: acts of rhetorical imagination are now responsive to and reflective of much more powerful and impersonal social conditions. And there is no convincing access or appeal to worlds other than the one we have, "the very world, which is the world / Of all of us."²⁶

What then renders Wordsworth's account of the making and unmaking of images so critical and critically historical is that it confronts the constraints of commodity form as *becoming* fully habitual and normative: it reproduces them but always with a staged awareness of doing so. At a later stage of modernity's evolution, when commodity form had become much more powerful, Adorno found that Benjamin had fully capitulated to it, and in the same terms he complained of the phantasmagoric aura of Wagner's art as the result of "the occultation of production by means of the outward appearance of the product," so that "the object that he has forgotten he has made is dangled magically before his eyes, as if it were an absolutely objective manifestation."²⁷ In Wordsworth the transcription of production is everywhere. He does make his own spectacles, and he is mistrustful of what he makes, aware that mere imaginative effort does not alone exempt the poet from the circle of commodification. Guy Debord would identify the dominance of the spectacle as symptomatic of the moment at which "the commodity has attained the *total occupation* of social life," at which point "everything that was directly lived has moved away into a representation" and takes its place in the "autonomous movement of the non-living" arrayed in "*frozen time*."²⁸ Wordsworth records the imminence and coming into being of this world but does not yet reflect or accept its definitive articulation. All the signs are there, and Wordsworth's narrators take all the false steps that come from following them, but they are not yet completely aligned in the same single direction. This residual indecision reflects the historical onset of a new and estranging world, but one that has not yet fully pervaded the whole lifeworld.

The encounter with death-in-life, for example, can even be adjusted to the apparatus of comedy and thus to the prospect of an alternative life. There is such a case in the second book of *The Excursion*, which opens with Wanderer and narrator walking through the landscape and dispensing suspiciously uncomplicated homilies about the past lives of strolling minstrels, the contemporary pleasures of rambling and the virtues of charity. They come upon a village "wake" whose positive sense here (as fair or festival) overrides and overwrites for the moment any hint of funereal ritual, although the scene is portentously "Half-veiled in vapoury cloud" (2: 131): a clue, given what we have seen elsewhere of such vapors, of something else to come. The narrator is tempted to linger but the Wanderer resists him with a short lecture on the importance of sticking to one's schedule in life, for they are on their way to meet the Solitary whose own story is then summarized. As they walk toward his dwelling across a "dreary plain" (l. 324) whose allegorical portent is already familiar from Book 1 (the rewrite of "The Ruined Cottage"), they enter an ominously figurative high valley: "Urn-like it was in shape, deep as an urn" (l. 332). The simile here picks up on the previously disavowed sense of "wake" (the logic of the *pharmakon* must unfold) as they do indeed then hear the approach of a "funeral dirge" (l. 376).[29] The Wanderer is quick to infer that this must signal the death of the person they have come to see, and thus sets up the narrator to witness another of the "moving spectacles" (l. 491) of the sort he has earlier projected in the story of Margaret. So it is with comic abruptness that the Solitary himself strides into view: "Behold the Man whom he had fancied dead" (l. 497).

This is comedy indeed, but the ironies are profound. The Wanderer has already put the Solitary to death in his own judgmental imagination by pronouncing him a disciple of Voltaire, a man "hardened by impious pride" (l. 486) while wasting his time "steeped in a self-indulging spleen" (l. 311). The ready presumption of his death is the apt imagination of a moralizing narrator who cannot seem to wait to be proven right: death-in-life has died after all, and so perish all infidels! The poet-narrator's corrective apostrophe, "behold the man," mimics the *ecce homo* announced by Pilate as he brings Jesus before the priests and officers who cry "crucify him, crucify him" (John 19: 5). So if the narrator is a Pilate figure then the Wanderer, who has already put the Solitary to death in his own mind and judgment, takes on the role of the priests, the upholders of the old law and the dispensers of the death penalty. His self-confident righteousness teeters throughout the poem on the edge of unappealing certitude; here it aligns him with those who are sure enough of themselves to put to death the founder of the same Christian faith he himself avows.

Things get yet more complicated as the poet-narrator explains *how* he recognizes the Solitary:

> I knew from his deportment, mien and dress,
> That it could be no other; a pale face,
> A meagre person, tall, and in a garb
> Not rustic – dull and faded like himself. (ll. 498–501)

Here again is a discharged soldier, old beggar and fisherman lookalike, a specter, still a figure of death-in-life even as he has been comically just restored to life in a narrative that assumed him dead. This attribution is in turn itself subverted by the invocation of a Luciferic energy:

> Vivid was the light
> That flashed and sparkled from the other's eyes;
> He was all fire: no shadow on his brow
> Remained, nor sign of sickness on his face. (ll. 514–17)

He passes from life to death to half-life to incandescent energy and seemingly eternal life, all in the space of this first brief encounter. All fire indeed, beyond aging, and roving still about the world like his Satanic alter-ego, or like the leech-gatherer who also had "a fire about his eyes" and who was imagined wandering "about the weary moors continually." At no point in the poem does the Solitary settle into final form or simple moral identity: he is always to be found triangulated between the self-righteous disapproval of the Wanderer and the vaguely admonishing but still hesitant gaze of the poet-narrator who seems to want to follow his Virgil but has yet some small signs of a mind of his own. This spectacle proves to be moving in a sense rather different from the one proposed by the Wanderer, who has in mind another morally uplifting encounter with human suffering; it becomes instead mobile, mysterious and inaccessible to final solutions.

Contradictions continue to emerge. Despite living within what the poet-narrator describes as a "wreck" (l. 660) of disorderly objects whose description would fit right into the most severe of George Crabbe's renderings of the cottages of the undeserving poor, the Solitary is able to play the "courteous Host" (l. 672) and to produce both clean napkins and delicious fresh food. Furthermore, he goes on to tell the story (ll. 730–95) of the man whose funeral they have just witnessed and to reveal that his own contribution to the sustenance of old age was considerably more active and engaged than was the Wanderer's for Margaret in her cottage on its way to ruin. The Wanderer, despite his self-declared tolerance, tends to discover differences in kind, differences between the saved and the damned and between good and evil: this certitude also informed his attempt in Book 1 to proffer the image of the cottage as, in Alan Liu's words, a "separate principle of form," an inalienable property whose value could not be detached from it and that thereby provided an assured possession of metaphysical "richness."[30] Liu suggests that this was a Wordsworthian initiative and thus aligns the poet with his protagonist, so that what is "shockingly dehumanizing" (p. 320) about imagery is something of which Wordsworth is implicitly not conscious.[31] The Wanderer/pedlar may indeed be imperfectly dramatic, to the point that readers are likely to continue to identify him with the poet, a tendency embodied in the narrator's own unsure relation to his mentor (which is thereby one of concern). But he becomes more and more dramatic in the later drafts of the poem and in Book 1 of *The Excursion*, so that we miss a rich vein of comic meaning if we align ourselves uncritically with him and with the biblical priests who "behold the man." We also commit ourselves to not-so-comic judgments that stem in their psychic operations from the worship of graven images and preestablished moral laws. This understanding retroactively calls into question the "so still an image of tranquillity" at the end of "The Ruined Cottage" and the first book of *The Excursion* (l. 946), that which allows the Wanderer/pedlar to view Margaret's tragedy as an instance of the "idle dream" of "passing shows of Being" and to compose himself into a state of nothing less than "happiness" (1: 951–52, 956). This is not company that we should passively opt to keep, nor do I think that Wordsworth finds himself comfortable with it either.

The comic or ironic framing of these spectacles and specters allows the poet to explore the undecidable and unpredictable limits of substitutability. The narrator who accompanies and reports on the Wanderer moves between approval and hesitant disapproval, both attracted to and suspicious of his emphatically resolute personality. The narrator cannot maintain the position of radical detachment and theoretical clarity that the Wanderer himself demonstrates, but neither can he identify with his stern companion: to do so would be to accede to a reified moral order and a fully habituated world. It is the Wanderer who returns to the ruined cottage in order to reaffirm its value as an unchanging commodity for gratifying the feelings, while it is Wordsworth who writes and publishes the poem, inscribing his narrator as an indecisive figure who is not sure of his affiliation to the story but who is still open to experiencing radical distress. The distress is both the fear of a failing career (the poet's calling) *and* the revived imagination of Margaret's life and death: the dynamics of concern establish both motivations as foundational insofar as the narrator really can imagine being Margaret or sharing her fate. The Wanderer cannot do so; he is immune to radical concern and as such is the poem's covert harbinger of death and death-in-life, as befits his career identification with the abstract circulation of goods. Wordsworth does not yet confirm the existence of the world Debord would describe, one where *all* life has become death and where "the spectacle in general, as the concrete inversion of life, is the autonomous movement of the non-living."[32] The effort at separation of subject and object that Wordsworth's narrators inscribe only to undermine, becoming what they behold and alienating what they think to become, still carries the energy of resistance to a condition of undifferentiated complicity in a diminished lifeworld. But Wordsworth does project as an evolving tendency the modern condition described by Debord wherein any effort to describe the spectacle speaks its language and "moves through the methodological terrain of the very society which expresses itself in the spectacle" (#11). The relationship that obtains here is "the opposite of dialogue" (#18); active living is displaced by "contemplation" as the subject's gestures "are no longer his own but those of another who represents them to him. This is why the spectator feels at home nowhere, because the spectacle is everywhere" (#30).

Homelessness again, and again commodification – because the spectacle, like the commodity, cannot be owned or inhabited but only experienced at a distance and as distance. For Wordsworth, "contemplation" has both an inward and outward sense: one contemplates something *in* the world and takes it into oneself as a way of withdrawing *from* the world. The Wanderer, always the most rhapsodically abandoned of Wordsworth's characters and the one who pushes what may seem to be received Wordsworthian doctrine to the point of its own hyperbolic collapse, invokes "contemplation" as an external entity or personified agent which he bids locate itself in the Solitary's high valley, though in a manner quite foreign to what the Solitary himself wishes to find there. Here is the Wanderer's Miltonic apostrophe:

> – "Hail Contemplation! From the stately towers
> Reared by the industrious hand of human art
> To lift thee high above the misty air
> And turbulence of murmuring cities vast;
> From academic groves, that have for thee
> Been planted, hither come and find a lodge
> To which thou mayst resort for holier peace, –

> From whose calm centre thou, through height or depth,
> Mayst penetrate, wherever truth shall lead;
> Measuring through all degrees, until the scale
> Of time and conscious nature disappear,
> Lost in unsearchable eternity!" (*Excursion*, 3: 101–12)

Deciphering as we must the contorted inversions of this high-pitched song, we can see traces of the narrator of *The Prelude* standing before the convent of Chartreuse and expressing similar desires for the place of eternity in time. But whereas Wordsworth confronted the ghostliness of things with an acknowledgment of his deep divisions and confusions about the boundaries between life and death and by extension between commodified and uncommodified imagination, the Wanderer more resembles one of Milton's angels (bad or good) lifting us up above the world and its "misty air" and tempting or inviting us to some sort of "calm centre" that does not admit any contiguity with either unseemly pride or imminent death. He mimics also Spenser's personification of contemplation as an old man (in *The Faerie Queene*, 1: x) who directs Redcrosse *toward* the city that is the new Jerusalem. The Wanderer's religiosity is more obscure than Spenser's, its model of eternity "unsearchable." We are left with inflation itself as a sort of free-standing literary effect. No wonder, then, that "a pause ensued" before the mundanely "courteous voice" of the Solitary resumes the conversation and reminds us that men see things according to their moods, so that this same scene can as well produce "depression" as "delight" (l. 155).

The Wanderer's investment in contemplation can thus seem far too sure of itself, and as such it bespeaks the brittle objectification that Debord claimed to be typical of a world in which dialogue and active living have been displaced. Lukács had made "contemplation" the hallmark of an alienated existence which in mature capitalism came to govern not only the position of the worker in relation to his automated labor but more generally that of the bureaucrat as he performed his tasks and watched himself perform them without either energy or creativity.[33] Margaret with her rope of hemp (or flax), the hunger-bitten girl being led by her heifer, the old Cumberland beggar on his rounds and the leech-gatherer in the mind's eye of the narrator all have this quality. They are the workers. The Wanderer too, as overseer, projects himself beyond time as the panoptical companion of that "contemplation" which stands at the "calm centre" and sees all the "truth" that goes on around it, but he thereby signals his own attitudinal abstraction and alienation. This kind of achieved contemplation is the dissolution of concern. Wordsworth seldom attains such lordship and mastery and when he does it is never for very long. He passes in and out of identification with the leech-gatherer, never fully either merging or maintaining complete detachment. Even when his narrator does not write himself into the drama of description, remaining aloof and quite literally overseeing as he does in "Poor Susan" and in "The Old Cumberland Beggar," there is a latent transcription of involvement. In "Poor Susan" this comes with the strident use of cliché and with the hyperbolic allusions to the seas of print that threaten to cover the street; in "The Old Cumberland Beggar," it is the grotesquerie of the old man's poeticized dismemberment that makes it impossible to ignore the role of the excited and dismayed observer writing the poem. Similarly self-conscious projections govern the spectral forms of soldier and fisherman as the figures of death-in-life and the sad sufferers of occupational mutilations.

Wordsworth profiled the world to come when he pondered a future governed by the "craving for extraordinary incident which the rapid communication of intelligence hourly gratifies."[34] But he was not yet ready to propose the full saturation of life with the deathly function of the commodity form, even as he intuits the proleptic symptoms of exactly that. There is a hesitation or indecision, an effort to postulate some openness to the making of images and to meditating upon them. Images and spectacles are not just or not only the negatively reified phenomena of panoramas and dumb-shows described in Book 7 of *The Prelude* but also the stuff of positive recollection and recreation, for instance as "living images" coming back to life in healthful ways and capable of "everlasting motion" and "deathless spirit" (6: 313; 1: 431; 5: 17). Images preordained in the mind can fall away and create disappointment, as at Yarrow and beneath Mont Blanc, but rich amends may still be forthcoming, new sets of images more promising for sustaining a creative mind through the passage of time. But then what is posited is often also in turn retracted or opened to question: the invocation of a "deathless spirit" is but *The Prelude*'s prelude to a meditation upon what perishes (5: 20ff.). The reported "rich amends" and reconcilement to realities that follow the disappointment of seeing Mont Blanc (6: 460ff.) has an aura of routine pastoral cliché – birds warbling, reapers binding sheaves – that, like the corresponding passages in "Poor Susan," too strongly aver their own adequacy and seem to refer to a world of nature that is not so much seen as read about in bad books.

The clichés we have seen at work in the "green pastures" and cottage-as-dove's-nest in "Poor Susan" and in the sight of the landscape below Mont Blanc work to distance the narrator (and not just his readers) from his own rhetoric and to mark it as the debased coin of a commercial poetry market while admitting that he may have no other recourse. He is, implacably, one among the *lumpen*. But there are other points at which nature has gone dead, or generates deathliness, that are among the high points of the Wordsworth canon. These passages do not employ playful and controlled allusions to a poetic diction commodified by others in a corrupted print market, and their importance suggests a more profound response whereby commodity form cannot be identified as simply the territory of the other. Sometimes it seems that deathliness is precisely what is admired, whether as memento mori or as emblem of endurance: Wordsworth often cannot have the one without the other. Such is the case with "Yew Trees," a poem whose importance as ghost story was brought out in a major essay by Geoffrey Hartman some years ago.[35] Hartman explored the spookiness of the personification whereby the human presence of the narrator is expunged and "the yews make a ghost of the speaker" (p. 133) in "some of the most ghostly poetry ever written" (p. 150). The poet, devoid of body or location, seems "to speak to us from the grave" (p. 136). The first transcript of the poem does not even fall into narrative or grammatical form, so hesitant is it to evoke anything modeling the passage of earthly time, so apparently determined to instance an eternity on the page.[36] Sentence fragments succeed one another but never make sentences, just as the body parts of the old Cumberland beggar or the fisherman in the mist seem never to make up a conventional human form in the eyes of their excited or benumbed beholders. "Yew Trees" parallels "Poor Susan" and "The Old Cumberland Beggar" in its elision of the place of narration, and even more obviously than those poems, it specifies its object as death-in-life. The first tree stands "in the midst of its own darkness" (p. 606) making darkness visible and itself visible as darkness, even though neither can, according to the limits of common sense, be *seen*. The tree is "living" but yet "produced too slowly ever to decay" and therefore not really living; the other yew trees provide the stage for a dance of death where "Ghostly Shapes / May meet at noontide" – the same noontide that befuddled the wits of the narrator of "The Ruined Cottage" with infernal imaginations. In its conflation of the living with the dead, of the already dead with the undead, the poem precisely recalls the scene at the convent of Chartreuse where the narrator celebrated the "ghostliness of things" and yet drew back from full immersion in its dark environs, looking to an alternative nature that, he avowed, could not know death, even as he named it Vallombre. Wordsworth's note on "Yew Trees" mentions a fallen tree that "must have been as old as the Christian era" as if it were a building, a convent or temple perhaps: "great masses of its ruins were strown about" (*Poems 1807*, p. 680). In this poem the evergreens that were dramatically misdescribed in *The Prelude* (1850) as "unapproachable by death" (6: 467) are specifically described as *always* dying and killing off the grass beneath them "By sheddings from the pining umbrage tinged / Perennially." Vallombre returns, and wins. What speaks here is neither fully tree nor narrator but something that is both and neither, something outside or beyond. The commodity does not speak, but if it could, it might sound (or look, from within its own darkness) something like this.[37]

TIME AND TIDINGS

There is in Book 10 of *The Prelude* a "spot-of-time" event (though it is not named as such) that sets out an uncommonly complex staging of the life and death of images – stilled lives and living images. It reports the scene in which the narrator first heard of the death of Robespierre while crossing Leven Sands. The story evolves from within the poet's narrated memories of France during the Terror. This larger story is halted in order to begin a "separate chronicle" of how and when Wordsworth heard the first report (in August 1794) that Robespierre and his faction were gone, that "this foul tribe of Moloch was o'erthrown" (10: 468). The poet is back in England though "gone abroad" (l. 471) from one village to another – the first of many stunning shifts of place and time. Everything seems easy and untroubled across "smooth Sands" and under "genial sun," though the rhetoric is even more than usually encrusted with and extruded through the Miltonic lexicon and especially through *Paradise Lost*, as if to advertise an imminent exploration of darker legacies. The light on the mountains is "like a diadem / Or crown of burning seraphs" (ll. 481–82) and the narrator gazes at this "fulgent spectacle" which "neither changed, nor stirred, nor passed away" (like Debord's "equilibrium of frozen time"), going on his way with "a fancy more alive" (ll. 486–88): a happy conversion of arrested time to enlivened temporality. But the unchanging state brings death upon the scene as we learn that the narrator's destination had been the grave of a beloved schoolmaster in Cartmell, one who has indeed "passed away" and does not stir but whose voice came back to him after "full eight years" while he stood before the grave (l. 503). There is, then, no earthly paradise. Time has, at the same time, both passed and not passed, and what has passed (his teacher) is offset by a return from the dead that is both compensatory and disturbing, "so that some few tears / Fell from me in my own despite" (ll. 505–6). The sense of stopping time is here welcomed and not deplored (as it was in "Gipsies") – all is "gentleness and peace" (l. 517) – but time does not stop. It begins to threaten movement in the image of crowds of travelers crossing the sands while the tide is out and the "great Sea . . . at safe distance, far retired" (ll. 528–29). Wordsworth wants to stop time once again, being "unwilling to proceed" (l. 530), but that tide must turn and the travelers must hurry. And it is just then that Wordsworth hears the "tidings" (l. 537) of Robespierre's death, and himself opts to speed up time – like a machine running out of control – in his "Hymn of triumph": "Come now ye golden times" (ll. 541–43). What he conjures up is an automated pattern of unimpeded progress, a providential engine allowing earth to "march firmly toward righteousness and peace" (l. 552). The predicted homogeneous motion of history is, however, articulated in "bursts" that are "uneasy" (l. 557) and that give way to yet another memory of passing along this same route as a schoolboy in a "wantonness of heart," one that recalls *Comus* by way of the recollected noise and revelry of a "joyous Crew" (l. 563).

The whole interpellated "separate chronicle" ends with evoking those schoolboys of past times who – perhaps before the death of their teacher (William Taylor) in 1786 when Wordsworth was sixteen – "beat with thundering hoofs the level Sand" (l. 566). *Beat* is one of those happy verbs that stays the same in present and historic tenses: we are out of time again. And this last line, which ends Book 10 in the published (1850) *Prelude*, happens to repeat verbatim line 144 of Book 2, as if two moments in the time of the writing of the poem are also collapsed into one along with the onset of the memory that is being written about. This entire episode is all about time and its embedding in the condition of mortal and perhaps sinful man: it is hard to avoid sensing a reference to the primal flood in the waters of the "great Sea" that may put the travelers at risk. The domestic scene is no more immune to death and destruction than were Robespierre and France, an alignment hinted at in William Taylor's reported comment to the young Wordsworth just before his death: "My head will soon lie low" (l. 501), as low as those of guillotined politicians. Personal and national-political history come together here, as do different times and places. The years 1786 and 1794, England and France, as well as the later time of writing, are all mixed up together in a poetic event that records neither progressive history nor frozen time but something between the two. The passage, indeed, from "traveling smoothly o'er the level Sands" (l. 507) by way of fantasies of marching "firmly toward righteousness and peace" (l. 552) to the recollection of a prior time when schoolboys "beat with thundering hoofs the level Sand" (l. 566) embodies a reading back through visions of unending peace and pleasure to memories of a more energized and turbulent "wantonness of heart" that is a more suitable analogue to the real history of men on earth. It is less paradisal than Satanic, taking us back to those "burning seraphs" (l. 482) whose biblical function is to display a vision of the Lord to Isaiah and to cleanse him of his sins by placing a burning coal upon his mouth (Isaiah 6: 1–6). In *Paradise Lost* it is Abdiel who is the "flaming seraph" warning Satan of his coming crime (5: 875); the "fiery seraphim" who surround him during the Stygian council (2: 512) are ambiguously both the fallen angels themselves and those sent by God to keep him in his place. Miltonic allusions in this passage of *The Prelude* seem to gather most obviously around the devilish figure of Robespierre, the leader of the "foul Tribe of Moloch" (l. 468), but it is the narrator who witnesses the "fulgent spectacle" in the sky and who is caught desiring no time when he was not as now. The density of this spot of time memorializes that desire (also a desire for an end to history) and holds it up to an implacable mortality that invokes another flaming brand, the one that forbids reentry into paradise. Death is at once regretted (William Taylor) and celebrated (Robespierre) and perhaps again willed forth in the shape of a spectacle which "neither changed, nor stirred, nor passed away" (l. 487).

This is extraordinary poetry whose depths I have only begun to fathom (and I will return to Leven Sands in my last chapter). Putting together the desired death of a bad man alongside that of a loved and admired teacher while alluding also to the passage of the poet's own lifespan and the grander hopes of global political change (and their well-known disappointment long before the time of writing), this passage, like the "spots of time," confronts explicitly the complex implications of wishing for either modified time or timelessness, and it reminds us that death-in-life is more than a merely rhetorical figuration. The inconstancies of imagined political time – passing all too slowly during the revolutionary phase governed by Robespierre but speeding up into a progressive history after his death – image an uneven development that governs both the personal life and the historical condition. Between and among these temporalities there is that of the narrator rediscovering not just a memory of youth but the exact *phrasing* of a prior moment in the writing of the poem. This is not cliché but repetition of an even more startling order: a citation of oneself. Here indeed is the moment that fulfills one fantasy of the spot-of-time motif: that something might emerge from the storehouse of the memory that turns out to be worth exactly what it was when it was deposited there. An apparently uncomplicated still-life moment where the narrator beholds a glorious sky turns out to be latent with past and future time. Meanwhile the great sea waiting to flood in and the fulgent spectacle of fiery seraphim introduce an empirical urgency and a literary-mythological overlay reminding us that human vision can only process experience in human ways and under human conditions. Death-in-life and life-in-death are not separable for mortal beings. No more separable are life and literature.

Devotees of the heritage-industry incarnation of Wordsworth would do well to look closely at his account of crossing Leven Sands and at other poems and passages that resemble it. The location into which the tidings flow in from France is a "far-secluded privacy" (l. 473) even by Lakeland standards, but it does not keep out the "rapid communication of intelligence" about the "great national events" that played its part in pressuring the mind with a power "unknown to former times."[38] Why else would Wordsworth remember "carelessly" asking a fellow traveler "If any news were stirring" (ll. 532–33)? He got what he asked for. Robespierre was executed on July 28, 1794. According to Mark Reed, the first English newspaper report was on August 16 – a delay presumably to be attributed to the difficulty of sending out information in wartime. Reed thinks that Wordsworth got the news on August 19 or 20, three or four days after the story broke in London.[39] By today's standards this is not exactly "rapid communication," but it does speak for the penetration of even the most far-flung regions by important "intelligence." Those "Coaches, Wains, and Travellers" (l. 525) hurrying across the sands before the tide turns are presumably engaged just as vigorously as their peers in the streets of London in the trucking and bartering of a modern commercial economy, and they would be obvious conduits of important tidings. Just as striking as the fact of transmission is Wordsworth's appetite for the news. In this he was perfectly representative of a culture which, according to J. Paul Hunter, had become attuned to responding to breaking news since the first daily papers began to appear in 1702 along with an increase in printed gossip, crime and disaster narratives and a pamphlet literature reporting on various ephemera of the day.[40] Stuart Sherman has since argued that the popularity of journal and travel writing in the eighteenth century habituated readers to a new notion of punctilious time, a "new precedence of measure over occasion."[41] He suggests that the postal service and the newspaper industry developed symbiotically, each dependent upon and flourishing with the other and together creating and sustaining a national appetite for the latest news (pp. 119–21). The syndrome was then not new to Wordsworth's generation: close to the start of the century, Addison had remarked on the incidence of a "perpetual Gape after Knowledge."[42] But improved roads and coach transport meant that London newspapers could travel more quickly by 1800. In a superb reading of Cowper's *The Task*, Kevis Goodman has shown the close affiliation between newspapers and high poetry: Cowper was an avid reader of the press and mined it for all sorts of poetic material, thus challenging in the 1780s the precise distinction between slow and fast reading and high and popular culture that Wordsworth worked so hard to refine and reestablish in competition with those "frantic novels" and "deluges of idle and extravagant stories in verse."[43]

Poetry *as* news, and in competition *with* the news: this is a fascinating connection, and says much about the atmosphere in which Wordsworth – a poet who was by no means as hostile to appearing in the newspapers as he sometimes suggested[44] – imagined on poor Susan's behalf those "bright volumes of vapour" gliding through Lothbury. The same connection informs the story of crossing Leven Sands, where the more than usually extravagant allusions to Milton rub against the brute, almost Gothic fascination of the news of the death of the leader of the "atheist crew" (10: 457), which is later displaced (as it was in lived time prefigured) by the "joyous Crew" (l. 563) of the poet's remembered youth. And it goes some way toward explaining why the deceased schoolmaster William Taylor meant so much to Wordsworth, for he had arranged for "a fragment from the Elegy of Gray" (l. 499) to be carved on his tomb:

> I thought with pleasure of the Verses, graven
> Upon his Tomb-stone, saying to myself
> He lov'd the poets, and if now alive
> Would have lov'd me, as one not destitute
> Of promise, nor belying the kind hope
> Which he had form'd, when I, at his command,
> Began to spin, at first, my toilsome Song. (10: 508–14)

Why Gray's elegy? The most popular and arguably hackneyed citation of the later eighteenth century and, according to John Guillory, the centerpiece of innumerable schoolbooks and manuals of style and elocution?[45] Is this the company Wordsworth wishes to keep – a disciple of that Thomas Gray whose sonnet on the death of Richard West he had publicized as exhibit A in the attack on poetic diction mounted in the Preface to *Lyrical Ballads*? The same Thomas Gray who was there exposed as "at the head of those who, by their reasonings, have attempted to widen the space of separation betwixt Prose and Metrical composition, and was more than any other man curiously elaborate in the structure of his own poetic diction"?[46] Or is it that, in such straightened times, any poetry, even poetry as old news, is better than none? Wordsworth is curiously elaborate in deploying the thick Miltonic encrustations marking almost every other line in this episode of his poem. Is he edging toward a confession of complicity with his own arch enemy, an admission of his own participation in a print culture that is full of citation, secondariness, and indeed (on this occasion) breaking news? Taylor said, we recall, that his head "would soon lie low" (l. 501) – as low as Robespierre's. The good man and the bad come together in death. So too perhaps the poet aspiring to be different is taxed by a suspicion that he is more of the same, spinning (as Margaret spins her flax) a "toilsome" song, the product of a labor painful to both writer and reader. And to be sure, Wordsworth was not wholly hostile to Gray, whose posthumously published *Journal of a Tour to the Lakes* he cited approvingly in his own *Guide to the Lakes*, and whose "Elegy" is used for the epigraph to one of his *Essays on Epitaphs*. Wordsworth might well indeed have envied one who did not for the most part write for money and did not himself (unlike Wordsworth) even bother to publish the journal of his tour to the lakes.

We cannot come away from thus reading the story of crossing Leven Sands with any simple model of a poet who merely desires a world now gone or fast disappearing – a detached participant in the endorsement of village culture over cosmopolitan anomie that took on definitive shape in the nineteenth century. Nor is Wordsworth given to expressions of the sorts of time–space compression deployed in late twentieth-century magic realism, where characters live improbably long or eternal lives and ignore all the laws of gravity, friction and inertia, and where the global system is imaged as marvelously unable to puncture the quality of imaginative life (magical indeed) and story-spinning energy in those far-flung corners of the earth that are empirically, economically and politically now increasingly subject to the undifferentiating laws of capital and commodity. Time indeed seems to stop or to have stopped and to be exfoliated into a protected space, but it is always restarted, and often jump-started, in ways that dramatize unevenness, substitutability and concern. Paul de Man made an insightful case for Romanticism as fixated on the idea of the image as a replacement for the lost object and therefore a sign and focus of nostalgia for both the object and for its origins.⁴⁷ The images of magic realism may then be read as the last best instances of this Romanticism, but it is not Wordsworth's. The celebratory or vivifying component of magic realism that makes magic itself the backbone of its stories is not what we find in the Wordsworthian incarnation even of slow time or still life. There the figure is that of death-in-life, where the staging of narrative action and responsibility cannot keep apart bringing to life and putting to death. Nor is there final endorsement of any trope of resurrection to conjure away the paradox. The leech-gatherer must be drained of life so that the narrator and his poem can live, and his attitude of profound contemplation is one imposed upon him both by his work discipline and by the yet more contemplative professional poet; and the lack of embodied charity toward the fisherman in the mist signals his prime function as that of a figment or specter and one made so by the ramblers, never alive but haunting forever, a living image of a stilled life, still hungry and still in need, an enduring icon of unexpended social concern.

Still ... the word speaks volumes, and never more fully than in Wordsworth's poetry. A still life is life still, or as much of it as a poet can have after the event and as much as his readers can have in the afterlife of a poet's allotted span. *Still* deploys a powerful ambiguity in English, one beloved of its poets and playing between adverbial and adjectival senses: generations of student readers have cut their critical teeth on Keats's "still unravished bride of quietness." In Wordsworth's more than beloved *Paradise Lost*, the double sense is peculiarly apt because it specifies the manner in which earthly and eternal time overlap in the career of the fallen angels. When Satan is "still" doing (i.e. yet doing) something, and doing it in the assumption that he may not do it forever, he is thinking of himself as still governed by the opportunities afforded by historical time, but he is in the reader's godlike eye *stilled*, inert and frozen, caught for all time in a posture of eternal death-in-life, with no prospect of change. He appears thus on the fringe of paradise and beholding the sexual bliss of the first couple yet unfallen, "Satan still in gaze, as first he stood / Scarce thus at length failed speech recovered sad" (4: 356–57); and again later, as he "still unfulfilled with pain of longing pines" (4: 511). Such instances are numerous and need not be exhaustively listed here: suffice it to say that the Miltonic precursor works extensively for Wordsworth but does so without the imprimatur of a theological irony and of a theological certitude: three closely printed columns of the concordance list Wordsworth's uses of "still," and that is only a partial listing. The inertia of being is underwritten by the suspension of action, as if in a spot of time.

So the leech-gatherer references not only his endurance through time but his figure in the space made by the poet's (and perhaps the incautious reader's) eye, his death-image, as he comments on the vanishing creatures he hunts: "yet still I persevere, and find them where I may."[48] In "The Old Cumberland Beggar," the word occurs four times, three of them registering both the continued activity of a protagonist in time and the fixedness of a still life out of time: thus the beggar, "still attempting to prevent the waste," is too still to stop it. In "The Brothers" the pathos of the double reading is almost unbearable as the returned seaman, Leonard Ewbank, is introduced "still lingering" by the grave of the dead brother whose image is a stream "flowing still" and who held until death his absent brother "still . . . at his heart" until he himself dies after being "still . . . unheard of."[49] The first book of *The Prelude* works the "stolen boat" episode to conflate the still increasing size of the cliff with its portent of punishment and death, "growing still in stature," and the same effect is used twice in the ice-skating scene (1: 409, 481–84). Perhaps most evocatively of all, the narrator who describes himself as one who "roamed from hill to hill, from rock to rock / Still craving combinations of new forms" (11: 191–92) is through his greed and craving for images at once the Satan figure who is in *Paradise Regained* (1: 33–34) "roving still / About the world" disposing death around him and stilled in this very movement, as well as (when he finds forms that are healthfully new) his creative antidote. He is fallen man, who is neither uncontaminated nor completely beyond hope, but whose lifeworld reflects the radical historical changes that make hope harder to maintain.

Wordsworth was not alone in his predilection for stopping time and for figuring his landscapes as stilled lives. The novels of Walter Scott and his American epigone James Fenimore Cooper continue to frustrate those readers who like a fast-paced story by stopping them in their tracks and embellishing a "scene" in every minute detail, as in the opening pages of *Ivanhoe* or the banqueting episode of *Waverley*. Cooper's stories seem to slow down to the most minimal motion as he regales us with the microscopic progress of an Indian through the underbrush. John Clare's poems can have the same effect, but it is in the cause of a scrupulous naturalism that is never devoid of the signs of life. With Scott and Cooper and with the Gothic novels from which they have learned their trade, it is as if we move from language to painting, from the temporal succession of syntax and the orderings of grammar to the projection of a visual field that we could take in all at once if it were not for the fact that we have only the words to imagine it, one at a time and bit by bit. The historical analogues here are the commercial panoramas where three dimensions were squeezed into two, and the dumb shows where what is dead is made to look like it is living (and vice versa), except of course that nothing in a novel is ever alive.[50] The structurally ironic, self-conscious interposition of the set pieces reminds us – and in a good story such reminders are always needed – that we are in the realm of artifice, and that the story we have temporarily left hanging is no less artificial than the interlude we feel being forced upon us. The visible commodity form of the interlude, which signals its affiliations with the panorama or the painting, only exposes the less apparent identity of the story as something other than a slice of life.

Wordsworth writes more naturalistically than Scott, with fewer unmissable signals of the artificiality of it all, but in Wordsworth too there is no easy adjudication of a clear and distinct difference between still (and stilled) lives and living images, and correspondingly no clear position of right reason and unencumbered, disinterested vision given to the poet with which to analyze commodity culture and the forms of social justice and injustice it sustains. We are so attuned to familiarized (and fully commodified) expressions of nostalgia for a past time that we tend not to make sense of the specific features of Wordsworth's engagement with time as something newly urgent in historical terms and something not psychoanalytically normative. What tells us that we are not yet in the world of uncontested postmodernity is Wordsworth's reluctance to settle for the "endless, unreal circulation" that Baudrillard finds in Los Angeles, or for the "single planetary petty bourgeoisie" of Agamben's potentially regnant community.[51] Death-in-life still surprises in its threatened ubiquity, as does the social distinction it displaces, and putting to death is of serious concern to a poet who wants to give life and thought for future years while still fearing himself and the historically prescient chthonic functions of his own creative mind. Just as images of life are shadowed by inseparable invocations of death, so the accounts of first-hand experience are mediated by the legacies of books, which are at once lifeless and sustaining of life. The letter killeth, but there is no spirit without the letter, and because of this the spirit never simply lives. We turn finally to books, and to their contribution to the qualities of Wordsworth's still unsettled poetics of social concern.

CHAPTER 7

The scene of reading

A BOOK OF BOOKS

The end of Book 4 of *The Prelude* describes a narrator who is seeking his "distant home" with "quiet heart" after discharging a discharged soldier upon the hospitality of a cottager woken from his sleep. Perhaps he saw himself sitting down by a warm fire with a good book. As we have seen, the telling of the story of the discharged soldier is full of bookishness (Dante, Homer, Virgil, Milton), as is so much of Wordsworth's poetry. Most often or perhaps most recognizably, it is the great precursors who frame Wordsworth's tales, Milton and Shakespeare above all. But there are other sources, for example Cook's voyages (in the "Point Rash-Judgment" poem). Then, in "Poor Susan," there is the impersonalized sea of print that vaporizes and drifts through the streets of London enlivening the reverie of its subject only with the consolations of cliché. The real leech-gatherer Wordsworth met on the road near his Grasmere cottage was about to try his luck as a used-book seller, and books by poets dead or living are very much behind the poem that Wordsworth writes about him.[1] Early in *The Prelude* Wordsworth remembers himself before he was ten years old deriving an "organic pleasure" from seeing the landscape arrayed as if it were a book, with its "level plain" and "lines of curling mist" (1: 592–93). The Cumberland beggar performs the functions of a bookkeeper, providing a "record" of what is otherwise "unremember'd" for those who cannot read, the "unletter'd Villagers" who thereby receive a thing "far more precious" than books themselves can provide.[2] But the old man himself tends toward the lifelessness of written books. The murderer whose gibbet forms part of the constellation of the first of the "spots of time" has his name carved nearby as "monumental writing" that is kept "fresh and visible" by the "superstition of the neighbourhood" and thus neatly sums up the price to be paid for a permanent inscription.[3] And, in the Leven Sands episode, Wordsworth splices together a whole range of items of print culture, placing high and interestingly overwrought Miltonisms next to the more dubious paradigm of Gray and setting both alongside the ephemeral yet commanding content of the newspapers.

This is indeed a poet whose distinctive originality lives not only through the books of others but also by constant reference to popular print culture. Perhaps no one who published a title called *Lyrical Ballads* could fully ignore the tastes and presence of a relatively unlettered readership.[4] Wordsworth's formal habits depend upon reflexivity, upon persuading his readers to make their own tales, without which they risk finding his poems inconsequential. The reflexivity is also historically self-conscious in its repeated bringing forward of its own allusiveness and dependence on sources too well known to be deemed objects of plagiarism.[5] Wordsworth stood on the shores of many lakes and rivers, but also on the shores and shoulders of a sea of print.[6] Book 5 of *The Prelude* declares itself to be about books and thus proposes itself as making some summary address to its author's life in letters. It is also about water, which is everywhere, as it has been from the start. The nom de plume of water poet had been taken before Wordsworth's time by John Taylor, who died in 1654, but in any fair competition among the immortals for the award of a golden oar, Wordsworth would surely outpace the Thames boatman. Wordsworth's waters are mightier, indeed: he deals in floods and torrents as often as gentle streams. And wherever there are books, in Wordsworth's poetry, water is not far away, whether vaporized as mist and cloud or roaring in rain and deluge. The apparent solidity of printed words melts into the fluid form of water, producing another indeterminate image that seems to belong neither to us nor to it, and registering another subject–object of concern. It is hard to talk about books without discussing water, but I shall try to do so for the first part of this chapter, if only to try to keep my own critical feet temporarily dry. And so we begin with books, as Wordsworth tells us to.

If we look to Book 5 of *The Prelude* for a confessional list of all the great writers who make up the allusive texture of the poem, then we will be disappointed; or, we would have to conclude that the most important influence upon his creative mind was an abbreviated edition of the *Arabian Nights*. To be sure, the poem intends an account of childhood reading and does not claim to set down the record of a lifetime among books. But that fuller record never comes. Book 5 is a list of luminous episodes at best haltingly connected up and loosely stitched together into a narrative whose overriding motif is one of loss and growing concern over an uncertain future for literary culture itself. It encases three of the most famous passages in the Wordsworth canon, those telling of the drowned man of Esthwaite, the dream of the Arab, and the Winander boy. All lovers of Wordsworth know them, but few can pass easily from the one to the others without sensing a radical retraction or distraction in the narrative voice. Wordsworth's account begins neither with a homage to the great books nor with a critique of the bad ones but with an avowed "sadness" at the "shrines so frail" (5: 10, 48) in which the records of man's deepest and finest thoughts are preserved: sadness at the vulnerable physical form of books. It is worth thinking about this emphasis. One might have expected the opposite from one who had had access to the treasured collections of college, public and some private libraries and who could look to well-preserved and cherished editions of Virgil and Homer as evidence for the powers of great poetry over time and change. One who has himself chosen the vocation of poetry might be expected to feel more hopeful. Instead, Wordsworth chooses to lament the material impermanence of books and their remoteness from the nature of the human mind itself: "we cannot choose but feel / That these must perish" (ll. 20–21). If fire be sent to burn up a sinful earth, then something of man would remain, he speculates, but not books. Why fire, here? The allusion is to another book. At the end of Book 11 of *Paradise Lost*, Michael has told the story of the flood and promises Adam that there will not be another one. Next time it will be fire: in other words a book burning, turning to ashes not only the piles of cheap print that Wordsworth felt were burying everyone around 1800 but also the classics, the best of the best. This anticipated conflagration leads, oddly, into the story of a dream that is after all about a flood (I am still trying to stay dry): his friend's dream of the Arab in the desert trying desperately and seemingly against the odds to save the book of geometry and the book of prophetic literature from destruction by "the fleet waters of the drowning world" (l. 136). The flood might put out the fire but does not guarantee protection against inundation.

This episode has been widely studied and has attracted much commentary on its content and significance. Its genesis is itself literary – Coleridge seems to have found it in an early life of Descartes, who was the original dreamer. And the dreamer in Wordsworth's poem has fallen asleep while reading Cervantes on the seashore, which leads the narrator to refigure the Arab in his own aroused imagination as a "Semi-Quixote" (l. 142). Books themselves, in other words, are what generated a dream about the precious frailty of books. And it is the shell of prophecy, in the dream, that forecasts its own imminent destruction and commands its own *burial*. Why is it that what is to survive must be buried? And what is a Semi-Quixote? Most obviously this figure is half-Quixote because also half-Bedouin. As a Quixote he is a figure in whom one scarcely believes, one who deceives himself and goes upon fools' errands, who (on the first page of Cervantes's novel) sells land to buy books. But is he only semi-embedded in self-deception and in a merely virtual, fictional existence, and perhaps thus half-credible: "the very Knight / Whose tale Cervantes tells, yet not the Knight" (5: 123–24)? In the published poem of 1850, the figure of the quixotic Arab is worked up through a first-person narration into a fully spectral persona: "distress and fear / Came creeping over me, when at my side / Close at my side, an uncouth shape appeared." The phrase harks back to the "uncouth shape" that was the discharged soldier, the last encounter reported in the previous book of the poem, and it repeats the experience of being startled by something undefined suddenly noticed as close at hand.[7] It is this figure whom the narrator feels he might become when he is holding a book of great poetry in his hand, anxious as he is about the "poor earthly casket" that it is.[8] If the book is already a casket, then it may as well be buried like one. The death of "immortal verse" seems thus to have already occurred even before the threatened deluge; it has occurred in the everyday world of commodified print. The threat to come has already happened; the great apocalypse can do no more damage than has been done by the daily round of trivial occupations and pursuits and by the gross and violent stimulants arising to compensate for their effects.

The discussion of "Poor Susan" in chapter 3 touched upon the developments in print culture that might well have caused acute anxiety in a neophyte poet. Wordsworth's notice of the rapid increase in the volume of middle-brow books was shared by many others: John Millar, for example, also commented on the onset of what Wordsworth called poetic diction, a language "coined and carefully collected from every quarter ... with prosaic tameness and languor ... in a pompous artificial diction."[9] Is the narrator-poet of *The Prelude* himself part of this process, so that he is prone to sense immortal verse as *already enshrined* in earthly *caskets*? Book 5 continues with a strangely contorted confession of guilt at having failed for so long to tell of the importance of early reading to the young narrator, who was too fully immersed in (or has been too exclusively recalling) the pleasures of unmediated nature to pay due homage to the influence of literature and folklore: "I was hurried forward by a stream, / And could not stop" (ll. 183–84). A stream of print or a stream of rushing water? And if the second, perhaps another invocation of the flood that is not supposed to happen again but just has, in the dream about the Bedouin Quixote? Just as we expect him to make the promised amends, there is another shift of direction as he brusquely resolves to leave all of this "where it lies hidden in its endless home / Among the depths of time" (ll. 197–98). This in turn is turned again by a long "and yet" sentence which proposes that perhaps he should (but will he?) after all attest to the honor and power of authors. Then instead we are given a long detour: an extended critique of modern education and its tendency to exclude or disparage fiction. It is easier to write about what is wrong with the general culture and its indifference to great books than to describe what exactly it is that they have done for him.

The first two hundred lines of Book 5 are almost impossible to paraphrase; they do not so much tell a story as stage a set of attitudes and options in a language so thorny and impacted as to seem at points almost indecipherable. It is hard not to puzzle over what motivates Wordsworth here: was it a discomfort about his own reliance on a bookish nature rather than on the open and original landscapes he professes to have favored, an anxiety of influences? If so, then these influences are hardly disguised. Indeed, the early citation (in l. 25) of Shakespeare's sonnet 64 is placed in quotation marks in both 1805 and 1850 texts: so he is citing Shakespeare in support of a lament about the frailty of the books in which his poems are printed.[10] Does the urge to invoke Shakespeare suggest a proud participation in what was already seen as a distinguished national tradition or an awkward confession of second-handedness, an effort to make a great precursor's words do the work that his own cannot complete? Was he wrestling with undigested memories of his dead mother, who was, we will soon be told, "the heart / And hinge of all our learnings and our loves" (ll. 257–58)? Is the failure or reluctance to do full justice to books connected in some way with her death? What is it that holds the narrator back from expressing his "perfect love" (l. 263)? Her positively coded "simple-mindedness" (l. 288) distinguishes her from the improperly book-driven modern educators, but did she perhaps also withhold, in her natural benevolence (like a parent hen) something of value or something desired?[11] Why is his urge to commemorate his early reading life at first avowed and then displaced, and why is it "hidden" in the "depths of time" as in an "endless home," one that seems between space and time but properly neither, or both at once?

Wordsworth does concede that he and his friend Coleridge were treated to a synthesis of books and nature – receiving nature itself as a book – in being permitted to wander "through heights and hollows, and bye-spots of tales / Rich with indigenous produce, open ground / Of Fancy, happy pastures ranged at will" (ll. 235–37). Spots of time and spots of tales; or "bye-spots," set aside from fully embodied spots?[12] Ranging at will through the pastures of literature does not, certainly, suggest a rigorous plan of reading and research, in the scholarly mode, and Wordsworth was quite reasonably never ashamed of that; but ranging happily at will along the shore of Grasmere Lake also brought on the self-rebuke of the "Point Rash-Judgment" poem. Time and space are scrambled here once again; the time of reading is imaged as a space, a bye-spot – not a byway or by-path but a *spot*, a punctilious place that is not for passing through or across but for stopping at, though not apparently a major stopping point, something for the fancy, perhaps, rather than the imagination. De Quincey may not be fully reliable but he made much of the contrast between Southey's "splendid library" and Wordsworth's "small book-collection," opining that his friend might not have "much lamented, on his own account, if all books had perished, excepting the entire body of English Poetry, and, perhaps, 'Plutarch's Lives.'" This was a man who, apparently, did not mind separating the pages of an uncut volume of Burke with a greasy butter knife.[13] So it is that desultory reading, outside the mainstream, feeds the fancy an ecologically correct diet of "indigenous produce" (garnished with local butter?) and provides an approved alternative to the force-fed diet of scientifically balanced nutrients imposed upon the modern child according to the utilitarian calculus of costs and benefits. That diet presumably includes some part of the prodigious volume of ephemeral print, the "bright volumes of vapour" that threaten to engulf the world in their own fleet waters of words, the products of a commodity culture whose material frailty might well not be regretted (the sooner they fall apart the better) were it not for the fact that they are setting the norm for all other books including those of the aspiring poet and his great precursors.

"My drift hath scarcely, I fear, been obvious" (ll. 291–92). By the time we are four hundred lines into Book 5, very little has been said about books other than indirectly. And when the narrative again finds its poetic feet with two justly well-known and well-loved episodes coming one after the other, the boy of Winander and the drowned man of Esthwaite, books again seem less than central. The first of these seems not to be about books at all, and thus might seem out of place, except that books are here aggressively dismissed. They appear as items *not* attended to by the "race of young Ones" (l. 432) to which the narrator belonged: "We might have fed upon a fatter soil / Of Arts and Letters, but be that forgiven" (ll. 433–34). He moves on with a benediction directed at modern youth, "May books and nature be their early joy" (l. 447), but it is nature we have heard about, not books, except the books he has not read. Even that reference is another citation, this time from *Henry IV, part 2*, IV.iv.54: "Most subject is the fattest soil to weeds."[14] Wordsworth resorts to the book of Shakespeare, in other words, to disavow the regret or resentment that he otherwise seems to have about not doing enough serious reading; he marks himself as not one among the aspirants to royal favor that King Henry's proverb refers to. This is something of a joke intended to show that the adult poet knows his Shakespeare; but along the way it suggests that arts and letters might rank among the modern weeds generated by the soiled sheets of commodified print.

There is also something troubling in the account of the favored "race of real children" (l. 436) that Wordsworth admires, and among whom he ranks his own childhood self. It comes in the shape of a traditional allusion specifying them as "mad at their sports like withered leaves in winds" (l. 440). These shades of Vallombrosa we have seen before, and will see again. What might it mean to image the healthy play of vigorous young children as akin to withered leaves in wind? The spring of life and the autumn of the year are conflated in a manner that fits all too sombrely into the pattern of death-in-life that governs much of Book 5. The unthinking young will die, as the Winander boy has died; they are his "mates" (l. 414) in more than one sense. So too will ephemeral print – and all print is ephemeral – wither and flutter in the wind, carried on the breezes that blow from Grub Street through the vale of Cheapside and beyond. The Horatian melancholy that proposes the fall of leaves from trees as analogous to the fate of both men and their writings – "we and our works are a debt owed to death" – is by around 1800 enforced and intensified by a debased literary marketplace that militates by the speed and volume of its circulation against its own best products.[15]

When we come to the drowned man, we are then fully primed for death's embrace, not only by the dead boy and his soon to wither playmates, but by the whole aura of anxiety and sadness at frail forms that begins Book 5, that carries through the dream of the Arab and the lament for the dead mother, and that governs more polemically the deathlike routine of the despised modern education where children are dwarf-men before their time and thus hasten yet more quickly than they need to do, and without ever having properly lived, toward their promised end. That same abbreviated chronology, as we have seen, is exactly what Marx finds in the operations of capital and Engels in the condition of the working class in England: children old before their time, men and women dying earlier than they should. Once again Wordsworth's privileged rural enclave shows itself as contaminated by the organizing energies of industrial time and factory routine: his anti-commodity subculture obeys in its deepest rhythms the logic of its antagonist. Those "withered leaves" are indeed also those of the book trade whose traditional investment in good-quality rag paper would soon give way to the cheaper material we have lately been working against the clock to preserve in our libraries of record. Death governs all, not just the shrunken lives of the coming proletariat (or *lumpenproletariat*) but also the sometimes yet intact but about to succumb existences of the country dwellers whose demise may be passed off as natural and necessary (everyone dies) but who are falling increasingly into step with the beat of the same dance of premature and untimely death.

A child wandering by a lake at the hour of "twilight" with "gloom" setting in (l. 459) might not then surprise us, thus prepared, as the recipient of another spectral vision, a "ghastly face; a spectre shape / Of terror even" (l. 472). Yes, there is the guillotine, still to come but already past and present at the time of writing, with its heads severed from bodies and its famous claim to terror. But the young poet does *not* report himself as having been afraid:

> and yet no vulgar fear,
> Young as I was, a Child not nine years old,
> Possessed me, for my inner eye had seen
> Such sights before, among the shining streams
> Of Fairy Land, the Forests of Romance:
> Thence came a spirit hallowing what I saw
> With decoration and ideal grace;
> A dignity, a smoothness, like the works
> Of Grecian art, and purest Poesy. (ll. 473–81)

What he sees does not upset him as much as it otherwise might, because he has been reading books and seeing in his mind's eye sights just like this. The body itself is a kind of book, embodying the "spirit . . . breath'd / From dead men to their kind" as books are elsewhere said to do.[16] What kind of books, one wonders, tell stories of dead men shooting out "bolt upright" from the surfaces of lakes? Celtic lore is mentioned, but it devolves into something classically proportioned, something Grecian, with its rough edges trimmed into pleasing shape. Gothic novels, perhaps – is Wordsworth's "Forests of Romance" an allusion to Radcliffe's *The Romance of the Forest*, published in 1791 and one of the naive Harriet Smith's favorite books in Jane Austen's *Emma*? Celtic and classical also combine in the mind of the idling narrator of the "Point Rash-Judgment" poem as he is trying to describe the stately fern he calls Queen Osmunda, finding her (it) lovelier than either Grecian "naid" or Arthurian "Lady of the Mere." This was not one of the Wordworthian narrator's finer moments: his scientific inaccuracy prefigures the more dramatically rash judgment about to come.[17] If this too fallible narrator has indeed been reading Gothic novels, he could have there learned his art of opposition; the Gothic plot often depends on the repeated promise of a terror that never comes or takes final form, whereas Wordsworth's terror comes unannounced. Or does it? The way is in fact prepared because the pile of clothes tells a "plain Tale" (l. 467) to those who can read it, which is why they are dragging the lake in the first place. Instead of expecting terror and not getting it, as in one version of the Gothic plot, Wordsworth's narrator does encounter terror but is not terrified. This is not the consequence of a sophisticated command of the aesthetics of the sublime, which also excludes mere terror in the service of its suggested analogy to moral education, but of childhood reading: he has read about such things.

Here again is the phenomenon of the *pharmakon* about which Derrida has written so brilliantly: the poison is one with the cure. The cure of literature is that it defends us from sheer terror by offering us proleptic imaginings, opportunities to try out in the mind's eye things we have not yet seen in the real world. The poison is that in so doing, it keeps us from experiencing the "freedom and power of real and substantial action and suffering," that which explores the whole range of human feeling and, not incidentally, provides the raw materials for the best poetry.[18] We may not wish for "vulgar fear," but perhaps a little more fear of some sort would be appropriate? Is this not indeed the ailment of the previously critiqued modern child, the monster-birth and dwarf man who is, in a passage a hundred or so lines earlier, described as

> fenced round, nay armed, for ought we know
> In panoply complete; and fear itself,
> Natural or supernatural alike,
> Unless it leap upon him in a dream,
> Touches him not. (ll. 314–18)

To one proud to have been fostered by both beauty *and* fear, who slips up (according to one reading of one of his most famous poems) in not having "human fears" and is repaid by the death of one he loves, or of some part of himself ("she neither hears nor sees"), does not this eerie proximity of the disavowed and fearless modern child to the approved fearless narrator demand being thought about?[19] Can we get away with inferring that the nine-year-old Wordsworth had an experience of fear that was not "vulgar," that was in some way authentic? I think not, since what *is* fear if not vulgar, common to all and prone to excite us in ways that we cannot control? Alan Bewell has read this passage as evidence of Wordsworth's engagement with the Enlightenment critique of the fear of death as an ideological tool for the disciplining of subservient populations; he finds him to be suggesting here a new idea of death as part of the proper education of the mind, not fully displacing its terror but not giving way to it either, navigating between the rationalist's indifference to death and the establishment ideologue's use of contrived terror.[20] Perhaps so; but this is to ignore the striking alignment Wordsworth presents between the modern child's lack of fear (of which he does not approve) and that of the young narrator by the lakeshore.

There is a noteworthy relation between this episode and Rousseau's case for the inhibiting effects of literature. As the writer of an epic autobiography, Wordsworth had good reason to be attentive to and cautious about Rousseau, whose *Confessions* had brought him a scandalous notoriety that was only further enhanced by his reputation as a formative influence on the outbreak of the French Revolution.[21] The young Rousseau was quite explicit about the effects of his own early reading upon the constitution of his adult personality: he and his father compulsively read novels he did not fully understand, leaving him with "bizarre and romantic concepts about human life" that have never gone away. Then he discovered Plutarch and began to fashion himself as an upright republican "impatient with the yoke and servitude which has tormented me my whole life."[22] The two primary elements of Rousseau's notoriety, his sexual sensibility and sentimentality and his political radicalism, are thus here attributed, right at the start of his autobiography, to the early influence of books. Wordsworth's reticence about this same subject, which he claims to want to leave hidden in the depths of time, and only comes to in Book 5 after reporting so much else about his childhood, may then have an extra motivation as a reaction to the too-bookish Rousseau and his learned cultivation of dangerous habits and false expectations. And yet the literary origins or insinuated analogues to his own poetry of so-called experience are often unmissable even when somewhat implicit: the Satanic narrators of "The Ruined Cottage" and

"Gipsies," the Odyssean aura of the discharged soldier who is on his way home from a distant war and places his trust not in begging but "in the eye of him that passes me," as if to position his fellow traveler as a reluctant Polyphemus who may regret his efforts at detaining him.[23] The proper sort of literature, one might rightly claim, is no bad example: better to be formed by Milton, Shakespeare, Virgil and their kind than by the "frantic novels, sickly and stupid German tragedies, and deluges of idle and extravagant stories in verse" that Wordsworth so despised.[24] But the possibility of not being formed at all, except by nature and its great and permanent objects, is also entertained and cherished by Wordsworth, who is as we have seen happiest about books when he can treat them as if they were already part of nature, as tales that are "bye-spots" among open fields.

Book 5 at least, by coming as late in the story as it does and by way of its thick and complex rhetoric, marks Wordsworth out as definitely not a Rousseau when it comes to confessing his early reading habits. So it is all the more striking that we can find in the drowned man episode a counter-reading that positions Wordsworth as rather close to another famous Rousseavian argument, the one made in the letter to D'Alembert against the introduction of theatres into the city of Geneva. Rousseau is not here speaking of novels or poems, but about the theatre, whose spectacular characteristics also troubled Wordsworth and made sure that he enjoyed them (and he did enjoy them) somewhat uncomfortably at best. The argument goes back to Plato and has to do with a suspicion of the political effects of inauthentic personalities upon both the actors and those who pay to watch them. Rousseau's polemic plays up the embeddedness of theatres in the modern luxury economy, another thing that worried Wordsworth even as he enjoyed them. And when Rousseau takes up the question of tragedy's effects on its audience, he speaks directly to Wordsworth's report on the place of reading in his response to the drowned man. Some, following Aristotle, thought that tragedy should inspire pity and terror, and a proper sense of human frailty. Rousseau finds otherwise. The pity aroused by tragic drama is no more than a "transitory and fruitless emotion, which lasts no longer than the emotion producing it ... a barren compassion indulging itself in a few tears, but never productive of any act of humanity." Tyrants have shown themselves quite able to weep tears in the theatre without ceasing from their real-life brutalities. Real misery requires us to respond with "assistance, relief and consolation": watching fictive misery on the stage does not encourage such interventions but tends to preempt them.[25]

Rousseau's concerns were not new: Dryden's translation of Lucretius had noted that "pains unfelt produce the pleasing sight," while Addison, Burke and Campbell had observed that our response to the spectacle of pain is principally conditioned by a sense of relief that others suffer instead of ourselves.[26] Cowper's virtuoso mock-heroic self-presentation of himself as a newspaper reader in *The Task* locates itself very seriously in this tradition: the pleasure of reading presupposes being far from the roar of the crowd, "At a safe distance, where the dying sound / Falls a soft murmur on th'uninjur'd ear."[27] The dying sound can be the sound of others dying, the music of death. In this state of imagined panoptical lordship and mastery, with all its Miltonic overtones soon to be Wordsworth's – "I behold / The tumult, and am still" – the poet can hear the sounds of war and pain but never so loudly as to threaten his peace of mind: he will "sigh, but never tremble, at the sound." Cowper here unsettles the very domestic bliss he is so often deemed to be celebrating by issuing reminders of what it must exclude in order to subsist. Others since have worried about how readily we manage any discomfort that might ensue from the sight of the pain or destruction of others. Hans Erich Nossack asks himself whether he should undertake the description of Hamburg after the firestorm of July 1943: "what if [those who will come later] read it only to enjoy something strange and uncanny and to make themselves feel more alive?"[28]

Wordsworth's formulation of the scene of reading in the drowned man episode does not align completely with any of these positions, but it touches on and conjures up all of them. He describes the power of reading to assist us in facing events that would otherwise prove perhaps too stressful to endure; without the forests of romance we would be overwhelmed to the point of trauma by the ghastly sight of the dead man rising. That overwhelming would cause us to lose self-control, casting us into a condition that the Gothic pretends to describe but so often conspires to fold back within the vocabulary of literary allusion and textual reflexivity.[29] The cost of this protective reading experience is a loss of immediacy and originality in response – access to real and substantial action and suffering – but the implication is that without such loss we could not cope. The cost of managing is thus the numbing of response, although if one is a poet who himself describes that numbing, as Wordsworth so often does, then the whole question of adequacy is passed on to those who come after, those who read his stories. In this way, to read Wordsworth is to read against the poet's account of his own reading, and to think about how and whether things might be different. What would it be to see a drowned man surface without having read those stories, and are there any positive emotions that are destroyed or impeded by such reading? Might the untutored heart see and feel something valuable that the reader of fairy tales and romances is missing? What is emphatically not settled in this passage is the debate about the ultimate value of books, which remains a matter of concern.

Nor is it settled in what follows. The account of the failed resolution to save up for and purchase other volumes of the "Arabian Tales" (l. 484) – which harks back to the "Arabian Waste" of the dream (l. 71) – is another instance of a "firmness" (l. 499) promised but not delivered, a falling away from full or committed investment in the need for and value of books, a breach indeed of a "league, a covenant" (l. 492) Wordsworth had made with his young friend. So, having just asserted the usefulness of such tales for keeping at bay the full impact of traumatic experience, the narrator reports himself as failing to equip himself with further reading, and reading that he claims to like a lot. The back-and-forth logic continues as he goes on to report his excitement at having access to his father's house and to the "golden store of books" (l. 503) from which he would select volumes to keep him company on fishing trips. So absorbed would he become in what he was reading that he found himself:

> Defrauding the day's glory, desperate!
> Till, with a sudden bound of smart reproach,
> Such as an idler deals with in his shame,
> I to my sport betook myself again. (ll. 512–15)

Here again is Wordsworth at his fascinating best. The act of reading is one of selfish absorption inspiring guilt, and here he responds (rather delicately) to the widely circulated eighteenth-century critique of reading, particularly novel-reading, as a masturbatory analogue and occasionally as itself a sex-tool: hence the jokes about the books one might read with one hand, jokes not lost on the confessional Jean-Jacques Rousseau among others, including perhaps the poet who delighted himself with the daffodils.[30] More familiarly Wordsworthian is the claim for the priority of unmediated experience of nature over second-hand descriptions, for the "hour of feeling" rather than of meditation: "Up! Up! my friend, and quit your books / Or surely you'll grow double."[31] Books do make us double, dividing the self into a reflexive dyad within which one watches oneself reading: an ontological equivalent of the professional deformation afflicting the old leech-gatherer bent double over the surface of the pond. Equally familiar is the instant half-retraction whereby what is rejoined after reading is a "sport," something between serious and trivial activity, something indulged in not out of necessity (as with the fisherman in the mist) but out of a pleasure drive; something that is not, perhaps, a full embrace of the glory of the day, though it is not quite an affront to it either. There is at least a tiny shock in this turning from reading to fishing being described as a kind of moral awakening, and such moments are common enough in Wordsworth to be deemed crafted and deliberate. Books are disavowed once again, but the world without them is not so pure and simple; it is the world of a child of education and relative leisure who can afford to spend his day fishing for sport rather than for subsistence. Children do this, of course, but this child is father to the too-happy idler who rambles along the shore of Grasmere Lake making rash judgments and who writes about his past in the light of just such later knowledge.

The last hundred or so lines of Book 5 do not at all resolve these bookish questions into a written (and thereby lifeless) book. The strangely nominated "forgers of lawless tales" (l. 548) – made but also faked, and *faked* as lawless – are redeemed by the invocation of a "gracious Spirit" (l. 516) that reconciles all things to each other, ennobling the "dumb yearnings, and hidden appetites" (l. 530) that books arouse and partly appease. But then there is the onset of a power complex analogous to the lordship and mastery generated by the spots of time. The authors of fiction's lawless tales are those who

> Make our wish our power, our thought a deed,
> An empire, a possession; Ye whom Time
> And Seasons serve; all Faculties; to whom
> Earth crouches, the elements are potter's clay,
> Space like a Heaven filled up with Northern lights;
> Here, nowhere, there, and everywhere at once. (ll. 552–57)

This is at once the ordinary, empirical psychology of much reading experience – the participation in a closed world where fantasy is king and there are no constraints on what can be imagined – and a distinctly megalomaniac experience in which there are no incentives to return to the everyday world where more exigent rules obtain. To make an empire of a thought (or is it the other way round?) is a positive tribute to the power of fiction: we can be satisfied with what we have as if it were everything. It is also the outcome of fiction's dubious art of persuading us to fill immensity with a single thought and to respond as if it were an empire. Poison and cure again come together, and cannot be clearly separated, any more than the enlivening and death-dealing attributes of images can be kept apart.

No sooner has Wordsworth recounted this (ambivalent) permission for authors to continue to flourish and to deserve approval than he moves us on to estimate a different sort of literature than the merely marvelous (ll. 558–67) and promptly rediscovers the sadness with which he began Book 5:

> I am sad
> At thought of raptures now forever flown,
> Even unto tears I sometimes could be sad
> To think of, to read over, many a page,
> Poems withal of name, which at that time
> Did never fail to entrance me, and are now
> Dead in my eyes as is a theatre
> Fresh emptied of spectators. (ll. 568–75)

This odd analogy suggests a sadness that is not just at the passing of literature but at the disappearance of forms of life. Books are ephemeral, Book 5 began by telling us, because we will not need them in an afterlife and because they are themselves materially frail, prone to fall apart and decay. But now it is their reader who is feeling the passing of time and the onset of dusty death. We do not respond to some books as we once did, although the texts are the same now as they were then. The poems are still performing their roles but the audience has left. This experience of loss and change is a personal analogue of the position of the so-called moderns in the early eighteenth century, those who claimed that past literatures are similarly destined to pass into obscurity and misunderstanding unless we subject ourselves to a rigorous scholarly immersion in the historical record (philological, archeological, cultural) to recover what we can of the meanings and contexts of times past. Pope, in defense of his translations of Homer, made the opposite case (along with the so-called ancients), claiming that the most important human truths have not changed and can be accurately recognized whenever and wherever they are encountered. But Rousseau, for example, lined up with the moderns: "there cannot be the least doubt that the very best tragedy of Sophocles, would be totally damned in our theatres. It is impossible for us to put ourselves in the place of people, to whom we bear no sort of resemblance."[32] It is as if the historical onset in the eighteenth century of an enormous nostalgia for the past, for the glories of Rome, Athens and (or) Sparta, comes to be compressed into the life of the single individual who looks back, as Wordsworth does, on his own childhood as a lost world seen at best by glimpses and sometimes not at all. This is one of the effects of modernizing time, of the temporality of modernization in which machine technology is implicated, that things happen so much faster – the circulation of news, the evolution of national events and conditions, the lifespan of persons who either really do die sooner than they used to (Marx and Engels's industrial proletariat) or feel that they will. One threatened result of that "multitude of causes unknown to former times" acting on modern life is the loss of the value and experience of great literature, so that Shakespeare and Milton are "driven into neglect."[33]

Both in *The Prelude* and in the lyric poems, Wordsworth meets or hears about numbers of people who seem to be about to die or who experience their own past as dead (the Winander boy was, as is well known, originally written up as Wordsworth himself). In this climate of feeling a sense of radical change and sadness can come from something as simple as growing out of one literary taste and into another, as Wordsworth claims that it does for him. What is lost is not just a line of verse or passage of prose but a whole field of experience and imagination and a trust in the continuity of any component of the past, one's own as well as that of the national culture at large. Wordsworth feared having to live "in reconcilement with our stinted powers" and the "meagre vassalage" that came with time (5: 541–42) not just because he had a happy childhood but because he saw in the maturation process of his own life a microcosm of a massive historical shift in the disposition of work and leisure, creation and reproduction, life and death themselves. Books can help, and the "forgers of lawless tales" keep us alive to our best origins, but books are also subject to passing away into dead letters, as well as to the copyright scandals and pirated publications forged by lawless entrepreneurs. They cannot thus be sustained simply as an alternative to the ravages of modernizing time because they are a symptom and expression of its processes. The topic of Book 5, the attempt to put into a book what other books meant and continue to mean, is not then for nothing awkward and obfuscatory and prone to the back-and-forth logic of pros and cons. Books enshrine the best of human thoughts but do so precisely as shrines, and they are shrines that are themselves increasingly impermanent, frail caskets. Their physical form images mortality, and reading them can deaden new experience though also make it bearable *because* it is deadened, as happens in the drowned man episode. We cannot or should not live without them, but living with them brings some doubtful side effects. And, when we read the stories favored in our youth and find them empty, we are brought up against our own passing away as still to come but not to be avoided. These are more than merely bookish thoughts.

The childhood memory narrative of Book 5 ends with recollections of a "never-ending show" (l. 606) in which poetry and nature were combined as the young poet and his friend recited verse amongst the flowers and the birdsong. The "show" that was the daffodils is enjoyed only in solitude, as if in a theatre empty of spectators. Here he has company, albeit that "full oft the objects of our love / Were false, and in their splendour over-wrought" (ll. 593–94). The lover of nature is also the lover of "glittering verse" (l. 615), as each embodies and offsets the other. But the show has ended, as all shows must. He cannot remain still on the "still borders of the misty Lake" (l. 587) without himself turning into a ghost. The most powerful of the attributions concluding Book 5 is chthonic: the "motions of the winds / Embodied in the mystery of words" embody a "darkness" populated by "a host / Of shadowy things" that live there as their "proper home" (ll. 621–22). The darkness is profound and also profoundly literary. Its lighter side is the twilight gloom of Gray's "Elegy" and of Milton's "Il Penseroso," though that is still dark enough. Gray, according to De Quincey, was one of the poets whom Wordsworth chanted by the lake and, although "far below the tone of high poetic passion," then found suitable to a time of life when "the profounder feelings were as yet only germinating."[34] Darker yet are the shades visited by Aeneas, Virgil and Dante, the abode of the dead who live again in poetry. And dark again is the unmissable allusion to *Measure for Measure*, and to Claudio's imagining his death "imprison'd in the viewless winds / And blown with restless violence round about / The pendant world" (III.i.124–25). Darkest of all, if one is a Christian or a Miltonist, is the depth into which the rebel angels are cast forever, the darkness that keeps them from the sight of God. Mixing up light and darkness, as Wordsworth does by finding in poetry's nature both this darkness and a "light divine" (l. 626), poses the question of whether their relation is orderly and divinely ordained, each giving way to the other in "perpetual round" and "grateful vicissitude" (*Paradise Lost*, 6: 6–8), or more mixed up and interfused, such that easy orientation (moral as well as diurnal) is no longer possible. The verse suggests the second, and the whole argument of Book 5 suggests the same. With books, one never knows the time of day.

There are at least three twilights in Book 5: that in which the young narrator comes upon the pile of clothes on the shore of Esthwaite (l. 459); the time of the Winander boy's mimic hootings (ll. 391–92, "when the stars had just begun / To move along the edges of the hills"); and "that twilight when we first begin to see / The dawning earth" (ll. 537–38). This last use is unusual – twilight can and does indeed describe the dawn but is not commonly used that way. The dawn of consciousness is indeed a passing away of something else (famously so in the "Intimations" ode) as it may also be a beginning. Twilight is a time between, looking back at "Being past" and forward to "the life to come" (ll. 534–35). Neither the twilight of dawn nor that of dusk are fully darkness, but they impinge upon it. Beginnings and endings, passages to and fro, are juxtaposed here in Book 5 in a superimposition that marks the entire narrative of this confessional poem, which is always looking back while moving forward, looking down while going up (as in the famous ascent of Snowdon in the dark), seeing what is above one's head reflected in the waters beneath one's feet, watching what is further away get bigger (as from the stolen boat). Everything is as if, Marx might have said, standing on its head. The movements in Book 5 are also framed by stillness: the dreamer sees the spectral Arab-Quixote while asleep, and that sleep is like the "deep entrancement" that *half*-possesses the narrator as reader (l. 162) – a kind of death-in-life. Twilight is the time of haunting and of ghosts. Beside the grave of the Winander boy the narrator stands mute for "a full half-hour" (l. 421) – death-in-life again. In the twilight by the lake of Esthwaite, the boy stands "long," watching for the corpse that will rise on the following day (l. 462); this watch too was, in the 1799 manuscript, specified as "half an hour."[35] Time is slowed and space is stretched, so that what is to come never comes when one expects it. The surface of the lake waits also in a "breathless stillness" for the uprising "spectre shape" to come (ll. 466, 472). It is *dead* calm, like Grasmere Lake on rash-judgment day. The life that is absent is at once removed by the adverting narrator, who needs to slow things down in order to have a properly tranquil and less lively experience, and independently apparent in a world that is peopled by dismembered bodies and alienated minds. Book 5 projects all of the ambivalences that govern Wordsworth's sense of the operations of images and imaginations, and focuses them specifically on the death-in-life that is the book. This poem that resists its own destiny as a finished story, one "exposed and lifeless as a written book" (8: 727), has much to say of books and continually both insinuates and rejects its own dependence upon the previously fashioned lives of deceased writers. Book 4 ended with its narrator saying farewell to the discharged soldier and lingering "near the door a little space (4: 503) before heading home. The ghostly soldier had more than a little of the literary about him. The beginning of Book 6, which follows the book about books, has the narrator telling us that

> The leaves were yellow when to Furness Fells,
> The haunt of shepherds, and to cottage life
> I bade adieu (6: 1–3)

and, like a bird lured by a fowler, returned to "Granta's Cloisters" (l. 6). Now it is Macbeth who is conjured up – for the bookish instruments of darkness do indeed tell truths – telling us that he has lived long enough, that his "way of life / Is fall'n into the sear, the yellow leaf" (V.iii.22–23). Perhaps Shakespeare's sonnet 73 is also invoked, where the yellow leaves bespeak "bare ruined choirs" and the twilight of life. The yellowing leaves certainly recall the yellow cover of the book of Arabian Tales (5: 483) as well as the happy youths imaged as "withered leaves in winds" (l. 440), aging thus before their time or turned to still life in the leaves of books. The leaves of trees and the leaves of books both turn yellow, like those who read them. Here again Wordsworth invokes that profound and extended tradition invoking falling leaves as dying human generations beloved of Homer, Virgil, Horace, Dante and Milton (and of a host of others), and embodied in the shady vale (Vallombrosa) that opens out its canopy only to wintry light.[36] The beginning of a new book in and on the life of the poet is autumnal, his passage that of a migrating bird lured to death by fowlers as it seeks a warmer clime. Sadness again, and frail shrines for memorial gestures. Books that tell of ghosts are themselves ghostly forms, virtual and more and more perishable in a world that wants to read them only once if at all. The young poet's ambitions, the subject of the first book of *The Prelude*, were ghostly from the first, "phantoms of conceit / That had been floating loose about so long" (1: 131–32), so many "gleams of light" (l. 135) that flash and disappear. His proposed subjects for poetry were the illustrious dead whom he might "summon back from lonesome banishment" (l. 175), among them William Wallace, whose deeds people the Scottish landscape "like a Family of Ghosts" (l. 217). And when, in Book 5, he sadly thinks upon the impermanence of books, he calls them "garments" (5: 23) that the "immortal being" will no longer need. So too the "heap of garments" (l. 461) left by Esthwaite's side that signal the drowned man. Books and water once again, and by the water's side.

In the first manuscript version of the drowned man passage included in the 1799 two-book *Prelude*, there is no summarizing of the event with a commentary on the effects of reading, protective or otherwise. But books are in play nonetheless: what follows the appearance of the ghastly face (not yet a spectral form) is a quotation from *Othello* and an invocation of other such local incidents that left indelible impressions on the narrator's mind:

> I might advert
> To numerous accidents in flood or field,
> Quarry or moor, or 'mid the winter snows,
> Distresses and disasters, tragic facts
> Of rural history that impressed my mind
> With images, to which in following years
> Far other feelings were attached, with forms
> That yet exist with independent life
> And, like their archetypes, know no decay.[37]

Here it is the real world to which the narrator adverts, not the realms of romance and folk tale. The impression is that he has witnessed these tragic facts himself, or at least been very close to them. But the citation of Othello's "moving accidents by flood and field" (I.iii.135) is unmissable and relocates this first-hand experience back within the very realm of fiction that it purports to refute. Peter Manning, in a fine reading of this episode in its 1799 form, has suggested that Wordsworth might have removed the Shakespeare reference because of a reluctance to affiliate himself with the murderous Othello.[38] And indeed, when the same affiliation resurfaces, it is attached to the discharged soldier who tells his "Soldier's tale" in Book 4 of the 1805 *Prelude* (l. 445) – it is he, not the narrator, who has been murdering in the service of his country. Manning notes the oddity of the 1805 narrative's presentation of a scene from adolescence in Book 4 (the discharged soldier) preceding one from childhood in Book 5 (the drowned man), and finds that it produces a sense of déjà vu (p. 99): the horror at the spectral soldier's "ghastly" mouth (4: 411) anticipates in the narrative the shock at the "ghastly face" (5: 472) of the drowned man which in autobiographical time preceded it.[39] Thus the "first" episode functions as if it were an example of the protective functions of preparatory reading, even though it is recounted as something that really happened (and happened later). It is also reported in a manner very visibly embedded in literary allusions to the traditions of visits to the underworld and encounters with the living dead. Life and literature chase each other's tails in a circular pattern. The 1799 invocation of distresses and disasters whose memories "know no decay" (1: 287) gives them the aura of written records that have not yet (as they will in 1805) become impermanent and all-too destructible. In taking them out of time – and they are indeed immediately succeeded in the 1799 manuscript by the spots-of-time passages (1: 288ff.) – they also become epitaphic, deathly permanent. The narrator has once again worked himself around to an act of putting to death as the ultimate option for preserving a life to come; the forms to come will have the *same* life and are thereby already fixed and dead, and as such they work to make provision for feelings that are "other." Time-bound and timeless agencies combine to return the inert commodified element back to a world of creative recomposition and circulation; the expense of spirit readies itself to be spent again, a "monumental writing" whose "letters are all fresh and visible."[40]

The 1799 theorization of the drowned man incident thus ends with an endorsement of the ideal synthesis between living image and still life, whereas by 1805 the whole event has been subsumed within the dubious penumbra cast by books – books which are themselves subject to material decay even as they make possible through their desensitizing powers (and repositories of images) the acceptance of otherwise unbearable experiences.[41] The letter killeth and the spirit restoreth, but not to complete life. Book 5 ends by confessing that it has offered only a "scanty record" of the importance of books to the young narrator, while their "later influence yet remains untold." So much is the plan of the poem expanding, we are told, that "further progress" would be unseemly if "these acknowledgments were left unpaid" (ll. 630–37). There is an almost grudging tone to this conclusion, as if the topic of books and reading were itself stilling or wasting time, interrupting an ongoing narrative with a dutiful payment of respects. Stilling, not killing time: the poet would rather be moving on to something else, something perhaps less infused with death, with thoughts of frail and perishable shrines and quixotic commercial circulations. The jolt we receive at the start of Book 6, with its yellowing leaves and birds caught in traps, is all the more notable because of the expectation that we are about to change direction, to make further progress, to mimic the motion of evolutionary life rather than the halted or static attributes of a being toward death. And when we are told that "we need not linger o'er the ensuing time" (6: 19) when "many books / Were read" according to "no settled plan" (ll. 26–27, 29), with the poet wishing to be no more than a "lodger" in the "House / Of Letters" (ll. 32–33), the disenchanting effect of reading is rendered all the more forcefully. Only the avowedly escapist trip to France (6: 331ff.), where the young revolutionary movement has not yet been polluted by dead letters and cruel laws, achieves a new turn and tone of eagerness and excitement. There the confines of college cloisters and the covers of books are briefly displaced by "dances in the open air" (l. 382) and happy encounters with a world made new.

The story of the "later influence" (l. 632) of books is never rejoined. Book 5 is all about the books read in childhood, like *The Arabian Nights*. In the last book of the poem, we are still being told how much has been omitted, "of books how much!" (13: 280). The most notable mention of books between Book 5 and the end of the poem is of "how books mislead us" in privileging the judgments of a "wealthy Few" (12: 207–8) or in reducing complex conditions to easy understanding, thereby flattering our "self-conceit" (l. 215). Shakespeare, Milton and all the other great precursors who are cited on almost every page of *The Prelude* remain undiscussed. The most visible book in *The Excursion*, another encyclopedia of allusion and citation, is the volume of Voltaire which is discovered beside the Solitary's seat and which the Wanderer indicts as both symptom and cause of his despair. Such a stern judgment might be expected of a poet whose reputation subsists on an avowed turn to nature precisely as respite from bookish values and crabbed contemplations: but Wordsworth exposes his Wanderer to critical irony in this section of the poem. Book 5 of *The Prelude* brings his book-bound state home to the poet himself as not so much a triumph as an enabling condition of his own survival, detouring the poem on his life through the bye-spots of an always pending death. And it is death not by fire but by water.

FLEET WATERS OF A DROWNING WORLD

If the "immortal spirit" abandons books as if they were "garments" (5: 23), is it then drowning, like the schoolmaster of Esthwaite who abandoned his own garments by the shore of the lake? Is its transubstantiation into eternal life doubled or displaced by its disappearing from sight beneath the waves? The Winander boy standing beside the calm lake at twilight hears something more portentous, the "voice of mountain torrents" (5: 409), and watches as the reflected images of the landscape are "receiv'd / Into the bosom of the steady Lake" (ll. 412–13) as if committed to the same act of burial that awaits the boy himself. Still water or water held back is both calming and threatening. Crossing Leven Sands while the "great Sea" stands back at "safe distance" (10: 528–29), the travelers must hurry. These were (and are) some of the most dangerous beaches in Britain, as the siting of the chapel (l. 52) perhaps acknowledges. Wordsworth's sense of standing outside time while beholding an unchanging spectacle (l. 486) is bracketed by the passing of critical time, the time of life and death – for Robespierre, for William Taylor and for those who need a guide to help them cross the "shallow Stream / Of inland water" (ll. 527–28), avoiding deep pools and quicksands while moving fast enough to beat the turning tide. The newspapers are not the only source of "tidings" that have "substantial truth" (l. 537). Here people can drown. De Quincey catches a distinct absurdity in the figure of the poet whom he positions as actually upon the sands at the time of hearing the news: "Immediately a passion seized him, a transport of almost epileptic fervour, prompting him, as he stood alone on this perilous waste of sands, to shout aloud anthems of thanksgiving for this great vindication of eternal justice."[42]

On Leven Sands, where he had best be at his most alert for the noise of waters, Wordsworth seems to forget the passage of time. More commonly he conjures up the sound of water even in the most unlikely places, as if he distrusts Michael's assurance that there will be no more universal floods, and that God will never again "let the sea / Surpass his bounds" or rain "drown the world" (*Paradise Lost*, 11: 893–94). Why, then, have we seen the vales of Cheapside shrouded in literary vapor and turned to a river in terms that recall Milton's description of Noah's flood (11: 738–45)? The primal flood, the waters of life and the waters of materialism flow together here as so often in Wordsworth's poems.[43] The sight of the blind beggar in the middle of London, and of the "written paper" that makes his story public, strikes Wordsworth "as with the might of waters."[44] So too the Shakespeare sonnet incorporated into the beginning of Book 5 and there converted into a lament for the impermanence of books alludes in its original form to the erosion of the land by the "hungry ocean" (l. 5). Getting away from the sea and from the "fog and damp" of the lowlands by ascending Snowdon leads the party only to another "huge sea of mist" whose chasms produce a chthonic roaring of the waters – the "homeless voice of waters" – seemingly left behind.[45]

There seems to be no escaping the sounds and senses of great bodies of water. Horatio warned Hamlet that following the ghost might lead him "toward the flood" (I.iv.69) and Wordsworth's ghostly shapes have similar propensities. The power of Wordsworth's moving accidents indeed can turn fields into floods, as they do most spectacularly in "Resolution and Independence," another poem that summons up Othello in its strange conjuration of a "moorish flood" (l. 81) that may also be a metathesis of another sea of mist, that to which Milton compares the cherubim at the very end of *Paradise Lost*, "Gliding metéorous, as evening mist / Ris'n from a river o'er the marish glides" (12: 629–30). If the flood is moorish and marish, then it gathers together Wordsworth's two greatest literary precursors as together putting pressure at the bizarre moment when the quite ordinary "little pond" is transfigured: "Beside the little pond or moorish flood / Motionless as a Cloud the Old Man stood."[46] Not every flooding is a deluge, of course, but with this poet it is hard to keep the sense of deluge at any distance, especially in a poem which begins with rain falling "in floods" (l. 2). Nighttime inundations may indeed have been converted to a "pleasant noise of waters" (l. 7), but dark thoughts supervene and incline the narrator toward a trance-like state in which the old man's voice becomes "like a stream" (l. 114) and his ghostly form departs on its career of eternal wandering "about the weary moors" (l. 137). He studies the surface of the pond "as if he had been reading in a book" (l. 88): again, the old man who gave Wordsworth the idea for the poem was indeed about to take up a career as a used-book salesman.

So the conflation of books with water that is all over Book 5 spills out into the rest of Wordsworth's poetry: the watery road where the discharged soldier is encountered, the river and vapor of Poor Susan's London streets, the roaring streams of life and death in the Vallombre that is also Vallombrosa. Rivers and streams connect life and literature. If the River Derwent composed and calmed the infant poet's thoughts and gave them measure, as he says it did in the first book of *The Prelude*, then it also haunted the adult narrator with a sense of imminent and uncontrollable deluge. Critics have noticed this fixation on water and contextualized it in various ways: Geoffrey Hartman, Alan Bewell and Theresa Kelley in particular have written well on this syndrome in psychoanalytic, geological and aesthetic terms.[47] It is true that the sight of masses of moving water evokes the sublime, and very unlikely that Wordsworth was unaware of the grand scale of geological time which proposed that the tops of mountains were once the bottoms of seas. It is true too that, as Laura Brown has recently suggested, water had a more recent history as the "fluid roadway" of travel, commerce and empire.[48] Here we can begin to sense why it might be that Wordsworth's images of water shift so radically from calm to torrent, stillness to apocalyptic motion, and why the contemplation of stillness so often recalls or prefigures some expectation of a flood. Real seas and rivers do this too. But Wordsworth's poems show this oscillation as once again a symptom of the radically unpredictable and uncontrollable space–time formations of an economy of circulation driven by machine time and a constantly out-of-control relation between labor, productivity, price and value. Brown relates the force of water to "the transforming power of capitalist economic expansion" in its "threat to engulf everything" (p. 118). Wordsworth, I have been arguing, saw this force as particularly apparent in the book trade and in the cultural sector, with its "bright volumes of vapour" and its spectral, persevering and endlessly mobile used-book salesman who gathers leeches to let blood and assist in medical cures against the tide of a history that is doing away with his trade.

The "weary moors" are given by prosopopoeia a life that the old man in his ghostliness does not have. Like the "black drizzling crags that spake by the way-side" (*Prelude*, 6: 562) of Gondo gorge – crags do not drizzle or speak, but rather are drizzled upon and spoken about – they indicate a world in which everything solid has turned into air, or water, where all social ranks [*alles Ständische*] as well as everything upright evaporates [*verdampft*]. Commodities do not speak, but if they could there would be talking books as well as tables standing on their heads and thinking of dancing. The stream that is traced from darkness and comes and goes throughout the poem remits a "feeling of life endless" (13: 183) which is not only that of spiritual continuity but also, and inseparable from it, that of commodity time: unpredictable, speeding up and slowing down without warning, being seen by glimpses and then disappearing, like the phantom that it is. Water is not just the conduit of economic circulation but, in its surgings and floodings, its hydraulic analogue, a tide in the affairs of men. When the leech-gatherer reads the pond as if it were a book, he is confirming again the vaporous qualities of print whose passage through the streets of London we have surmised as one of the subjects of "Poor Susan." Cobbett's national debt is a thing with "no place at all," wherein gold and silver have turned to paper and been circulated out of existence and out of the pockets of investors whose only satisfaction is to have their names "written in a book."[49] The deistic regularity of a cosmic process that subsists by ceaseless motion is mimicked and overtaken by the mechanisms of modern psychic and economic life. Paper money and printed books beget more paper money and printed books.

Wordsworth's preoccupation with floods counters, as I have said, Michael's assurance that there will be no more deluges, that the next earth-changing event will be fire to "purge all things new" (*Paradise Lost*, 11: 900). It does so at least partly as a secular image of unpredictable and dangerous fluid circulation – the tides at Leven Sands come in fast, even if the tidings of Robespierre's death take a little longer – but it is also a reminder that the sins of this earth have not yet been punished nor the world made new for modern Noahs and their beasts. Wordsworth here invokes a Christian providential history, whose covenant he seems to have rejected as governing the world he sees around him, as a figure of commodification. Tides and torrents are the stuff of the sublime, but their analogues in seas of print threaten to engulf us and thus to breach the mind's sense of its own inviolability, which is exactly what makes the sublime a source of pleasure rather than terror. They model that rapid communication of intelligence whose effects Wordsworth feared, and against which he devised his own model of emotion recollected in tranquillity and the slow reading it calls for. In the most obvious sense, this slow or close reading – which would become the bedrock of literary pedagogy in the modern academy – offers a vigorous alternative to the time–space dislocations and speed reading that govern the modern economy and media cultures. In modeling the identity of a subculture of trained and deep readers who are immune to the seductions of first impressions, it also holds open the possibility that a few natural hearts can remain uncorrupted by the slick surfaces and fast moves of ordinary life under the sway of commodity form and commodity time. Deidre Lynch's *Economy of Character* makes exactly this case for the function of "rounded" characters in the later eighteenth-century novel (and beyond): they insist on being read over and over again if we are to decipher or speculate about their motives, and as such they offer us a virtual role outside the hectic cycle of consumerism wherein every item is rapidly replaced by another just like itself. To show a proper appreciation of Jane Austen's novels, for example, we must train ourselves to detect an authentic "language of undertone, uttered under a blanket of noise" (p. 239). At the same time, Lynch argues, we can sense in some of those same Austen novels a world in which "mechanical reproduction is perceived to be operating overtime and running amok" (p. 226) to the point that the privileged heroes and heroines themselves are not completely immune to its persuasions.[50] Austen at times seems unsettled by the power of her own fiction to conjure up the aura of real life – hence those famously flagrant reminders that we are after all still reading a novel, and one that cannot be completely immune to the materiality of the very print culture it critiques. And yet these do remain novels premised on the integrity of deep subjectivity, just as Lynch surmises.

There are no such characters in Wordsworth's poetry, not even himself. What is so disturbing about it is that the operations of close reading do not produce, I have argued, a deepening identity with a person or an inner life, but a prolonged reckoning with a dispersed literary tradition and with the bewitching functions of rhetoric and figure. The very authenticity desired and sometimes declaimed is not achieved. There is no one in "Yew Trees" or "Poor Susan" in whom to get deeply interested, and coming close to narrators or protagonists like the Wanderer produces as much or more critique as affection or identification. The poems are often made up of stories about ghosts told by ghosts. When we do explore a supposed interior life – for example in the narrator of "Gipsies" – what surfaces for inspection is not an exemplary individuality, something resistant to the pressures of commodification, but a more exact and detailed anatomy of commodification itself. As reading slows and meditation supervenes, modern temporalities and superficial sights are indeed challenged, but what comes to occupy the space is something akin to what Hartman (reading back from Conrad and from proverbially numberless college literature courses) calls a "heart of darkness."[51] Some of this has to do with books – the books that Wordsworth compulsively cites and incorporates into his diction, which is by no means as simple as he claims it to be. When the recourse is to cliché, as it is in "Poor Susan" or "Simon Lee," or in describing the descent after crossing the Alps, the effect is to dramatize this poetry's affiliations with the very traditions it claims to want to displace, the "mechanical adoption" of "figures of speech" that constitutes "what is usually called poetic diction."[52] Wordsworth's interest in and use of cliché is much too complex to be explained as merely a homage to the simplicity of ballad conventions. When it is Shakespeare or Milton who thicken the mixture, then we might suppose an effort to dignify the verse by writing into it the unmissable signatures of the best-loved and best-known English poets. In a case like "Gipsies," where Shakespeare and Milton inhabit the poem along with dramatic borrowings from a despised sonnet by Thomas Gray, something more ambivalent is going on, something suggesting the actual or potential equivalence of these and every other literary precursor, whether they be the property of high, middle or low culture.[53] If, in the pool of precursive rhetoric available to the excited mind of the judgmental narrator, Shakespeare, Milton and Gray are thus grouped together, does this not suggest a flattening out of the peaks and valleys of literary history into one featureless plain of polemical opportunity? Would this not be a poetics of commodification? From Coleridge and Hazlitt on, this poem has shocked its readers as some sort of false coining, morally or poetically deficient and perhaps both. I would counter that it is Wordsworth's genius along with an astonishing immunity to embarrassment that allows him to produce a paradigm poem for the times, so much so that the times could not understand its breaching of the boundaries between high- and middle-brow culture, high poetic vocation and petulant bourgeois moralism. Each becomes the other without quite ceasing to be itself. The complexities of the Shakespearean and Miltonic allusions are such as to deepen by their very deciphering the gravity of the poem, while the incorporation of "what is usually called poetic diction" shackles its rhetoric with epiphenomenal gestures that affront the steady gaze of cultivated readers. Persisting with that gaze while opening oneself to crossing the very boundaries that close reading was otherwise designed to preserve – between high and low-middle culture, between the philosophic-aesthetic mind and the second-hand appeal of prefabricated poeticisms – permits an understanding of the poem as a stunningly articulate symptom of the very thing it so histrionically decries. To be able to *think* of seeing the table standing on its head or dancing is to think within the world created by the fetishism of the commodity. The absurdity of that gesture held, for Marx, the potential for critique. Similarly, to be able to think of oneself as Wordsworth's pompous narrator, walking for "twelve bounteous hours" without ever saying what the bounty might be, is to think oneself within a world that encases us but which we prefer not to recognize as our own. The routines of fastidious taste that render "Gipsies" a bad poem only deepen the self-deception that we are not, after all, we who are deep readers, touched by the fetishism of the commodity that governs everyone else, including those who "appreciate" Thomas Gray's sonnet.

These insights, which affiliate Wordsworth with Keats, the Della Cruscans and the sentimental poets in a common willingness to engage with the shopworn components of poetic language, only add further complexities to a body of poetry that, I have argued, uncommonly and perhaps uniquely records what it is like to live within a culture impacted for the first time by the full dispersal of commodity form throughout the economic system and the social imaginary. No one works harder than Wordsworth to mount an exemplary critique of these forces taking on seemingly irresistible powers in the years around 1800, and no one registers with greater clarity the extent and depth of their capacity to remake human beings in their own image.[54] Wordsworth is the eloquent poet of what Agamben calls substitutability, the potential for each of us to become the other, not in some saving theological way (an equivalence in the sight of God) but according to the harsh logic of exchange wherein any thing or person will do as well as any other and cannot be assured that it will not have to play the part of the other. The inherited truisms about mutability and mortality – *debemur morti nos nostraque* – are renovated here only to put us to death all over again by the engines of a modern world of which Horace could have known nothing. It is not just money, which had been around for centuries, nor private property, nor class, which were similarly long-durational in different forms, nor even luxury and consumption, which were the objects of righteous protests for several centuries before Wordsworth's time, that created the urgency apparent in this poetry. What gathers all of these symptoms together and makes them into a quite new historical formation is the power of machine-driven production under rapidly developing capitalist conditions of valorization and exchange coincident with the phenomenon of mass warfare. This the world had not seen before. Wordsworth saw all around him the ghosts who walked the earth as the figures of an existing *lumpenproletariat* which already included many of his kind, the subculture of working or aspiring writers, and would have warmly welcomed him too into its ranks. No wonder he could not distinguish himself fully from the homeless and destitute figures who haunted his poetry and his dreams. No wonder he could not fully articulate his relationship to books beyond telling about his early love of fairy tales – a narration which already carried him far from shore and into very deep waters. No wonder that his social-political address, when it is pursued (as it must be) beyond our inherited assumptions, produces a poetics of social concern. Wordsworth's greatest gift to literary history, and his greatest contribution to an understanding *of* history, is that he was never sure that he knew what to say, or how to say it. His failure of resolution and independence which, however conscious it was, was in every important sense deliberate and is as such open to careful intellectual and theoretical articulation, aligns him with those readers of the twenty-first century who are engaged in trying to understand the dynamics of their own society as that society becomes, increasingly since 1989 and again after 9/11, more and more obliged to confront the possibility that the very mechanisms with which it purports to alleviate its concerns are themselves significantly implicated in their continued and urgent existence.

Notes

INTRODUCTION

1 Ferry, *Limits of Mortality*, pp. 51, 70.
2 See Hartman, *Wordsworth's Poetry*.
3 McGann, *Romantic Ideology*, p. 88.
4 See, for example, de Man, *Rhetoric of Romanticism*, pp. 67–81; *Romanticism and Contemporary Criticism*, pp. 74–94.
5 Wordsworth, *Prose Works*, I: 128.
6 Exemplary instances can be found in, respectively, Agamben, *Coming Community*; Deleuze and Guattari, *Nomadology*; Hardt and Negri, *Multitude*.
7 A good summary of the trope of the *Muselmann* can be found in Anidjar, *The Jew, the Arab*, pp. 113–49. See also Simpson, *9/11*, pp. 160–70.
8 Santner, *On Creaturely Life*. The "spectral materialism" that Santner traces in Sebald's writing works well enough as summary of Wordsworth's poetry as I here understand it.
9 Heidegger, *Being and Time*, pp. 159, 169.
10 Marx, *Capital One*, p. 163.
11 But at least one writer ascribes to consumerism the same level of mystery that Marx finds surrounding the commodity: Campbell, *Romantic Ethic*, p. 37, writes that "a mystery surrounds consumer behaviour, or, at least, there is a mystery surrounding the behaviour of consumers in modern industrial societies." He finds the whole question to have been poorly theorized, with attention given primarily to vividly particular examples.
12 Mitchell, *Iconology*, p. 161. Mitchell's own brief discussion of the commodity (pp. 185–90) is both incisive and generative.
13 Thus Appadurai, in *Social Life of Things*, while commendably setting out to restore a "calculative" dimension (p. 12) to premodern societies, preserves pride of place for a "subject" whose "judgment" constitutes value and thus for the primary role of a "politics" (p. 3). But commodity form is not about "human transactions and calculations that enliven things" (p. 5); it is about things relating to one another independently of human knowledge and control. Marx, as so often, turns conventional expectations upside down.
14 Lefebvre, *Production of Space*, pp. 306, 340. As commodities, things become resolved into pure "relations" (p. 402), but relations with real power over lived experience. See also pp. 340–43.

15 Marx, *Capital One*, p. 128.
16 Lukács, *History and Class Consciousness*, pp. 87, 90.
17 See Marx, *Capital Two*, pp. 121ff., 207.
18 Marx, *Capital One*, p. 176.
19 Marx, *Capital Two*, p. 221.
20 Wordsworth, *Prose Works*, I: 128.
21 Levinson, *Keats's Life of Allegory*, p. 292.
22 Liu, *Wordsworth*; Langan, *Romantic Vagrancy*.
23 Keats, *Letters*, I: 281.
24 Millar, *Historical View*, pp. 725, 777.
25 Marx, *Capital One*, p. 163.

AT THE LIMITS OF SYMPATHY

1 Sachs, *End of Poverty*, pp. xvii, 1.
2 Wordsworth, *Thirteen Book Prelude*, 9: 519–26. Here and generally throughout, I quote from the AB-Stage reading text dating from 1805–6, henceforth cited as *Prelude*. Exceptions will be noted.
3 See Gareth Stedman Jones, *An End to Poverty?*, who argues for the importance of Paine's writings to the late eighteenth-century discussion of welfare, and describes the efforts in the early French republic to establish a committee overseeing the right to subsistence, estimated to be lacking for an eighth of the population of France (pp. 110–19).
4 Wordsworth found the same image apt in summing up the situation of the child suffering under a "modern" education: "String'd like a poor man's Heifer, at its feed / Led through the lanes in forlorn servitude" (*Prelude*, 5: 240–41).
5 The guillotine was not used in a public execution until April 1792 and did not figure significantly in the September Massacres of that year. But Wordsworth is of course writing well after these events and in the light of the violent traditions relating to knitting during the "Terror." The "knitters" were specifically Montagnards who did handwork in the galleries of the political clubs in 1792–93 and beside the guillotine. Many of them may have been seamstresses, others shredding linen: see Godineau, *Women of Paris*, pp. 212, 301. Beaupuy left with his regiment for the Rhineland in late July; he and Wordsworth did not meet again.
6 Wordsworth, *Fourteen Book Prelude*, p. 193 (9: 510f.).
7 Marx, *Capital One*, p. 148.
8 Thus Berg, *Age of Manufactures*, p. 196: "the classic textile innovations were all developed initially within rural dispersed manufacture." The mechanization of small-unit production was often undertaken to preempt the competition of the larger factories. The first Arkwright mills were "located in the countryside close to sources of water power" (p. 230). See pp. 236–41 for further details.
9 Hufton, *Poor of Eighteenth-Century France*, pp. 25–42.

10 Berg, *Age of Manufactures*, p. 254. For a detailed history, see Mantoux, *Industrial Revolution*, p. 399f.
11 This word "heartless" is massively overdetermined: it contrasts with the name of Vaudracour who is about to appear in the early drafts of Book 9 of the poem. Vaudracour ("heartsworth" and/or "courtsworth") is the displaced Wordsworth figure separated from his lover by the cruel father in alliance with the state. He is punished for his lovemaking while being nominated as one who would like to make love (*il vaudra faire la cour à*).
12 Marx, *Capital One*, p. 152.
13 Arnold, "The Study of Poetry," pp. 4, 2. The Wordsworth concordance indeed lists sixty-nine uses of the word *sustain*, twice as many as Shakespeare and Milton combined.
14 Take, for instance, the extraordinary embrace of Putnam's *Bowling Alone* by the same political and media classes which had previously fastened on Etzioni's *The Spirit of Community* as the best new recipe for social regeneration. The mood is nowhere better captured than in the title of Elster's (edited) *The Roundtable Talks*.
15 Anthony Giddens, in Beck, Giddens and Lash, *Reflexive Modernization*, pp. 97, 100.
16 MacIntyre, *After Virtue*, p. 263.
17 Some of these questions have been recently focused for the Romantic period in Russell and Tuite (eds.), *Romantic Sociability*. Much more work has been done on this topic in the eighteenth century.
18 Wordsworth, *Poems 1807*, p. 128.
19 They can of course be either, as much of the recent work on sentiment and sympathy has made clear: see, among others, Mullan, *Sentiment and Sociability*, who stresses the discordant social effects of sentiment carried to the point of a medical condition; Marshall, *Surprising Effects of Sympathy*, who explores the eighteenth-century concerns about faking sentiment; and Pinch, *Strange Fits of Passion*, who addresses the paradoxes of the felt need for the management of what is apparently spontaneous. See also Barker-Benfield, *Culture of Sensibility*; Ellison, *Cato's Tears*; and Averill, *Wordsworth*, pp. 21–54, who sees sentimentalism as proto-Wordsworthian in its reflexive self-consciousness and far from spontaneous because of its explicitly literary heritage: "the sentimental poet looks out into the world of guilt and sorrow to discover himself" (p. 52).
20 Mackenzie, *Man of Feeling*, p. 59.
21 Marx, *Capital One*, p. 144n. To complete a circle, Žižek suggests that Marx's model of commodity form is also the paradigm of the Freudian symptom: see *Sublime Object*, pp. 11–53.
22 Coleridge, *Biographia*, II: 127, 129.
23 Although the current "war on terror" might seem to have superseded the currency of a civility-ideal, its ongoing appeal is apparent in the demands placed upon a radically dismantled Iraqi "state" to reproduce a recognizable dialogic democracy.

24 Beck, Giddens and Lash, *Reflexive Modernization*, p. 39. This is needless to say a far cry from what his coeditor Anthony Giddens hopes for by way of a "cosmopolitan conversation of humankind" (p. 100). However might that happen?
25 It must be said that the appeal of dialogism is not restricted to neoliberal political scientists, as the formative but flexible role of Habermas's work makes clear. Marshall Berman, for example, responds to the internationalist strand in the Communist Manifesto in finding that "one of the things that can make modern life worth living is the enhanced opportunities it offers us – and sometimes even forces on us – to talk together, to reach and understand each other." See *All That Is Solid*, p. 9. Recall also the rhapsodic prospect in Marx's 1844 manuscripts of communist artisans embodying the unity of theory and society in the routines of everyday conversational sociability: "the brotherhood of man is no mere phrase with them, but a fact of life" (Marx and Engels, *Collected Works*, III: 313). A further variant is the Bakhtinian dialogism wherein the diversities represented are formally irreducible and not a matter of authorial choice, though Bakhtin himself notoriously denies that poetry can achieve this representation, which properly belongs to the novel form.
26 Habermas, *Communicative Action*, p. 70.
27 Bewell, *Wordsworth*; Derrida, "Structure, Sign and Play."
28 Or we may resort, as Coleridge did, to Kantian projections of assumed consensus that are defensible because they remain transcendental: Simpson, *Figurings of the Real*, pp. 1–20.
29 Smith, *Moral Sentiments*, p. 12.
30 Wordsworth, *Prose Works*, I: 138.
31 Coleridge, *Biographia*, II: 129, 136.
32 Wordsworth, *Prose Works*, I: 138.
33 Bialostosky, *Wordsworth*, pp. 55–133, does make the case for a Bakhtinian syndrome at work in the poetry but makes clear that what is at issue is not actual dialogue but a play of internalized voices within the poetic psyche. This does not establish communication, but it does render the poems as something other than the "self-indulgent single voice of the ideologue" (p. 73).
34 Bentham, *Principles*, pp. 15–17, 43ff.
35 A character in Thelwall's *Peripatetic*, pp. 139–40, makes just this case in arguing that reciprocity of feeling only exists between those who are not separated by extreme class distinctions.
36 Simmel, *On Individuality*, p. 132.
37 See, for example, Marshall, *Figure of Theater*; Klein, *Shaftesbury*; Carter, *Men and the Emergence of Polite Society*; Davidson, *Hypocrisy*. The ongoing modern inquiry into this topic was significantly initiated by the work of Norbert Elias.
38 Kant also suggests that it is the idea of communicability itself that is the source of pleasure in the aesthetic judgment. Form would then be the secondary element whose lack of purposiveness is assumed but need never be proven.

39 Marx, *Capital One*, p. 149.
40 Wordsworth, *Poetical Works*, V: 20. The italics are in the text.
41 See Simpson, *Wordsworth's Historical Imagination*, pp. 160–84, which discusses sympathy by resorting to pertinent but not decisive historical-contextual explanations. Hartman, *Fateful Question*, has written on "the sympathy paradox" (pp. 141–64) as central to the mission of literature in modern culture: art must encourage sensibility but thereby risks desensitizing us. Brooks, "Wordsworth and Human Suffering," remains a central statement of the issues.
42 The best reading I have seen of the poem's opening is in Hickey, *Impure Conceits*, pp. 25–36. Literary allusion is here adduced as inaugurating the "decentering impulse that motivates the poem as a whole" (p. 26). Hickey's book does fine work in rescuing *The Excursion* from the Victorians and their modern acolytes.
43 Swann, "Suffering and Sensation"; see pp. 84, 93. The first extended treatment of Wordsworth's interest in suffering women was by Jacobus, *Tradition and Experiment*. See also Ross, "Naturalizing Gender," which argues that the figure of woman transforms history into ideology by way of shoring up "the male need for self-identity" (p. 391). For a more nuanced and extended treatment, see Page, *Wordsworth*.
44 Wordsworth, *Ruined Cottage*, pp. 43–45. I cite from the 1799 ms. copy (Ms. B). The "dewy shade" is ambivalent, and portends Milton's "Etrurian shades" of Vallombrosa (*PL*, 1: 303), in which Wordsworth has, as we will see, a sustained interest. It is somewhat comic to suggest that being within the dewy shade of postlapsarian tree cover could be a comfortable spot. Between plain and shade, there is really no place to go, unless the world be already redeemed.
45 Compare, for example, the "dark encounter" of warring clouds at *PL*, 2: 718.
46 Kames, *Essays*, pp. 19–20.
47 Homans, *Women Writers*, p. 25, finds him "a bit too consoled. This natural peace, exquisite as it is, is paid for by the woman's death." Brooks, "Wordsworth and Human Suffering," is "not at all sure" how this story promotes wisdom and finds the Wanderer more a "poetic creation" than the exponent of "plausible arguments" (pp. 385, 387). The fullest account of Wordsworth's image of suffering is Averill, *Wordsworth*: see especially pp. 128–46 for an excellent account of the varieties of Greek and Roman attitudes to the desirability and possibility of suffering with others. Averill's own preference is to regard Wordsworthian protagonists as inviting an experience of Aristotelian *katharsis*.
48 The function of still life in Wordsworth's aesthetic repertoire will be discussed in chapter 6.
49 Wordsworth, *Poetical Works*, V: 20. Hickey, *Impure Conceits*, p. 36, notes the "rather crass revision" of Miranda's lines from *The Tempest*: "I have suffered / With those that I saw suffer" (I.ii.13). Crassness is all.
50 Liu, *Wordsworth*, pp. 341–58.

51 See also Fumerton, *Unsettled*, pp. 3–4, 38, on the earlier legal constraints on pedlars by way of the vagrancy acts.
52 See also Levinson, *Romantic Fragment*, pp. 221–30, which finds the poem to be engaged in the transposition and sublimation of social history into aesthetic ideology.
53 Langan, *Romantic Vagrancy*, p. 229. Langan's extended account (pp. 225–60) has contributed much to my thinking here. She builds upon an equally important account by Marjorie Levinson, who argues that Keats's "Lamia" is an allegory of "the evolution of value forms and their corresponding social forms," with Lamia herself as "the money form" and her magic "the fabulous face of the exchange system" (*Keats's Life of Allegory*, pp. 261, 285, 288).
54 In the first book of *The Excursion*, flax is replaced by hemp (1: 885). Langan, *Romantic Vagrancy*, p. 251, notes that this places her at the bottom of the economic ladder, requiring the intervention of a "mediated exchange value" to place her goods into the marketplace. There is no "immediate use value." Mantoux notes that the jenny, "the simplest of all spinning machines," at first benefited the "smaller masters" though it was unpopular with their underlings: see Mantoux, *Industrial Revolution*, pp. 263–69. Liu, *Wordsworth*, pp. 329–31, has a valuable account of the differences in the home weaving economies of the West Country and the Lakes, both of which Wordsworth knew at first hand. Wordsworth's insight into the phenomenon of proleptically alienated labor in places seemingly not yet literally touched by the factory work pattern is discussed in Simpson, *Figurings of the Real*, pp. 31–38.
55 This is Langan's suggestion: see *Romantic Vagrancy*, p. 238.
56 Simmel, *Philosophy of Money*, p. 227.
57 Thus Scarry, *Body in Pain*, p. 7: "to have great pain is to have certainty; to hear that another person has pain is to have doubt." The pain of the other can neither be denied nor confirmed, so little so that it can be denied or ignored altogether (p. 4). While it would be excessive to deduce the activities of the torturer from the merely pompous bad faith of the pedlar, both are implicated in the (modern) psychic economy that Scarry describes.
58 See Barrell, *Spirit of Despotism*, pp. 210–46.
59 See Bermingham, "The Simple Life," pp. 37–62.
60 Harrison, *Wordsworth's Vagrant Muse*, pp. 18, 57ff.
61 Marx, and Engels, *Collected Works*, 3: 282.

AT HOME WITH HOMELESSNESS

1 Wordsworth, *Salisbury Plain*, p. 33.
2 De Quincey, *Collected Writings*, II: 242.
3 Wordsworth, *Poems 1807*, p. 408. Nor was this Wordsworth's only refiguring of the real: the "old man almost double" who had been a leech-gatherer was, when encountered on October 3, 1800, begging while on his way to Carlisle "where he should buy a few godly books to sell." See Dorothy Wordsworth, *Journals*, I: 63. The leech-gatherer's career as a used book salesman speaks

to a connection between books, poverty and commodity we will encounter again.
4 Wallace, *Walking*, pp. 1–66.
5 Bakhtin, *Dialogic Imagination*, p. 98.
6 Moretti, *Graphs*, pp. 58–59.
7 Wordsworth, *Salisbury Plain*, pp. 38, 34.
8 Wordsworth, *Lyrical Ballads*, p. 58.
9 Wordsworth, *Salisbury Plain*, p. 152.
10 For an important recent account of the poem(s), see Benis, *Romanticism on the Road*, pp. 57–93.
11 *The Excursion*, 9: 445–51, in *Poetical Works*, V: 300. For a fuller reading of this passage, see Hickey, *Impure Conceits*, pp. 157–65.
12 Virilio, *Speed and Politics*.
13 See Jameson, *Postmodernism*, pp. 16–19.
14 Adorno, *Minima Moralia*, pp. 38–39.
15 Heidegger, "Building, Dwelling, Thinking."
16 Agamben, *Means Without End*, p. 15.
17 Wordsworth, *Poems 1807*, p. 186.
18 Agamben, *The Coming Community*, p. 23.
19 Hardt and Negri, *Multitude*, p. xvii.
20 I have written at greater length on the first two poems in *Wordsworth's Historical Imagination*, pp. 22–55, 175–77, and further thoughts on "Gipsies" appear in "Figuring Sex."
21 Debord, *Society of the Spectacle*, #168.
22 Liu, *Wordsworth*, pp. 4, 6, 10.
23 Hartman, *Wordsworth's Poetry*, pp. 3–30.
24 Woodring, *Wordsworth*, p. 54. See also Brooks, "Wordsworth and Human Suffering."
25 Chandler, *Wordsworth's Second Nature*, pp. 84–92.
26 See Simpson, *Wordsworth's Historical Imagination*, pp. 162–74; Harrison, *Wordsworth's Vagrant Muse*, pp. 139–71; Benis, *Romanticism on the Road*, pp. 116–23. Harrison and Benis offer especially rich accounts of the eighteenth-century charity debates. Robin Jarvis, "Wordsworth and the Uses of Charity," explores the private charity debate and finds it still current in then-contemporary Britain. See also Connell, *Romanticism, Economics*, which argues for a connection with Malthus (pp. 19–30); and Dick, "Poverty, Charity, Poetry," which explores the analogy between begging and unproductive poetry.
27 Foucault, *Discipline and Punish*.
28 See Shershow, *The Work and The Gift*, esp. pp. 115–35, for a compelling account of the purposively slippery relations between work and charity at the turn of the twenty-first century.
29 Lamb, *Preserving the Self*, pp. 136–44. On the coexistence and interaction of gift and commodity exchanges in modern Papua New Guinea, see Gregory, *Gifts and Commodities*.

30 Wordsworth, *Lyrical Ballads*, p. 233.
31 Marx and Engels, *Collected Works*, III: 274; *Werke*, supplementary volume, p. 514.
32 Bentham, *Writings on the Poor Laws*, pp. 91–140.
33 *Ibid.*, p. 25.
34 Garber, *Wordsworth*, p. 106; Johnston, *Wordsworth and the Recluse*, p. 41; Benis, *Romanticism on the Road*, p. 113.
35 It is interesting to note that the narrator has this both ways. His first account of the scene with the birds has the beggar "still attempting to prevent the waste" (l. 17), while his final, hyperbolic benediction bids us allow the old man to "share his chance-gather'd meal" with the "little birds" (ll. 186–87). (*Lyrical Ballads*, pp. 229, 234). If this is sharing, it is not the result of any benign intent.
36 See Agamben, *Remnants*.
37 I draw here upon the fine analysis by Lynch, *Economy of Character*, pp. 24–28. Frow, *Time and Commodity Culture*, pp. 162–79, discusses the international trade in human body parts as a later stage in the logic of commodification.
38 Rousseau, *Discourse*, p. 23.
39 La Mettrie ascribes a social function to eating: "Joy revives in a sad heart, and infects the souls of comrades" (*Man a Machine*, p. 93).
40 Levi is thus cited in Santner, *On Creaturely Life*, p. 25. Creaturely life is Santner's term for the state of being occupying gaps in the "space of meaning" and subsisting beyond sociological categories like "the poor" (pp. xv, xviii).
41 See Agamben, *The Open*.
42 Marx and Engels, *Collected Works*, III: 274–75.
43 Cowper, *Poems*, II: 155.
44 See note 40 above.
45 See Rabinbach, *Human Motor*.
46 Both cited in Schivelbusch, *Railway Journey*, pp. 9, 13.
47 Marx, *Capital One*, p. 481.
48 Lynch, *Economy of Character*, pp. 192–99, 211–13.
49 Mandeville, *Fable of the Bees*, II: 142.
50 Smith, *Wealth of Nations*, I: 20.
51 Wordsworth, *Letters: Early Years*, p. 434.
52 It is striking that Wordsworth calls this a *dislocation*, or shifting of place, in describing a change in metrical time. The place–time conflation in Wordsworth is discussed in chapter 5 below.
53 Underwood, *Work of the Sun*, p. 17. See also pp. 33–34 and ff.
54 Dorothy Wordsworth, *Journals*, I: 109. Compare Dorothy's notice of Ellis the letter-carrier: "He goes at that slow pace every morning, and after having wrought a hard day's work returns at night, however weary he may be, takes in all quietly" (I: 108). For an account of the fir-grove path, see Simpson, *Figurings of the Real*, pp. 31–38. In *The Excursion* the Solitary's cottage is fronted by a "plot of green-sward … for reiterated steps / Smooth and

commodious" (4: 242, 245–46) where the ramblers walk up and down during the Wanderer's long homily. Wordsworth himself often paced back and forth while composing.
55 Marx and Engels, *Collected Works*, III: 236.
56 Marx, *Capital One*, pp. 458, 460.
57 Mayr, *Authority, Liberty*, p. 139. Mayr finds a declining incidence of clockwork metaphors because they were incompatible with liberal models of movement. Newtonian paradigms were more adaptable to ideas about the necessity of constant adjustment (p. 98). See pp. 62–101 for an account of Descartes's model of animals (including humans) as automata.
58 Langan, *Romantic Vagrancy*, pp. 59–138. This is in many ways the key argument in her book.
59 Wordsworth, *The Excursion*, 8: 322, 324, in *Poetical Works*, V: 276.
60 See, for example, Southey's 1807 *Letters from England*, pp. 207–12.
61 Godwin, *The Enquirer*, p. 188; Rousseau, *Reveries*, pp. 49–52.
62 Simpson, *Wordsworth's Historical Imagination*, pp. 22–55; and "Figuring Sex."
63 Derrida, *Specters*, pp. 42–45.
64 Wordsworth, *Poems 1807*, p. 211.
65 Also at issue here is Michael's rebuking Adam's eager sight of sexual pleasure under "the evening star / Love's harbinger" (*PL*, 11: 588–89).
66 Derrida, *Specters*, p. 45.

FIGURES IN THE MIST

1 See Simpson, "What Bothered Charles Lamb." I have been rather briskly taken to task by Adela Pinch for the "construction of a fantasy" about the connections between prostitutes and servant girls (*Strange Fits of Passion*, p. 104), for identifying both with a critique of the culture of commodification, and (most oddly of all) for a prurient impulse blaming Susan for her own demise! My point was, and is, that these connections were commonplace at the time, as I demonstrate at length, and that Susan is a victim, as I hope will be quite clear to most readers. See also Peter Manning's "Placing Poor Susan," the first version of which appeared simultaneously with my own essay in 1986 and shares some of its arguments.
2 See Manning, "Placing Poor Susan", p. 313.
3 See Harrison, *Wordsworth's Vagrant Muse*, pp. 41–49 (drawing on the work of Sean Shesgreen and John Barrell). T. J. Clark, *The Painting of Modern Life*, pp. 79–146, gives a thorough account of the anxieties and desires associated with unattached women in the city. We might note at least the oddness of Wordsworth's own narrated focus on "the Magdalene of le Brun" (*Prelude*, 9: 78) as the summation of his Paris visit in 1791. Marx wrote of the "universal prostitution" created by money in *Grundrisse*, p. 163; Simmel developed the association between money and prostitution by way of the "completely fleeting inconsequential relationship" which can be "radically terminated" by

the exchange of money (*Philosophy of Money*, p. 376). The association of Corinth with both commercial sex and spectral or apparitional form is discussed in Levinson's reading of Keats's "Lamia": see *Keats's Life of Allegory*, p. 273. Wordsworth is famous for the ghostly girls of the Lucy poems, and for his demystification of Gothic femininity in "The Thorn" and "Goody Blake and Harry Gill," where what looks to be supernatural is explained as ordinary experience. But his ghost-figures are otherwise mostly old men, for reasons that may have to do with either or both displacement and identification. Mary Jacobus, *Romanticism*, argues that the placing of Dorothy "simultaneously figures the repression of sexuality and the refusal of sexual difference. Women are all the same (as the young Wordsworth)" (p. 208).

4 Here I am drawing upon Moretti, *Atlas*, p. 83 n.5.
5 Rogers, *Grub Street*, p. ix.
6 See Jacobus, *Romanticism*, pp. 222–26.
7 Lynch, *Economy of Character*, p. 35.
8 Johnston, *Hidden Wordsworth*, p. 242. Johnston gives a detailed account of the culture and geography of the old city. See also Barrell, *Spirit of Despotism*, pp. 16–74.
9 Liu, *Wordsworth*, pp. 311–58. Other studies have described the extent and complex poetic manifestation of Wordsworth's anxieties about professionalism and poetic labor. See, for example, Simpson, *Wordsworth's Historical Imagination*; Eilenberg, *Strange Power of Speech*; Erickson, *Economy of Literary Form*, pp. 49–69; Schoenfield, *The Professional Wordsworth*; Pfau, *Wordsworth's Profession*; Janowitz, *Lyric and Labour*.
10 Wordsworth, *Prose Works*, I: 128; *Prelude*, 7: 209–10, 177.
11 See Ferdinand, "Selling it to the Provinces."
12 Gatrell, *City of Laughter*, pp. 86–87, 248–49.
13 In "Lines Written Near Richmond," published in 1798, Wordsworth exposes the fantasy of poets who follow a "faithless gleam" upon the water and expect that "colours shall endure" (*Lyrical Ballads*, p. 105). Poor Susan and her poet see them fade. See also the "lines of curling mist" of *Prelude*, 1: 590.
14 Johnston, *Hidden Wordsworth*, p. 245.
15 Wordsworth, *Poetical Works*, V: 269 (8: 123–27).
16 Cowper, *Poems*, 2: 116–17.
17 See Johnston, *Wordsworth and the Recluse*, pp. 37–43.
18 Two readings in particular have informed my discussion here: Bewell, *Wordsworth*, pp. 81–93; and Langan, *Romantic Vagrancy*, pp. 193–207.
19 The text can be found in *Lyrical Ballads*, pp. 277–82.
20 Langan, *Romantic Vagrancy*, p. 197. She also suggests the imaging of soldier and narrator as a single, split subject, a tandem of the transcendental spirit and the reduced empirical form (p. 195).
21 Bewell, *Wordsworth*, p. 85.
22 Langan, *Romantic Vagrancy*, pp. 204–5, notes that in 1803 Parliament was to allow the privilege of begging without culpability to be extended to returning veterans on their way from the ports to their home towns. The explicit

connection between soldiers and vagabonds is one that we will soon explore further.
23 Johnston, *Wordsworth and the Recluse*, p. 39.
24 Wordsworth, *Ruined Cottage*, p. 75.
25 Bewell, *Romanticism and Colonial Disease*, esp. pp. 108–19. In his vagueness about dates Wordsworth may be repressing or ignoring the slave revolts in Saint Domingue that were the principal cause of Britain's military efforts in the Caribbean in the 1790s: see Jacobus, *Romanticism*, pp. 73–74. But he could not have intended or indeed managed to disavow the effects of these campaigns on the men who conducted them. See also the discussion of the tropics in Barrell, *Infection of Thomas De Quincey*.
26 Linebaugh, *London Hanged*, reports that "in December 1796 the 32nd Regiment sailed with 650 men for St Domingo and by February only 80 were fit for service" (p. 412).
27 Simpson, "Wordsworth and Empire." The allusion to Cook is also argued in Bolton, "Taking Possession."
28 Bewell, *Wordsworth*, pp. 71–105; see also Wiley, *Romantic Geography*, pp. 79–126. Relevant earlier accounts are Garber, *Wordsworth*, pp. 113–17; and Simpson, *Irony and Authority*, pp. 72–76.
29 Wordsworth, *Lyrical Ballads*, p. 249, ll. 48, 64–68.
30 See Smith, *European Vision*, pp. 20–21. For more on the Patagonian giants, see Lamb, *Preserving the Self*, pp. 93–96; and Lamb, Smith and Thomas (eds.), *Exploration and Exchange*, pp. 46–66. In *Preserving the Self*, pp. 227, 234–35, Lamb reports on a tradition of satire attending exploration narratives, and on the habit of setting up English gardens mimicking Pacific landscapes.
31 Thelwall, *Peripatetic*, p. 73.
32 As does Ferry, *Limits of Mortality*, pp. 160, 171.
33 Wordsworth, *Prose Works*, II: 58.
34 Bewell, *Romanticism*, pp. 51, 69.
35 Wordsworth, *Lyrical Ballads*, p. 143.
36 Beer, *Wordsworth*, p. 194. See also Garber, *Wordsworth*, p. 116, on the poem's function as a memento mori.
37 Rousseau, *Discourse*, pp. 84–85.
38 Derrida, *Specters*, p. 99. See also p. 39.
39 The *cogito* in Descartes's French, *je pense, donc je suis*, can also be heard as a pun on the verb *suivre*, reading *je suis* as "I follow." I am therefore I follow, what I know of being consists in following … these are fitting ontologies for the Wordsworthian subject.
40 Derrida, *Acts of Religion*, p. 361.
41 Derrida, *Of Hospitality*, pp. 47–49.
42 Hazlitt, *Complete Works*, IV: 45.
43 Marx and Engels, *Selected Works*, I: 442.
44 *Ibid.*
45 Stallybrass, "Marx and Heterogeneity," p. 73, also pertinently notes the comparison to Wordsworth's view of London, as well as offering a thorough

review of the literature on the topic of the *lumpenproletariat*. See also *Capital One*, p. 797, where Marx seems to want to distinguish the "actual lumpenproletariat" from the three other categories of pauper.

46 Rancière, *Philosopher and his Poor*, pp. 96, 102.
47 See Marx, *Capital One*, pp. 1041–44.
48 Cited in Katz, *The Jews*, p. 294.
49 Endelman, *Jews of Georgian England*, p. 171. See also pp. 181–83.
50 *Ibid.*, p. 182.
51 Erickson, *Economy of Literary Form*, pp. 19–48.
52 Coleman, *British Paper Industry*, pp. 90, 166–67. According to Shorter, *Paper Making*, p. 41, some £200,000 p.a. was still being spent on imported rags in 1800.
53 Mayhew, *London Labour*, II: 138. Mayhew estimates that the ragpickers, who overlap with the bone-finders, the cigar-end finders and the dogs'-dung collectors, were annually producing some 1,240,000 lbs. of rags (p. 140).
54 Adorno's letter to Benjamin is cited in Jameson (ed.), *Aesthetics and Politics*, p. 130.
55 Marx and Engels, *Selected Works*, I: 478.
56 Emsley, *British Society*, pp. 164, 173.
57 See Halpern, *Poetics of Primitive Accumulation*, pp. 61–75; Fumerton, *Unsettled*, esp. pp. 153–56.
58 Marx, *Capital Three*, p. 343.
59 See Lefebvre, *The Great Fear*.
60 Cobbett, *Selected Writings*, I: 9–16.
61 See Linebaugh, *London Hanged*, pp. 130–34; and Fumerton, *Unsettled*, pp. 84ff.
62 Wordsworth, *Poems 1807*, p. 569.
63 Marx and Engels, *Selected Works*, I: 487.
64 Marx and Engels, *Collected Works*, IV: 329. See also Southey, *Letters from England*, pp. 209–10.
65 Marx and Engels, *Selected Works*, I: 109, 111, 115.

TIMING MODERNITY: AROUND 1800

1 Wordsworth, *Prose Works*, I: 128.
2 Lentricchia and McAuliffe, *Crimes*, pp. 18–22.
3 Horkheimer and Adorno, *Dialectic*, p. 137.
4 Wordsworth, *Prose Works*, I: 128.
5 Horkheimer and Adorno, *Dialectic*, pp. 121, 157.
6 At least one historian claims that in Britain "the loss of life among servicemen was proportionately higher between 1794 and 1815 than between 1914 and 1918." See Emsley, *British Society*, p. 169. Lukács's *The Historical Novel* argues for the role of citizen armies, raised in France by conscription, in creating a historically new sense of shared national identity. Wordsworth's critique of the Convention of Cintra approves of "massification" when it takes the form

of a populist opposition to the French invaders (*Prose Works*, I: 233–34, 289–90, 294, 300) but also registers its negative reflection in the "formal machine" governed by a despotic political overseer able to command "concentration of effort" and "rapidity of motion" (306, 312) from his subjects.
7 Wordsworth, *Prose Works*, I: 116.
8 Williams, *Politics and Letters*, p. 164.
9 See Fairer, "The Year Runs Round."
10 Benjamin, *Charles Baudelaire*, pp. 35, 38, 58. Chandler and Gilmartin, in *Romantic Metropolis*, pp. 1–41, make a case for London around 1800 as historically prior to Baudelaire's Paris in being pervaded by Benjamin's idea of the panoramic; so too they argue for Wordsworth's anticipation of Simmel's account of the modern metropolis. See also Kaufman, "Red Kant."
11 Altick, *Shows of London*, makes clear that spectacles of various sorts (including automata) were themselves commodities and made available as such to the paying public.
12 Benjamin, *The Arcades Project*, p. 460.
13 Benjamin, *Selected writings*, IV: 391.
14 See Halpern, *Shakespeare*, pp. 251–53; see also, for a fine account of Benjamin's idea of allegory, pp. 1–14.
15 Johnston, *Wordsworth and the Recluse*, e.g. pp. 174, 207. These passages have been widely discussed as central to the modeling of the Wordsworthian self. The classic psychoanalytic reading is Onorato, *Mind of the Poet*, pp. 205–19, 243–45, 253–54. See also Beer, *Wordsworth in Time*, pp. 29–52.
16 Chandler, *Wordsworth's Second Nature*, pp. 185, 187, 199.
17 Liu, *Wordsworth*, pp. 204, 446f.
18 Hartman, *Wordsworth's Poetry*, p. 12.
19 de Man, *Rhetoric of Romanticism*, p. 78.
20 Wordsworth, *Home at Grasmere*, pp. 38, 62.
21 Wordsworth, *The Prelude, 1798–99*, p. 50; *Prelude*, 11: 272–73; *Fourteen Book Prelude*, 12: 221.
22 This is the distinction between space and place important to Edward Casey's *The Fate of Place*, which argues that the displacement of place by space, lived situation by abstract site, is typical of early modernization, leaving place a "reduced residuum" and an "empty name" (p. 141).
23 Kant, *Pure Reason*, p. 77.
24 Hume proposes that even where objects do not change, we "fancy" that they do by revisiting them as embedded in "a continual succession of perceptions in our mind." See *Treatise*, p. 65.
25 Lindenberger, *Wordsworth's "Prelude,"* p. 131.
26 Cooper (ed.), *Concordance*, p. 616.
27 Quintilian, cited in Yates, *Art of Memory*, p. 22. See also Carruthers, *Book of Memory*, pp. 27–32, 71–79.
28 Carruthers, *Book of Memory*, pp. 30, 116.
29 Wordsworth, *Sonnet Series*, p. 604.
30 Marx, *Capital One*, p. 164.

31 Lukács, *History and Class Consciousness*, pp. 89–90. Postone, *Time, Labor*, p. 293, helpfully paraphrases Lukács's model of abstract space. See also Debord, *Society of the Spectacle*, #147, where "commodity-time" is described as "an infinite accumulation of equivalent intervals" or, as Wordsworth might have said, a series of tracks "Impress'd on the white road, in the same line / At distance still the same" (*Lyrical Ballads*, p. 230). Henri Lefebvre, *The Production of Space*, argues that under the conditions of modernity "lived time" loses both its place in nature and "its form and its social interest" (p. 95).

32 Bottomore (ed.), *Dictionary of Marxist Thought*, p. 506. One element of the controversy is the attempt to propose use-value as primary or original and thus to imagine its rediscovery as a utopian goal. Gayatri Spivak calls this "continuist romantic anti-capitalist" interpretation a "domestication": see *In Other Worlds*, pp. 155–56, 161. Postone and others take the position that use-value figures in Marx's theory as describing only what happens when someone buys something, i.e. it is already within value and one with "exchange" value. An earlier case for a theory of value devolving from the cooperative labor of poet and reader is Heinzelman, *Economics of the Imagination*, pp. 196–233.

33 Harvey, *Limits to Capital*, p. 338.

34 The dynamic tendency of this abstract form is further developed by the credit system, which does away with money and "accelerates the velocity of the metamorphosis of commodities," puts more and more capital in the hands of those who do not own it, and speeds up the rate of crisis and contradiction: see Marx, *Capital Three*, pp. 566–67, 572, and pp. 657–58. See also Ryan, *Marxism and Deconstruction*, pp. 178–84.

35 Postone, *Time, Labor*, p. 191.

36 Marx, *Capital One*, pp. 294, 296.

37 Terdiman, *Present Past*, p. 12. Memory and commodity, he notes, are linked by a "common resistance to analysis" (p. 10), and thus by a common aura of secrecy.

38 Yates, *Art of Memory*, p. 113.

39 Liu, *Wordsworth*, p. 204.

40 Postone, *Time, Labor*, p. 296. Salvesen, *Landscape of Memory*, captures just this sense in describing how the spots of time "make a kind of *instantaneous* space of the memory ... a pure present ... which does not denote duration or locality" (p. 193).

41 Hegel, *Phenomenology*, p. 492.

42 Compare the passage in the later *Philosophy of Mind*, p. 227, where the theoretical intelligence takes "possession" of its own "property" through the rational organization of memory data; thought and being come together and the self is indeed a lord and master.

43 "In the value form of the commodity the question [of the concrete forms of labor] is stood on its head ... [in] the equivalent form ... concrete labour

becomes the form of manifestation of its opposite, abstract human labour" (Marx, *Capital One*, p. 150).
44 Lindenberger, *Wordsworth's "Prelude,"* pp. 162, 187.
45 Marx, *Capital One*, p. 148.
46 Hume, *Treatise*, pp. 273–74.
47 Jacobus, *Romanticism*, p. 19.
48 Carruthers, *Book of Memory*, pp. 33–45.
49 Locke, *Essay*, p. 150.
50 Recall, once again, the bookish immersion of poor Susan: "Bright volumes of vapour through Lothbury glide . . . And the colours have all pass'd away from her eyes" (*Lyrical Ballads*, p. 178).
51 Locke, *Essay*, pp. 152–53. Hume picks up the same image in describing the self's past ideas as inhabiting a dark storage locker: "these spirits always excite the idea, when they run precisely into the proper traces, and rummage that cell, which belongs to the idea" (*Treatise*, p. 61).
52 Althusser and Balibar, *Reading Capital*, p. 99.
53 Ian Baucom, in *Specters of the Atlantic*, distinguishes between an "actuarial historicism" whose "key figure is the average, aggregate, and abstract type" devised by the insurance industry (p. 216) and a "romantic historicism" that stands in opposition to it and is committed to "melancholy realism" (p. 43). If we construe this as a distinction between the general equivalent form (substitutability) and a case-specificity embodying the essence of a place and time in an exemplary individual, then Wordsworth's spot of time stands for neither – or both at once.
54 Sohn-Rethel, *Intellectual and Manual Labor*, pp. 72, 56. See also the discussion in Žižek, *Sublime Object*, pp. 16–21, where Freudian as well as Kantian subjectivity is seen to correspond with the logic of commodity form.
55 At least until recently this late medieval/early modern transition was the assumed chronology of Hegel's rendering of European history. But Susan Buck-Morss, in "Hegel and Haiti," makes the very persuasive case that Hegel's master–slave dialectic is a response to the immediate events of the Haitian revolution, where the slave's risking of death was very recent and widely known about. Baucom's *Specters of the Atlantic* performs a similar task in making clear the exemplary status of the slave economy, and in particular the 1781 drowning of slaves by the master of the *Zong*, for an understanding of the contemporary logic of the value form and its impact on human lives.
56 Burke, *Reflections*, pp. 310, 181.
57 Pocock, *Virtue, Commerce and History*, p. 112. See esp. pp. 103–23, 193–212.
58 Debord, *Society of the Spectacle*, #192. See also Adorno, *In Search of Wagner*, p. 87.
59 Milton, *Paradise Lost*, 1: 253.
60 Wordsworth, *Fourteen Book Prelude*, 6: 429.
61 Lukács, *History and Class Consciousness*, pp. 110–21.
62 Marx, *Capital One*, p. 144n.

THE GHOSTLINESS OF THINGS

1. Gayatri Spivak has critically monitored Derrida's uses of Marx in a series of seminal essays over the years: see, for example, "Scattered Speculations"; "Speculations on Reading Marx"; "Limits and Openings"; "Ghostwriting." See also (and among others) Ryan, *Marxism and Deconstruction*; Halpern, "Impure History of Ghosts"; and Sprinker (ed.), *Ghostly Demarcations*.
2. See Simpson, *Figurings of the Real*; and *Fetishism and Imagination*. See also Keenan, "The Point is to (Ex)change It," which offers a powerful account of figurative language in relation to the value form, with particular reference to Marx's ghosts.
3. See, for example, Clery, *Rise of Supernatural Fiction*, p. 7. Castle, "Spectralization of the Other," notes that by the end of the eighteenth century the specter was coming to seem increasingly "real" (p. 247).
4. Wordsworth, *Prose Works*, I: 128, 130, 150.
5. Derrida, *Specters*, pp. 156–57.
6. Wordsworth, *Fourteen Book Prelude*, 6: 424 (p. 124). Unless otherwise noted, citations of the description of the visit to the convent of Chartreuse are from this edition.
7. Moorman, *William Wordsworth*, pp. 135–38.
8. Wordsworth, *Prelude*, 2: 104 (6: 430ff.). There is another lament at the sight of a convent "dismantled . . . by violence abrupt" later in the ms. (9: 480).
9. Milton, *Shorter Poems*, p. 262.
10. "Debemur morti nos nostraque." See Horace, *Ars Poetica*, l. 63. Horace's landscape here is in a state of total and continual transformation, but for living things there is only death: *mortalia facta peribunt* (l. 68).
11. Butler (ed.), *Burke, Paine*, pp. 111, 164.
12. See Underwood, "Romantic Historicism," who proposes that "the pleasure Romantic poems take in projecting historical difference onto the inanimate world is related to the pleasure of seeing (or imagining that one sees) a ghost" (p. 238). One could read this experience as a promise of life after death, as Underwood, following Terry Castle, does (p. 242); one could also see it as a confirmation of death-in-life, as I am doing, and as such a figure of commodity form. Lefebvre, *Production of Space*, pp. 234–41, describes a category of "absolute space" of which the Chartreuse convent would be a prime example as it proposes to embody natural forces and to assimilate the living to the dead.
13. Marx and Engels, *Selected Works*, I: 25.
14. Derrida, *Specters*, p. 156.
15. Marx, *Capital One*, pp. 163–64; Marx and Engels, *Werke*, XXIII: 85–86.
16. Marx, *Capital One*, p. 128; Marx and Engels, *Werke*, XXIII: 52.
17. Some very helpful commentary on this narrative predicament can be found in Harvey, *Limits to Capital*, pp. 1–4; and Postone, *Time, Labor*. Postone's powerful reading has been of enormous importance to my own understanding here. He argues that Marx's order of exposition is neither

conventionally logical, as if implying a "transhistorical standpoint" (p. 141), nor simply historical, as if "leading from the first appearance of commodities to a fully developed capitalist system" (p. 129), but something more elusive whereby the nature of the commodity is "validated retroactively by the argument as it unfolds" (p. 141), so that "what seems to be a historical unfolding is actually a projection backward, based on a logical reconstruction of the dynamic character of the social form of capital, a dynamic character that it acquires only when it is fully developed" (p. 285). The difficulties of reading by way of a "projecting backwards" are serious enough for Althusser to recommend skipping the first part of *Capital One* and coming back to it later and repeatedly: see *Lenin and Philosophy*, pp. 71–106. Marx's recourse to a critique which "takes no standpoint outside of its object, but rests, instead, on the full unfolding of the categories and their contradictions" (Postone, *Time, Labor*, p. 170) causes the same difficulties for its reader as does Wordsworth's poetic narration.

18 This is the implication in much of Goux's *Symbolic Economies*, which proposes a long durational causality deriving from the money form as foundational to "sociohistorical structuration" and thus implicitly diminishes Marx's claim for the qualitative shift accruing with industrial capitalism (p. 14). A similar emphasis is to be found in Shell, *Economy of Literature*, which discusses early Greek theories of the simultaneous origins of money, tyranny and philosophy as cognate forms of invisible agency: spectral powers. See also Sohn-Rethel, *Intellectual and Manual Labor*, pp. 94–98. Gayatri Spivak specifies a similar problem in Derrida's conflation of industrial capitalism with the money circuit in general, a move she sees as allowing him to project Marx as no more than a kinsman of Plato and Aristotle ("Ghostwriting," pp. 65, 73).

19 Wordsworth, *Prose Works*, I: 128.

20 Marx, *Capital One*, p. 152. Thus Postone (*Time, Labor*, p. 366): "With the historical emergence of capital – of the commodity as a totalizing social form – a mode of social mediation comes into being that is abstract, homogeneous, and general ... the commodity form of social mediation generates a form of equality that potentially is universal, establishing commonality among objects, among labors, among commodity owners, and potentially among all people." Here democracy means substitutability and life means death; thus the Carthusian monks are one with their built abode in signifying the ghostliness of things.

21 De Bolla, *Discourse of the Sublime*. See esp. pp. 103–40.

22 According to Johnston, *Hidden Wordsworth*, the cost of living "approximately doubled" in the mid-1790s (p. xx), though no sources or authorities are cited.

23 Mantoux's *The Industrial Revolution* is the foundational study, and the debates on this topic are usefully summarized in Berg, *Age of Manufactures*, pp. 13–76. One of the most influential arguments for a radical shift in the economy around 1800 is Polanyi, *The Great Transformation*, which sees the onset of a belief in the benefits of self-adjusting markets without state control

as the first step toward the disasters of twentieth-century politics. For Polanyi the dominance of machine production sponsored the automation of land, labor and money as purely market-regulated; this "commodity fiction" was the direct result of the factory system (see pp. 57, 73–75, 131).

24 Consumerism is, as I have said, easier to study than commodity form because it is vividly attached to objects and related to an inherited theological concern about luxury. See, among others, Brewer, McKendrick and Plumb (eds.), *Birth of a Consumer Society*; and Brewer and Porter (eds.), *Consumption*. Commodity form is the ghostly framework of the consumption debate in the later eighteenth century. Its poetics are extensively engaged in Morton, *Poetics of Spice*, esp. pp. 90–104.

25 Paine blamed the twentyfold increase of the debt in the century after 1697 on the increased circulation of paper money, an "emission of art" rather than nature, "at best a bubble" printed out of nothing, and speeding up time in the "accelerating velocity" of its depreciation, with payment only ever to come in "anticipation": see *Complete Writings*, II: 404, 654, 409, 659, 665. Cobbett made similar comments: see *Selected Writings*, III: 13, 23, 167. For Marx's sense of the critical role of credit, see Ryan, *Marxism and Deconstruction*, pp. 178–84.

26 Marx, *Capital One*, pp. 138–39; Marx and Engels, *Werke*, XXIII: 62. The early sections of *Capital* do not, for example, discuss profit or mechanical production. They are not (and are not intended as) a complete account of the commodity form in the modern world. But we can only read one step at a time.

27 Postone describes how the unseen component of the twofold identity of commodity form, like the socially abstract element of labor as distinguished from its concrete emanation, is newly critical in developed capitalism, where it becomes for the first time a "structuring social category" (p. 128). What is seen draws its most important attributes from what cannot be seen.

28 Patrick Murray, Lord Elibank, cited in de Bolla, *Discourse of the Sublime*, p. 116.

29 Marx, *Capital One*, pp. 342, 367. For a fine account of Marx's use of the vampire motif, see Neocleous, *The Monstrous and the Dead*.

30 See Keenan, "The Point is to (Ex)change It," pp. 157–58.

31 Marx, *Capital One*, p. 163; Marx and Engels, *Werke*, XXIII: 85.

32 Marx's *als wenn* for *als ob* is apparently an item of Rhenish dialect. It opens up at least the ghost of a temporal narrative (reading *als wenn* as "as when") but this pending sense is refuted by the strong subjunctive of *zu tanzen begänne*. We are after all reading Rhenish and not German. Derrida "misreads" the table as dancing, as does Keenan, whose account of Marx's prosopopoeia "The Point is to (Ex)change It," (pp. 177–85) is otherwise very insightful. My thanks to Gerhard Richter for shedding light on Marx's teasing little sentence.

33 Derrida gets the active, competitive sense of this relation (*er stellt sich allen andren Waren gegenüber*) in saying that "it faces them or opposes them," "in a

competition or in a war," because "the market is a front, a front among fronts, a confrontation" (*Specters*, pp. 151, 155).
34 Marx, *Capital One*, p. 165.
35 For a fine study of this passage, see Stallybrass, "Marx's Coat," which notes that "the fetishism of the commodity inscribes *im*materiality as the defining feature of capitalism" (p. 184). It is no accident that Marx picks on coats and linen. The textile industry was both central to British industrial development in the late eighteenth century and also (and therefore) a tried and true figure of economic theory. Mandeville, *Fable of the Bees*, I: 169–70, employs it, as does Smith (*Wealth of Nations*, I: 22–23). In each of these cases, the complexity of coat-production is imaged as the result of human cooperation and purposive division of labor. Marx figures things differently, putting the commodities themselves in the driving seat.
36 Marx, *Capital One*, p. 148; Marx and Engels, *Werke*, XXIII: 71.
37 Coleridge, *Biographia*, II: 6.
38 Debord, *Society of the Spectacle*, #217.
39 Marx and Engels, *Collected Works*, XXIX: 303.
40 Freud, "The Uncanny," p. 948.
41 Marx, *Capital One*, pp. 163–73; Marx and Engels, *Werke*, XXIII: 85–94.
42 de Man, "Epistemology of Metaphor," p. 19.
43 Paul de Man, after bringing up exactly the "long series of mutilated bodies" that includes "Wordsworth's mute country-dwellers and blind city beggars," oddly displaces what he has thus asserted by adding that "one should avoid the pathos of an imagery of bodily mutilation and not forget that we are dealing with textual models, not with the historical and political systems that are their correlate" (*Rhetoric of Romanticism*, p. 289).
44 Smith, *Wealth of Nations*, II: 782–83.
45 Ferguson, *Essay*, pp. 173–74.
46 Marx and Engels, *Collected Works*, IV: 396, 455.
47 Scarry, *Body in Pain*, pp. 243–77, has written powerfully on how Marx's awareness of suffering bodies structures the narrative of the first volume of *Capital*.
48 Factory work patterns were especially well advanced in the shipyards, where Taylorized methods and a 24-hour shift system were in place in the 1790s: see Linebaugh, *London Hanged*, pp. 64–68, 126–33. For an account of the incremental standardization of both domestic and industrial labor in the eighteenth century, see Styles, "Manufacturing, Consumption." As I have said, a major institution like the cotton industry called upon all kinds of commodification and divided labor components: armies, navies, banks, machines and a mobile labor force.
49 Marx and Engels, *Collected Works*, IV: 384; Marx, *Capital One*, p. 852.
50 Marx, *Capital One*, p. 165.
51 Dorothy Wordsworth, *Journals*, I: 131–32.
52 de Man, *Romanticism and Contemporary Criticism*, p. 79.

53 de Man, *Rhetoric of Romanticism*, p. 287.
54 Wordsworth, *Poems 1807*, pp. 207–8.
55 Although these images would likely have seemed more surprising at the time. See the further discussion in chapter 6, below.
56 de Man, *Rhetoric of Romanticism*, p. 265.
57 Kleist, "Marionette Theatre", p. 14. The "operator" is, in the German, *der Maschinist* (Kleist, *Werke*, III: 474). I am very grateful to Alysia Garrison for sending me to Kleist in this context. Six years later, in 1816, E. T. A. Hoffman would publish his story "The Sandman," so important in Freud's essay on "The Uncanny," one instance of which is the uncertainty about whether the figure in the story is a human being or an automaton.
58 Coleridge, *Biographia*, II: 136.
59 Hartman, *Wordsworth's Poetry*, p. 5; Ferry, *Limits of Mortality*, p. 10.
60 Wordsworth, *Lyrical Ballads*, p. 117.
61 See Laqueur, *Solitary Sex*, which claims that the notion of masturbation in its modern sense, as overlaid with moral and economic associations, took form in the early 1700s. Its expense of spirit can thus be seen as partaking in the economics of commodification.
62 I owe thanks to Steven Blevins for noticing this connection.
63 Derrida, *Specters*, p. 153.

LIVING IMAGES, STILL LIVES

1 Cowper, *Poems*, II: 15, 17.
2 Wordsworth, *Last Poems*, pp. 184–85. I would not have noticed this poem had it not been given a seal of approval in a brilliant reading by Timothy Morton, "Wordsworth Digs the Lawn," which establishes the cultural-historical fullness of this empty space of the lawn as, among other things, a purposive rhetorical confusion of figure and ground, and a suburban-republican icon that inevitably evokes what it apparently seeks to exclude.
3 Lamb, "Modern Metamorphoses," pp. 134, 137. See also Lynch, *Economy of Character*, pp. 95–102, 112–19, and the various essays collected in Blackwell (ed.), *Secret Life of Things*. Liz Bellamy's essay in this volume (pp. 117–46) provides a very helpful bibliography.
4 Marx and Engels, *Collected Works*, III: 309.
5 Another such element would be the "newness" of the image which convinces us that, like the value form, it "has no past," and thus communicates a sense of "freedom" and "mastery" only by freezing time. This is the account of poetic creation offered by Bachelard, *Poetics of Space*, pp. xvi, xxvii.
6 de Man, "Epistemology of Metaphor," p. 19. See, again, Keenan, "The Point is to (Ex)change It," which is creatively influenced by de Man's work.
7 Coleridge, *Biographia*, II: 6.
8 Wordsworth, *Prose Works*, I: 138.
9 Wordsworth, *Lyrical Ballads*, p. 351. Frances Ferguson, *Wordsworth*, explores the interdependence of organicism and death, the living and the dead, spirit

and counter-spirit, in Wordsworth's work. See also Keach, *Arbitrary Power*, pp. 28–30.
10 Marshall Brown notes that the term *cliché* itself only came into use at all in 1797 – it was a French term for a new printing process – and that its modern sense arose in the later nineteenth century: see *The Gothic Text*, p. 163. Brown's discussion of Radcliffe and the cliché (pp. 161–82), which includes a fascinating interpretation of the uses of "astonishment," pays important attention to the functions of conventional words and phrases as motivated by Freudian secondary revision. His reading of Radcliffe's slippages between the figured and the real and between narrator and character would accord very happily with an argument for the dominance of commodity form.
11 Wordsworth, *Poems 1807*, p. 126; *Prose Works*, III: 32.
12 Marx, *Frühschriften*, p. 529.
13 Onorato, *Mind of the Poet*, p. 238n.
14 See, preeminently, Hartman, *Fateful Question*.
15 Wordsworth, *Prelude*, 8: 431.
16 In Jameson (ed.), *Aesthetics and Politics*, pp. 127, 129.
17 Langan, *Romantic Vagrancy*, p. 142, has suggested that the poet's habit of *showing* himself walking (and, I would add, making himself a spectacle) has the effect of rupturing "the desire for formal completion and autistic self-enclosure that the poem may thematically represent." So also it breaches the stillness of death, but only to emphasize the imperfections of the living as tending toward death.
18 Derrida, *Specters*, p. 18.
19 Rousseau, *Essay on the Origin of Languages*, pp. 294–95. This passage is discussed in detail in Bewell, *Wordsworth*, pp. 79–80, as a prototype for Wordsworth's interest in the "primitive encounter," and thereafter by Langan, *Romantic Vagrancy*, p. 198. Vico had proposed a materialist explanation for the archaic existence of giant humans: see his *New Science*, sections 369, 371–72.
20 Heidegger, *Introduction to Metaphysics*, p. 158.
21 Derrida, *Specters*, pp. 156–57.
22 Agamben, *Coming Community*, p. 79.
23 Wordsworth, *Prelude*, 8: 723, 741.
24 Hegel, *Philosophy of Mind*, pp. 220, 223. Yates sees a movement away from images in favor of pure dialectic as latent in Quintilian, emergent in Erasmus and definitive in the Ramist treatises; see *Art of Memory*, pp. 127, 234, 273.
25 Derrida, *Specters*, p. 147.
26 Wordsworth, *Prelude*, 10: 725–26.
27 Adorno, *In Search of Wagner*, pp. 85, 92.
28 Debord, *Society of the Spectacle*, ##42, 1, 2, 200.
29 See Hickey, *Impure Conceits*, pp. 47–49, on the purposive duplicities of this passage. She finds, for example, a hint of betrayal in the crowing of the cock – a hint richly developed, I shall argue, in what follows.
30 Liu, *Wordsworth*, pp. 311, 324, 325.

31 Liu's association of this "richness" with the later evaluative vocabulary of New Criticism is important and convincing; I would simply say that the pedlar rather than Wordsworth is the originator of this tradition, and that Coleridge is its house theorist. Wordsworth was not the poet Coleridge wanted him to be.
32 Debord, *Society of the Spectacle*, ##1–2.
33 Lukács, *History and Class Consciousness*, pp. 98–100.
34 Wordsworth, *Prose Works*, I: 128.
35 See Hartman, "Use and Abuse of Structural Analysis."
36 Transcripts of the first two versions can be found in *Poems 1807*, pp. 605–6.
37 Hartman, in a short passage that is highly prescient for my extended argument, notes (pp. 147–48) that the drama of "Yew Trees" might allude to "a modern ghostliness" that has something to do with the conditions of war and industry.
38 Wordsworth, *Prose Works*, I: 128.
39 Wordsworth, *Prelude*, note to 10: 467.
40 Hunter, *Before Novels*, pp. 167–94.
41 Sherman, *Telling Time*, p. 117.
42 Cited in *ibid.*, p. 173.
43 Wordsworth, *Prose Works*, I: 128; Goodman, *Georgic Modernity*, pp. 67–105.
44 See Hessel, "The Opposite of News."
45 Guillory, *Cultural Capital*, pp. 85–133. Guillory argues that Gray's poem was central to the establishment of a commonly acknowledged polite diction for middle-class readers who could identify with the poet's "classic literacy" and "immense learning . . . at a *discount*, at the cost only of acquiring the vernacular literacy requisite to reading the poem" (p. 121).
46 Wordsworth, *Prose Works*, I: 133.
47 de Man, *Rhetoric of Romanticism*, pp. 6–7.
48 Wordsworth, *Poems 1807*, p. 129.
49 Wordsworth, *Lyrical Ballads*, pp. 229, 143, 147, 155, 156.
50 On the ubiquity of these and other such media and on their formative importance for Romantic aesthetics, see Wood, *Shock of the Real*. Still life is always about the exclusion of the human and almost always evokes the relation between commodities and death: see Norman Bryson's brilliant study *Looking at the Overlooked*.
51 Baudrillard, *Simulations*, p. 26; Agamben, *Coming Community*, p. 64.

THE SCENE OF READING

1 Dorothy Wordsworth, *Journals*, I: 63.
2 Wordsworth, *Lyrical Ballads*, pp. 231–32; ll. 81–82, 162, 104.
3 Wordsworth, *Prelude*, 11: 295–99.
4 See Rajan, *Supplement of Reading*, pp. 144–53, on the publication and circulation of *Lyrical Ballads*.
5 There are various discussions of Wordsworth's literariness. Hartman's work is fully attentive to this dimension: see, for example, "Words, Wish, Worth"

and "Diction and Defense." Averill, *Wordsworth*, and Jacobus, *Tradition and Experiment*, among others, both give extended evidence of Wordsworth's sources. Goodman, *Georgic Modernity*, p. 28, notes that Wordsworth's sources (especially in Virgil and Milton) were themselves already highly allusive texts. For a superb account of *The Prelude*'s use of Milton, see Jarvis, *Wordsworth, Milton*, esp. pp. 106–35. Jarvis anticipates my sense that the act of allusion renders the poetry "ungovernable" and interpretation "potentially endless" (pp. 106, 112). As such it both reflects and resists the to-handedness of a commodity print market.

6 Wordsworth could be tetchy about admitting this. He explains that *The Excursion* avoids bookishness lest he be accused of pedantry "as Milton has been," and thought of as "having a mind which could not support itself but by other mens labours." This is, however, a reactive response to what seems to have been a negative view of his lack of learning and dignity. See *Letters: The Middle Years*, part 2, p. 191.

7 Wordsworth, *Fourteen Book Prelude*, 5: 73–75; 4: 387.

8 Wordsworth, *Prelude*, 5: 164.

9 Millar, *Historical View*, pp. 815, 817–18. See also Price, *The Anthology and the Rise of the Novel*, which shows that even novels, especially after the end of perpetual copyright in 1774, were popularized and marketed in abbreviated forms. On the increase in newspaper production in the later 1790s, see Liu, *Wordsworth*, pp. 413f.

10 Pinch, *Strange Fits of Passion*, pp. 168–71, has written well on the disturbance of simple authenticity that comes with this quotation.

11 For an account of Book 5 that stresses the importance of the death of the parents, see Shakir, "Books, Death, and Immortality."

12 Goodman notes that Virgil's "by-ways" in the *Georgics* were appreciated by Addison as conducive to the pleasures of indirection (*Georgic Modernity*, pp. 17, 32). Wordsworth's characteristic twist on the phrase places it unignorably in the mysterious space–time coordinate of the "spots of time."

13 De Quincey, *Collected Writings*, II: 335, 287–88, 313.

14 See Owen, *Fourteen Book Prelude*, note to 5: 411.

15 "debemur morti nos nostraque": Horace, *Ars Poetica*, l. 63.

16 Wordsworth, *Lyrical Ballads*, p. 108.

17 *Ibid.*, p. 248. See Simpson, "Wordsworth and Empire," for a detailed account of the botanical misconceptions.

18 Wordsworth, *Prose Works*, I: 138.

19 "A slumber did my spirit seal," in *Lyrical Ballads*, p. 164.

20 Bewell, *Wordsworth*, pp. 215–17. Bewell has a fine extended account (pp. 187–234) of the place of death in Wordsworth's aesthetic.

21 See Mitchell, "Influence, Autobiography."

22 Rousseau, *The Confessions*, p. 8.

23 Wordsworth, *Lyrical Ballads*, p. 282. There is also here a journey into the underworld, in the manner of Virgil and of Dante, and of Satan's meeting with Sin and Death, as noted by Bewell, *Wordsworth*, pp. 85–86.

24 Wordsworth, *Prose Works*, I: 128.
25 Rousseau, *Miscellaneous Works*, III: 34–35. Rousseau's analogous concerns about the effects of novel-reading in generating false responses are discussed at length in Marshall, *Surprising Effects of Sympathy*. See also Pinch's account of Wordsworth's theory of meter in *Strange Fits*, pp. 85–97.
26 I draw here on Averill, *Wordsworth*, pp. 128–29. This is another element of the problem of sympathy discussed in chapter 1.
27 Cowper, *Poems*, II: 142.
28 Nossack, *The End*, pp. 36–37.
29 Cynthia Chase, "The Accidents of Disfiguration," notes that this "book of accidents" constantly reveals the literal as an "effaced figure" (pp. 547, 556) and sees in the drowned man "the surfacing of an effaced figure" (p. 561). The historical figure was, she notes, that of a local schoolmaster, here included in a book taking lengthy issue with the effects of modern schooling.
30 For a detailed history see Laqueur, *Solitary Sex*.
31 Wordsworth, *Lyrical Ballads*, pp. 64, 109.
32 Rousseau, *Miscellaneous Works*, III: 27.
33 Wordsworth, *Prose Works*, I: 128.
34 De Quincey, *Collected Writings*, II: 265.
35 Wordsworth, *Prelude, 1798–99*, p. 49 (1: 270).
36 For a fine abbreviated history of this trope, see Harrison, *Dominion of the Dead*, pp. 125–36, 177–78. Wordsworth fashioned another poetic encounter with Vallombrosa in 1837, one where the sprightly anapaestic tetrameters are unable fully to suppress another allusion to the flood (l. 3) and to the relation between the falling leaves and the leaves of books: see *Sonnet Series*, pp. 775–77. Jarvis, *Wordsworth, Milton*, pp. 84–105, has a fascinating and detailed reading of this poem.
37 Wordsworth, *Prelude 1798–99*, p. 50 (ll. 279–87).
38 Manning, "Reading Wordsworth's Revisions," p. 92. See also Wolfson, "Illusion of Mastery." Goodman, "Making Time for History," reads the 1799 version of this episode as an example of both sustaining and working through traumatic experience and thence as an instance of a non-repressive attitude to history.
39 The effect is further compounded in the 1850 text where, as we have seen, the "uncouth shape" of the Arab-Quixote also recalls that of the discharged soldier.
40 Wordsworth, *Prelude*, II: 295, 299.
41 Lindenberger, *Wordsworth's "Prelude,"* pp. 300–4, notes that allusions to Milton are worked into the 1804–5 revisions of the poem; they are scarcer in the earlier drafts.
42 De Quincey, *Collected Writings*, II: 281. De Quincey's note further elaborates on the perils of Leven Sands, where many have drowned "when baffled and perplexed by mists." One such case is mentioned by none other than "Gray the poet" who himself figures in Wordsworth's telling of this episode. For a detailed account of the dangers of this estuary, see Baker, *Time and Mind*,

pp. 161–63. This was no place to stand around as if captivated by a spot of time!
43 How apt it is that Dove Cottage had a former life as a pub called The Dove and Olive.
44 Wordsworth, *Prelude*, 7: 614, 617.
45 Wordsworth, *Prelude*, 13: 16, 43, 63.
46 Wordsworth, *Poems 1807*, p. 126. Milton also uses the forms *moorish* (*Comus*, l. 433) and *moory* (*Paradise Lost*, 2: 944). Spenser's "Ruins of Time" has *moorish fens*.
47 Hartman, "Blessing the Torrent"; Kelley, *Wordsworth's Revisionary Aesthetics*, pp. 170–92; Bewell, *Wordsworth*, pp. 257–79. See also Hertz, "Wordsworth and the Tears of Adam."
48 Brown, "Oceans and Floods," p. 109.
49 Cobbett, *Selected Writings*, III: 23.
50 This is the burden of Lynch's fine discussion of Burney on pp. 164–206.
51 Hartman, *Fateful Question*, p. 70.
52 Wordsworth, *Prose Works*, I: 160.
53 Gray's line "And Reddening Phoebus lifts his golden fire" is of the same species as Wordsworth's "Then issued Vesper from the fulgent West." See Simpson, *Wordsworth's Historical Imagination*, p. 30.
54 Levinson's *Keats's Life of Allegory* claims at least an equal clarity for Keats.

Bibliography

Adorno, Theodor, *In Search of Wagner*, trans. Rodney Livingstone (London: Verso, 1984).
  Minima Moralia: Reflections From Damaged Life, trans. E. F. N. Jephcott (London: Verso, 1985).
Agamben, Giorgio, *The Coming Community*, trans. Michael Hardt (Minneapolis and London: University of Minnesota Press, 1993).
  Means Without End: Notes on Politics, trans. Vincenzo Binetti and Cesare Casarino (Minneapolis and London: University of Minnesota Press, 2000).
  Remnants of Auschwitz: The Witness and the Archive, trans. Daniel Heller-Roazen (New York: Zone Books, 2002).
  The Open: Man and Animal, trans. Kevin Attell (Stanford: Stanford University Press, 2004).
Althusser, Louis, *Lenin and Philosophy and Other Essays*, trans. Ben Brewster (New York and London: Monthly Review Press, 1971).
Althusser, Louis, and Etienne Balibar, *Reading Capital*, trans. Ben Brewster (London: Verso, 1986).
Altick, Richard, *The Shows of London* (Cambridge, MA and London: Harvard University Press and Belknap Press, 1978).
Anidjar, Gil, *The Jew, the Arab: A History of the Enemy* (Stanford: Stanford University Press, 2003).
Appadurai, Arjun, *The Social Life of Things: Commodities in a Cultural Perspective* (Cambridge: Cambridge University Press, 1986).
Arnold, Matthew, "The Study of Poetry," in *Essays in Criticism: Second Series* (London: Macmillan, 1935), pp. 1–39.
Averill, James H., *Wordsworth and the Poetry of Human Suffering* (Ithaca and London: Cornell University Press, 1980).
Bachelard, Gaston, *The Poetics of Space*, trans. Maria Jolas (Boston: Beacon Press, 1994).
Baker, Jeffrey, *Time and Mind in Wordsworth's Poetry* (Detroit: Wayne State University Press, 1980).
Bakhtin, M. M., *The Dialogic Imagination*, trans. Caryl Emerson and Michael Holquist (Austin: University of Texas Press, 1985).

Barker-Benfield, G. J., *The Culture of Sensibility: Sex and Society in Eighteenth-Century Britain* (Chicago and London: University of Chicago Press, 1996).
Barrell, John, *The Infection of Thomas De Quincey: A Psychopathology of Imperialism* (New Haven and London: Yale University Press, 1992).
  The Spirit of Despotism: Invasions of Privacy in the 1790s (Oxford and New York: Oxford University Press, 2006).
Baucom, Ian, *Specters of the Atlantic: Finance Capital, Slavery, and the Philosophy of History* (Durham and London: Duke University Press, 2005).
Baudrillard, Jean, *Simulations*, trans. Paul Foss, Paul Patton and Philip Beitchman (New York: Semiotext(e), 1983).
Beck, Ulrich, Anthony Giddens and Scott Lash, *Reflexive Modernization: Politics, Tradition and Aesthetics in the Modern Social Order* (Stanford: Stanford University Press, 1994).
Beer, John, *Wordsworth and the Human Heart* (London: Macmillan, 1978).
  Wordsworth in Time (London and Boston: Faber and Faber, 1979).
Bellamy, Liz, "It-Narrators and Circulation: Defining a Subgenre," in Blackwell (ed.), *The Secret Life of Things*, pp. 117–46.
Benis, Toby R., *Romanticism on the Road: The Marginal Gains of Wordsworth's Homeless* (London and New York: Macmillan and St. Martin's Press, 2000).
Benjamin, Walter, *Charles Baudelaire: A Lyric Poet in the Era of High Capitalism*, trans. Harry Zohn (London and New York: Verso, 1983).
  The Arcades Project, trans. Howard Eiland and Kevin McLaughlin (Cambridge, MA and London: Harvard University Press and Belknap Press, 1999).
  Selected Writings, Volume IV, 1938–40, ed. Howard Eiland and Michael W. Jennings (Cambridge, MA and London: Harvard University Press and Belknap Press, 2003).
Bentham, Jeremy, *The Principles of Morals and Legislation* (New York: Hafner, 1963).
  Writings on the Poor Laws, Vol. I, ed. Michael Quinn (Oxford: Clarendon Press, 2001).
Berg, Maxine, *The Age of Manufactures: Industry, Innovation and Work in Britain, 1700–1820*, 2nd edn. (London and New York: Routledge, 1994).
Berman, Marshall, *All That Is Solid Melts into Air: The Experience of Modernity* (New York: Penguin Books, 1988).
Bermingham, Ann, "The Simple Life: Cottages and Gainsborough's Cottage Doors," in Peter de Bolla, Nigel Leask and David Simpson (eds.), *Land, Nation and Culture, 1740–1840: Thinking the Republic of Taste* (Houndmills: Palgrave-Macmillan, 2005), pp. 37–62.
Bewell, Alan, *Wordsworth and the Enlightenment: Nature, Man and Society in the Experimental Poetry* (New Haven and London: Yale University Press, 1989).
  Romanticism and Colonial Disease (Baltimore and London: Johns Hopkins University Press, 1999).
Bialostosky, Don, *Wordsworth, Dialogics and the Practice of Criticism* (Cambridge: Cambridge University Press, 1992).

Blackwell, Mark (ed.), *The Secret Life of Things: Animals, Objects, and It-Narratives in Eighteenth-Century England* (Lewisburg: Bucknell University Press, 2007).
Bolton, Carol, "Taking Possession – Romantic Naming in Wordsworth and Southey," in Fiona L. Price and Scott Masson (eds.), *Silence, Sublimity, and Suppression in the Romantic Period* (Lewiston: Edwin Mellen, 2002), pp. 149–68.
Bottomore, Tom (ed.), *A Dictionary of Marxist Thought* (Cambridge, MA: Harvard University Press, 1983).
Brewer, John, Neil McKendrick and J. H. Plumb (eds.), *The Birth of a Consumer Society: The Commercialization of Eighteenth-Century England* (London: Hutchinson, 1983).
Brewer, John, and Roy Porter (eds.), *Consumption and the World of Goods* (London: Routledge, 1983).
Brooks, Cleanth, "Wordsworth and Human Suffering: Notes on Two Early Poems," in Frederick W. Hilles and Harold Bloom (eds.), *From Sensibility to Romanticism: Essays Presented to Frederick A. Pottle* (New York: Oxford University Press, 1965), pp. 373–87.
Brown, Laura, "Oceans and Floods: Fables of Global Perspective," in Felicity A. Nussbaum (ed.), *The Global Eighteenth Century* (Baltimore and London: Johns Hopkins University Press, 2003), pp. 107–20.
Brown, Marshall, *The Gothic Text* (Stanford: Stanford University Press, 2005).
Bryson, Norman, *Looking at the Overlooked: Four Essays on Still Life Painting* (Cambridge, MA: Harvard University Press, 1990).
Buck-Morss, Susan, "Hegel and Haiti," *Critical Inquiry* 26 (1999–2000), pp. 821–65.
Burke, Edmund, *Reflections on the Revolution in France*, ed. Conor Cruise O'Brien (Harmondsworth: Penguin Books, 1976).
Butler, Marilyn (ed.), *Burke, Paine, Godwin, and the Revolution Controversy* (Cambridge: Cambridge University Press, 1984).
Campbell, Colin, *The Romantic Ethic and the Spirit of Modern Consumerism* (Oxford: Blackwell, 1987).
Carruthers, Mary J., *The Book of Memory: A Study of Memory in Medieval Culture* (Cambridge: Cambridge University Press, 1990).
Carter, Philip, *Men and the Emergence of Polite Society: Britain 1660–1800* (Harlow: Longman, 2001).
Casey, Edward S., *The Fate of Place: A Philosophical History* (Berkeley, Los Angeles and London: University of California Press, 1998).
Castle, Terry, "The Spectralization of the Other in *The Mysteries of Udolpho*," in Laura Brown and Felicity Nussbaum (eds.), *The New Eighteenth Century: Theory, Politics, English Literature* (New York and London: Methuen, 1987), pp. 231–53.
Chandler, James K., *Wordsworth's Second Nature: A Study of the Poetry and Politics* (Chicago and London: University of Chicago Press, 1984).

Chandler, James K., and Kevin Gilmartin (eds.), *Romantic Metropolis: The Urban Scene of British Culture, 1780–1840* (Cambridge: Cambridge University Press, 2005).
Chase, Cynthia, "The Accidents of Disfiguration: Limits to Literal and Rhetorical reading in Book V of *The Prelude*," *Studies in Romanticism* 18 (1979), pp. 547–65.
Clark, T. J., *The Painting of Modern Life: Paris in the Art of Manet and his Followers* (New York: Knopf, 1985).
Clery, E. J., *The Rise of Supernatural Fiction, 1762–1800* (Cambridge: Cambridge University Press, 1995).
Cobbett, William, *William Cobbett: Selected Writings*, 6 vols., ed. Leonora Nattrass (London: Pickering and Chatto, 1998).
Coleman, D. C., *The British Paper Industry, 1495–1860: A Study in Industrial Growth* (Oxford: Clarendon Press, 1958).
Coleridge, Samuel Taylor, *Biographia Literaria*, ed. James Engell and W. Jackson Bate, 2 vols. (Princeton: Princeton University Press, 1983).
Connell, Philip, *Romanticism, Economics, and the Question of "Culture"* (Oxford: Oxford University Press, 2001).
Cooper, Lane (ed.), *A Concordance to the Poems of William Wordsworth* (London: Smith, Elder and Co., 1911).
Cowper, William, *Poems by William Cowper*, 3rd edn., 2 vols. (London: J. Johnson, 1787).
Davidson, Jenny, *Hypocrisy and the Politics of Politeness: Manners and Morals from Locke to Austen* (Cambridge: Cambridge University Press, 2004).
De Bolla, Peter, *The Discourse of the Sublime: Readings in History, Aesthetics and the Subject* (Oxford: Blackwell, 1989).
"Mediation and the Division of Labour," unpublished paper.
Debord, Guy, *Society of the Spectacle* (Detroit: Black and Red Press, 1983).
Deleuze, Gilles, and Felix Guattari, *Nomadology: The War Machine*, trans. Brian Massumi (Semiotext(e), 1986).
de Man, Paul, "The Epistemology of Metaphor," in Sheldon Sacks (ed.), *On Metaphor* (Chicago and London: University of Chicago Press, 1979), pp. 11–28.
The Rhetoric of Romanticism (New York: Columbia University Press, 1984).
Romanticism and Contemporary Criticism, ed. E. S. Burt, Kevin Newmark and Andrzej Warminski (Baltimore and London: Johns Hopkins University Press, 1993).
De Quincey, Thomas, *Collected Writings of Thomas De Quincey*, ed. David Masson, 14 vols. (Edinburgh: Adam and Charles Black, 1889–90).
Derrida, Jacques, "Structure, Sign and Play in the Discourse of the Human Sciences," in Richard Macksey and Eugenio Donato (eds.), *The Structuralist Controversy: The Languages of Criticism and the Science of Man* (Baltimore and London: Johns Hopkins University Press, 1970), pp. 247–72.
Specters of Marx: The State of the Debt, the Work of Mourning, and the New International, trans. Peggy Kamuf (New York and London: Routledge, 1974).

    Of Hospitality: Anne Dufourmontelle Invites Jacques Derrida to Respond, trans. Rachel Bowlby (Stanford: Stanford University Press, 2000).
    Acts of Religion, ed. Gil Anidjar (New York and London: Routledge, 2002).
Dick, Alex J., "Poverty, Charity, Poetry: The Unproductive Labors of 'The Old Cumberland Beggar,'" *Studies in Romanticism* 39 (2000), pp. 365–96.
Eilenberg, Susan, *Strange Power of Speech: Wordsworth, Coleridge, and Literary Possession* (New York and Oxford: Oxford University Press, 1992).
Ellison, Julie, *Cato's Tears and the Making of Anglo-American Emotion* (Chicago and London: University of Chicago Press, 1999).
Elster, Jon (ed.), *The Roundtable Talks and the Collapse of Communism* (Chicago and London: University of Chicago Press, 1996).
Emsley, Clive, *British Society and the French Wars, 1793–1815* (Totowa: Rowman and Littlefield, 1979).
Endelman, Todd M., *The Jews of Georgian England, 1714–1830: Tradition and Change in a Liberal Society* (Philadelphia: Jewish Publication Society of America, 1979).
Erickson, Lee, *The Economy of Literary Form: English Literature and the Industrialization of Publishing, 1800–1850* (Baltimore and London: Johns Hopkins University Press, 1996).
Etzioni, Amitai, *The Spirit of Community: Rights, Responsibilities and the Communitarian Agenda* (New York: Crown, 1993).
Fairer, David, "'The Year Runs Round': The Poetry of Work in Eighteenth-Century England," in Lorna Clymer (ed.), *Ritual, Routine and Regime: Repetition in Early Modern British and European Culture* (Toronto: University of Toronto Press, 2006), pp. 153–71.
Ferdinand, C. Y. "Selling it to the Provinces: News and Commerce Round Eighteenth-Century Salisbury," in Brewer and Porter (eds.), *Consumption and the World of Goods*, pp. 393–411.
Ferguson, Adam, *An Essay on the History of Civil Society*, ed. Fania Oz-Sulzberger (Cambridge: Cambridge University Press, 1995).
Ferguson, Frances, *Wordsworth: Language as Counter-Spirit* (New Haven and London: Yale University Press, 1977).
Ferry, David, *The Limits of Mortality: An Essay on Wordsworth's Major Poems* (Middletown, CT: Wesleyan University Press, 1959).
Foucault, Michel, *Discipline and Punish: The Birth of the Prison*, trans. Alan Sheridan (London: Allen Lane, 1977).
Freud, Sigmund, "The Uncanny," in Vincent Leitch (general ed.), *The Norton Anthology of Theory and Criticism* (New York: W. W. Norton, 2001), pp. 929–52.
Frow, John, *Time and Commodity Culture: Essays in Cultural Theory and Postmodernity* (Oxford: Clarendon Press, 1997).
Fumerton, Patricia, *Unsettled: The Culture of Mobility and the Working Poor in Early Modern England* (Chicago and London: University of Chicago Press, 2006).
Garber, Frederick, *Wordsworth and the Poetry of Encounter* (Urbana: University of Illinois Press, 1971).

Gatrell, Vic, *City of Laughter: Sex and Satire in Eighteenth-Century London* (New York: Walker and Co., 2007).
Godineau, Dominique, *The Women of Paris and Their French Revolution*, trans. Katherine Streip (Berkeley, Los Angeles and London: University of California Press, 1998).
Godwin, William, *The Enquirer: Reflections on Education, Manners, and Literature, in a Series of Essays*, facsimile reprint (New York: Augustus M. Kelley, 1965).
Goodman, Kevis, "Making Time for History: Wordsworth, the New Historicism, and the Apocalyptic Fallacy," *Studies in Romanticism* 35 (Winter 1996), pp. 563–77.
  Georgic Modernity and British Romanticism: Poetry and the Mediation of History (Cambridge: Cambridge University Press, 2004).
Goux, Jean-Joseph, *Symbolic Economies: After Marx and Freud*, trans. Jennifer Curtiss Gage (Ithaca: Cornell University Press, 1990).
Gregory, C. A., *Gifts and Commodities* (London and New York: Academic Press, 1982).
Guillory, John, *Cultural Capital: The Problem of Literary Canon Formation* (Chicago and London: University of Chicago Press, 1993).
Habermas, Jürgen, *The Theory of Communicative Action, Vol. I: Reason and the Rationalization of Society*, trans. Thomas McCarthy (Boston: Beacon Press, 1984).
Halpern, Richard, *The Poetics of Primitive Accumulation: English Renaissance Culture and the Genealogy of Capital* (Ithaca and London: Cornell University Press, 1991).
  Shakespeare Among the Moderns (Ithaca and London: Cornell University Press, 1997).
  "An Impure History of Ghosts: Derrida, Marx, and Shakespeare," in Jean E. Howard and Scott Cutler Shershow (eds.), *Marxist Shakespeare* (London and New York: Routledge, 2001), pp. 31–52.
Hardt, Michael, and Antonio Negri, *Multitude: War and Democracy in the Age of Empire* (New York: Penguin Press, 2004).
Harrison, Gary, *Wordsworth's Vagrant Muse: Poetry, Poverty and Power* (Detroit: Wayne State University Press, 1994).
Harrison, Robert Pogue, *The Dominion of the Dead* (Chicago and London: University of Chicago Press, 2003).
Hartman, Geoffrey H., *Wordsworth's Poetry, 1787–1814* (New Haven and London: Yale University Press, 1977).
  The Unremarkable Wordsworth (Minneapolis: University of Minnesota Press, 1987).
  "Blessing the Torrent," in *The Unremarkable Wordsworth*, pp. 75–89.
  "Words, Wish, Worth," in *ibid.*, pp. 90–119.
  "Diction and Defense," in *ibid.*, pp. 120–28.
  "The Use and Abuse of Structural Analysis," in *ibid.*, pp. 129–51.
  The Fateful Question of Culture (New York: Columbia University Press, 1997).

Harvey, David, *The Limits to Capital*, new edn. (London and New York: Verso, 2006).
Hazlitt, William, *The Complete Works of William Hazlitt*, ed. P. P. Howe, 21 vols. (London and Toronto, 1930–34).
Hegel, Georg Wilhelm Friedrich, *Philosophy of Mind*, trans. William Wallace (Oxford: Clarendon Press, 1971).
  The Phenomenology of Spirit, trans. A. V. Miller (Oxford: Clarendon Press, 1979).
Heidegger, Martin, *Being and Time*, trans. John Macquarrie and Edward Robinson (London: SCM Press, 1962).
  "Building, Dwelling, Thinking," in *Poetry, Language, Thought*, trans. Albert Hofstadter (New York: Harper and Row, 1975), pp. 143–61.
  An Introduction to Metaphysics, trans. Ralph Manheim (New Haven and London: Yale University Press, 1977).
Heinzelman, Kurt, *The Economics of the Imagination* (Amherst: University of Massachusetts Press, 1980).
Hertz, Neil, "Wordsworth and the Tears of Adam," in *The End of the Line: Essays on Psychoanalysis and the Sublime* (New York: Columbia University Press, 1985), pp. 21–39.
Hessel, Nikki, "The Opposite of News: Rethinking the 1800 *Lyrical Ballads* and the Mass Media," *Studies in Romanticism* 45 (2006), pp. 331–55.
Hickey, Alison, *Impure Conceits: Rhetoric and Ideology in Wordsworth's "Excursion"* (Stanford: Stanford University Press, 1997).
Homans, Margaret, *Women Writers and Poetic Identity: Dorothy Wordsworth, Emily Brontë and Emily Dickinson* (Princeton: Princeton University Press, 1980).
Horace, *Satires, Epistles and Ars Poetica*, trans. H. Rushton Fairclough (Cambridge, MA: Harvard University Press, 1939).
Horkheimer, Max, and Theodor Adorno, *Dialectic of Enlightenment*, trans. John Cumming (New York: Continuum, 1986).
Hufton, Olwen H., *The Poor of Eighteenth-Century France, 1750–1789* (Oxford: Clarendon Press, 1974).
Hume, David, *A Treatise of Human Nature*, ed. L. A. Selby-Bigge (Oxford: Clarendon Press, 1973).
Hunter, J. Paul, *Before Novels: The Cultural Contexts of Eighteenth-Century English Fiction* (New York and London: W. W. Norton, 1990).
Jacobus, Mary, *Tradition and Experiment in Wordsworth's "Lyrical Ballads (1798)"* (Oxford: Clarendon Press, 1978).
  Romanticism, Writing, and Sexual Difference: Essays on "The Prelude" (Oxford: Clarendon Press, 1989).
Jameson, Fredric (ed.), *Aesthetics and Politics* (London: New Left Books, 1979).
  Postmodernism; or the Cultural Logic of Late Capitalism (Durham: Duke University Press, 1991).
Janowitz, Anne, *Lyric and Labour in the Romantic Tradition* (Cambridge: Cambridge University Press, 1998).

Jarvis, Robin, *Wordsworth, Milton, and the Theory of Poetic Relations* (London: Macmillan, 1991).
  "Wordsworth and the Uses of Charity," in Stephen Copley and John Whale (eds.), *Beyond Romanticism: New Approaches to Texts and Contexts, 1780–1832* (London and New York: Routledge, 1992), pp. 200–17.
Johnston, Kenneth R., *Wordsworth and the Recluse* (New Haven and London: Yale University Press, 1984).
  The Hidden Wordsworth: Poet, Lover, Rebel, Spy (New York and London: W. W. Norton, 1998).
Kames, Henry Home, Lord, *Essays on the Principles of Morality and Natural Religion*, 3rd edn., ed. Mary Catherine Moran (Indianapolis: Liberty Fund, 2005).
Kant, Immanuel, *Critique of Pure Reason*, trans. Norman Kemp Smith (London: Macmillan, 1973).
Katz, David S., *The Jews in the History of England, 1485–1850* (Oxford: Clarendon Press, 1996).
Kaufman, Robert, "Red Kant, or the Persistence of the Third Critique in Adorno and Jameson," *Critical Inquiry* 26 (2000), pp. 682–724.
Keach, William, *Arbitrary Power: Romanticism, Language, Politics* (Princeton and Oxford: Princeton University Press, 2004).
Keats, John, *The Letters of John Keats*, ed. Hyder E. Rollins, 2 vols. (Cambridge, MA: Harvard University Press, 1972).
Keenan, Thomas, "The Point is to (Ex)change It: Reading *Capital*, Rhetorically," in Emily Apter and William Pietz (eds.), *Fetishism and Cultural Discourse* (Ithaca and London: Cornell University Press, 1993), pp. 152–85.
Kelley, Theresa M., *Wordsworth's Revisionary Aesthetics* (Cambridge: Cambridge University Press, 1988).
Klein, Lawrence E., *Shaftesbury and the Culture of Politeness: Moral Discourse and Cultural Politics in Early Eighteenth-Century England* (Cambridge: Cambridge University Press, 1994).
Kleist, Heinrich von, *Werke und Briefe*, 4 vols, ed. Siegfried Streller (Berlin and Weimar: Aufbau-Verlag, 1978).
  "On the Marionette Theatre," trans. Idris Parry, *Hand to Mouth and Other Essays* (Manchester: Carcanet, 1981), pp. 13–18.
La Mettrie, Julien Offray de, *Man a Machine*, ed. Gertrude Carman Bussey (La Salle, IL: Open Court, 1912).
Lamb, Jonathan, *Preserving the Self in the South Seas, 1680–1840* (Chicago and London: University of Chicago Press, 2001).
  "Modern Metamorphoses and Disgraceful Tales," *Critical Inquiry* 28 (2001–2), pp. 133–66.
Lamb, Jonathan, Vanessa Smith and Nicholas Thomas (eds.), *Exploration and Exchange: A South Seas Anthology, 1680–1900* (Chicago and London: University of Chicago Press, 2000).
Langan, Celeste, *Romantic Vagrancy: Wordsworth and the Simulation of Freedom* (Cambridge: Cambridge University Press, 1995).

Laqueur, Thomas, *Solitary Sex: A Cultural History of Masturbation* (New York: Zone Books, 2003).
Lefebvre, Georges, *The Great Fear of 1789: Rural Panic in Revolutionary France*, trans. Joan White (London: New Left Books, 1973).
Lefebvre, Henri, *The Production of Space*, trans. Donald Nicholson-Smith (Oxford: Blackwell, 1991).
Lentricchia, Frank and Jody McAuliffe, *Crimes of Art and Terror* (Chicago and London: University of Chicago Press, 2003).
Levinson, Marjorie, *The Romantic Fragment Poem: The Critique of a Form* (Chapel Hill: University of North Carolina Press, 1986).
  Keats's Life of Allegory: The Origins of a Style (Oxford: Blackwell, 1988).
Lindenberger, Herbert, *On Wordsworth's "Prelude"* (Princeton: Princeton University Press, 1963).
Linebaugh, Peter, *The London Hanged: Crime and Civil Society in the Eighteenth Century* (Cambridge: Cambridge University Press, 1992).
Liu, Alan, *Wordsworth: The Sense of History* (Stanford: Stanford University Press, 1988).
Locke, John, *An Essay Concerning Human Understanding*, ed. Peter H. Nidditch (Oxford: Clarendon Press, 1979).
Lukács, Georg, *History and Class Consciousness: Studies in Marxist Dialectics*, trans. Rodney Livingstone (Cambridge, MA: MIT Press, 1972).
  The Historical Novel, trans. Hannah and Stanley Mitchell (Lincoln and London: University of Nebraska Press, 1983).
Lynch, Deidre Shauna, *The Economy of Character: Novels, Market Culture and the Business of Inner Meaning* (Chicago and London: University of Chicago Press, 1998).
MacIntyre, Alasdair, *After Virtue: A Study in Moral Theory*, 2nd edn. (Notre Dame: University of Notre Dame Press, 1984).
Mackenzie, Henry, *The Man of Feeling* (New York: W. W. Norton, 1958).
Mandeville, Bernard, *The Fable of the Bees; or, Private Vices, Publick Benefits*, ed. F. B. Kaye, 2 vols. (Indianapolis: Liberty Fund, 1988).
Manning, Peter, "Placing Poor Susan: Wordsworth and the New Historicism," in *Reading Romantics: Texts and Contexts* (New York and Oxford: Oxford University Press, 1990), pp. 300–320.
  "Reading Wordsworth's Revisions: Othello and the Drowned Man," in *Reading Romantics*, pp. 87–114.
Mantoux, Paul, *The Industrial Revolution in the Eighteenth Century: An Outline of the Beginnings of the Modern Factory System in England* (Chicago and London: University of Chicago Press, 1983).
Marshall, David, *The Figure of the Theater: Shaftesbury, Defoe, Adam Smith and George Eliot* (New York: Columbia University Press, 1986).
  The Surprising Effects of Sympathy: Marivaux, Diderot, Rousseau and Mary Shelley (Chicago and London: University of Chicago Press, 1988).
Marx, Karl, *Die Frühschriften*, ed. Siegfried Landshut (Stuttgart: Kröner, 1953).

Grundrisse: Foundations of the Critique of Political Economy, trans. Martin Nicolaus (New York: Random House, 1973).
Capital, Volume One, trans. Ben Fowkes (New York: Vintage, 1977).
Capital, Volume Two, trans. David Fernbach (New York: Vintage, 1981).
Capital, Volume Three, trans. David Fernbach (New York: Vintage, 1981).
Marx, Karl, and Friedrich Engels, *Werke*, 39 vols. (Berlin: Dietz, 1957–68).
Selected Works, 3 vols. (Moscow: Progress Publishers, 1970).
Collected Works, vol. III (London: Lawrence and Wishart, 1973).
Mayhew, Henry, *London Labour and the London Poor*, 4 vols. (New York: Dover Reprints, 1968).
Mayr, Otto, *Authority, Liberty and Automatic Machinery in Early Modern Europe* (Baltimore and London: Johns Hopkins University Press, 1989).
McGann, Jerome J., *The Romantic Ideology: A Critical Investigation* (Chicago and London: University of Chicago Press, 1983).
Millar, John, *An Historical View of the English Government (1803)*, ed. Mark Salber Phillips and Dale R. Smith (Indianapolis: Liberty Fund, 2006).
Milton, John. *Paradise Lost*, ed. Alastair Fowler, 2nd edn. (London and New York: Longman, 1993).
Complete Shorter Poems, ed. John Carey, 2nd edn. (London and New York: Longman, 1997).
Mitchell, W. J. T., *Iconology: Image, Text, Ideology* (Chicago and London: University of Chicago Press, 1986).
"Influence, Autobiography, and Literary History: Rousseau's *Confessions* and Wordsworth's *The Prelude*," *ELH* 57 (1990), pp. 643–64.
Moorman, Mary, *William Wordsworth: A Biography. The Early Years, 1770–1803* (Oxford: Clarendon Press, 1969).
Moretti, Franco, *Atlas of the European Novel, 1800–1900* (London and New York: Verso, 1999).
Graphs, Maps, Trees: Abstract Modes for a Literary History (London and New York: Verso, 2005).
Morton, Timothy, *The Poetics of Spice: Romantic Consumerism and the Exotic* (Cambridge: Cambridge University Press, 2000).
"Wordsworth Digs the Lawn," *European Romantic Review* 15 (2004), pp. 317–27.
Mullan, John, *Sentiment and Sociability: The Language of Feeling in the Eighteenth Century* (Oxford: Clarendon Press, 1988).
Neocleous, Mark, *The Monstrous and the Dead: Burke, Marx, Fascism* (Cardiff: University of Wales Press, 2005).
Nossack, Hans Erich, *The End: Hamburg 1943*, trans. Joel Agee (Chicago and London: University of Chicago Press, 2005).
Onorato, Richard J., *The Mind of the Poet: Wordsworth in "The Prelude"* (Princeton: Princeton University Press, 1971).
Page, Judith W., *Wordsworth and the Cultivation of Women* (Berkeley, Los Angeles and London: University of California Press, 1994).

Paine, Thomas, *The Complete Writings of Thomas Paine*, ed. Philip S. Foner, 2 vols. (New York: Citadel Press, 1945).
Pfau, Thomas, *Wordsworth's Profession: Form, Class, and the Logic of Early Romantic Cultural Production* (Stanford: Stanford University Press, 1997).
Pinch, Adela, *Strange Fits of Passion: Epistemologies of Emotion, Hume to Austen* (Stanford: Stanford University Press, 1996).
Pocock, J. G. A., *Virtue, Commerce and History* (Cambridge: Cambridge University Press, 1985).
Polanyi, Karl, *The Great Transformation: The Political and Economic Origins of Our Time* (Boston: Beacon Press, 1957).
Postone, Moishe, *Time, Labor, and Social Domination: A Reinterpretation of Marx's Critical Theory* (Cambridge: Cambridge University Press, 2003).
Price, Leah, *The Anthology and the Rise of the Novel: From Richardson to George Eliot* (Cambridge: Cambridge University Press, 2000).
Putnam, Robert, *Bowling Alone: The Collapse and Revival of American Community* (New York: Simon and Schuster, 2000).
Rabinbach, Anson, *The Human Motor: Energy, Fatigue, and the Origins of Modernity* (New York: Basic Books, 1990).
Rajan, Tilottama, *The Supplement of Reading: Figures of Understanding in Romantic Theory and Practice* (Ithaca and London: Cornell University Press, 1990).
Rancière, Jacques, *The Philosopher and his Poor*, trans. John Drury, Corinne Oster and Andrew Parker (Durham and London: Duke University Press, 2003).
Rogers, Pat, *Grub Street: Studies in a Subculture* (London: Methuen, 1972).
Ross, Marlon, "Naturalizing Gender: Woman's Place in Wordsworth's Ideological Landscape," *ELH* 53 (1986), pp. 391–410.
Rousseau, Jean-Jacques, *The Miscellaneous Works of Mr. J.J. Rousseau*, 5 vols. (London: Becket and De Hondt, 1767).
  Discourse on the Origins of Inequality, ed. Roger D. Masters and Christopher Kelly (Hanover and London: University Press of New England, 1992).
  The Confessions, trans. Christopher Kelly (Hanover and London: University Press of New England, 1995).
  "Essay on the Origin of Languages" and Writings Related to Music, trans. John T. Scott (Hanover and London: University Press of New England, 1998).
  The Reveries of the Solitary Walker, Botanical Writings, and Letter to Franquières, ed. Christopher Kelley (Hanover and London: University Press of New England, 2000).
Russell, Gillian, and Clara Tuite (eds.), *Romantic Sociability: Social Networks and Literary Culture in Britain, 1770–1840* (Cambridge: Cambridge University Press, 2002).
Ryan, Michael, *Marxism and Deconstruction: A Critical Articulation* (Baltimore and London: Johns Hopkins University Press, 1982).
Sachs, Jeffrey D., *The End of Poverty: Economic Possibilities for our Time* (New York: Penguin Press, 2005).

Salvesen, Christopher, *The Landscape of Memory: A Study of Wordsworth's Poetry* (Lincoln: University of Nebraska Press, 1965).
Santner, Eric L., *On Creaturely Life: Rilke, Benjamin, Sebald* (Chicago and London: University of Chicago Press, 2006).
Scarry, Elaine, *The Body in Pain: The Making and Unmaking of the World* (Oxford and New York: Oxford University Press, 1985).
Schivelbusch, Wolfgang, *The Railway Journey: The Industrialization of Time and Space in the Nineteenth Century* (Berkeley and Los Angeles: University of California Press, 1986).
Schoenfield, Mark, *The Professional Wordsworth: Law, Labor and the Poet's Contract* (Athens and London: University of Georgia Press, 1996).
Shakir, Evelyn, "Books, Death, and Immortality: A Study of Book V of *The Prelude*," *Studies in Romanticism* 8 (1969), pp. 156–67.
Shell, Marc, *The Economy of Literature* (Baltimore and London: Johns Hopkins University Press, 1978).
Sherman, Stuart, *Telling Time: Clocks, Diaries, and English Diurnal Form, 1660–1785* (Chicago and London: University of Chicago Press, 1996).
Shershow, Scott Cutler, *The Work and the Gift* (Chicago and London: University of Chicago Press, 2005).
Shorter, A. H., *Paper Making in the British Isles: An Historical and Geographical Study* (Newton Abbott: David and Charles, 1971).
Simmel, Georg, *On Individuality and Social Forms: Selected Writings*, ed. Donald L. Levine (Chicago and London: University of Chicago Press, 1971).
  The Philosophy of Money, trans. Tom Bottomore and David Frisby (Boston: Routledge and Kegan Paul, 1978).
Simpson, David, *Irony and Authority in Romantic Poetry* (London: Macmillan, 1979).
  Fetishism and Imagination: Dickens, Melville, Conrad (Baltimore and London: Johns Hopkins University Press, 1982).
  Wordsworth and the Figurings of the Real (London: Macmillan, 1982).
  "What Bothered Charles Lamb About Poor Susan?" *Studies in English Literature* 26 (1986), pp. 589–612.
  Wordsworth's Historical Imagination: The Poetry of Displacement (New York: Methuen, 1987).
  "Figuring Sex, Class and Gender: What is the Subject of Wordsworth's 'Gipsies'?" *South Atlantic Quarterly* 88 (1989), pp. 541–67.
  "Wordsworth and Empire – Just Joking," in Peter de Bolla, Nigel Leask and David Simpson (eds.), *Land, Nation and Culture: Thinking the Republic of Taste, 1740–1840* (Basingstoke: Palgrave Macmillan, 2005), pp. 188–201.
  9/11: The Culture of Commemoration (Chicago and London: University of Chicago Press, 2006).
Smith, Adam, *The Theory of Moral Sentiments*, ed. D. D. Raphael and A. L. Macfie (Oxford: Clarendon Press, 1976).

An Inquiry into the Nature and Causes of the Wealth of Nations, ed. R. H. Campbell, A. S. Skinner, W. B. Todd, 2 vols. (Oxford: Clarendon Press, 1976).
Smith, Bernard, *European Vision and the South Pacific, 1768–1850: A Study in the History of Art and Ideals* (London: Oxford University Press, 1969).
Sohn-Rethel, Alfred, *Intellectual and Manual Labor: A Critique of Epistemology* (Atlantic Highlands: Humanities Press, 1983).
Southey, Robert, *Letters from England*, ed. Jack Simmons (London: Cresset Press, 1951).
Spivak, Gayatri, "Scattered Speculations on the Question of Value," in *In Other Worlds: Essays in Cultural Politics* (London and New York: Methuen, 1987), pp. 154–75.
  "Speculations on Reading Marx: After Reading Derrida," in Derek Attridge, Geoff Bennington and Robert Young (eds.), *Poststructuralism and the Question of History* (Cambridge: Cambridge University Press, 1987), pp. 30–62.
  "Limits and Openings of Marx in Derrida," in *Outside in the Teaching Machine* (New York and London: Routledge, 1993), pp. 97–119.
  "Ghostwriting," *Diacritics* 25.1 (1995), pp. 65–69.
Sprinker, Michael (ed.), *Ghostly Demarcations: A Symposium on Jacques Derrida's "Specters of Marx"* (London and New York: Verso, 1999).
Stallybrass, Peter, "Marx and Heterogeneity: Thinking the Lumpenproletariat," *Representations* 31 (1990), pp. 69–95.
  "Marx's Coat," in Patricia Spyer (ed.), *Border Fetishisms: Material Objects in Unstable Spaces* (New York and London: Routledge, 1998), pp. 183–207.
Stedman Jones, Gareth, *An End to Poverty? A Historical Debate* (London: Profile Books, 2004).
Styles, John, "Manufacturing, Consumption and Design in Eighteenth-Century England," in Brewer and Porter (eds.), *Consumption and the World of Goods*, pp. 527–44.
Swann, Karen, "Suffering and Sensation in *The Ruined Cottage*," *PMLA* 106 (1991), pp. 83–95.
Terdiman, Richard, *Present Past: Modernity and the Memory Crisis* (Ithaca and London: Cornell University Press, 1993).
Thelwall, John, *The Peripatetic*, ed. Judith Thompson (Detroit: Wayne State University Press, 2001).
Underwood, Ted, "Romantic Historicism and the Afterlife," *PMLA* 117.2 (2002), pp. 237–51.
  The Work of the Sun: Literature, Science and Economy, 1760–1820 (Basingstoke and New York: Palgrave Macmillan, 2005).
Vico, Giambattista, *New Science*, trans. David Marsh (London: Penguin, 2001).
Virilio, Paul, *Speed and Politics* (New York: Semiotext(e), 1986).
Wallace, Anne, *Walking, Literature, and English Culture: The Origins and Uses of Peripatetic in the Nineteenth Century* (Oxford: Clarendon Press, 1993).
Wiley, Michael, *Romantic Geography: Wordsworth and Anglo-European Spaces* (London: Macmillan, 1998).

Williams, Raymond, *Politics and Letters: Interviews with New Left Review* (London: Verso, 1981).
Wolfson, Susan J. "The Illusion of Mastery: Wordsworth's Revisions of 'The Drowned Man of Esthwaite,' 1799, 1805, 1850," *PMLA* 99 (1984), pp. 917–35.
Wood, Gillen Darcy, *The Shock of the Real: Romanticism and Visual Culture, 1760–1860* (New York and Houndmills: Palgrave, 2001).
Woodring, Carl, *Wordsworth* (Boston: Houghton Mifflin, 1965).
Wordsworth, Dorothy, *Journals of Dorothy Wordsworth*, ed. E. de Selincourt, 2 vols. (London: Macmillan, 1952).
Wordsworth, William, *The Poetical Works of William Wordsworth*, ed. E. de Selincourt and Helen Darbishire, 5 vols. (Oxford: Clarendon Press, 1940–49).
  The Letters of William and Dorothy Wordsworth: The Early Years, 1787–1805, ed. E. de Selincourt, 2nd edn. rev. Chester L. Shaver (Oxford: Clarendon Press, 1967).
  The Letters of William and Dorothy Wordsworth: III. The Middle Years, Part 2, 1812–1820, ed. E. de Selincourt, 2nd edn. rev. Mary Moorman and Alan G. Hill (Oxford: Clarendon Press, 1970).
  The Prose Works of William Wordsworth, ed W. J. B. Owen and Jane Worthington Smyser, 3 vols. (Oxford: Clarendon Press, 1974).
  The Salisbury Plain Poems of William Wordsworth, ed. Stephen Gill (Ithaca and Hassocks: Cornell University Press and Harvester Press, 1975).
  Home at Grasmere, ed. Beth Darlington (Ithaca: Cornell University Press, 1977).
  The Prelude, 1798–99, ed. Stephen Parrish (Ithaca: Cornell University Press, 1977).
  The Ruined Cottage and The Pedlar, ed. James Butler (Ithaca and Hassocks: Cornell University Press and Harvester Press, 1979).
  "Poems, in Two Volumes," and Other Poems, 1800–1807, ed. Jared Curtis (Ithaca: Cornell University Press, 1983).
  The Fourteen Book Prelude, ed. W. J. B. Owen (Ithaca and London: Cornell University Press, 1985).
  The Thirteen Book Prelude, ed. Mark L. Reed, 2 vols. (Ithaca and London: Cornell University Press, 1991).
  "Lyrical Ballads," and Other Poems, 1797–1800, ed. James Butler and Karen Green (Ithaca: Cornell University Press, 1992).
  Last Poems, 1821–1850, ed. Jared Curtis (Ithaca and London: Cornell University Press, 1999).
  Sonnet Series and Itinerary Poems, 1820–45, ed. Geoffrey Jackson (Ithaca and London: Cornell University Press, 2004).
Yates, Frances A., *The Art of Memory* (Chicago: University of Chicago Press, 1972).
Žižek, Slavoj, *The Sublime Object of Ideology* (London and New York: Verso, 1989).

Index

9/11 (September 11, 2001) 14–15, 61

Adorno, Theodor W. 59, 62, 104, 109, 183, 189, 246, 249
  see also Horkheimer
Agamben, Giorgio 3, 60, 61, 62, 66, 68, 187, 205, 233
Althusser, Louis 25, 135, 251
Altick, Richard 247
Anidjar, Gil 235
Appadurai, Arjun 235
Aristotle 94, 151, 154, 177, 216, 239, 251
Arnold, Matthew 5, 6, 22, 24, 28, 117, 121
Augustine 134
Austen, Jane 27, 73, 167, 214, 231
automation 8, 12, 18, 47, 48–49, 63, 72–80, 93, 160, 161, 162, 165, 169, 172, 173
  see also machine labor
Averill, James 237, 239, 257, 258

Bachelard, Gaston 254
Bakhtin, Mikhail 55, 238
Barker-Benfield, G. J. 237
Barrell, John 240, 243, 244, 245
Baucom, Ian 249
Baudrillard, Jean 205
Beck, Ulrich 29
Beer, John 101, 247
Bellamy, Liz 254
Benis, Toby 64, 67, 241
Benjamin, Walter 109, 119–21, 183, 189, 247
Bentham, Jeremy 36–39, 64, 65–67, 75
Berg, Maxine 236, 251
Berman, Marshall 238
Bewell, Alan 31, 93, 95, 99, 215, 229, 244, 245, 255, 257
Bialostosky, Don 238
Blake, William 3, 175
Blevins, Steven 254
Bono, 17
book trade 14, 87–90, 107–9, 126–27, 196, 206–34, 241

Brooks, Cleanth 56, 239
Brown, Laura 229
Brown, Marshall 255
Bryson, Norman 256
Buck-Morss, Susan 249
Burke, Edmund 30, 64, 65, 122, 137–38, 140, 149, 154, 211
Burney, Fanny 73

Campbell, Colin 235
Casey, Edward 247
Castle, Terry 250
Chandler, James 64, 121, 137–38
  and Gilmartin, Kevin 247
Chase, Cynthia 258
Chesterfield, Lord 24, 38
civil society, civility 22–32, 40
Clare, John 204
Clark, T. J. 243
Clery, E. J. 250
Cobbett, William 112, 230, 252
Coleridge, Samuel T. 144, 161, 178, 179, 208, 238, 256
  "The Rime of the Ancient Mariner" 9, 71, 94, 100
  on Wordsworth 28, 31, 32, 33, 168–69, 170, 171, 174, 175
commodification, commodity form 5–10, 20, 22, 38, 39, 52, 114, 118, 140, 143, 150, 183, 187, 189, 205, 231, 233, 255
  theory of 5–10, 14, 116–17, 120, 144, 252, 235
  and Wordsworth 13, 14, 20, 27, 40, 45–46, 49, 63, 83, 90, 122, 148, 184, 192, 193, 195, 196, 197, 232
  see also Marx
concern, *see* Wordsworth
Connell, Philip 241
Cook, James 31, 65, 95–96, 206, 245
Cooper, James Fenimore 204
Cowper, William 69–70, 91, 175–77, 201, 217

Dante 41, 93, 94, 147, 222
De Bolla, Peter 154, 252

274

Index

de Man, Paul 2, 122, 162, 166, 168, 177–78, 179, 202–4, 253
De Quincey, Thomas 54, 96, 211, 222, 228, 258
Debord, Guy 4, 120, 138–39, 161, 187, 189, 193, 194, 197, 248
Derrida, Jacques 31, 80, 81, 104, 150, 160, 161, 173, 187, 214
   on Marx 4, 13, 14, 80, 81, 102–3, 143–44, 145, 153, 157, 158, 160, 161, 162, 165–66, 172, 183, 187, 188, 250, 251, 252
   see also specters
Descartes, René 208, 245
dialogue, dialogism 11, 23–32, 50, 238
Dick, Alex 241

Eden, Sir Frederick 17
Edgeworth, Maria 108
Elias, Norbert 238
Ellison, Julie 237
Elster, Jon 237
Emsley, Clive 246
Engels, Friedrich 113, 163, 164
   see also Marx and Engels
Erickson, Lee 244, 246
Etzioni, Amitai 237

Ferguson, Adam 138, 163
Ferguson, Frances 254
Ferry, David 4, 143, 169, 245
Fielding, Henry 36
Freud, Sigmund 59, 73, 124, 162, 237, 254
Frow, John 242
Fumerton, Patricia 240, 246

Garber, Frederick 67, 245
Garrison, Alysia 254
Gatrell, Vic 89
ghosts, ghostliness 27, 184, 222, 223, 234
   see also specters
Giddens, Anthony 237, 238
gift giving 64–65
Godineau, Dominique 236
Godwin, William 78, 149
Goodman, Kevis 201, 257, 258
Gothic novel 45, 114, 144, 155, 204, 213–14, 217, 244
Goux, J.-J. 251
Gray, Thomas 201, 202, 207, 222, 232, 233, 256, 258, 259
Gregory, C. A. 241
Guillory, John 201, 256

Habermas, Jürgen 11, 29–32, 39, 50–51, 238
Halpern, Richard 246, 247, 250
Hardt, Michael, and Antonio Negri 62

Harrison, Gary 52, 241, 243
Harrison, Robert Pogue 258
Hartman, Geoffrey 7, 63, 122, 143, 169, 196, 228, 232, 239, 255, 256
Harvey, David 128–29, 250
Hazlitt, William 32, 105
Hegel, G. W. F. 131, 137, 149, 188, 248
   see also Marx on
Heidegger, Martin 5, 59, 104, 124, 187
Heinzelman, Kurt 248
Hertz, Neil 259
Hickey, Alison 239, 241, 255
Hoffman, E. T. A. 73
Homans, Margaret 239
homelessness 54–82, 90, 103, 113–15, 193
   see also lumpenproletariat
Homer 94, 98, 181, 216, 220
Horace 147, 148, 212, 233, 250
Horkheimer, Max, and Adorno 118, 119
hospitality 104–5
Hume, David 124, 134, 247, 249
Hunter, J. Paul 200

Jacobus, Mary 239, 244, 257
Jarvis, Robin 241, 257, 258
Johnson, Samuel 177
Johnston, Kenneth 67, 87–88, 90, 94, 121, 244, 251

Kames, Lord 43, 50
Kant, Immanuel 37, 124, 125, 141, 146, 179, 238
Kaufman, Robert 247
Keach, William 255
Keats, John 10–11, 203, 233
Keenan, Thomas 156, 250, 252, 254
Kelley, Theresa 229
Kleist, Heinrich von 166, 168, 171

La Mettrie 72, 242
Lamb, Jonathan 65, 175, 245
Laqueur, Thomas 254, 258
Langan, Celeste 10, 46, 77, 80, 93, 182, 240, 244, 255
Lefebvre, Henri 6, 235, 248, 250
Lentricchia, Frank, and Jody McAuliffe 117
Levi, Primo 3, 68, 69, 72
Levinson, Marjorie 10, 240, 244, 259
Lewis, M. G. 144
Lindenberger, Herbert 124, 132, 258
Linebaugh, Peter 245, 246, 253
Liu, Alan 10, 45–46, 63, 77, 88, 122, 131, 192, 240, 256, 257
Locke, John 134–35
Lukács, Georg 6, 127, 141, 194, 246, 248

lumpenproletariat 12, 97, 105–15, 119, 142, 155, 170, 196, 234, 246
  see also Marx on, ragpickers
Lynch, Deidre 73, 87, 231, 242, 254, 259

machine labor 8, 20, 55, 75–79, 83, 116, 126–28, 136, 138, 140, 154, 221, 229
  see also automation, Marx on
MacIntyre, Alasdair 23–24
Mackenzie, Henry 26, 36
Mandeville, Bernard 73, 253
Manning, Peter 225, 243
Mantoux, Paul 237, 240, 251
Marshall, David 237, 238, 258
Marx, Karl 8, 10, 20, 73, 77, 111, 124, 166, 173, 223, 238, 250, 251, 252, 253
  on the commodity 5–6, 7–9, 10, 16, 21–22, 28, 38, 128–34, 150–66, 174–77, 179, 182, 230, 237, 248
  see also Derrida on
  and Engels 78, 114, 138, 181, 213, 221
  on fetishism 151, 156, 158, 188, 233
  and figurative form/language 4, 7, 10, 13, 156–61, 164, 171, 172, 174, 176, 183, 230
  and/on Hegel 28, 131, 142, 150, 151, 157–58
  on the *lumpenproletariat* 12, 97, 105–15, 112, 164, 246
  on machine labor 20, 52, 66, 69, 73, 152, 155, 160
  on money 34, 74, 80–82, 155, 162, 176, 182, 243
  on primary accumulation 111
  on value 128–34, 153, 159
Mayhew, Henry 108–9, 246
Mayr, Otto 77, 243
McGann, Jerome 2, 8
memory systems, classical and medieval 126, 134
Mill, J. S. 5, 117, 121
Millar, John 15, 209
Milton, John 11, 40–41, 86, 90–91, 124, 125, 174, 188, 202, 257, 258
  Comus 198, 259
  Paradise Lost 43, 44, 59, 80–81, 91–92, 98–99, 139, 147, 172, 175, 194, 197, 199, 201, 203, 208, 222, 228, 230, 239, 243
  Paradise Regained 204
  Samson Agonistes 44, 147, 148, 149
Mitchell, W. J. T. 6, 235, 257
Mitford, Mary Russell 51, 56
Modernism 117, 177
modernity 1, 4–5, 12–13, 24, 39, 50, 116–42
Moorman, Mary 145
Moretti, Franco 56, 87, 244
Morton, Timothy 252, 254
Mullan, John 237
Muselmann 3, 68, 69, 72, 93, 96, 181, 235

Neocleous, Mark 252
Nossack, Hans Erich 217

Onorato, Richard 181, 247

Page, Judith 239
Paine, Thomas 149, 154, 236, 252
Pinch, Adela 237, 243, 257, 258
Pocock, J. G. A. 138
Polanyi, Karl 251–52
Pope, Alexander 27, 87, 91, 124, 220
Postone, Moishe 129–30, 132, 248, 250, 251, 252
poverty 17–22, 116
Price, Leah 257
Putnam, Robert 237

Quintilian 126, 134, 177, 255

Rabinbach, Anson 74
Radcliffe, Anne 214, 255
ragpickers 107–9
Rajan, Tilottama 256
Rancière, Jacques 85, 106–7, 164
Reed, Mark 145, 200
Richter, Gerhard 252
Rogers, Pat 87
Ross, Marlon 239
Rousseau, Jean-Jacques 55, 68, 78, 101, 184–85, 186, 215–17, 218, 220, 258
Russell, Gillian, and Clara Tuite 237
Ryan, Michael 248, 250, 252

Sachs, Jeffrey 11, 17–19, 116
Salvesen, Christopher 248
Santner, Eric 3, 235, 242
Scarry, Elaine 240, 253
Schivelbusch, Wolfgang 242
Scott, Walter 204, 205
Sebald, W. G. 3
Shaftesbury, Third Earl, 24, 38
Shakespeare, William 41, 44, 80–81, 124, 125, 174, 176, 210, 212, 222, 224–25, 228
Shakir, Evelyn 257
Shelley, P. B. 177, 186
Sherman, Stuart 200
Shershow, Scott 241
Shell, Marc 251
Shesgreen, Sean 243
Simmel, Georg 27, 29, 42, 49, 243, 247
Smith, Adam 24, 29, 32–39, 43, 50, 61, 73, 77, 106, 163, 182, 253
Sohn-Rethel, Alfred 136–37, 251
Southey, Robert 88, 211, 243, 246

space and time, refiguring of 7, 8, 12, 21, 76–77, 78–79, 83, 116–42, 197, 202–4, 211, 221, 229, 231, 242
  see also Wordsworth, spots of time
spectacle 81, 117, 120, 138, 161, 187–205
  see also Debord
specters, spectrality 1–2, 213, 224–26, 235, 139
  Derrida on 4, 102–4, 145, 150, 157, 161, 166, 187
  see also ghosts, uncanny
  in Wordsworth 4, 11–13, 14, 19, 40, 44–45, 49–50, 56, 63, 70–71, 83, 86, 92–105, 114, 140, 143–73, 209, 212, 213, 224–26
Spenser, Edmund 40, 62, 170, 194, 259
Spivak, Gayatri 248, 250, 251
Stallybrass, Peter 106, 245, 253
Stedman Jones, Gareth 236
Sterne, Laurence 68
Stewart, Dugald 73
Styles, John 253
substitutability 8, 15, 22, 52, 61–63, 66, 68, 71, 89, 93, 107, 109, 110–11, 136, 142, 160–61, 164, 192, 233
Swann, Karen 40, 239
Swift, Jonathan 86
sympathy 11–12, 17–53, 97, 114, 258

Taylor, John 207
Terdiman, Richard 130
textile industry 8, 20–21, 46, 236, 253
Thelwall, John 55, 73, 97, 238
Todorov, Tzvetan 144

uncanny 9, 13, 19, 55, 59, 65, 73, 74, 75, 83, 90, 91, 125, 162, 254
  see also ghosts, specters
Underwood, Ted 74–75, 250
value, value form 12–13, 21, 38, 39, 106, 128–42, 240, 250
  see also commodification, Marx

Vico 255
Virgil 40, 41, 58–59, 93, 147, 217, 257
Virilio, Paul 59

Wallace, Anne 55
Wolfson, Susan 258
Wood, Gillen 256
Woodring, Carl 64
Wordsworth, Dorothy 55, 57, 140, 166, 242, 244
Wordsworth, William
  and cliché 14, 41, 88, 89, 167, 170, 171, 174–75, 179–80, 195, 196, 199, 206, 232, 233
  see also commodification

and concern 5, 7, 14, 25, 39, 40, 53, 60, 98, 103–4, 105, 115, 116, 120, 141, 187, 193, 195, 203, 234
and contemplation 193
on crowds 3, 112, 119, 167
Essays on Epitaphs 202
on homelessness 12, 54–82, 90
  see also lumpenproletariat
Lyrical Ballads, preface 9, 33, 117–21, 144, 152, 195, 202, 216, 221, 232
  see also Milton
and money 27, 35, 46, 49, 77, 80–82, 182
poems: "Alice Fell" 27, 54
  "Beggars" 31, 62, 86
  "The Brothers" 100, 204
  The Excursion 13, 57, 75, 242, 257; bk. 1 (*see* "The Ruined Cottage"): 36, 39–53, 162, 192; bk. 2: 190–91, 227; bk. 3: 193–94; bk. 8: 78, 91, 111–12; bk. 9: 58–59
  "Home at Grasmere" 54, 57, 123
  "I wandered lonely as a cloud" 55, 130, 166–73, 174, 175, 180, 186, 218
  "Gipsies" 12, 32, 62, 80–82, 83, 85, 168–69, 170, 182, 188, 198, 232–33
  "Lines written near Richmond" 244
  "Michael" 31, 109, 110
  "The Old Cumberland Beggar" 3, 12, 16, 25, 31, 35, 63–80, 83, 85, 90, 92, 100, 110, 113, 114, 139, 140, 150, 156, 162, 178, 182, 195, 196, 204, 206
  "Old Man Travelling" 25, 31, 113
  "Point Rash-Judgment" 12, 95–105, 150, 156, 178, 203, 206, 211, 214, 223
  "Poor Susan" 12, 84–91, 92, 99, 107–8, 109, 110, 114, 150, 178, 179, 195, 196, 201, 206, 209, 211, 230, 231, 249
  The Prelude 14, 76, 125, 134, 136, 197–202, 244
    bk. 1: 186, 204, 206, 224; bk. 4: 223; bk. 5: 236; bk. 6: 223, 226, 230; bk. 8: 179, 183; bk. 9: 250; bk. 11: 204; bk. 12: 227; bk. 13: 227, 228, 230
    on books and reading (bk. 5) 14, 99, 195, 207–27
    the convent of Chartreuse (bk. 6) 13, 140, 145–50, 165, 197
    the discharged soldier (bk. 4) 12, 91–95, 100, 105, 110, 112, 114, 125, 150, 156, 181, 206, 225
    dream of the Arab (bk. 5) 208–9
    the drowned man of Esthwaite (bk. 5) 212–18, 224–26
    in France (bk. 6) 113, 226
    the hunger-bitten girl (bk. 9) 11, 18–23, 47, 61, 77, 78, 142, 156

Wordsworth, William (*cont.*)
    Leven sands, crossing (bk. 10) 13, 197–202, 206, 227–28, 230
    London (bk. 7) 79, 86, 88, 119, 125, 133, 195, 228
    and memory 12–13, 133, 141
    in Paris (bk. 9) 243
    the spots of time (bk. 11) 12, 13, 121–42, 174, 189, 197–202, 199, 200, 206, 211, 219, 225
    the Winander boy (bk. 5) 166, 211–12, 222, 223, 227
Poems 1815, preface 180
"Resolution and Independence" 3, 13, 25, 55, 150, 156, 162, 180–87, 191, 203, 204, 206, 218, 228–29, 230
"The Ruined Cottage" 11, 22, 23, 39–53, 83, 88, 95, 147, 162, 178, 192, 192, 196
    see also The Excursion, bk. 1
Salisbury Plain poems 56–57
"Simon Lee" 26, 187
"The Solitary Reaper" 54
"Steamboats, viaducts and railways" 127, 130
"Stepping Westward" 60
"This Lawn, a carpet all alive" 175
"The Thorn" 31, 62, 85, 244
"Tintern Abbey" poem 31, 170
"We Are Seven" 31, 35
"When to the attractions of the busy world" 112
"Yew Trees" 196–97, 231, 256
see also Shakespeare, space and time, specters

Yates, Frances 130, 247, 255

Žižek, Slavoj 237, 249

CAMBRIDGE STUDIES IN ROMANTICISM

GENERAL EDITOR
JAMES CHANDLER, University of Chicago

1. *Romantic Correspondence: Women, Politics and the Fiction of Letters*
   MARY A. FAVRET

2. *British Romantic Writers and the East: Anxieties of Empire*
   NIGEL LEASK

3. *Poetry as an Occupation and an Art in Britain, 1760–1830*
   PETER MURPHY

4. *Edmund Burke's Aesthetic Ideology: Language, Gender and Political Economy in Revolution*
   TOM FURNISS

5. *In the Theatre of Romanticism: Coleridge, Nationalism, Women*
   JULIE A. CARLSON

6. *Keats, Narrative and Audience*
   ANDREW BENNETT

7. *Romance and Revolution: Shelley and the Politics of a Genre*
   DAVID DUFF

8. *Literature, Education, and Romanticism: Reading as Social Practice, 1780–1832*
   ALAN RICHARDSON

9. *Women Writing about Money: Women's Fiction in England, 1790–1820*
   EDWARD COPELAND

10. *Shelley and the Revolution in Taste: The Body and the Natural World*
    TIMOTHY MORTON

11. *William Cobbett: The Politics of Style*
    LEONORA NATTRASS

12. *The Rise of Supernatural Fiction, 1762–1800*
    E. J. CLERY

13. *Women Travel Writers and the Language of Aesthetics, 1716–1818*
    ELIZABETH A. BOHLS

14. *Napoleon and English Romanticism*
    SIMON BAINBRIDGE

15. *Romantic Vagrancy: Wordsworth and the Simulation of Freedom*
    CELESTE LANGAN

16. *Wordsworth and the Geologists*
   JOHN WYATT

17. *Wordsworth's Pope: A Study in Literary Historiography*
   ROBERT J. GRIFFIN

18. *The Politics of Sensibility: Race, Gender and Commerce in the Sentimental Novel*
   MARKMAN ELLIS

19. *Reading Daughters' Fictions, 1709–1834: Novels and Society from Manley to Edgeworth*
   CAROLINE GONDA

20. *Romantic Identities: Varieties of Subjectivity, 1774–1830*
   ANDREA K. HENDERSON

21. *Print Politics: The Press and Radical Opposition in Early Nineteenth-Century England*
   KEVIN GILMARTIN

22. *Reinventing Allegory*
   THERESA M. KELLEY

23. *British Satire and the Politics of Style, 1789–1832*
   GARY DYER

24. *The Romantic Reformation: Religious Politics in English Literature, 1789–1824*
   ROBERT M. RYAN

25. *De Quincey's Romanticism: Canonical Minority and the Forms of Transmission*
   MARGARET RUSSETT

26. *Coleridge on Dreaming: Romanticism, Dreams and the Medical Imagination*
   JENNIFER FORD

27. *Romantic Imperialism: Universal Empire and the Culture of Modernity*
   SAREE MAKDISI

28. *Ideology and Utopia in the Poetry of William Blake*
   NICHOLAS M. WILLIAMS

29. *Sexual Politics and the Romantic Author*
   SONIA HOFKOSH

30. *Lyric and Labour in the Romantic Tradition*
   ANNE JANOWITZ

31. *Poetry and Politics in the Cockney School: Keats, Shelley, Hunt and their Circle*
   JEFFREY N. COX

32. *Rousseau, Robespierre and English Romanticism*
   GREGORY DART

33. *Contesting the Gothic: Fiction, Genre and Cultural Conflict, 1764–1832*
   JAMES WATT

34. *Romanticism, Aesthetics, and Nationalism*
   DAVID ARAM KAISER

35. *Romantic Poets and the Culture of Posterity*
   ANDREW BENNETT

36. *The Crisis of Literature in the 1790s: Print Culture and the Public Sphere*
   PAUL KEEN

37. *Romantic Atheism: Poetry and Freethought, 1780–1830*
   MARTIN PRIESTMAN

38. *Romanticism and Slave Narratives: Transatlantic Testimonies*
   HELEN THOMAS

39. *Imagination Under Pressure, 1789–1832: Aesthetics, Politics, and Utility*
   JOHN WHALE

40. *Romanticism and the Gothic: Genre, Reception, and Canon Formation, 1790–1820*
   MICHAEL GAMER

41. *Romanticism and the Human Sciences: Poetry, Population, and the Discourse of the Species*
   MAUREEN N. MCLANE

42. *The Poetics of Spice: Romantic Consumerism and the Exotic*
   TIMOTHY MORTON

43. *British Fiction and the Production of Social Order, 1740–1830*
   MIRANDA J. BURGESS

44. *Women Writers and the English Nation in the 1790s*
   ANGELA KEANE

45. *Literary Magazines and British Romanticism*
   MARK PARKER

46. *Women, Nationalism and the Romantic Stage: Theatre and Politics in Britain, 1780–1800*
   BETSY BOLTON

47. *British Romanticism and the Science of the Mind*
   ALAN RICHARDSON

48. *The Anti-Jacobin Novel: British Conservatism and the French Revolution*
   M. O. GRENBY

49. Romantic Austen: Sexual Politics and the Literary Canon
   CLARA TUITE

50. Byron and Romanticism
   JEROME MCGANN AND JAMES SODERHOLM

51. The Romantic National Tale and the Question of Ireland
   INA FERRIS

52. Byron, Poetics and History
   JANE STABLER

53. Religion, Toleration, and British Writing, 1790–1830
   MARK CANUEL

54. Fatal Women of Romanticism
   ADRIANA CRACIUN

55. Knowledge and Indifference in English Romantic Prose
   TIM MILNES

56. Mary Wollstonecraft and the Feminist Imagination
   BARBARA TAYLOR

57. Romanticism, Maternity and the Body Politic
   JULIE KIPP

58. Romanticism and Animal Rights
   DAVID PERKINS

59. Georgic Modernity and British Romanticism: Poetry and the Mediation of History
   KEVIS GOODMAN

60. Literature, Science and Exploration in the Romantic Era: Bodies of Knowledge
   TIMOTHY FULFORD, DEBBIE LEE AND PETER J. KITSON

61. Romantic Colonization and British Anti-Slavery
   DEIRDRE COLEMAN

62. Anger, Revolution, and Romanticism
   ANDREW M. STAUFFER

63. Shelley and the Revolutionary Sublime
   CIAN DUFFY

64. Fictions and Fakes: Forging Romantic Authenticity, 1760–1845
   MARGARET RUSSETT

65. Early Romanticism and Religious Dissent
   DANIEL E. WHITE

66. *The Invention of Evening: Perception and Time in Romantic Poetry*
CHRISTOPHER R. MILLER

67. *Wordsworth's Philosophic Song*
SIMON JARVIS

68. *Romanticism and the Rise of the Mass Public*
ANDREW FRANTA

69. *Writing against Revolution: Literary Conservatism in Britain, 1790–1832*
KEVIN GILMARTIN

70. *Women, Sociability and Theatre in Georgian London*
GILLIAN RUSSELL

71. *The Lake Poets and Professional Identity*
BRIAN GOLDBERG

72. *Wordsworth Writing*
ANDREW BENNETT

73. *Science and Sensation in Romantic Poetry*
NOEL JACKSON

74. *Advertising and Satirical Culture in the Romantic Period*
JOHN STRACHAN

75. *Romanticism and the Painful Pleasures of Modern Life*
ANDREA K. HENDERSON

76. *Balladeering, Minstrelsy, and the Making of British Romantic Poetry*
MAUREEN N. MCLANE

77. *Romanticism and Improvisation, 1750–1850*
ANGELA ESTERHAMMER

78. *Scotland and the Fictions of Geography: North Britain, 1760–1830*
PENNY FIELDING

79. *Wordsworth, Commodification and Social Concern: The Poetics of Modernity*
DAVID SIMPSON